Creating the Other

AUSTRIAN HISTORY, CULTURE, AND SOCIETY
General Editor: Gary Cohen, Center for Austrian Studies,
University of Minnesota

CREATING THE OTHER

Ethnic Conflict and Nationalism in Habsburg Central Europe

Edited by

Nancy M. Wingfield

Berghahn Books
New York • Oxford

First published in hardback in 2003 by
Berghahn Books

www.berghahnbooks.com

First paperback edition published in 2004

Reprinted in 2005.

© 2003, 2004 Nancy M. Wingfield

Library of Congress Cataloging-in-Publication Data

Creating the other : ethnic conflict & nationalism in the Habsburg Central Europe / edited
by Nancy M. Wingfield.
    p. cm. -- (Austrian history, culture & society ; v. 5)
    Includes bibliographical references and index.
    ISBN 1-57181-384-5 (hc : alk. paper); ISBN 1-57181-385-3 (pbk : alk. paper)
    1. Nationalism--Europe, Central --History--19th century. 2. Nationalism--Europe,
Central--History--20th century. 3. Europe, Central--Ethnic relations. 4. Austria--Ethnic
relations. 5. Austria--Politics and government--1789-1900. 6. Racism--Europe,
Central--History--19th century. 7. Racism--Europe, Central--History--20th century. 8.
Europe, Central--Politics and government. I. Wingfield, Nancy M. (Nancy Meriwether) II.
Austrian history, culture, and society ; v. 5.

DAW 1050.C74 2003
943'.009'034--dc21   2002043679

British Library Cataloguing in Publication Data

A catalogue record for this book is available from
the British Library.

Printed in Canada on acid-free paper

CONTENTS

PREFACE

Gary B. Cohen

The essays in this volume are the fruit of a sea change in research on ethnic and national identification that has occurred in the past two decades. Since the late nineteenth century, ethnic and national conflicts and the rise of nationalist political movements have been major concerns for students of modern Central and East-Central Europe. Until the 1980s, however, most historians and political scientists tended to assume that nationalist politics in Europe rested on preexisting cultures and identities of ethnic groups. To a great extent scholars tended to study the dynamics of modern nationalism from within the boundaries of nationalist perspectives. Perceptive contemporary observers during the nineteenth and early twentieth centuries recognized that popular loyalties and identities were constructed and transformed in the context of ongoing political and social development, but before the 1980s few scholars analyzed the creation and transformation of popular ethnic and national identities in Central and East-Central Europe as dynamic cultural phenomena.

In the last two decades scholars interested in the Habsburg Monarchy and the Tsarist and Ottoman empires and their successor states have begun to examine modern ethnic and national loyalties as dynamic, socially constructed artifacts, using concepts and methods drawn from cultural anthropology, political sociology, postmodernist discourse analysis, and cultural studies. As the essays in this volume vividly illustrate, these researchers have begun to reinvent studies of modern nationalism, nationality conflicts, and national political movements in Central and East-Central Europe. In the process they are developing a sophisticated new understanding of the cultural meaning and social dynamics of ethnic and national identification in everyday life. For most ethnic and national loyalties in modern societies, the creation of a group identity included, and indeed usually required, defining the Other or Others who stood outside the ethnic or national group. As these essays remind us, establishing what characteristics and qualities defined one's own group, who belonged and who did not, and what were the chief economic and political needs of the group typically required as a direct corollary a process of identifying and characterizing the group's rivals and adversaries. The linking of self-definition with notions of alterity only underscores how the development of national rivalries and political conflicts involved an ongoing, multisided cultural process.

This volume follows in the series on Austrian History, Culture, and Society published by Berghahn Books. The essays presented here are selected, revised, and expanded versions of papers originally given at the international symposium "Creating the Other: The Causes and Dynamics of Nationalism, Ethnic Enmity, and Racism in Central and Eastern Europe," held by the Center for Austrian Studies at the University of Minnesota in Minneapolis in May 1999. This gathering was one of the series of international, interdisciplinary conferences that have been organized by the Center for Austrian Studies annually or biannually since 1978 to discuss major issues in contemporary scholarship regarding culture, society, economics, and politics in Austria and the other Central European lands that share the Habsburg heritage. The generous endowment given the Center by the Austrian people in 1976 has helped make possible all the conferences as well as the other programs of the Center. The authors and editors of this volume are grateful to the Austrian Cultural Forum in New York, the Commission for the Modern History of Austria, the College of Liberal Arts, the Institute for Global Studies, the Center for Holocaust and Genocide Studies, and the Immigration History Research Center at the University of Minnesota for cosponsoring the 1999 symposium. Professor Richard L. Rudolph, director of the Center for Austrian Studies between 1996 and 1999, conceived and organized the conference. Barbara Krauss-Christensen, executive secretary of the Center; Daniel Pinkerton, editor; and Matthew Lungerhausen, the Center's conference coordinator in 1998-99, were responsible for the logistics and publicity for the symposium.

Particular thanks is due to Nancy M. Wingfield of Northern Illinois University for the great care, finesse, and efficiency that she has brought to the task of bringing together and editing the essays for this volume. The authors and editors are also grateful to Seulky McInneshin, the editorial assistant for the Center for Austrian Studies, and to Marion Berghahn and the staff of Berghahn Books for their fine production work.

Gary B. Cohen
University of Minnesota
General Editor,
Series on Austrian, History,
Culture, and Society

NOTES ON CONTRIBUTORS

Hugh LeCaine Agnew is Associate Professor of History and International Affairs at the George Washington University. He is the author of *Origins of the Czech National Renascence* (1993) and a number of articles on Czech and Habsburg history.

Regina Bendix is Professor of Volkskunde and European Ethnology at the Georg-August Universität in Göttingen. Her latest book is *In Search of Authenticity: The Formation of Folklore Studies* (1997). In addition to the history of ethnology, she has published monographs and articles on such topics as festive display and popular theater, narrative, and cultural tourism.

Peter Haslinger received his Ph.D. in history from the University of Vienna in 1993. The author of *Hundert Jahre Nachbarschaft. Die Beziehungen zwischen Österreich und Ungarn 1895-1994* (1996) and articles on modern East Central European history, he is a researcher at the Collegium Carolinum in Munich.

Pieter M. Judson is Professor and Chair of the Department of History at Swarthmore College. He is the author of *Exclusive Revolutionaries: Liberal Politics, Social Experience, and National Identity in the Austrian Empire, 1848-1914* (1996), which won the American Historical Association's Herbert Baxter Adams Prize in 1997 and the Austrian Cultural Institute's book prize in 1998.

Karl Kaser heads the Department for Southeastern European History at the University of Graz. He has published widely on the social history of the Balkans, most recently, *Südosteuropäische Geschichte und Geschichtswissenschaft* (2002).

Peter Loewenberg is Professor of History and Political Psychology at the University of California, Los Angeles. He is the author of many books and articles, including *Decoding the Past: The Psychohistorical Approach* (1996). The Dean of the Southern California Psychoanalytic Institute, he received the first

Edith Sabshin Award of the American Psychoanalytic Association (1999) for excellence in the teaching of psychoanalytic concepts.

Breda Luthar is Head of the Communication Studies Department at the University of Ljubljana. Her research is in media culture and popular culture.

Oto Luthar is Associate Professor of History at the University of Ljubljana. He has written on cultural history and the history of historiography, including *"O žalosti niti besede": Uvod v kulturno zgodovino vélike vojne* (2000).

Irina Popova is an independent scholar who received her Ph.D. in history from Central European University in 2000. She has published articles on the Habsburg Monarchy.

Christian Promitzer is an Academic Assistant in the Department for Southeastern European History at the University of Graz. He is coeditor of *Human Rights in Bosnia and Herzegovina* (1999). He has published articles on minorities, nation-building, racism, and ethnic stereotypes in the former Yugoslavia.

Jiří Štaif is Associate Professor of History and Vice Director of the Institute of Economic and Social History at Charles University, Prague. Most recently, he is author of *Historici, dějiny a společnost. Historiografie v českých zemích od Palackého a jeho předchůdců po Gollovu školu, 1790-1900* (1997) and coeditor of *K novověkým sociálním dějinám českých zemí* (1999).

Kai Struve is a Research Fellow at the Simon Dubnow Institute for Jewish History and Culture at the University of Leipzig. He is coeditor of *Nationalismus und nationale Identität in Ostmitteleuropa im 19. und 20. Jahrhundert* (2000) and *Die Grenzen der Nationen. Identitätenwandel in Oberschlesien in der Neuzeit* (2002).

András Vári is Professor of History at Miskolc University. He was trained as an economist at Budapest University. He is the author of a number of works on the nineteenth- and twentieth-century social history of Hungary, Austria, and Germany. His book, *Az agrárius mozgalom Magyarországon 1830-1909,* will be published in 2003.

Nancy M. Wingfield is Associate Professor of History at Northern Illinois University. She has published books and articles on Czech and Habsburg history. Most recently, she is co-editor, with Maria Bucur, of *Staging the Past: The Politics of Commemoration in Habsburg Central Europe, 1848 to the Present* (2001).

INTRODUCTION

Nancy M. Wingfield

Historians and other social scientists interested in the construction of national identity have increasingly employed the term, "Other," applying it in connection with the identity-building process. In examining the Other, we are examining the relationship between reality and invention. But what is this Other? How does it function? The Other, which is fundamentally different than "We/Us," is part of the process of symbolic exclusion.[1] It is a general expression that applies to situations in which linguistic and other cultural differences are recognized. This was particularly the case in Habsburg Central Europe, with its rich cultural legacy of multinational exchange, during the emergence of self-defined ethnic groups and exclusive national identity beginning in the late nineteenth century.

At least since the Enlightenment, there has been a Western European discourse on a lesser-developed, lesser-civilized Eastern Europe that conjures up overlapping images of the exotic: the Balkans, the East, the Orient.[2] This internal Other is usually marginal, often located at the edge or even beyond the "edge of civilization." Marginal places are not necessarily on geographic peripheries, of course, but rather on peripheries of cultural systems of space, as many of the contributors to this volume note. Others then "carry the image and stigma of their marginality, which becomes indistinguishable from any basic empirical identity they may once have had."[3]

An important aspect of the Other is the Enemy, which is always an Other, although the reverse is not necessarily true. "Enemy Images," a concept derived from psychology and social psychology, are "commonly held, stereotyped, and dehumanized images of the outgroup." The Enemy appears when "We/Us" and "They/Them" are thought to be fundamentally different, emerging from the Other in times of war and other societal violence.[4] While the authors writing here do not assume primordial antagonisms, some do trace the transition of Other to Enemy, particularly in the Balkans during the twentieth century. Their contri-

---

Notes for this section begin on page 15.

butions thus illuminate some of the dangers inherent in the essentializing of other peoples.

At certain times, the identity of the Other as Enemy has been both a legitimate and a unifying force in Habsburg Central Europe. In fact, the identity of this (Christian) region was dependent on the identification of an Other as Enemy, for example, the (Muslim) Ottoman Empire prior to its defeat at Vienna in September 1683 at the hands of forces led by the Polish King Jan Sobieski. Soon afterward, Prince Eugen of Savoy routed the Turks from all of Hungary and later from the rest of the Danubian Basin. The Habsburg military campaigns against this very real enemy resulted in the formation of the so-called Military Frontier along the border regions of the Monarchy, on the other side of which lived the Other.

During much of the "short" twentieth century, the Soviet Union/Russia/communism constituted the Other as a real enemy in Habsburg Central Europe. The attempted internationalization of identity in the Soviet satellite countries after the Second World War fueled the attitude among some peoples of the region that their native communist parties represented an occupying power, rather than a domestic political organization. These views were ascendant in 1989, by which time many citizens of these countries considered communism inimical to the survival of their national identities. While communist parties and their successors, if not the Soviet Union/Russia, remain the Enemy in the eyes of some, it remains to be seen if this Other will have the staying power of the Ottoman Turk.

Many of the essays in this volume build upon recent contributions to nationalism studies, especially those focusing on the construction of national identity. Some of the most important literature in the field traces its origins to the Habsburg Monarchy, including the work of Otto Bauer, Karl Deutsch, Ernest Gellner, and Hans Kohn.[5] A spate of recent publications, including Rogers Brubaker's influential *Nationalism Reframed: Nationhood and the National Question in the New Europe*, attests to the ongoing interest that this region holds for many theorists of nationalism.[6] Indeed, many of the most explosive European national issues of the 1990s have their roots in the geopolitical settlements that resulted from the Paris Peace Conference and the end of the First World War. Certainly, with the breakup of multinational Czechoslovakia and Yugoslavia, the first half of the 1990s saw the revitalization/rebirth of the nation-state with the reconfiguration of political space along national lines in Habsburg Central Europe, even if one does not subscribe to Anthony D. Smith's assertion that nations and nationalism continue to provide the "only realistic socio-cultural framework for a modern world order."[7]

Maria Todorova and Edward W. Said have also influenced many of the contributors to this volume. One of the threads running through these chapters is the relationship of dominant versus subordinate nationalities. These relationships are reflected in a distancing from and denigration of different peoples to the east and southeast that is common throughout Habsburg Central Europe. At the heart of Todorova's pathbreaking book, *Imagining the Balkans*, is consideration of how the Balkans came to be viewed as distinct from the West and why the term "Balkans" came to have pejorative connotations. Todorova identifies a hierarchy of self-identification among the peoples of the Balkans in which virtually every group considers itself more Western and less Balkan than its neighbors to the east and southeast.[8] She subjects Western treatments of the Balkans to a thorough critique, similar to Said's critique of Western discourse on the Orient in his now classic work *Orientalism,*[9] asserting that Balkanism is a similar, though not identical, phenomenon.

The historic myths of a people or nation play an important role in the creation and consolidation of the basic concepts from which the self-image of that nation derives. Such myths vary widely, from the Czech "natural democratic spirit" through the Polish "Bulwark of Christendom" and "Christ of Nations" to the Serbian Kosovo Polje.[10] These myths incorporate not only images of the nation itself, but also images of other peoples, who range from competitors to enemies. Such images, of course, are fluid: a one-time competitor may become an enemy as circumstances change.

Although the creation of ethnic stereotypes during the "long" nineteenth century initially had other functions than the simple homogenization of particular cultures and the attempt to exclude the Other from the public sphere, the evaluation of peoples according to criteria that included "level of culture or civilization" yielded subjective classifications of ethnic groups in Austria-Hungary based on their perceived level of culture and modernization. Different élites increasingly considered it their mission to bring "advancement" and "civilization" to other—usually linguistically different—groups within the Monarchy. These rankings provided the basis for later, more divisive ethnic characterizations of exclusive nationalism. While the Hungarians claimed a civilizing mission over the non-Magyar minorities in Transleithania, the best-known example is the traditional German civilizing mission in Central and Eastern Europe, which began when German-speaking colonists established outposts in "barbarian" Slavic territory during medieval times. The increasingly nationalist nineteenth-century German rhetoric on colonizing missions would be transformed into constructs of German racial superiority during the interwar period.

Not only Slavs, especially those in the Balkans, have been designated Other within Habsburg Central Europe. Indeed, Jews and Roma have historically been among the best-known Others in the Habsburg Monarchy. This is perhaps because both of them are, as Zoltan Barany has suggested, transnational and traditionally non-territorially based peoples (both lacked a home state, until the formation of Israel in 1948).[11] Kai Struve examines the construction of the Jew as Other in rural nineteenth-century Galicia in his contribution to this volume. Peter Haslinger traces the elaboration, beginning during the First World War, of the incompatibility of an alleged Magyar character with Europeanness by the advocates of the Czechoslovak state. Breda and Oto Luthar, in contrast, discuss a strategy—the use of majority popular culture in self-naming—employed by Roma, who are part of the multinational society in northwestern Slovenia.

Some of the essays in this volume locate development of the Other within the context of modernization reflected in the transformation of the rural landscape in parts of the Habsburg Monarchy or in the growth of what Jürgen Habermas has termed the bourgeois public sphere.[12] As Geoff Eley has noted, this public sphere is linked to the growth of urban culture as an arena of a locally organized public life, including concert halls, lecture halls, museums, opera houses, and theaters. It is also connected to a new infrastructure of social communication, the rise of a reading public, improved transportation, and adapted centers of sociability; as well as to the rise of voluntary associations.[13]

In Habsburg Central Europe, the emergence of a public sphere by the mid-nineteenth century was paralleled by the beginnings of national conflict throughout the region. Both were reflected in the voluntary associations into which the various peoples of the Monarchy increasingly organized their social lives in the late nineteenth century, which involved issues of interest, power, and prestige. Vital to the moral authority of the bourgeoisie in towns and cities was the visible performance of civic duties: sitting on charitable or philanthropic committees, improving public amenities, patronizing the arts, promoting education, organizing public festivals, or commemorating historic events.[14] National and civic conflicts resulted in multiple—and riven—public spheres with contestation for dominance among competing interests, including conflicting concepts of national civic society.

This interdisciplinary collection addresses issues of ethnic and national enmity in Habsburg Central Europe from the late eighteenth century to the present. It focuses on the roots, growth, and results of ethnic and national conflict from a variety of historical and theoretical concerns and perspectives. The contributors examine the mutually reinforcing behavior of different groups in the construction and maintenance of a convincing national Other. The topics the essays consider include the role of geography in ethnic identity and stereotyping, the formation of civil society *(bürgerliche Gesellschaft)*, the importance of increasing administrative centralization in the attempt to create homogenous territory and patterns of behavior, the contestation of administrative centralization from the margins, the transformation of the rural landscape and the formation of peasant national identity, and the psychology of nationalism.

The volume is divided into three parts. In the first section, "The Origins and Changing Images of the Other to 1848," Irina Popova, András Vári, and Hugh LeCaine Agnew trace the changes from multiple, varied, anational identities in the Monarchy to the beginnings of exclusive national identities at mid-century. They address the creation of an Other against the background of change due to the state-building efforts and enlightened dynasticism commonly associated with the enlightened absolutist Habsburg Emperor Joseph II, who ruled from 1780 to 1790.[15] In the late eighteenth century, he attempted to organize the Habsburg Lands more rationally by forming a central, unified bureaucracy serving a well-organized state. Joseph II encouraged both the spread of education, fostered from above, and economic liberalization. The Josephine reforms relaxed censorship,

introduced religious tolerance, and instituted linguistic standardization to facili-
tate ease of communication, one of the keys to modernization. Joseph II's impo-
sition of German as the *lingua franca*, both because there were more German
speakers in more provinces than any other national group and because German
had an established literary tradition, angered other linguistic élites throughout
the Monarchy. The German language and culture as the language and culture of
the economic, political, and social élites of the Monarchy would be increasingly
contested from the margins during the nineteenth century. The patterns of dominance and subordination implicit in cultural power relations form another
common thread running through many of the contributions to this volume.[16]

Modern European maps both represented the institutional consciousness of
territory and organized it for state needs. The progress of mapmaking was thus
an indicator of state strength and the state's ability to formulate its strategies
clearly. In chapter one, "Representing National Territory: Cartography and
Nationalism in Hungary, 1700-1848," Popova argues that the history of the
Habsburg Monarchy exemplifies the complexities of the construction of territory, because both the Monarchy and its national élite attempted to identify the
geographic limits of their power. In her examination of the imperial-national
nexus, Popova focuses on Hungary, discussing mapmaking as a method of constructing (supra)national territory. She asserts that national territory was created
as a result of the cultural and political interaction of national élite within the
Monarchy. Moreover, loyalty to the Monarchy was embedded in cartographically expressed national identities.

The mapping of Hungary was the result of the interplay of Habsburg and
local Hungarian institutional activities and individual cartographic practices.
Hungarian mapmakers were implicated in the transformation of imaginable
national groups into imagined communities. This transformation affected elements of cartographic language, such as design, cartouches, symbols, measurements, standards, and the choice of prime meridian.

Ethnic stereotypes in the post-Josephine era from the 1790s to the 1830s had
functions other than homogenization of culture and the exclusion of the Other
from the public sphere. So argues Vári in chapter two, "The Functions of Ethnic
Stereotypes in Austria and Hungary in the Early Nineteenth Century." Early ethnic stereotypes insisted on characteristics that all people, irrespective of culture,
should have, because such characteristics were conducive to the realization of civil
society. These early stereotypes were, in fact, about the way different social segments could live together. Evaluation of people according to criteria of advancement in civilization, however, yielded rankings of ethnic groups. Whatever the
intent, these rankings provided the basis for later, more divisive ethnic characterizations during the era of exclusive nationalism in the late nineteenth century.

Employing descriptive statistical works from the national and regional level,
statistical ethnography, and political pamphlets, Vári investigates writings of two
generations of authors who produced the statistical material *(Statistik)*. The first
group hailed from throughout the Monarchy, the second from Transleithania

only. Vári dates the first period of creating modern stereotypes—differentiated by political intent and content—from 1780 to 1810. The authors of this period employed stereotypes with the intent of reaching and instructing people in order to transform and broaden public opinion. Publications from the second period, 1810 to 1830, mirrored the slow realization of a certain rivalry among languages that had the possibility to act as modernizing agents. This recognition was reflected in the fact that the statistical authors of this era addressed the language issue, which the first generation had not. Although the second generation of authors maintained liberal and anational views, public and political life was going in another direction, precisely because of the open, educational, and recruiting character of stereotypes.

Hugh LeCaine Agnew and Jiří Štaif examine literary sources by Bohemian/ Czech/German authors that not only aided in the construction of the Self and Other in Bohemia but also provided support for the Czech claim of Bohemian state rights *(české státní právo/Staatsrecht)* in the era of modern nationalism. Agnew focuses on the *Vormärz* era, while Štaif concentrates for the most part on the mid-nineteenth century and later. They analyze a number of texts, including major works by Czech patriots Josef Jungmann, František Martin Pelcl, and František Palacký. In addition, Agnew and Štaif discuss the famous forgeries, the Královédvorský/Königinhof and Zelenohorský/Grünberg manuscripts, which played so large a role in the efforts of the Czech "National Awakeners" to bolster Czech claims to a heroic past and to counter traditional negative stereotypes about the Slavs, especially the Czechs, propagated by the Germans.

In chapter three, "Czechs, Germans, Bohemians? Images of Self and Other in Bohemia to 1848," Agnew analyzes the process of national differentiation and integration in Bohemia, which he argues set the stage for increasing Czech-German national-political conflict in Bohemia after 1848. He posits a flexible Bohemian identity that was neither Czech nor German through the mid-nineteenth century. This identity contained three elements that would affect later Czech and German self-images: a "territorial patriotism" that asserted Bohemian uniqueness and loyalty to Bohemia as political entity, which derived in part from Czech culture, history, and language; a German sense of belonging to Bohemia, which was associated with other Habsburg-German territories as well as with the Holy Roman Empire; and social relations in Bohemia, where language was long the most reliable index of social status.

During the nineteenth century, there was a transition from instrumentalizing language as a means of communication to identifying nation with language which would have momentous consequences. The Czechs no longer considered German influence a civilizing one. Indeed, some Czech patriots, while recognizing the virtues of German culture, opted for competition and emulation, rather than assimilation to German culture. Thus, they increasingly formulated their national identity in opposition to the Germans. Perhaps not the quintessential symbol of ethnicity, language is certainly a prototypical element in the modern social construction of nationality, as the Czech case demonstrates.

Beginning during the Revolution of 1848, Bohemian identity was increasingly superceded by Czech and German identities.[17] Although most Jews initially sought acculturation or assimilation with the Germans rather than the Czechs, under the Emperor Francis Joseph and in the First Czechoslovak Republic, some Jews became Czechs, while others became Germans. During the interwar period, some asserted a Jewish national identity. Almost all of them—irrespective of which nationality they claimed—would be killed in the Holocaust. The ultimate Czech victory over the Germans for domination of the Bohemian Lands was confirmed by the internationally sanctioned expulsion of the Germans from Czechoslovakia and elsewhere in Habsburg Central Europe immediately after the Second World War.[18]

In the essays in the second section of the volume, "Austria-Hungary in the Age of Nationalism," Štaif, Struve, Pieter M. Judson, and Regina Bendix consider creation of the Other against the background of the great economic, political, and social changes that rent the Monarchy during its last decades. Following the Revolution of 1848, when nationalism asserted itself in Habsburg Central Europe via the Frankfurt Parliament and the Prague Slav Congress, the subsequent absolutist experiments in the wake of 1848, and the *Ausgleich* in 1867, the Cisleithanian half of the Monarchy began moving slowly toward constitutional monarchism. The vote was repeatedly expanded until universal, equal, male franchise in elections to the imperial Reichsrat was finally achieved in 1907. In contrast, Transleithania would remain politically unitary, ruled by the centralized, nationalistic, and almost solely Magyar bureaucracy.

In chapter four, "The Image of the Other in the Nineteenth Century: Historical Scholarship in the Bohemian Lands," Štaif argues that the development of historiography during this period had a major impact on the process of modern national creation, in which images of the Other played a fundamental role. By the nineteenth century, a Czech nationalist historiography had developed based on a set of assumptions that included these claims: the Czechs were the first people to settle permanently in the Bohemian Lands, they formed their own state and it survived. From the thirteenth century, however, and especially following the defeat of the Czech-speaking Protestant nobility at the hands of the Roman Catholic Habsburg forces at the Battle of White Mountain in 1620, German culture gained ground at the expense of Czech culture.

Štaif focuses particularly on Palacký, the nineteenth-century historian, statesman, and leader of the Czech National Revival. He traces the development of the bilingual Palacký's ideas, beginning with the magisterial *Geschichte von Böhmen* (The History of Bohemia, which appeared in German beginning in the 1830s) and which he began publishing in early 1848 in Czech as *Dějiny národu Českého v Čechách a v Moravě* (History of the Czech Nation in Bohemia and Moravia). Czech nationalists disseminated variations on Palacký's arguments, including his conception of the Germans as an aggressive nation, for popular consumption by the broad Czech national society.

Differing, often opposing, interpretations of the shared past would have fundamental effects on the mentality of both the Czechs and the Germans. With the rise of nationalism during the second half of the nineteenth century, the image of the Other shifted from one of cultural difference to one of the Enemy. This view of the Other survived well into the twentieth century and became part of the respective national histories with disastrous consequences for both peoples during and after the Second World War.

Struve and Judson both examine the modernization of the rural landscape and the formation of peasant national identities. While Struve focuses specifically on Galicia, Judson looks more broadly at Cisleithania. The two authors build upon arguments laid out in *Peasants into Frenchmen*, Eugen Weber's classic discussion of the relative lateness of European peasant identity with the nation in whose borders they reside.[19]

Struve analyzes the complicated and shifting relations among different segments of Galician society in chapter five, "Gentry, Jews, and Peasants: Jews as Others in the Formation of the Modern Polish Nation in Rural Galicia during the Second Half of the Nineteenth Century." He examines the peasants' changing perception of the Jewish Other during the era of modernization. Prior to the development of modern Polish identity in Galicia, which postdated the *Ausgleich,* collective peasant identity had incorporated religious, social, and territorial elements, rather than national elements. The typical village was culturally, physically, and politically isolated. Sharp social tensions had long divided the peasants from their Polish landlords. Polish peasants traditionally identified the Polish gentry with the national state and landlords as the Other. Indeed, when the peasants rebelled in 1846, they attacked members of the landlord class, rather than Jews, who constituted an Other, but not an Enemy. Struve argues that the Jews constituted the strongest personification of alien or Other in the traditional peasant world, precisely because they represented more of a presence in that world than did other outsiders.

After 1867, the nationally engaged intelligentsia worked to overcome peasant distrust of Polish nationalism and to improve the social situation of the peasants. They sought to inculcate temperance among the peasants in part by relocating the center of village life from the taverns and driving away the predominantly Jewish tavern-keepers. Moreover, the Polish peasant movement, which articulated peasant interests as well as stressed their Polish national identities, emerged as a result of cooperation between the nominally left-wing intelligentsia and those peasants who sought change at the local level.[20] This movement propagated the foundation of credit and savings organizations to oust Jewish moneylenders and of Christian shops to redirect trade from "Them"—the Jews to "Us"—the peasants. The latter was similar to the contemporary Czech nationalist movement, *svůj k svému* (each to his own), an economic boycott of German production in the Bohemian Lands. In both cases, national economic competition helped to differentiate the Other.[21] The phenomenon of continuing antisemitism in contemporary Poland (and elsewhere in the region), despite the virtual absence of Jews, reflects the continuing resonance of the Jewish Other.

Judson considers the broadening of the national movement to include peasants in chapter six, "Nationalizing Rural Landscapes in Cisleithania, 1880-1914." One of the striking developments in the multilanguage rural areas of Austria between 1880 and 1914 was the increase in violent incidents that were traceable to nationalist agitation. Judson argues that the changing construction of the national Other propagated by German national associations that struggled, but failed, to gain a foothold in rural areas, coupled with the transformation of the rural world around 1900, produced an attempt to nationalize the rural landscape. While nationalist activism took hold in the Austrian countryside after 1900, it did not necessarily involve mobilization of the peasants. As Judson notes, the expanding networks of commercial markets, communications, and state administration resulted in an influx of civil servants, railway officials, and the like into the countryside. Growing national success in rural areas after 1900 depended in large part on the activism, influence, and loyalties of these new figures in the local landscape.

Judson employs examples of fiction aimed at rural audiences gleaned from German nationalist almanacs to illustrate the transformation of rural life in Cisleithania. The early fiction, recounting private tragedies that resulted from dangerous social interaction—marriage, for example—between different peoples, was a didactic trope aimed at the peasants. Although it initially focused on the rural Other as peasant, after 1910 the fictional context for the national conflict looked decidedly different. So, too, did the rural Other, which now might be a municipal councilor or school board official, relative newcomers to the countryside, who had become authentic subjects of fiction about the rural world. The later trope of "evil regional administrator" was no longer didactic nor particularly aimed at peasants. However, these new characters had to remain vigilant in the face of a national enemy who had numerous means available to gain desperate ends: Slav predominance over the Germans.

Under the patronage of Crown Prince Rudolf, the *Kronprinzenwerk*, which was conceptualized as a scholarly ethnographic work presenting a comprehensive image of the peoples of the Habsburg Monarchy, appeared in twenty-four volumes between 1886 and 1902.[22] Prince Rudolf hoped that these volumes, which were to offer the reader an "ersatz journey" through Austria-Hungary, would generate a love for the Monarchy based upon recognition of the power and strength of cultural diversity. In chapter seven, "Ethnology, Cultural Reification, and the Dynamics of Difference in the *Kronprinzenwerk*," Bendix argues that the work confirmed cultural differences. Rather than fostering Rudolf's patriotic goal, however, it contributed to the growing nationalist tendencies throughout the Monarchy.

Bendix describes the artists, authors, and scholars from across Austria-Hungary who contributed to the undertaking, which employed the newest print technology. Although the contents were negotiated, the potentially liberating impulse inherent in cultural self-preservation was at odds with the Viennese editorial committees, which maintained artistic and intellectual control of the project. Therefore, the vision of the *Kronprinzenwerk* remained paternalistic. Moreover, the language of publication—it appeared in both German and Hungarian, with the contents of the six volumes devoted to the Kingdom of Hungary completely under the control of Hungarian editors—would become a point of contestation. Indeed, the dual-language publication both raised the issue of printing parts of work in other languages of the Monarchy and undermined the common imperial imagination.

The *Kronprinzenwerk* built upon existing scholarship, rather than innovating cultural representation and ethnography. Therefore, it fits within the rich Central European discourse of exhibitions, pictorial traditions, and a variety of other efforts to account for cultural particularism.[23]

In the third section of this volume, "The Legacy: Where Images Collide," Haslinger, Christian Promitzer, Karl Kaser, and the Luthars examine the legacies of Habsburg Central Europe since the end of the First World War. While German speakers had been dominant in Cisleithania, none of the diverse national or anational groups living in the Austrian half of the Monarchy had been specifically obliged to regard itself as a minority. Indeed, the "Iron Ring" government of Count Eduard Taaffe, who served as Minister President of Austria from 1879 to 1893, generally favored agrarian-feudal, clerical, and Slavic interests at the expense of German, liberal ones. The interwar states that replaced the Habsburg Monarchy and the three other defeated empires that had dominated Central and Eastern Europe, however, explicitly regarded themselves as nation-states. Thus, if the formation of the relatively mononational Republic of Austria resolved the issue of nationally mixed regions for the German speakers there, the lot of the numerous interwar minorities elsewhere was politically more demeaning than had previously been the case.[24] Czechoslovakia and Yugoslavia were the most ethnically diverse of the nascent interwar states. The efficacy of the artificial construction of each country's majority, as expressed in Czechoslovakism and Yugoslavism, would be contested during the course of the interwar period, both from within and from without, as the essays in this section of the volume demonstrate.

Czechoslovakism, the official national narrative for the foundation and maintenance of the First Czechoslovak Republic, is a concept advocated by the first Czechoslovak President Tomáš G. Masaryk and others. It argues that the Czechs and Slovaks were two branches of a single Slavic nation, or even that the Slovaks constituted part of the Czech nation and that their language was a form of Czech.[25] Czechoslovakism has received much attention, particularly from those interested in Czech-German relations during the interwar period. Haslinger, in contrast, examines the role of Hungary as Other in the creation of Czechoslovakism in chapter 8, "Hungarian Motifs in the Emergence and the Decline of a Czechoslovak National Narrative, 1890-1930." Haslinger looks at Slovak reception of Czechoslovakism in his analysis of the formulation of discourse strategies around the concept. Indeed, he focuses on the development of the "Slovak question," arguing that the incorporation of Hungarian elements into the national narrative was destabilizing over the long term because neither the Czech nor Slovak adherents of Czechoslovakism proved able to conceptualize adequately the new imagined national community. This was in part because the project remained fluid during the 1920s. Slovak contributions to the national narrative remained, in any case, marginal.

Haslinger traces the limited contacts between the Czechs and Slovaks from the *Ausgleich* through 1914, a period when the Czech-Slovak relationship could be characterized as one of mutual sympathy blurred by substantial differences in perception of one another. One aspect of this misperception was the Czech construction of a Slovak *Naturmensch*, with an idealized vision of the Slovaks as archaic and noble savages. The author also addresses a variety of anti-Hungarian elements that found their way into the Czechoslovak national narrative: the incompatibility of the so-called Magyar national character with Europeanness, the policy of aggressive Magyarization after 1867 that resulted in Slovak subservience, and a deviant Slovak political culture due to the system of values the Slovaks had absorbed under Hungarian rule.

Both administrative difficulties and the failure of Czechsolovakism to meet the needs of the majority of nationally conscious Roman Catholic Slovak intelligentsia diminished the effectiveness of the Czechoslovak national narrative.[26] The Slovak intelligentsia shifted to resistance in the late 1920s. By the end of the first decade of the republic, an independent Slovak discourse, incompatible with Czechoslovakism, had formed, due to Slovak perceptions of structural similarities of pre-1918 Hungary and post-1918 Czechoslovakia, despite differences in the historic context and the political systems. One of the key elements of Slovak national emancipation during this period was the term "Judeo-Magyar," an Other that had been part of Slovak discourse in Transleithania at the turn of the century. When repopularized during the interwar era, stressing antisemitism, it became part of the counterdiscourse to Czechoslovakism, which did not include antisemitic elements.

A major weakness of Czechoslovakism was the lack of a convincing shared Other. For the Czechs, the Other was first and foremost the Germans living in the border regions and linguistic islands of the Bohemian Lands. For Slovak autonomists, however, the Czechs increasingly replaced an earlier Other, the Magyars. While the Czechs' imagined community included Slovaks but not Germans, as Agnew also notes in his essay, the Czech vision of national or imagined territory did not include Slovakia.

By 1992, of course, it was apparent that neither the Czechoslovak identity proposed in 1918, nor between 1945 and 1948, nor even in 1989, was satisfactory to many Slovaks. Thus, the so-called Velvet Divorce resulted in the division of Czechoslovakia into the Czech Republic and Slovakia on 1 January 1993. In post-Velvet Divorce Slovakia, streets and squares have been renamed as historic figures who were rejected, not only by the Czechoslovakists of the interwar period, but also by the communists in the postwar period and the Czechoslovak democrats after 1989, have been claimed. The renaming reflects both the Slovak nationalist aspirations of the interwar era and the previously discredited wartime Parish Republic.

Promitzer employs academic publications to trace changes in Austrian anti-Slavic tradition from the nineteenth century through the present in chapter nine,

"The South Slavs in the Austrian Imagination: Serbs and Slovenes in the Changing View from German Nationalism to National Socialism." He concentrates on the Slovenes of Cisleithania and the Serbs of the Kingdom of Serbia. Austrian perception of the two differed, because they occupied different cultural frontiers in the Austrian imagination. The Slovenes formed one part of a cultural frontier marking the German core lands of Habsburg Central Europe, while the Serbs were located in the Balkans.

Following the *Ausgleich*, the Czech and South Slav national élites also sought compromise with Vienna, but the Germans, seeking to protect their national *Besitzstand* —national assets in terms of property, land, population, and, more elusively, cultural capital—in the frontier areas of the Monarchy, refused. These were not frontiers in geographic or economic terms, but rather indicated that German speakers in these territories lived among people who spoke other languages.[27] By the turn of the twentieth century, German nationalism had absorbed the Austrian anti-Slavic tradition. After the First World War, Austrian study of the South Slavs was concentrated mainly on the Slovenes both within and bordering Austria. This discourse of mourning was concerned with the allegedly unjust borders decided upon at the Paris Peace Conference. Meanwhile, the German-language study of Southeastern Europe during this period became centered in Germany. In 1928, the Weimar German government provided funds to found the first of several institutes for the study of what would be termed *Südostforschung* with a focus on the German minorities of Southeastern Europe. Nazi ideology permeated this research more and more following the seizure of power in 1933, and following the *Anschluß*, Austrian Nazis aided in *Südostforschung*'s transition from a discipline of Austro-German national revisionism to a tool of National Socialist geopolitics.

Promitzer concludes that the location of Slovenia—Central Europe or the Balkans—remains an issue today. Since 1989, the Slovenes, along with the Croats, have emphatically situated themselves within Central Europe. They declined, for example, to attend the first-ever Balkan summit in November 1997, because they did not consider themselves Balkan. The Serbs, however, remain on the southeastern side of the boundary between Habsburg Central Europe and the Balkans.

Kaser decodes the ethnographic representations of two leading social scientists from Yugoslavia, the Serbian geographer Jovan Cvijić and the Croatian sociologist Dinko Tomašić, to demonstrate how closely geographic and ethnic perspective are linked in the Balkans. The point of comparison in chapter ten, "Peoples of the Mountains, Peoples of the Plains: Space and Ethnographic Representation," is Cvijić's and Tomašić's ethnographic representation of the Serbs (the Dinaric Mountain people) and the Croats (the plains people). Kaser details the respective work of these two scholars, separated by a generation, on this topic. He argues that their work represents characteristic constructions of cultural otherness: they portray the Other from different historic contexts and national perspectives.

With the wars of Yugoslav succession in the 1990s, traditional images of the Other have resurfaced on all sides. After years of neglect, the works of Cvijić in

Serbia and Tomašić in Croatia have again become popular. Their messages have been politicized and recycled in a kind of Balkanization of the Balkans by contemporary nationalists, some of whom assert that Croatia and Slovenia tend toward western cultural values, while Serbia and Montenegro do not.

Kaser explicitly employs Todorova's theoretical framework in his conclusion. Describing Cvijić as a cultural relativist and Tomašič's work as reflecting "discursive hardening," he calls for a correction of their selective perceptions. He suggests a broadly comparative approach to the Balkans, one that explores not only local and regional cultures but also overarching phenomena.

The Luthars investigate the fluidity of Central Europe as a concept from before the First World War, when it—as *Mitteleuropa*—referred to regions of German cultural and political hegemony, primarily within the German Empire and the Habsburg Monarchy, through the post-1989 era, when Central Europe has been pushed east. Because they are closely linked with the changing concept of Europe and its eastern territories, Central Europe's boundaries remain sites of contestation. Beyond its geographic, historic, and social dimensions, Central Europe also has a fictional dimension, and practices of inclusion and exclusion are dependent on the way it perceives itself and others. The Luthars argue in chapter eleven, "Marking the Difference or Looking for Common Ground? Southeast Central Europe," that the imaginary borders of civilization in Southeastern Europe are always south of one's own geographic territory. Each group considers its southern neighbor a space for primitive ethnic conflict and exotic underdevelopment. First formulated in the fifteenth century, the stereotypical Turk, the threatening Oriental Barbarian from the south, has been recycled in the contemporary right-wing political discourse of the region. The historic Turk has become emblematic of an entire range of contemporary Oriental/Other figures, including two generations of economic migrants, primarily Bosnians from the former Yugoslavia and refugees.

By way of contrast to the hegemonic notion of ethnic citizenship, the Luthars offer the example of traditionally multiethnic Prekmurje in northeastern Slovenia. Intercultural practices still thrive in this region, which includes Hungarians, Roma, and Slovenes of different confessions. Moreover, prior to their deportation by the Nazis in 1944, Prekmurje also contained two Jewish communities. The authors argue that identity is the product of cultural, political, historical and other discourses. They assert the importance of exploring the constructed nature of national identity as well as both the fictional and real nature of the concept of Central Europe. This is necessary to get beyond reassertion of traditional essentialist allegiances and identities.

Rather than a regional case study, the last chapter in this volume, "The Psychology of Creating the Other in National Identity, Ethnic Enmity, and Racism," considers the psychological dimensions of national identity. Peter Loewenberg argues that humanistic and psychoanalytic understandings of national identity incorporate inner subjective dimensions of experience necessary for understanding history and politics. Loewenberg cites examples from two of the great literary figures of the twentieth century, James Joyce and Robert Musil, to support his argument that national identity is constructed in a variety of ways. The author identifies a major character from *Ulysses*—Leopold Bloom, born in 1866 to a Hungarian-Jewish father and a gentile mother—as a modern Odysseus who reflects the tensions of chauvinist twentieth-century identity politics. Loewenberg argues that in *The Man without Qualities*, Musil challenged the concept of national character, deconstructing the essentialist concept of identity by describing the multiple identities of each individual.

Loewenberg critiques three main social science approaches to national identity, arguing that the family communication model, one of the older models, offers the most relevance for research on issues of the topic. It draws upon the concept developed by Austro-Marxist Bauer that a nation is a community shaped by shared experiences. Arguing that nationalism begins in the family and home, Loewenberg asserts that we are not daily born anew—we carry internalized pasts within us.

The contributors to this volume offer compelling perspectives on creating the Other in Habsburg Central Europe from a number of disciplinary and geographic views. They address the formation and transmission of numerous intellectual traditions in the modern era, providing scholars with new avenues of approach for the study of the region's past and present. The case studies presented here do not address every Other that has been constructed from peripheral and diaspora peoples during the last several hundred years in Habsburg Central Europe. Rather, these articles invite comparisons with subaltern/subordinate peoples throughout the region, and indeed, throughout the world. These examinations of changing construction and meaning of the Other are contributions to a larger discussion on national identity and ethnic enmity. Moreover, the authors provide cautionary examples for those who assume primordial identities of the peoples of Habsburg Central Europe and/or static relations among them. Such examples are especially important because assumptions of age-old ethnic/national enmities among the peoples of the region still dominate much of the popular and at least some of the academic discourse.

Notes

1. I have taken the terminology for much of my discussion of the Other from Vilho Harle, "On the Concepts of the 'Other' and the 'Enemy'," *History of European Ideas* 19,nos. 1-3 (1994): 27-34.

2. On the construction of Eastern Europe, see Larry Wolff, *Inventing Eastern Europe: The Map of Civilization on the Mind of the Enlightenment* (Stanford, Calif.: Stanford University Press, 1994); on overlapping images of the East, the Orient, and the Other, see Milica Balić-Hayden, "Nesting Orientalisms: The Case of Former Yugoslavia," *Slavic Review* 54, no. 4 (Winter 1995): 917-31.

3. Rob Shields, *Places on the Margin: Alternative Geographies of Modernity* (London: Routledge, 1991), 3.

4. Harle, " Concepts of the 'Other,'" 27-28.

5. Otto Bauer, "Die Nationalitätenfrage und die Sozialdemokratie" (Vienna, 1908); Karl Deutsch, *Nationalism and Social Communication: An Enquiry into the Foundations of Nationality*, 2nd ed. (Cambridge, Mass.: MIT Press, 1966); Ernest Gellner, *Nations and Nationalism* (Oxford: Basil Blackwell, 1983); Hans Kohn, *The Idea of Nationalism* (New York: Collier-Macmillan, 1944).

6. Rogers Brubaker, *Nationalism Reframed: Nationhood and the National Question in the New Europe* (Cambridge: Cambridge University Press, 1996). See also Eric J. Hobsbawm, *Nations and Nationalism since 1780: Programme, Myth, Reality*, 2nd ed. (Cambridge: Cambridge University Press, 1992); and Anthony D. Smith, *Nations and Nationalism in a Global Era* (Cambridge: Polity Press, 1995); also Jeremy King's recent discussion of the historiography of nationalism in nineteenth-century Habsburg Central Europe and writings on nationalism more generally, "The Nationalization of East Central Europe: Ethnicism, Ethnicity, and Beyond," in *Staging the Past: The Politics of Commemoration in Habsburg Central Europe, 1848 to the Present*, ed. Maria Bucur and Nancy M. Wingfield (West Lafayette, Ind.: Purdue University Press, 2001), 112-52.

7. On the revival of the nation-state and the reconfiguration of political space along national lines, see Brubaker, *Nationalism Reframed*, 2; and Smith, *Nations and Nationalism*, 159.

8. On Balkan self-designation, see Maria Todorova, *Imagining the Balkans* (New York: Oxford University Press, 1997), chapter 2.

9. Edward W. Said, *Orientalism* (New York: Random House, 1978).

10. See, for example, Thomas Emmert, *Serbian Golgotha Kosovo* (Boulder: East European Monographs, 1997) and the chapters on Czechs and Poles in Geoffrey Hosking and George Schöpflin, eds., *Myths & Nationhood* (New York: Routledge, 1997).

11. Zoltan Barany has made this point as part of his analysis of the continued marginalization of Roma in *The East European Gypsies: Regime Change, Marginality, and Ethnopolitics* (Cambridge: Cambridge University Press, 2002); "Memory and Experience: Anti-Roma Prejudice in Eastern Europe," Woodrow Wilson Center for Scholars, East European Studies, Occasional Paper 50 (July 1998); "Orphans of Transition: Gypsies of Eastern Europe," *Journal of Democracy* 3 (1998): 142-56. The literature on the Jew as Other is enormous. A recent collection on the topic is Robert S. Wistrich, ed., *Demonizing the Other: Antisemitism, Racism, and Xenophobia* (Amsterdam: Harwood Academic, 1999).

12. See Jürgen Habermas's seminal work, *The Structural Transformation of the Public Sphere: An Enquiry into a Category of Bourgeois Society*, trans. Thomas Burger with the assistance of Frederick Lawrence (Cambridge, Mass.: MIT Press, 1992). A number of historians and other social scientists have elaborated upon this topic. See, for example, Geoff Eley, "Nations, Publics, and Political Cultures: Placing Habermas in the Nineteenth Century," in *Culture/Power/History: A Reader in Contemporary Social Theory*, ed. Nicholas B. Dirks et al. (Princeton, N.J.: Princeton University Press, 1994), 297-335; and Harold Mah's critique of

both, "Phantasies of the Public Sphere: Rethinking the Habermas of Historians," *Journal of Modern History* 72, no. 1 (March 2000): 152-82.

13. Eley, "Placing Habermas," 298-99.

14. Ibid., 303.

15. The complicated character of Emperor Joseph II has excited numerous biographers. Among the most recent is T.C.W. Blanning, *Joseph II* (London: Longman, 1994).

16. On cultural politics, see, for example, Peter Jackson, *Maps of Meaning: An Introduction to Cultural Geography* (London: Allen and Unwin, 1989), 4-8.

17. On the change from non-national to national identities, see most recently, Jeremy King, *Budweisers into Czechs and Germans: A Local History of Bohemian Politics, 1848-1948* (Princeton: Princeton University Press, 2002).

18. There is a vast literature on this topic. See Peter Heumos, ed., *Heimat und Exil. Emigration und Rückwanderung, Vertreibung und Intergration in der Geschichte der Tschechoslowakei* (Munich: R. Oldenbourg Verlag, 2000); and Alfred J. Rieber, ed., *Forced Migration in Central and Eastern Europe, 1939-1950* (London: Frank Cass Publishers, 2000).

19. Eugen Weber, *Peasants into Frenchmen: The Modernization of Rural France, 1870-1914* (Stanford, Calif: Stanford University Press, 1976).

20. Patrice M. Dabrowski and Keely Stauter-Halsted have both stressed the role of commemorations in the development of Polish peasant nationalism. See Dabrowski, "Folk, Faith and Fatherland: Defining the Polish Nation in 1883," *Nationalities Papers* 28, no. 3 (September 2000): 397-426, and Stauter-Halsted, "Rural Myth and the Modern Nation: Peasant Commemorations of Polish National Holidays, 1879-1910," in *Staging the Past*, 153-77.

21. On the politics of economic differentiation in the Bohemian Lands, see Catherine Albrecht, "Pride in Production: The Jubilee Exhibition of 1891 and Economic Competition between Czechs and Germans in Bohemia," *Austrian History Yearbook* 24 (1993): 101-18, and "The Rhetoric of Economic Nationalism in the Boycott Campaigns of the Late Habsburg Monarchy," *Austrian History Yearbook* 32 (2001): 47-67.

22. *Die Österreichisch-ungarische Monarchie in Wort und Bild* ("Kronprinzenwerk"), 24 vol. (Vienna: k. & k. Hofdruckerei, 1886-1902).

23. The nationalities section of the 1908 Emperor's jubilee parade—all participants were required to wear folk costume—was at the zenith of a variety of regional and national exhibitions that included people as representatives of "living cultures," during the last decades of the Habsburg Monarchy. See Elisabeth Grossegger, *Der Kaiser-Huldigungs-Festzug, Wien 1908* (Vienna: Verlag der Österreichischen Akademie der Wissenschaften, 1992).

24. On postwar territorial arrangements, see Joseph Rothschild, *History of East Central Europe between the World Wars* (Seattle: University of Washington, 1974).

25. On Masaryk's idea of Czechs and Slovaks as two branches of one Slavic nation, see Roman Szporluk, *The Political Thought of Thomas G. Masaryk* (Boulder, Colo.: East European Monographs, 1981), 39.

26. On the religious limitations of Czechoslovakism, see, for example, the reaction of militant Slovak populists to Jan Hus commemorations in 1925 in Cynthia J. Paces, "Religious Heroes for a Secular State: Commemorating Jan Hus and Saint Wenceslas in 1920s Czechoslovakia," in *Staging the Past*, 209-35.

27. On national *Besitzstand*, see Pieter Judson, "'Not Another Square Foot!': German Liberalism and the Rhetoric of National Ownership in Nineteenth-Century Austria," *Austrian History Yearbook* 26 (1995):83-97. On frontiers, see Judson, "Frontiers, Islands, Forests, Stones: Mapping the Geography of a German Identity in the Habsburg Monarchy, 1848-1900," in *The Geography of Identity*, ed. Patricia Yaeger (Ann Arbor: University of Michigan Press, 1996), 395.

Part One

THE ORIGINS AND CHANGING IMAGES OF THE OTHER TO 1848

Chapter 1

REPRESENTING NATIONAL TERRITORY

Cartography and Nationalism in Hungary, 1700-1848

Irina Popova

Historians have viewed the construction of national territory as a "civilizing mission" of the state, which broke local particularism by means of administrative centralization, mapping, transportation, markets, schooling, and the army, and created homogeneous territory and patterns of behavior.[1] One of the critiques of this argument came from political scientists and political sociologists, who reflected on the contemporary separatist movements and challenged the idea of total homogenization, paying attention to territorial cleavages and spatially different ways of political mobilization within the national states.[2]

The history of multinational states and the Habsburg Monarchy in particular provides a good example of complexities of the construction of territory, since both the Monarchy and its national élite attempted to identify the geographic limits of their power. Research into the eighteenth-century history of the Monarchy has pointed to the political and cultural sense of community, the imperial supranational identity transcending the local traditions that started to emerge in the Monarchy during the eighteenth century.[3] However, students of nineteenth-century Habsburg history have virtually put aside the multinational milieu of the Monarchy that stimulated emerging national movements. Furthermore, researchers are used to considering only inner resources of national groups, claiming that the Habsburg Monarchy delayed the building of national states and failed to accommodate the nationality problem.[4]

This essay offers a different perspective on the "nation-empire" nexus and addresses Hungarian mapmaking to show the interplay of imperial and national contexts in cartographic representations of national territory.[5] It argues that maps

Notes for this section begin on page 33.

became a tool for constructing national identity, and that national identities expressed through cartographic production contained loyalty to the Habsburg Monarchy as an integral part.

Discussing the evolution of Hungarian mapmaking and its Habsburg context, this essay pays tribute to the postmodernist enthusiasm for the idea of the world as a representation with the emphasis on discourse and narrative.[6] Following current intellectual developments, historians of cartography have utilized methods of literary theory and cultural anthropology with their extended understandings of textuality and Foucault's vision of discourses constructing their objects.[7] Therefore, the map and atlas are understood as representations and discursive texts embedded in reality and creating it. From this perspective, the content of maps can only be grasped when the ethnic, religious, social, and cultural environment that produced them is taken into account.[8]

Research into the cartographic representations of national territory has been concerned with several aspects of mapmaking. Scholars have pointed out that European governments used maps as a tool for administrative centralization. Learned communities of Western Europe made maps instrumental in conceptualizing the eastern part of the continent and creating a discourse on it.[9] Maps were also involved in the international efforts of small and great powers to secure their influence in some regions of Europe such as Macedonia, and to "prepare the way for establishment of local hegemony."[10] Additionally, the ethnographic maps of Macedonia reflected developing ethnic and national identities there, and proved to be an identity-shaping factor. In interwar Germany, joint efforts by scholars and nationalists "created a network of institutions engaged in the production and distribution of suggestive maps and managed to establish a system of coercion which ensured a unified nationalist message."[11]

This essay views the mapping of Hungary as the interplay between Habsburg and local Hungarian institutional activities and individual cartographic practices. It substantiates the involvement of Hungarian mapmakers in the transformation of imaginable national groups into imagined communities, and shows the ways that this transformation affected the elements of their cartographic language such as design, measurement standards, cartouches, symbols, the choice of prime meridian, and the languages cartographers utilized.

Hungarian Cartography in the Habsburg Context

Modern European maps signified the institutionalized consciousness of territory and organized it for state needs. The progress of mapmaking was an indication of both the state's strength and its ability to clearly formulate its strategies. To generate this ability, the Habsburgs turned mapmakers into its employees with regular salaries, and imposed the function of regular mapping on special military bodies such as the Corps of Engineers.[12]

Until 1747, when the Corps was created and subordinated to the Headquarters of the Quartermaster General (*Generalquartiermeisterstab*), the Habsburg administration and military authorities had relied mainly on foreign private cartographers and engineers, and had commissioned maps of single provinces and their borders. In the seventeenth century, maps were a tool of propaganda for the dynasty, a record of the famous battles, and a definition of particular territorial units. In the eighteenth century, maps proved to be at the center of the struggle between the imperial administration and provincial estates, which turned maps into a tool that rendered "political rights as a spatial abstraction" to oppose them to the imperial centralization.[13]

The first comprehensive description and mapping of the Monarchy was undertaken between 1763 and 1787, and covered the borders and borderlands of the Habsburg possessions. Drawing a comprehensive map of the dynasty's dominions was hindered by the lack of uniformity in the methods of taking measurements. This effort involved the institution of new departments within the military administration, such as the Department of Topography of the Military Archive established in 1764.

The first comprehensive measurement of the Habsburg Monarchy denoted a new perception of its territory among the rulers and administration. Maps penetrated the decision making of cameralist bureaucrats and their spatial behavior. Maps served the Austrian state and "assisted the Habsburgs and their ministers in carrying out the social and political responsibilities prescribed by the eighteenth century for the enlightened government." On the other hand, the ministers believed that the state was the center of society and of cartographic concern, and maps therefore became a tool of the governments to "meddl[e] with society." Large-scale programs of educational reform, highway building, health care, and industrial growth streamed from the Viennese government. The maps of the period both reflected and stimulated this expansion by the state.[14] Furthermore, by 1768, when the first comprehensive measurement was in progress, Emperor Joseph II had started to treat the Monarchy as a single unit and not as an agglomeration of provinces, and his travels, which covered a major part of the Austrian dominions and their frontier regions, supported his conviction.[15]

The creation of the Austrian Empire and the dissolution of the Holy Roman Empire in 1804-1806 turned the king-estates dualism into the dualism of king and nation(s).[16] All the functions of the state were defined as "Austrian," and imperial (military) cartography, which had been inspired by Napoleon's achievements, was involved in creating the identity of a new state.[17] Institutionally, the Topographic Bureau of the General-Quartermaster Headquarters created in 1844 and the Institute for Military Geography established in 1839 were in charge of executing these new tasks.[18] The second comprehensive mapping of the Monarchy (1806-1869) standardized local spatial practices within the Austrian *Kaiserstaat*. At the same time, the beginning of ethnographic mapping challenged Metternich's "imperialization of the Empire," which was based on the German-directed centralism. Ethnographic maps outlined the territories of national groups, and the national political élite began to use these maps in order to represent their spatially concrete political and cultural claims.[19]

The interaction of the imperial and Hungarian administration can be clearly seen in the institutionalization of Hungarian cartography, both in the Empire's reliance on Hungarian resources, and in the mapping of the Austrian-Hungarian border.

At the beginning of the eighteenth century, Hungarian mapmaking and engineering developed mainly in aristocratic estates and estates of the Hungarian Treasury, which was "part and parcel of the financial system of the Habsburg lands."[20] The Hungarian Treasury hired private engineers to map and maintain the royal estates and to execute the regulation of the rivers that started in the 1720s in the southern parts of Hungary. To deal with growing problems of transportation (mainly navigation) and the colonization of depopulated areas in the 1760s and 1770s, the Hungarian Treasury staffed its newly created technical departments and its network of local offices with professional engineers, who had been trained by Austrians, Bohemians, and Germans at the Collegium Oeconomicum in Szenc (1763-1776) and the Studium Cameraticum in Tata (1776-1780). During the first comprehensive measurement of the Monarchy, the engineers of the Hungarian Treasury were required to assist imperial military surveyors.

The imperial experiment of instituting a technical advisory body, the Allgemeine Ober-Hofbau Direction (1783-1788), subordinated to the Austrian-Bohemian Chancellery, reflected the difficulties and unreasonableness of centralized control over all the territory of the Monarchy. However, decentralization and the establishment of the Directory for Navigation and Construction for Hungary in 1788 brought administrative confusion as its result, since the new body was financed by the Hungarian Treasury and exploited its network of local offices, and had the candidates for positions in the central office nominated by the Hungarian Vice-regal Council.[21] Throughout the first half of the nineteenth century, the Vice-regal Council tenaciously attempted to gain full control over the Directory.

The Directory for Navigation and Construction was concerned primarily with navigation. With the exception of the large-scale mapping of the Danube between 1823 and 1838 and the projects of the Tisza regulation in the late 1840s, the engineers of the Directory focused on local projects. It was the Vice-regal Council's Departments of Postal Service and Public Transportation, county engineers, and private Hungarian cartographers and engineers, as well as the engineers of the Habsburg army, who prepared the maps of the whole country and showed its connections with the Hereditary Lands.[22]

Throughout the first half of the nineteenth century, Hungarian engineers, who worked in the counties, and maps they attached to their projects introduced and popularized the idea of large-scale national construction projects aimed at homogenizing the country's space and modernizing its landscape. In 1807, István Vedres, the city engineer of Szeged, suggested using the Hungarian financial contribution to the Monarchy to create a national transportation network, which would consist of canals and navigable rivers and would be a part of the imperial and European transportation networks. According to his meticulous and lengthy proposal, income generated by the canals could finance Hungary's industry, trade, education, sciences, and national culture.[23] Until the 1840s, Hungarian engineers continued to consider canals the foundation of the country's transportation, although already by the late 1820s, some engineers regarded the artificial waterways as an anachronism compared to the advantages of railways in Europe and the Habsburg Lands.[24] In the 1830s and 1840s, Hungarian lawmakers and the government came to realize the need for integrating the country's territory through transportation. Law 1836:XXV identified strategic aims for transportation development in Hungary, and was followed by private construction works in the sphere of public transportation. On the very eve of the Revolution of 1848-49, Count Széchenyi and his collaborators in the Transportation Committee of the Vice-regal Council developed a comprehensive program for Hungarian construction works.[25] At the same time, Hungarian engineers and politicians started to regard the map as a tool for strategic economic planning for the country.[26]

From the 1730s onwards, the Vice-regal Council supported Hungarian private cartographic projects. It endorsed the initiatives of Mátyás Bél and Sámuel Mikoviny to complete the geographic description and mapping of the country, and requested that the local authorities assist in and proofread the description. Yet the Vice-regal Council had to struggle with the counties, which were reluctant to send back the required information, and cited a number of reasons (including the costs of proofreading, complex property relations, workload, the worthlessness of Bél's work, and the postal service) for the delays and lack of cooperation. Bél's project developed into five volumes of geographic description of the counties (with enclosed maps).[27] During the first half of the nineteenth century, the Vice-regal Council and the Archduke-Palatine Joseph sustained the endeavors of private cartographers to draw general maps and atlases of the country and coordinated local cartographic activities which were reinforced by the Institutum Geometricum (1782-1850) with German and Latin as the languages of instruction. The members of its faculty were born and educated in Hungary and had been teaching in Hungary and Austria before being appointed professors at the Institutum.[28]

The comprehensive mapping of the Hungarian Kingdom was a prerogative of the military institutions of the Monarchy. The Hungarian Court Chancellery was instrumental in providing the coordination of the imperial military cartographic operations in the Hungarian counties. In the course of the first comprehensive measurement of the Monarchy, the Chancellery required the assistance of Hungarian civil surveyors for the mapping of Maramaros county in 1766. The services of the counties' authorities and engineers were also requested for proofreading the local names on the map of Colonel Baron Andreas von Neu, which was a result of the military mapping of Hungary between 1782 and 1785.[29] In 1784, the Chancellery tried to adjust the usage of the Austrian census pattern in Hungary and to allay noble unrest and resistance to the census. Two years later, the Chancellery was instrumental in promoting the cooperation of military and county engineers, when Joseph II ordered the cadastral mapping in order to support the administrative reform of Hungary.[30] The work of civil engineers was hindered by the lack of cooperation on the part of the nobility, who again resisted the royal initiative. The military had to supervise civil engineers, and the meticulousness and strictness of the former were somewhat irritating to the latter.[31] Occasionally, the civil engineers made their maps and measurements independently.

With the superseding of Latin as a language of mapmaking by German and, to a far lesser extent, Hungarian and Slavic languages, the mapping and description of Hungary contributed to Joseph II's policy of introducing German as the official language of the Monarchy, and reflected his vision of this language as the most suitable to create cultural progress in the Monarchy. Hungarian engineers who took part in the imperial measurements later painfully reflected on this period and claimed that Hungarians became aliens in their own country due to the language policy of the Emperor.[32]

In terms of career opportunities within the Habsburg Monarchy as a whole, Hungarians were underrepresented in the imperial cartographic establishment. The cases of Mikoviny and an army officer, János Lipszky, were exceptions to the general career pattern, which usually began with an assistantship to a county engineer, then continued at the Institutum Geometricum (more rarely at the Engineering Academy and Polytechnical Institute in Vienna) and abroad (a short-term scholarship for studies), and developed into either a position in the county, or work for the Directory for Navigation and Construction.[33] During the 1830s and 1840s, the extensive usage of Hungarian in cartography and engineering intensified Hungarian cartographic exclusiveness.

Mapping the Austrian-Hungarian Border

Issues of property relations in the frontier region emerged out of the question of the border between Austria and Hungary. This border was produced by the dialectic of local, national, and imperial interests, and was constructed out of local social relations in the border region.[34] The first to map the Austrian-Hungarian border were estate engineers and surveyors. Between 1717-18 and 1828-30, mapping was a part of the work of the demarcation commissions appointed by the Hungarian Court Chancellery and approved by the Diet and the administration of the respective Habsburg territory. The Hungarian arguments to a great degree incorporated elements of public national discourse. For instance, the commission often stressed that it was negotiating on behalf of the constitutional state and the Hungarian (noble) nation.[35] In 1793-94, following the stormy anti-Habsburg Diet of 1790-91, the commission emphasized that Hungary was acting as a state independent of the other Hereditary Lands.[36] Hungarians insisted that the Hungarian Holy Crown exercised the right of property over all the territory of the country, and that strips of the Hungarian territory incorporated into Austria were incorporated only temporarily.[37] These claims notwithstanding, the continuous Austrian control over parts of the Hungarian western frontier led to their inclusion as part of Austria, and the Hungarians somewhat reluctantly accepted these alterations in the Compromise arrangements of 1867.[38]

Maps of the border were the outcome of the demarcation commissions' proceedings and visualized the arguments of the negotiating sides, but it was not until 1828-30 that the discussion turned from historical and constitutional issues to the actual maps. The manuscript maps of the border, usually prepared in only a few copies, isolated the frontier zone as a specific region of contact of the two powers, and portrayed a variety of local social and political structures, as well as the mutability of the natural borders. It was the printed maps of Hungary and the Empire that fixed borders as indisputable and encoded all the aspects of the Hungarian state existence.

Mapping Hungarian Identity

This part of the essay argues that (national) identity is a complex and changing structure, which can be hardly reduced to only one of its constituents.[39] Imperial loyalty was one of these elements, and was constantly a focus of attention among the Hungarian political and cultural élite. This essay shows three periods in the evolution of identities of private mapmakers and outlines their changing visual representations of Hungary.

Between 1700 and the 1780s, the European and Austrian maps of Hungary identified the kingdom of St. Stephen as a semi-European Catholic state with rich historical traditions and traditions of wars with the Turks.[40] The European and Austrian maps, atlases, and geographic descriptions were unanimous in portraying and describing Hungary in the broad sense with the territories that belonged to the kingdom in the fourteenth century. In doing this, European maps referred first of all to historical tradition and political realities, and to a far lesser extent "transposed the ancient lands of Asia onto modern maps of Europe," as Larry Wolff has claimed.[41] The European maps also delineated Hungary's participation in the Habsburg anti-Turkish wars by depicting military fortifications as a part of the Hungarian landscape and by referring to the victorious Habsburg army. The latter and the ruling dynasty were the subject of constant laudations on the part of Austrian mapmakers. Georg Mattheus Seutter, for instance, showed the representatives of the lands of the Holy Crown humbly offering their coats of arms to the Emperor Leopold I.[42] Hungarian geographers, who had an allegiance to the Holy Roman Emperor (and simultaneously the king of Hungary) in their set of loyalties, made the borders of the Holy Roman Empire, together with the ethnically mixed areas within Hungary, a topic of scholarly expertise.[43]

Hungarian maps of the period showed the country in a narrow sense as consisting of Hungary proper, Slavonia, and the Hungarian counties of Transylvania. The major part of Hungarian maps was topographical, which delineated Hungarian localities and counties. The maps showed the relief, borders, social and political structures, transportation systems, historic events, and people in national costumes together with allegoric figures, thus signifying the very beginning of the transformation of the universalism of the Baroque and Classicism into the realism of national culture. Sámuel Mikoviny, the key figure in the development of modern Hungarian mapmaking, symbolically united his individual maps of the counties into a narrative by choosing the Hungarian prime meridian, which passed through the northeastern tower of the royal castle in Pozsony. The mapmakers of the period from 1700 through the 1780s envisaged the application of maps in military and civil administration, history writing, and anticipated strategic economic planning based on the cartographic production.[44]

Hungarian self-definitions of this period included class (nobility), polity, and terrltory, which was a common homeland for all nationalities and ethnic groups (*natio Hungarica*).[45] Hungarians also identified themselves through region and religion, and far less often through language. Cartographers, who originated mainly from the ethnically mixed areas of Upper Hungary, reflected the multiculturalism of the region and of the Hungarian Kingdom in their work. Hungarian maps of the period assigned particular domains for each language—Latin names for the political institutions and legends to the maps, German names for cities, and Hungarian and Slavonic names for towns and villages.[46] In this respect, the attempts of contemporary scholars to prove the Magyar or Slovak identity of the intellectuals and mapmakers appear fruitless, for the multilingualism of the national élite makes evident their Hungarian and not Magyar or Slovak feelings.[47]

Hungarian mapmakers believed that the multiplicity of national groups and multiculturalism were the unique features of Hungary. Mikoviny's manuscript map of Upper Hungary associates the country with a fountain surrounded by people resting and drinking from it. The figure of a traveler on this map symbolically connects localities of the region. Mikoviny portrays this traveler as taking his trip on foot and stopping for a moment to look at the map, and thus implies the emerging modern spatial behavior.[48]

Region and religion were closely interconnected in the identity of Hungarian mapmakers. The majority were Protestants and were born in Upper Hungary, which was populated predominantly by Lutherans, who toiled to turn the region into a national center of education.[49] The financial support of the Hungarian Lutheran parishes made it possible for the mapmakers to receive their higher education in Germany, and the Hungarian maps of the period conceptualized Hungarian data through German scientific paradigms. Hungarian Lutheran gymnasiums taught geography with the help of maps, which were usually brought to Hungary from Germany or the Netherlands. Additionally, the teaching methods of Bél, the rector of the Lutheran gymnasium in Pozsony, widened the geographical framework of his students beyond the limits of their native villages. To achieve this, Bél made the students describe Hungarian counties with the help of a questionnaire that he developed.[50]

The works of János Tomka-Szászky, who succeeded Bél as the rector of the Pozsony Lutheran gymnasium, introduced a historical perspective to Hungarian mapmaking.[51] Tomka-Szászky buttressed the idea of continuity in the Hungarian territoriality with historic evidence and maps, and stressed Hungary's identity as a multinational state located on the borderland between Habsburg-dominated Central Europe and Eastern Europe.[52] His atlas tells a story of loyalty to Queen Maria Theresa, and its title page portrays her sitting on the throne surrounded by faithful subjects.[53]

Between the 1790s and the 1810s, the administrative integration of the Habsburg realm and creation of the Austrian Empire offered a dual challenge for cartographers—first to portray the Empire as a political unit, and second to reflect upon the nature of the Austrian-Hungarian relationship. Austrian maps proposed an image of imperial space without inner borders bound by the use of the German language, by the imperial measurement standard, by the Viennese meridian, and by portraits of the members of the Habsburg dynasty.[54] On the other hand, Austrian and European maps stressed all the attributes of Hungarian statehood, such as the coat of arms and Latin as the official language, and utilized the Hungarian measurement standard, thus debilitating the integrity of the new Empire.[55]

The Hungarian reaction to these new political developments was complicated. The Hungarian élite kept its political and linguistic distance from Vienna, though it preferred Austrian educational and publishing opportunities to the intellectual attractions and resources of Germany.[56] The reliance of Hungarian cartographers on imperial databases grew considerably, though some authors, such as Ézsaiás Budai, continued to use German sources.[57] Eduard (Edvárd) Greipel's atlas of Hungary represented the Austrian Empire as a unified territory, but at the same time highlighted Hungary by using the Hungarian language and emphasizing its borders within the empire.[58]

Dedications to members of the Habsburg dynasty and the usage of the German language by Hungarian mapmakers also brought Hungary closer to the Empire, though it was not accepted for a Hungarian patriot of the period to speak German or to wear German dress. János Berken(y) provided German equivalents for the most important places in Hungary on his map of Europe, and intended this map to be dedicated to Archduke Charles.[59] János Mátyás Korabinszky, who prepared an atlas of Hungary, followed the arguments of the so-called Hungarian or patriotic trend in the national movement. Members of this group, one of whom—a Lutheran priest and a teacher, Sámuel Bredeczky (Bredetzky)—was close to Korabinszky, came from multinational Upper Hungary and associated themselves with the conservative trend within the Hungarian political élite.[60] Bredeczky accentuated patriotism—"a holy fire which drives a noble good citizen to noble actions" and opposed it to nationalism, or "pernicious creeping fervor, which carbonizes the pillars of the building and prepares its collapse."[61] Korabinszky's atlas claimed to profess Hungarian patriotism using German, which Korabinszky preferred to the other languages (Hungarian, Slovak, and Croatian) with which he was familiar.[62] German is preeminent among the variety of vernaculars on Korabinszky's general map of Hungary.[63]

The issue of the national language and the problem of Hungary's Europeanness entered Hungarian political discourse and became important to the self-definition of mapmakers in the 1790s. The language movement emerged as a result of the education reform of 1777, the influence of the German Enlightenment, and the centralizing and Germanizing assault of Joseph II. Hungarian opposition to the Emperor's far-reaching reforms resulted in Law 1791:X, which stated that Hungary was free and independent with respect to its entire administration and constitution, and was to be ruled and governed by the constitutionally crowned king. The language innovation designed by Ferenc Kazinczy, whose map collection contained sixty-five maps of Hungary and fifty-four maps of foreign territories, supplemented political initiatives of the Hungarian nobility.

Latin was the official language of the Hungarian Kingdom, though as the language of education, church services, and cartography, it steadily yielded to Hungarian and, to a far lesser extent, German. A tendency to extend the usage of Hungarian in mapmaking became salient in the 1790s and manifested itself in the linguistic engagement of mapmakers, for instance, in the works of Demeter Görög and György Szaller. Görög, a court governor in Vienna, contributed to Hungarian periodicals and advanced plans to create a Hungarian learned society. Both Görög and Szaller supported the dissemination of the national language; the former offered prizes for the best Hungarian grammar book and dictionary and the best essays on the importance of the national language, and the latter composed a popular Hungarian grammar book, which was then translated into Slavic languages.[64] Görög had many prominent Hungarian writers as his friends and was perceived by contemporaries as a self-made person, who advocated the interests of Hungary in the Empire.[65] Görög's position at the court enabled him to access imperial cartographic collections for preparing his maps of the counties. County engineers trained in the Institutum Geometricum made a number of maps for this project. Bound in an atlas, these maps were published with the generous support of Count György Festetich, to whom Görög dedicated forty-one of the sixty-two maps. The atlas emphasized political functions of the counties and their constitutional autonomy. At the same time, the atlas of Görög and the map of Szaller provided Hungarian versions of local names and reflected a trend toward delineating the territory of Hungary as linguistically homogeneous.[66]

The maps of the Hungarian Kingdom showed the expanded territorial authority of the Vice-regal Council and the Hungarian Treasury, and started to depict Hungarian natural resources and religious and national groups. Together with geography textbooks, they demonstrated that Hungarian local and regional identities were steadily replaced by strong identification with the territory of the country. Korabinszky, for instance, implemented Bél's method of teaching geography, believing that the study of the subject should start with one's native county. The students were then to make an imaginary journey across their counties and the entire country. These imaginary journeys became those of encounter with the national community and a kind of "domestication" and personalization of national space. Korabinszky himself maintained a strong regional (Upper Hungarian) identity, though his regionalism had imperial and Protestant connotations.[67] When depicting the Danube as disproportionally large on his map of Hungary, Korabinszky expressed his belief that the river was an inherent element of the country's identity.[68] At the same time, he underlined a supranational regional identity that he believed the inhabitants of the Danubian Basin had developed.

The idea of Europeanness appeared in Hungarian public thought due to the increased number of foreign travelers in the country. The accounts of international visitors represented Hungary as a transitional zone from backwardness to civilization. Both Hungarian and international authors pointed to multilingualism as a sign of backwardness, and the promotion of a single national language in Hungary looked in this respect essentially European.[69] Hungarian mapmakers believed that the national language, maps, and freedom of thought were all prerequisites for the spread of civilization in Europe, and they toiled to disseminate the Hungarian language and maps in the sphere of education. Foreign stereotypes and ignorance of the region proved a constant challenge for Hungarian geography and cartography. Facing the lack of knowledge of Hungary in Europe, Hungarian mapmakers intended their works as a source of information on the country, and their maps became part of Hungary's image as it was constructed in the West.[70]

A widely disseminated Hungarian map that was highly regarded abroad was that of a Hungarian officer in the Habsburg army, János Lipszky, who identified the precise geographical location of five hundred settlements in Hungary.[71] The map was the product of his service in the military cartographic commission of Colonel Neu. Lipszky enjoyed the powerful backing of imperial and Hungarian authorities and was able to use new measurements, astronomical observations, and maps from the Festetich family archive. The multiplicity of measurement standards on Lipszky's map (German, Hungarian, Austrian, Polish, Italian, Turkish, English, and Russian) reveals the author's intention to have it used in Europe, and thus to expose Hungary to the rest of the continent. The picture on his map of peasants and surveyors taking measurements brought localities and remote areas into the context of the nation and the Empire.

From the 1820s to the 1840s, Austrian cartographers continued their work of incorporating Hungary into the Empire, but at the same time, emphasized the economic division of the Empire by marking the borders of tariff zones with a special symbol.[72] The translation and publication of Austrian maps in Hungary was a factor for the rapprochement of the Empire's two halves.[73] The attempts of the Hungarian gentry to achieve linguistic uniformity revealed its efforts to establish itself as a ruling élite. Hungarian steadily replaced Latin in all spheres of administration and public life including mapmaking, especially after 1844, when it became the official language of the Kingdom.[74]

During their travels around Hungary, members of the Magyar political and cultural élite propagated an image of the rural population preserving all the attributes of the nationality such as the pure Hungarian language. At the same time, the élite strove to replace the oral transmission of culture within isolated rural communities with the "more abstract realities" of science, technology, and formal learning throughout the whole country.[75] The Hungarian language, textbooks, and maps made in Hungarian were to support the educational endeavors of the élite, but encountered the opposition of the non-Magyar nationalities, who constructed narratives of resistance and narratives about maps but did not have sufficient resources to defy the Magyars cartographically.[76]

Ferenc Karacs, an engraver and a prominent mapmaker, supported the language movement and was an active member of the Calvinist community in Pest. One of his major works—the first wall map of Hungary made in Hungarian for an educational institution—went far beyond the scope of his parish and the needs of the Pest Calvinist school, showing a linguistically uniform and politically independent country.[77] One more educational cartographic project—the Hungarian globe of István Nagy and Antal Vállas—attributed importance to geography and cartography within the structure of modern education.[78] Mihály Táncsics tirelessly worked to extend elementary education in Hungarian among children and adults in Hungarian urban centers, and his slim textbook on geography with a map of Hungary was part of a large educational project.[79]

Hungarian mapmakers joined the political reform movement of the nobility and the language movement of the *literati* and thus contributed to the identity change, which broadened the framework of the traditional understanding of nation beyond the noble estate.[80] The increasingly popular definition of the nation included the territorial community of citizens braced by the constitution, speaking the same language, and contributing to the economic progress of the country, which was a part of the Habsburg Empire and Europe. The mapmakers were of non-noble or low noble origin, but their political maps of Hungary emphasized the counties as a foundation of the Hungarian polity and custodians of the Hungarian noble nation opposed to the Viennese government.[81] Geography textbooks and the works of Ferenc Karacs, Antal Vállas, Sámuel Blaschnek, and Lajos Schedius expressed these ideas and corroborated the country's Europeanness, which was one of the vital elements of Hungarian national identity.[82]

The idea of isolation of Magyars in Europe and the idea of the country's position between East and West was a determinant of national self-awareness over the centuries, together with the idea that the Magyars were the shield of the Christian world.[83] Hungarian authors wrote about their people's Asiatic past, a time when the Magyars were moving across the Asian steppes without any name in history, in order to emphasize the level of contemporary development of the country whose geographic location was at the epicenter of the European-Asiatic encounter. Likewise, Hungarian geography textbooks and linguistic studies attributed a positive meaning to the Asianness of the Magyars, singled them out among the nationalities of the Kingdom, gave them a right of conquest and leadership within the Danubian Basin, and claimed that the Magyars derived the best features of their national character (freedom, pride, faithfulness, and courage) from the "Asiatic" period in their history.[84] Emerging Hungarian ethnographic cartography involved itself in debates over the Europeanness or Asianness of Hungary and the Magyars. Heufler's map pointed to the Asian origin of the Magyars, stating that the people from Asia were among those whom the Austrian Empire united.[85]

The opposition to the idea of Hungarian "Asianness" came from several sources, first of all from Europe itself and European cartographic production, which considered Hungary a European country.[86] János Csaplovics, the author of an ethnographic map of Hungary, drew parallels between Hungary and England, and called Hungary a Europe in miniature in the sense that Hungary, just like Europe, was home to numerous nations. Csaplovics' comparison attracted criticism from "fantasts indulged in the Romantic notions of an Oriental Magyarism."[87] The works and projects of the Hungarian engineers, who followed Western technological achievements, encouraged the nation to look westward; so too did mapmakers such as Karacs with his *Hungarian Atlas of Europe*.[88] The dedications on the maps of this atlas, which was made with the assistance of his son Ferenc and with the support of the Vice-regal Council, underscored Hungary's prospects in the Habsburg Monarchy and in Europe, gave emphasis to the Hungarian counties as a basis of the political system, and showed the author's attention to the problems of education.

The maps of Lajos Schedius, member of the Academy of Sciences, editor, playwright, poet, and the first Protestant appointed professor at Pest University, summed up the evolution of Hungarian mapmaking in the period. The works of Schedius were a cartographic response to Klemens von Metternich's policy of gradual incorporation of Hungary into the Empire, to the Austrian maps, which showed Hungary as a Habsburg province, and to the attempts to create a new Austrian identity.[89] As early as 1802, Schedius lamented that Hungarian geographic knowledge was not precise, bitterly remarking that one could hardly find a map of the country created on the basis of measurements and astronomic data.[90] Thirty years later, he suggested his own vision of Hungarian territory. His map was preceded by one that the Secretary of the Vice-regal Council, József Aszalay, and Ferenc Ortlischek made in Latin.[91] The wall-size map by Schedius made in German and Hungarian had the meridian of Buda as prime meridian, embodied the latest achievements of cartography, and featured the Hungarian large coat-of-arms and images of the national capitals Pozsony, Buda, and Pest. The Hungarian coat-of-arms on the map had a special meaning given the penchant of the Habsburg imperial government of extending the usage of imperial symbols into Hungary in the 1830s.[92] Two editions of this map furnished more details on the country's educational institutions (schools, academies, universities) and public transportation (railways), and completely marginalized Latin as the language of mapmaking.[93]

The Circulation of Maps in Hungary

One of the most difficult questions for research concerns the effect that maps produced on the reading public. In a novel published in the 1840s, Jozef Miroslav Hurban, a loyal Hungarian, described a young noble, Vladimír Boleslavský, who spent his leisure time climbing the highest peaks of the Tatra Mountains with his friend and tutor. Resting on the rocks with a map in front of them, they both conveyed their thoughts about the Slovak people and the splendor of national landscapes.[94] Hurban turned the landscape into a powerful object of identification of the Slovak élite, calling Slovaks the Tatra Slavs, and writing of the Tatra as a made-of-stone expression of the Slav idea.[95] For him, the map proved a link between national feelings, perception of the national landscape, and the national territory. The lack of sources, however, makes it impossible to assess whether anyone followed the example of Hurban's characters, though in the 1840s the phrase "let us look at the map of the country" penetrated Hungarian political discourse, and the Hungarian élite began to think of maps in terms of economic prosperity and national security.[96]

Nevertheless, the circulation of maps was small, and their publication often encountered financial problems, as in the case of the atlas of Karacs, which had only 250 subscribers, and the author himself and then his widow continued to publicize this work in order to have the costs of the edition covered. An examination of forty-five family map collections in the Hungarian National Archive reveals that educational institutions and wealthy collectors such as the families Festetich, Batthyány, and Károlyi did not miss a chance to purchase foreign or local cartographic publications concerning Hungary. They also sponsored the making of maps, their dissemination, and the training of mapmakers.[97] The less well-off purchased maps of the Hungarian counties, the Hereditary Lands, and, more rarely, maps of Hungary. Among the most popular works were those of Mikoviny and Görög, the historical maps by Karacs, and the wall map by Schedius.

To attract public attention to Hungarian maps, publishers appealed to readers' patriotism and claimed that maps and atlases were as important as newspapers, thus impelling a potential audience to support national cartographic production.[98] In 1825, one of the deputies of the Hungarian Diet proposed a law that school maps of the counties would have to be prepared by certified engineers using an approved scale. Official reply to this initiative stated that it was a private opinion, which could not be considered an official proposition.[99] Some Hungarian authors, such as Károly Kiss, thought it was necessary to spread high-quality military cartographic works throughout the country, making maps tools for learning about other cultures.[100]

Conclusion

As John Agnew and Stuart Colbridge have put it, "Spatial practices and representations of space are dialectically interwoven."[101] As an expansion of this statement it may be suggested that the dispositions of localities, nations, and supranational space in the Habsburg Monarchy intermingled in spatial representations of Hungary. Modern spatial behavior was formed in Hungary by the extensive mapping of national territory, through the institutionalization of mapmaking, and the dissemination of maps. The growing accuracy of maps and the consequent correct depiction of the borders influenced it: "A firmer grasp of the nature of linear frontier developed, one that was possibly associated with improved mapping and a more definite perception of the nature of the political sovereignty."[102] The increased availability of maps made them an inalienable element of modern spatial behavior and education.

Identifying its territory the Habsburg Monarchy reached into Hungarian localities and acted as a modernizer of local spatial practices. At the same time, the Empire set a pattern for the cartographic conceptualization of Hungarian territory and thus prompted Hungarian national cartographic projects. It activated Hungarian cartographic resources and created the institutional support and databases of sources for the development of the Hungarian cartographic school. On the other hand, the Empire did not provide enough possibilities for career promotions and thus limited cartographic activity to the national framework. Hungarian mapmaking drifted from heteroglossia to the supremacy of the Hungarian national language, and the aggrandizement of the Hungarian national movement had the cartographic layout of the national territory as one of its manifestations. Therefore, the national movement emerged as the "acquisition" of national space by means of cartography and as the creation of a national project of European progress.

Notes

1. This thesis was exemplified by the work of Eugen Weber, *Peasants into Frenchmen: The Modernization of Rural France, 1870-1914* (Stanford, Calif.: Stanford University Press, 1976).
2. John Agnew, *Place and Politics. The Geographical Meditation of State and Society* (Boston, Mass.: Allen & Unwin, 1987).
3. Ernst Wangermann, *The Austrian Achievement* (London: Thames and Hudson, 1973), 19.
4. László Szarka, *Szlovák nemzeti fejlődés—magyar nemzetiségi politika: 1867-1918* (Poszony: Kalligram Könyvkiadó, 1995), and Jiří Kořalka, *Tschechen im Habsburgerreich und in Europa 1815-1914* (Vienna: Verlag für Gescichte und Politik; Munich: R. Oldenbourg Verlag, 1991).

5. Jánoo Sallai, *Magyarország történelmi határai a térképeken* (Budapest: Püski, 1995); Lajos Szántai, *Atlas Hungaricus. Magyarország nyomtatott térképei, 1528-1850*, vols. 1-2 (Budapest: Akadémiai Kiadó, 1996); *Granice Hrvatske po zemljovidima od 12. do 20 stoljeca* (Zagreb: Muzej za umjetnost a obrt, 1992).

6. Homi Bhabha, "DissemiNation: Time, Narrative, and the Margins of the Modern Nation," in *Nation and Narration*, ed. Homi Bhabha (London: Routledge, 1990), 297.

7. Michel Foucault, *The Archaeology of Knowledge* (New York: Routledge, 1972), 44, 205-6.

8. Trevor J. Barnes and James S. Duncan, eds., Introduction, *Writing Worlds: Discourse, Text and Metaphor in the Representation of Landscape* (London: Routledge, 1992), 5.

9. Larry Wolff, *Inventing Eastern Europe: The Map of Civilization on the Mind of the Enlightenment* (Stanford, Calif.: Stanford University Press, 1994).

10. Henry Robert Wilkinson, *Maps and Politics. A Review of the Ethnographic Cartography of Macedonia* (Liverpool: Liverpool University Press, 1951), 6.

11. Gunthram Henrik Herb, *Under the Map of Germany: Nationalism and Propaganda, 1918-1945* (New York: Routledge, 1997), 179.

12. John Marino, "Administrative Mapping in the Italian States," in David Buisseret, ed., *Monarchs, Ministers, and Maps: The Emergence of Cartography as a Tool of Government in Early Modern Europe* (Chicago: University of Chicago Press, 1992), 5-25.

13. James Vann, "Mapping under Austrian Habsburgs," in *Monarchs, Ministers, and Maps*, 160-67.

14. Ibid., 167.

15. Derek Beales, *Joseph II*, vol. 1 (Cambridge: Cambridge University Press, 1987), chapter 8.

16. János Mailáth, *Gedrängte Geschichte des österreichischen Kaiserstaates bis auf die neue Zeit* (Vienna: Schweiger, 1851), 291.

17. Franz Wilhelm Klenner, *Topographische Handelskarte des österreichischen Kaiserstaates* (Vienna: Druck Freyertag, 1833).

18. Oskar Regele, *Generalstabschefs aus 4 Jahrhunderten* (Vienna: Verlag Herold, 1966); Lajos Szabó, *Katonai térképeink* (Budapest: Pesti könyvnyomda-részvénytársaság, 1910).

19. Jakov F. Golovatskij, *Etnograficheskaja karta russkogo narodnaselenija v Galichine, severovostochnoj Ugrii i Bukovine* (Vena, 1800); Pavel Šafářik, *Slovanský zemevid* (Prague, 1842).

20. Béla Király, *Hungary in the Late Eighteenth Century; The Decline of Enlightened Despotism* (New York: Columbia University Press, 1969), 101.

21. Klára Dóka, *A vízmunkálatok irányítása és jelentősége az ország gazdasági életében, 1772-1918* (Budapest: A mezőgazdasági ugyvitelszervezési Iroda, 1987), 12-27, 52-103; Győző Ember, "A magyarországi építészeti igazgatóság történetének vázlata (1788-1867)," *Levéltári Közlemények* 20-23 (1942-45): 345-75.

22. The Department of Postal Service relied heavily upon the county engineers and senior post officers (Hungarian State Archive, Országos Levéltár [OL], S. 12, Div. XVIII).

23. István Vedres, *Eggy nemzeti jószág, mellyet Magyar ország és a hozzá kapcsolt tartományok számára 's javára szerzett Vedres István* (Szeged: Grünn Orbán, 1807), 76-87, 10-11, 18-19.

24. József Beszédes, *Mérnöki irányzatok* (Pest: Trattner–Károlyi, 1843), 153-67, and the map of the canals' network in southern Hungary attached to the book.

25. István Széchenyi, *Javaslat a magyar közlekedési ügy rendezésérül* (Poszony: Belnay, 1848).

26. Jozsef Petzelt, *Elöadásai útépítészetböl* (Pest, 1847-48, the manuscript record of Petzelt's lectures in the Institutum Geometricum), 3-4.

27. Mátyás Bél, *Notitia Hungariae novae historico geographica*, vols. 1-5 (Vienna: Johann Peter van Ghelen, 1735-42); Lajos Haan, *Bél Mátyás*. (Budapest: M.T. Akadémia könyvkiadó-hivatala, 1879), 39-40, 42-48.

28. Ferenc Fodor, *Az Institutum Geometricum. Az egyetem bölcsészeti káran 1782-töl 1850-ig fennállott mérnöki intézet* (Budapest: Tankönyvkiadó, 1955).

29. Andor Borbély and Julia Nagy, *Magyarország I. katonai felvétele II. József korában* (Budapest: M[agyar] kir[ályi] állami térképeszet, 1932). Map collection of the Institute of Military History, Budapest, B IX a 1116.

30. Zoltán Dávid, "Magyarország első katasteri felmérése (1786-1789). Forrástanulmány," *Történeti Statisztikai Évkönyv* (1960): 33-58.

31. OL, P 717, the archive of the Zichy family, cs. 572, l. 25-37, 42, 50.

32. Paul Mitrofanov, *Joseph II. Seine politische und kulturelle Tätigkeit* (Vienna: C.W. Stern, 1910), 262-63. Vedres, *Eggy nemzeti jószág*, 30-33. Vedres' maps of Kistelek and Tápé, in Csongrád county, both in Hungarian, are in OL, S. 77, #709:2, #717.

33. The data on the Institutum graduates are calculated on the basis of 312 biographies of Hungarian engineers collected by Fodor, in *Magyar vízimérnököknek a Tisza-völgyben a kiegyezés koráig végzett felmérései, vízi munkálatai és azok eredményei* (Budapest: Tankönyvkiadó, 1954).

34. Peter Sahlins, *Boundaries: The Making of France and Spain in the Pyrenees* (Berkeley: University of California Press, 1989), 8.

35. OL, Acta Limitanea A 115 [AL], Collection of microfilms [MT], 31623, l. 254, 256; 31622, l. 27.

36. A memo from the Hungarian demarcation commission to Austrian demarcation commission, 5 July 1793. OL, AL, MT 31621, l. 378.

37. Memo of 5 July 1793. OL, AL, MT 31621, l. 381.

38. Andrew Burghardt, *Borderland: A Historical and Geographical Study of Burgenland, Austria* (Madison: University of Wisconsin Press, 1962), 79.

39. Anthony Smith, *National Identity* (Reno: University of Nevada Press, 1991), 14.

40. [Luigi Ferdinando] Marsigli, *Carte de la Hongrie et des pays qui en dependoient autrefois* (Paris, 1703); idem, *La Hongrie et le Danube* (La Haye, 1741); Magda Jászay, "Marsigli, a katona, diplomata és tudós Magyarországon a török kor alkonyán," *Történelmi szemle* no. 1-2 (1999): 31-52.

41. Wolff, *Inventing Eastern Europe*, 185; Szántai, *Atlas Hungaricus*, vol. 1, 68, 247, 170, 276.

42. Szántai, *Atlas Hungaricus*, vol. 1, 324, 173, vol. 2, 582.

43. Haan, *Bél Mátyás*, 69-71. See Bél, *Institutiones lingvae Germanicae* (Hala [Magdeburg]: J.E. Fritsch, 1730), Introduction, § IX; idem, *Der ungarische Sprachmeister oder kurze Anweisung zu der edlen ungarischen Sprache* (Preßburg: Johann Paul Royer, 1729), Introduction, II, § 3.

44. László Bendefy, *Mikoviny Sámuel megyei térképei*, vols. 1-2 (Budapest: MTAK, 1976), vol. 1, 269-73.

45. Tofik M. Islamov, "From *natio Hungarica* to Hungarian Nation," in *Nationalism and Empire: The Habsburg Monarchy and the Soviet Union*, ed. Richard L. Rudolf et al. (New York: St. Martin's Press, 1992), 166-67.

46. Samuel Krieger, *Regni Hungariae in suos Circulos et Comitatus divisi Tabula Nova ex recentioribus Astronomicum et Geometrarum observationibus concinnata*, 1785.

47. See, e.g., Ján Tibenský, "Matej Bel a Apológia Trenčianskej stolice," *Historický časopis* 25, no. 2 (1977): 251, 257.

48. Mikoviny, *Liberae regiaeque et montanae civitates*, a manuscript map from the Map Collection of the National Széchényi Library, Országos Széchényi Könyvtár [OSzK].

49. Bél, *Der ungarische Sprachmeister*, 67-68. János Tomka-Szászky, *Introductio in orbis antiqui et hodierni geographiam*, vol. 1 (Pozsony: Johann Michael Landerer, 1777), 525.

50. Lubomír Prikryl, "Matej Bel a vyučovanie zemepisu," in *Pedagóg Matej Bel, 1684-1749* (Bratislava: Slovenská pedagogická knižnica a Ústav školskýh informácií v Bratislave, 1985), 224-30.

51. Tomka-Szászky, *(Atlas Parv[us] Hung[ariae]). Regn[um] Hungariae* (Pozsony, 1750-51).

52. Tomka-Szászky, *Conspectus introductionis, in notitiam regni Hungariae, geographicam, historicam, politicam et chronologicam* (Pos[z]ony: Johann Michael Landerer, 1759), C. 1, § 1, C. 3, § 8-12.

53. György Radvánszky, with whom Tomka-Szászky corresponded, had audiences with the Queen and attended her coronation in Prague in 1743. OL, P 566, III. A., LIII. cs./c, 60, 84-87. On the atlas as a narrative, see J.R. Ackerman, "Structuring of Political Territory in Early Printed Atlases," *Imago Mundi* 47 (1995): 139.

54. Szántai, *Atlas Hungaricus*, vol. 1, 169, vol. 2, 490, 632-34.

55. Samuel Dunn, *Hungary and Transylvania; with Croatia and Sclavonia; also Moldavia and Valakia* (London, 1774, 1789, 1794, 1810).

56. János Berken(y), *Új Posta mappája Magyar és Erdély Országoknak a' Posták legujjabb elintézések szerént* (Bécs, 1806) published with the support of Count Lajos Rhédei. Berken(y) to letter to Ferenc Széchényi, 24 July 1793 OL, P 623, cs. 31, 9, p. 1.

57. Ézsáias Budai, *Oskolai magyar Új Átlás* (Debrecen: Ref. Kollegium, 1804).

58. Wood, "Pleasure in the Idea," 30, 36; Eduard Greipel, *A nemzeti atlasz* (Pest: Greipel, 1819).

59. Berken(y), *Új Posta mappája*; Berken(y) to Széchényi, 8 November 1797, OL, P 623, cs. 31, 9, p. 6.

60. Moritz Csáky, "Die Hungarus-Konzeption. Eine 'realpolitische' Alternative zur magyarischen Nationalstaatsidee?" in *Österreich unter Maria Theresia und Joseph II. Neue Aspekte im Verhältnis der beiden Länder. Texte des 2. Österreichisch-ungarischen Historikertreffens, Wien, 1980*, ed. Anna Drabek, Richard Plaschka and Adam Wandruszka (Vienna: Verlag der österreichischen Akademie der Wissenschaften, 1982), 81-84.

61. Samuel Bredetzky (Bredeczky), *Reisebemerkungen über Ungern und Galizien*, vol. 1 (Vienna: Doll, 1809), 185-86.

62. János Mátyás Korabinszky, *Geographisch-historisches und Produkten Lexicon von Ungarn* (Preßburg: Weber und Korabinskische Verlag, 1786).

63. Korabinszky, *Vorstellung des Königreichs Ungarn nach den Poststationen für Reisende* (Preßburg, 1786); idem, *Atlas Regni Hungariae portatilis* (Vienna: Schaumburg, 1804), III.

64. Among the people who responded to the appeal of Görög was Vedres, *A' magyar nyelvnek a' magyar hazában való szükséges voltát tárgyozó hazafiui elmélkedések* (Vienna: David Hummel, 1790); see also György Szaller, *Hungarica Grammatica Latine et Germanice* (Pozsony: Simon Peter Weber, 1794).

65. József Márton, *Görög Demeter életleírása* (Vienna: Haykul Antal, 1834), 30; Ferenc Kállay, "Görög Demeter tiszteletbeli tag felett (emlékbeszéd)," *Tudománytár* (1834): 139-85.

66. Demeter Görög, *Magyar Átlás, az az Magyar, Horvát, és Tót országok' Vármegyéji', 's Szabad Kerületei és a határ-őrző Katonaság' Vidékinek közönséges és különös Tábláji* (Vienna: Auctor, 1802). Szaller, *Magyar Ország elosztva Vármegyékre, mellyeknek Neveit a' hasonló Nevű Helységek vagy várok viselik, hol melléjek irattak* (Pozsony, 1796).

67. Korabinszky, *Geographisch-historisches und Produkten Lexicon*, 4-5, 145-60, 475-98.

68. [Korabinszky], *Almanach von Ungarn auf das Jahr 1778* (Vienna and Preßburg: Verlag der Gesellschaft, 1778), 158. Two engravings attached to his *Almanach* are views of Kassa and Eperjes.

69. Szaller, *Hungarica Grammatica*, VIII-IX, X-XII.

70. Bredetzky, *Beiträge zur Topographie des Königreichs Ungarn*, vol. 2 (Vienna: Camesinaische Buchhandlung, 1803), V, 34-35, 37.

71. János Lipszky, *Mappa generalis regni Hungariae partiumque adnexarum Croatiae, Slavoniae et Confiniorum Militarium, magni item principatus Transilvaniae, geometricis partium dimensionibus, recentissimisque astronomicis observationibus superstructa* (Pest: Kilian, 1806).

72. *Postkarte der österreichische Monarchie* (Vienna 1829), and the reference book *Reise-Buch zur der Postakarte der österreichischen Monarchie* (Vienna, 1829).

73. Johann Schönberg, *Karte von dem Königreiche Ungarn mit den Königreichen Kroatien und Sklavonien und dem Grossfürstenthum Siebenbürgen* (Vienna, 1826). The map was published in Hungarian in 1840 under the name *Magyarország és Erdély*.

74. On the language policies in Hungary, see László Péter, "Language, the Constitution, and the Past in Hungarian Nationalism," in *Európa vonzásában*, ed. Ferenc Glatz (Budapest: MTA Történettudományi Intézete, 1993), 193-204.

75. Paul Claval, *An Introduction to Regional Geography* (Oxford: Oxford University Press, 1998), 133, 135.

76. Ján[os] Csaplovics, *Rozgjmánj o zmadařowánj zemé Uherské, aneb o Nemadarů w Uhřich na Madary obracowánj* (Prague: Jan Pospissil, 1842), 5-6, 17-18, 20.

77. Ferenc Karacs, *Magyarországnak és a hozzá kapcsoltatott Horváth és Tóth Országoknak a határorzo katonai vidékeknek nem külömben az Erdélyi Nagy Fejedelemségnek vármegyékre és szabad területekre osztatott s a legjobb mappák szerént készitetett közönséges táblája* (Pest, 1813).

78. Antal Vállas, *Az égi és földtekék' használáta* (Vienna: J.P. Sollinger, 1840), VI.

79. Mihály Táncsics, *Életpályám* (Budapest: Révai Könyvkiadó, 1949), 98, 126-28; idem, *Általános földleirás és magyar tartományok' leirása* (Pest: Emich Gusztáv, 1845) with the map *Magyar ország és Erdély földabrosza*; idem, *Magyar nyelvtudomány* (Buda: M[agyar] Kir[ályi] Egyetem, 1840).

80. Péter, "Language, the Constitution, and the Past in Hungarian Nationalism," 196.

81. [Gusztáv Rauschmann], *Magyar és Erdély ország közönséges földképe* in the atlas of Alajos Bucsánszky, *Az egész világ felülete* (Pozsony, 1845).

82. [n.a.], *Magyar Ábéce, a fiú és leány oskolák számára* (Debrecen: Tóth Ferenc, 1831), 13, 14.

83. Gyula Ortutay, "Between East and West," in *Europa et Hungaria. Congressus ethnographicus in Hungaria*, ed. Gyula Ortutay and T. Bodrogi (Budapest: Akadémiai Kiadó, 1965), 265.

84. Károly Puky, *A magyar haza* (Pest: Trattner–Károlyi, 1833), 40, 42-43.

85. J.V. Heufler, *Sprachenkarte der österreichischen Monarchie sammt erklärender Übersicht der Völker dieses Kaiserstaates, ihrer Sprachstämme und Mundarten, ihrer örtlichen und numerishcen Vertheilung* (Pest, 1846).

86. Szantai, *Atlas Hungaricus*, vol. 1, 19-21.

87. Ortutay, *Between East and West*, 268. See also János Csaplovics, *England und Ungarn. Eine Parallele* (Halle: Renger, 1842), 1, 122-26; idem, *Gemälde von Ungarn*, vol. 1 (Pest: Hartleben, 1829), 13, 14 and the ethnographic map of Hungary, *Ethnographische Karte des Königreichs Ungarn sammt Croatien, Slavonien, der ungrischen Militärgrenze und der Seeküste nach Lipszky*.

88. Petzelt, *Előadásai útépitészetből*, 3-4. See also the map attached to Széchenyi, *Javaslat a magyar közlekedési ügy rendezéséről*; Karacs, *Európa magyar Átlása* (Pest, 1821-1838).

89. A. Floder, *Strassen Karte der Oesterreichischen Monarchie* (Vienna, 1835).

90. Quoted in Fodor, Fodor, *A magyar térképirás története*, (Budapest, Honvéd Térképészeti Intézet, 1953), vol. 2, 178.

91. József Aszalay and Ferenc Ortlischek, *Mappa generalis topographico-ecclesiastico-ethnographico statistica regni Hungariae partiumque adnexarum Croatiae Slavoniae et Confiniorum Militarium Magni Item Principatus Transzlvaniae* (Vienna: Aszalay, 1825). The map was reprinted in 1830-38, 1840, 1844, and 1848.

92. See József Laszlovszky, *A magyar címere története* (Budapest: Pythenas, 1989), 27-28.

93. The first edition of this map was published in 1838 in Hungarian and German, *Magyarországnak, mellék-tartományainak és Erdély földabrosza*. The second edition was prepared with Sámuel Blaschnek and published in 1847.

94. Jozef Miroslav Hurban, "Prítomnost a obrazy zo života tatranského," in Hurban, *Dielo*, vol. 1 (Bratislava: Tatran, 1983), 254.

95. Hurban, "Slovensko a jeho život literárny," in *Dielo*, vol. 2, 23.

96. Miklós Skerlecz, "A kereskedelmi bizottság által az állam gazdaságának fejlesztése érdekében ajánlott törvények és azok megokolása," in *Skerlecz Miklós Báró művei*, ed. Pál Berényi (Budapest: Grill Károly könyvkiadóvállalata, 1914).

97. OL, p. 623, the correspondence of Ferenc Széchényi, cs. 31; OSzK, KT, Levelezes, Budai's letters to Széchényi.

98. *Tudományos Gyüjtemény* 1. éfv., k. 3 (1844): 100-101; *Honművész* (1836): 396, 397; (1837): 685-86.
99. OL, N. 64, Lad. XX, #16, Fasc. B, #2, 18.
100. Károly Kiss, "A hadi földképekröl és tervrajzokról," *Félső magyarországi Minerva* IV (1836)," 36, 46.
101. John Agnew and Stuart Colbridge, *Mastering Space: Hegemony, Territory, and International Political Economy* (New York: Routledge, 1995), 47.
102. Jeremy Black, *Maps and History: Constructing Images of the Past* (New Haven, CT.: Yale University Press, 1997), 17.

Chapter 2

THE FUNCTIONS OF ETHNIC STEREOTYPES IN AUSTRIA AND HUNGARY IN THE EARLY NINETEENTH CENTURY

András Vári

A nalysis of ethnic stereotypes in the Habsburg Monarchy between the 1790s and the 1830s reveals that they had functions other than the homogenization of culture and the exclusion of the Other from the public sphere. Rather, ethnic stereotypes insisted on properties that all people, though culturally different, should have. Such properties were thought to be conducive to the realization of a "civil society." These criteria served as filters; some people were fit, while others were not fit to participate in the construction of a new society. However, membership to this imagined community of builders of a new society was open to all. Evaluating people according to criteria of advancement in civilization yielded "rankings" of ethnic groups that provided the basis for the later, more divisive, ethnic characterizations of which mature nationalism was made. The contemporary significance of the stereotypes and related discourse lay elsewhere. They were part of the effort to integrate multistructured societies of social orders into a civil society. This integration, resting on the ideas of legal equality of individuals and of regulating social relationships in legal forms, is not the same as cultural homogenization. To map the course of the program of social change present in the stereotypes, it is necessary to look at them in context, to reconstruct the historical conditions of early discourse on ethnic peculiarities.

Creating the Other through Stereotypes?

The process of negative creation is investigated here through examination of the ethnically relevant set of social stereotypes. Ethnic enmity, symbolized in later generations by nineteenth-century stereotypes, is not simply the result of Enlightenment ideas turned sour. The age of Enlightenment provides a starting point, however, because at this time a substantial body of literature containing sets of ethnic stereotypes appeared. The bias in these works is that of a group of anational intellectuals. This literature produced pictures and characterizations that remained influential for several generations. Although these stereotypes were redrawn in more divisive nationalist fashion during the second half of the nineteenth century, through the end of the 1820s no such redrawing had occurred and the set of stereotypes created some forty years before was still employed. What was national or ethnically relevant in these stereotypes created before the age of national states? What were these stereotypes, how were they employed and by whom and for what purpose?

The Function and Context of Stereotypes and the "Science of the State" that Produced Them

Stereotypes have, commonly cited drawbacks aside, an orienting function in complex societies.[1] This orienting function may be abused at every turn of popular mobilization and especially in campaigns of nationalist mobilization. Abuse has its limits, however, beyond which the set of stereotypes collides with common sense and the everyday experience of multinational societies in the Habsburg territories.

Given the orientational function of stereotypes, there must have been naive concepts of difference among ethnic groups to which we have no access. What we can examine, however, are the concepts embedded in the political discourse of the era of enlightened absolutism and thereafter. Within this discourse an effort will be made to consider works that had great impact on contemporary popular opinion. Rather than analyzing outstanding political/literary figures and their ideas, which might be illuminating but are idiosyncratic and individual, works of contemporary practical social sciences, which both the imperial government and the public used, will be employed as sources. The contemporary "practical social science" to be focused on is *Statistik*, the study of state and society with the aim of making rational improvements possible. *Statistik* is a scientific undertaking with political consequences.

Two scientific disciplines, political arithmetic and descriptive statistics, are relevant here. The predecessor of modern statistics, political arithmetic was the first school of thought to apply systematically mathematical methods to the general problems of society and economy. However, its methods could only be utilized for a fairly narrow range of problems. Independent of this school, scholars in late-seventeenth-century Germany proposed a line of scientific inquiry that aimed at the integrated description of the states with all their significant public aspects, together with such geographical features as topography and descriptions of settlements or productive resources but without numerical analysis. This became known as descriptive statistics. In late-eighteenth-century Germany Gottfried Achenwall and August Ludwig Schlözer opened up descriptive statistics to new methods developed by political arithmetic. Those aspects that could be numerically analyzed, above all, the development of population and state finances, were characterized by elementary numerical-statistical methods in combination with the then available censuses and tax and military sources.

The new, more complex descriptive statistical approach (called *Statistik* or *Staatenkunde*) developed in two more directions. One produced comprehensive works aiming to present statistics of entire countries or even entire empires from the 1780 onwards.[2] The history of a country was omitted and three elements remained: the basic strength of the state; *Grundmacht* (data on population, production and consumption, natural resources); constitution as the basic structure of the state, then the *Verwaltung* (the functions and units of state administration). The other direction was a return to the geographic approach. It resulted in topographical lexica, which provided elementary descriptions of each settlement in alphabetical order.[3]

In the search for ethnic stereotypes, this article examines a variety of descriptive statistical works at both the national and the regional level as well as works of statistical ethnography, supplemented by political pamphlets. Only part of the relevant literature contains stereotypes. Moreover, in the works that present such images, only stereotypical characterizations of groups that were significant in the eyes of the contemporary commentators will be considered: the German, the Magyar, the Slav, and the Romanian. Two generations of authors produced these works. The first group of eleven authors was born between 1745 and 1770,[4] the second between 1770 and 1800.[5]

Two Stages of Discourse; Two Generations of Statistical Authors

The first group of authors was imbued with Enlightenment ideas. Irrespective of where they came from in the Monarchy, they enthusiastically supported the social-political reforms of the enlightened-absolutist Habsburg Emperor Joseph II. Indeed, both the Enlightenment ideological context and the Josephine reform fervor were phenomena common throughout the Monarchy. Josephine internationalism was possible because there was no claim to some supremacy of a particular national culture at this stage. This is important, since studies on "creating the Other" pursue the prospects of finding antecedents. There are, in my view, few.

There has, however, long been distancing: the most often cited "evil" figures in Hungarian folk songs are highwaymen and Turks. This was a result of the practices of seventeenth-century Turkish armies, which included looting, raping, devastating crops, and burning villages, as well as regular, large-scale slave taking and slave trading. To apply the modern label "xenophobia" to the abhorrence of the victims, apolitical and anational peasants rejecting looting, burning, and slave taking as "valid cultural practices" of their conquerors is inappropriate. This is an instance of a generalized and determinate distancing from another culture, with no political charge, intent, or consequence.

Propaganda paralleled the regular fighting between the feudal Hungarian estates and their absolutist kings. But no ethnic stereotypes accompanied the propaganda. Both sides employed the terms "Hungarian" and "foreigner" exclusively in the sense of "subject and non-subject of the Hungarian crown," or "member and non-member of the Hungarian 'body politic,'" respectively. That modern nationalism builds on and is determined by traditional antecedents cannot obscure its novelty.[6] Nineteenth-century nationalism was an effort to enlarge the political scene by cultural means, increasing both the numbers and competencies of people participating in political decisions.[7] This was a modernizing undertaking with emancipatory content. The creation and proliferation of politically charged distinctions among cultural groups, that is, the creation of modern ethnic stereotypes aided the drive to mobilize groups hitherto uninitiated into politics. In some cases, these stereotypes were real products, substantially new formulations of experiences, pictures, and popular themes that were already stock items. In others, for example, stereotypes of Germans, "modern" stereotypes closely resembled those employed earlier by one or another segment in a society of estates. Their political intent and content is what makes these stereotypes modern. Ethnic stereotypes exemplify different ways of life, different attitudes, and values that fit into different types of societies and political communities. Their application is an exercise in social cognition with as much political relevance as the study of state and society. When stereotypes occur in statistical descriptions, their appearance is not self-explanatory. Although modern stereotypes, like those appearing in statistical science, might closely resemble their antecedents, a "message" is attached to them—a political message, in a broad sense.

The Image of the German, the Hungarian, the Slovak, the Croat, and the Romanian during the First Period

The German/Central European tradition of Achenwall and Schlözer meant a comprehensive *Staatenkunde*. The authors discussed below all had contact with the descriptive statistical school in Germany. With one exception, they wrote in German, which connected them with a great cultural space in which a variety of ethnic-and other-stereotypes roamed the plains from the Baltic to the Adriatic and from Lower Saxony to Bukovina. It is difficult to identify the origin of a particular contribution to the sets of stereotypes or the path it traveled when one author after another borrowed it. Well-developed stereotypes from this time include those of Germans and Hungarians.[8]

Let us first look at the stereotypes of Germans in Hungary and Transylvania at the turn of the nineteenth century. In 1792 the Saxon-born statistician

Michael Lebrecht positively characterized the Saxons of Transylvania. After sketching historical developments since the time of "die alten gothischen Deutschen," he stressed the disconnect between contemporary Saxons and those of earlier, heroic times:

> One finds them in large villages, market towns, and cities, that are kept rich and tidy ... in their villages and market towns great walls have been put up around their churches, within which they keep their stock of corn safe from fire and prowling foes. In this way they have turned from poor vagrants into sedentary people and useful and solid citizens of the state. The passion for war, robbery, and abandonment that were common in all of the older peoples ... has been transformed into its opposite.[9]

Lebrecht also noted that in addition to peacefulness and a sedentary way of life, contemporary Germans' chief characteristics were economy and diligence. The Germans were mainly responsible for whatever the land produced by way of manufacture and crafts.

A pioneer in statistical science, Martin Schwartner, was more restrained in his descriptions of the "German," from whom the order of the burghers in Hungary originated. In his opinion, German achievements were by no means restricted to economics and industry, however: "The Hungarian national costume, which he ... has taken up early on, has been, like burgher loyalty purely preserved among these inhabitants of the Alps. Finally, it was he [the German] who let the teaching of Luther spread earlier in Hungary than elsewhere."[10]

Lucas Joseph Marienburg presented a similar picture of the Germans in Transylvania (1813). Like their brothers in Germany, who were soft, compliant, and thoughtful, the Germans in Transylvania were also "industrious and thrifty, capable in the arts, sciences, handicrafts; orderly and well-accomplished."[11] The restrained and peaceful German character was coupled with excellence in industry; even peasants engaged in both handicrafts and farming. Marienburg included the sterling military qualities traditionally attributed to the Germans, as well.

Between the publication of Schwartner's and Marienburg's works, similar descriptions appeared in the work of Johann Andreas Demián and Lebrecht, who like Schwartner and Marienburg came from Lutheran, German-speaking burgher backgrounds.[12] At the beginning of the nineteenth century, authors from other backgrounds wrote similarly. For example, the distinguished legal expert Antal Szirmay, a Slovak-Hungarian Catholic noble from northern Hungary, discussed the Germans' unfavorable physical traits, but conceded that they were civilized, honest people with good morals.[13]

The first generation of writers produced this characteristic picture of Hungarians: mainly engaging in cattle raising, they were less diligent and orderly than the Germans and the Slovaks. Schwartner noted that the Hungarians abhorred city life, believing that only open fields were adequate for their independence.[14] Lebrecht provided a detailed, sophisticated, and positive picture of the Hungarian, who had all the virtues and faults that result from the glut of fires in a sanguine type of man. Warfare is still his first passion, but only in service of his prince and his country, for it is to these that he believes himself boundlessly indebted. The Roman saying *pro patria mori* is felt by no people more passionately than the Hungarian.[15]

Lebrecht also provided an essay on the psychology of the Hungarians, contrasting them with the sedate and disciplined Germans:

> He is warmhearted. He is extraordinarily brave when he is able to act freely. But the Hungarian is just as generous as brave. Another attractive trait is his hospitality and his straightforwardness, his open-heartedness in contact and communication.[16]

This liveliness, however, had its drawbacks: the Hungarians were also described as "having a vain, hot-tempered, irascible nature."[17] Their rash and capricious temperament impeded their economic progress: "That is why they have too little economic spirit, little drive to industriousness, too little order in their houses and activities."[18] Demián adopted these characterizations verbatim in his 1804 work.[19] Moreover, Lebrecht's original characterization, unchanged and unacknowledged, eventually entered the German statistical literature.[20] Marienburg painted a similar picture of the Hungarians, one reiterated by subsequent authors: Hungarians were lively, even fiery, bellicose; honor and luxury were both dear to them. They were sincere, trusting, courteous, sharp-witted, hospitable, but not overly keen on handicrafts.[21]

The statistician Pál Magda, writing twenty-seven years after Lebrecht, shifted the characterization of Hungarians from the earlier depictions as emotional and hot-tempered, "wild," to embodying bravery and warm-hearted honesty.[22] He contrasted the Hungarians with the Germans, the leaders of the civilization race, thus: "[The German] has advanced further with regard to civilization than the Hungarian or Slovak. He loves the Hungarian fatherland, but, if I [Magda] understand correctly, does not have the Hungarian fire, force or energy."[23] This is the first example I have found in which the "fiery" character of the Hungarian has been redefined as "energetic" and is valued more than obviously politically constructive traits usually considered "German."

In the publications of the first generation of the scholars, the Germans appeared as symbols of cultural achievement, diligence, industrial undertaking, and orderliness, a continuation of earlier images. Hungarian high spirits, pride, bravery, straightforwardness, and military virtues emphasized at the turn of the nineteenth century represented a radical departure from earlier characterizations that had stressed laziness and simplicity in addition to warm hearts.

Demián, who worked on the statistical conscription of the military frontier, is an excellent source of information on the South Slavs. Demián described the inhabitants of the military frontier zone as a fine, big, and upright sort who were remarkably long-lived. These hardy people seldom became ill, but if they did, they healed themselves, "like wild animals."[24] He detailed the food, clothing, housing, and family life of the military frontier, concluding that:

The moral character of the border soldier is a mixture of good and evil. He is generous to the point of being prodigal, magnanimous, obliging, interested, easy to teach, undemanding, he maintains his spirit when in trouble … his hospitality is quite extraordinary … his unstoppable drive to steal, vengefulness, cruelty, even to close relatives; and pretense are his peculiar vices.[25]

Other publications from this era reflect similar patterns of meanings and references. Indeed, a decade before Demián, Lebrecht, who had first-hand knowledge of the Romanians in Transylvania, presented a picture of Romanians that was similar to the one Demián created of the Croats. Their Croats and Romanians were both *Naturmenschen*: hardened, lazy, wild, sensual, poor, extravagant, and drunken. Schwartner, whose widely quoted work served as one of Demián's sources, had created a *Naturmensch* modeled on the Romanians in 1798, writing: "An undemanding nature coupled with laziness, endurance with vengefulness, superstition without healthy morals are the main virtues and vices of this people."[26] Cultural backwardness was not without consequence, as Schwartner, the scholar of *Statistik*, spelled out with regard to the Romanians: "Their undemanding nature and moderation must be the chief factor conducive to their rapid proliferation."[27]

In contrast to Schwartner, who described both the positive and the negative attributes of Romanians and tried to establish the whole characterization with "reference to a grade of culture," Anatal Szirmay was less tolerant: "The Vlachs [of Szatmár county] are of medium stature, with extremely broad shoulders, very strong, but lazy, sly, drunken and vengeful, superstitious. But their women are plump and especially beautiful."[28] Szirmay's description would become the standard image of the Romanians and could be found in the dictionaries of the 1840s.[29]

Szirmay's cruder language compared to his predecessors may be a consequence of the inflation of stereotypes, which once created, proliferated in ever more colorful, eye-catching variants in the emerging market for textbooks and reference books.[30] The real breakthrough in the use of stereotypes had occurred already in the 1790s and the first decade of the 1800s. At this time, Lebrecht, Schwartner, Demián, and Joseph Rohrer represented Romanians, Croats, and Serbs as *Naturmenschen*. Geographers and statisticians writing before the 1780s, that is, before our first generation of the authors began publishing, offered nothing similar.[31] The lack of ethnic stereotypes or depictions of Christian peoples as *Naturmenschen* in the best-known statistical-geographical works of a decade or two earlier shows that around the turn of the century a new point of orientation had been needed. The *Naturmensch* was created as a negative image, in contrast to the "civilized" people.[32]

There were parallel developments in the stereotypes of the Germans, the Hungarians, and the Romanian/Croatian wild peoples. The negative attitude toward the last-named group was clearly a reflection of the attributes of the civilized people. First, the image of the Germans took on additional significance, rapidly assuming model validity. The Germans became the *Musterknaben* of progress and civilization.[33] At the same time the authors delineated the "wild peoples" ever more sharply to enhance the distance from them and to depict the identity of their own people, who were becoming "civilized," in contrast to these *Naturmenschen.*

There was an educational quality, a certain prodding to "get civilized," in the stereotypes of the "wild peoples." Such depictions contained a postscript noting that these people could better themselves if and when they advanced in civilization. The schoolmaster-statistician was handing out high and low marks to peoples who were pupils in a school of civilization studies. The stereotypes that the most informed contemporary commentators created were, of course, dependent on the values of the creators themselves. Can we explicate these values by looking at the social background and careers of the authors? What social factors explain their views?

Their social backgrounds provide only a partial explanation of the type of stereotypes that they developed. The people cultivating the new statistical sciences in the two halves of the Monarchy differed. The common denominator was that most of them were outsiders, new to public life. Thus, they depended on the benevolence of the bureaucratic élite, and they tried to be of some use to it. Indeed, Rohrer wrote that "a scholar of the people is not just a good man, but a good citizen of the state, a good public servant."[34]

Apart from being outsiders, who were the new scientists who tried to adapt themselves to the needs of the state administration? The term "intellectuals" best describes these men. The salient feature of the group is the flow of publications and literary activity. This constituted, on the one hand, a network of social connections, and on the other, the model of a new social role. Jürgen Habermas has discussed the theoretical implications of the formation of public opinion at length.[35] But the social history of the people in the Habsburg Lands who operated the institutions of public opinion, the patrons, members, and activists of learned societies, theaters, and journals, remains to be written.[36] It is important that the scale of reference of this social group was always larger than "ethnic" group, and larger than the national scene of politics. The authors seldom acknowledged national affiliation, and when they did it was to a patria, a motherland, which was home to many groups, peoples, nations. The *Gelehrtenrepublik*, the republic of the learned, was their horizon.

Anational though the two generations of authors may have been, the stereotypes they forged characterized concrete groups of people. Though not by design, the characteristics that the authors chose for comment and the comparisons they made helped construct a picture of a hierarchy of more and less civilized nations. Although the authors from the two halves of the Monarchy had different social backgrounds, all of them were part of the educated classes. These heterogeneous educated classes were theoretically open to everyone, though the range of educational paths and professional positions that their members occupied was limited. What counted was education and accomplishment. This has implied above all a certain communicative practice, that of pursuing a reasoned discourse over matters of public interest.

Did intellectuals attempt to strengthen their claims by particular communicative practices, for example, "professionalization," the monopolization of the trust of the public through unification and canonization of scientific practice? *Statistik*, on its long march from an aspect of geography to a universally applicable methodology of social life in the last third of the nineteenth century, might well be considered a process of professionalization. Certainly, the representatives of the two generations under review were the first to become university professors of an autonomous scientific discipline. However, the scientific content of the process of professionalization is the application of the methodology of political arithmetic to the description of structures and forces of the states. Most of the works discussed here treat first those elements that can be quantified, appending those elements that can only be described verbally as colorful annexes. Nevertheless, the annexes remained for some sixty years, until the 1850s. Why their persistence, if they were considered of secondary scientific significance?

Perhaps the readers liked them. This was what critics who protested one or another stereotypical characterization argued: an author stooped low for effect, to ingratiate himself into the public's favor.[37] Another reason for the persistence of these descriptions might have been that the authors sought to impress the political élite precisely with the colorful annexes. The colorful ethnic descriptions were fuzzy fragments straight out of the threatening jungle of reality whose outlines could only have been mapped by scientific methods. The scholar held up those fragments in a gesture to inspire awe in the public at large and more specifically in the political leadership. The gesture united the threat of unfathomable reality with the promise of further progress of science. In the age of Joseph II and, later, Emperor Francis, people, houses, roads, and settlements were numbered, counted, measured, and mapped. Fragmentary descriptions of until then unfathomable collective behavior of groups of people were quite suitable to impress public and élite alike.

Thus it cannot be only their social background that determined the authors' values and attitudes, which were reflected in the ethnic stereotypes. Rather, it was their common social position, that is, their semidependence on the state, on the municipalities, and on their respective churches that put a stamp on their writing. Both the concepts of "civil society" that they professed and the special skills they ascribed to themselves were the intellectuals' tools of emancipation.

The concrete ethnic stereotypes and descriptions they produced were largely lectures in civilization studies. Because of this quality, they were acceptable to both the modernizing state and the modernizing estates. The reproaches and admonitions were directed at the uncivilized people, "the lesser breed without the Law." The modernizing state and public opinion was—primarily implicitly—shown and given a new responsibility: a new educational role in helping civilize the backward. The set of stereotypes of the statistical and geographical authors and scholars with the implied mission of civilization was not inconvenient for the political players, the estates, or the absolutist monarchy.

To answer the question, then, of what made our writers write the things that they wrote, the following can be ventured. The ethnic stereotypes and descriptions did not develop as they did due to the authors' social background or their membership in a certain class. Rather, they developed under the influence of where these intellectual groups wanted to get to, that is, onto the national stage, into an emancipated position vis-à-vis the traditional stars of the play. The stage for the drama of enfolding national movement and ideology can be examined in the context of the concrete Central European societies. To learn what was said on this stage that our intellectuals constructed to present the drama of nation-building on, we shall return to our texts and authors.

Later Generations of Authors and Continuity in Ethnic Stereotypes

From 1815 through the 1830s, in addition to statistical literature producing descriptions of entire countries or empires, works on particular counties or cities increased greatly. The first ethnographical inquiries appeared, as well. The proliferation of the associations, publication outlets, and the interest of the public was already largely motivated by a desire to have a national scientific life and a national literature. Thus, in this period at least the two halves of the Monarchy need to be separated. The ten authors that we consider here were born between 1770 and 1800. They had their careers in the Kingdom of Hungary, which was also the focus of their interest. Their publications under discussion appeared before 1840.

These authors came from a more varied social background than the first generation. Lutheran authors were in a minority among the Calvinists and Catholics.[38] The literature that they produced was also more varied than the literature of the earlier generation. It is all the more striking that among the wide range of texts no new stereotypes occurred. To be sure, this was a phase of criticism when the detailed descriptions modified and countered the more fanciful allegations in the large-scale studies of the earlier generation. Basically, however, the new detailed studies followed the directions set down before, and as they documented, illustrated, and explicated the earlier works, they tended to confirm the earlier depictions. This can be demonstrated by examining some topics repeatedly reported on: the quality of material life; behavior patterns with regard to peacefulness and orderliness; and finally, attitudes toward diligence and saving.

Patterns of Material Culture

What the authors commented on above all was the pattern of everyday consumption: food, drink, and clothing. Some preference for sophisticated consumption and temperance appears in the descriptions of the food and drink of the "primitive" Croat, Serb, and Romanian. The authors sometimes wondered how primitive and primitively processed food sufficed to keep the body and soul of these peoples together. Issues of waste and frugality cropped up: Demián remarked that the Croats with their badly built ovens had to bake every day, because the bread produced in these ovens did not keep like good bread did.[39]

Comments on drink invariably addressed both quality and quantity. There is a distinction between wine and beer on the one hand and gin and Schnapps/ Slivovitz on the other. The authors understood, perhaps even condoned, the consumption of the former, while they considered the latter harmful and more addicting than the former. They praised the subjects for drinking in moderation or scolded them for habitually drinking too much. The Romanians were criticized for their consumption of spirits, while the light country wines of the predominantly Hungarian lowlands were explicitly recognized as a rational alternative to unhealthy well water. Indeed, Hungarians, Romanians, and Croats were universally praised for their high-quality wines.

These authors produced detailed and straightforwardly ethnocentric descriptions of housing conditions. The Lutheran priest Ladislaus Bartholomaides compared Hungarian, German, and Slovak buildings in Gömör County in northern Hungary:

> The Slavs and the Germans build their houses differently than the Hungarians. The former plaster walls made from planks smoothed by plane, with clay and lime, thus making them appear as if they were made of stone. They render their roofs, whether made of straw or shingles, more symmetrical and more solid than the Hungarians. Hungarian houses and villages show no such diligence. They build their walls of coarse beams, some of which protrude at the corners more, some less.[40]

The concept of orderliness of everyday life was applied unhesitatingly as a criterion of evaluation of ethnic groups even by those writers who emphatically rejected "nationalism." Samuel Bredetzky, for example, believed that scientific authors should refrain from idle, unscientific, and above all hate-inspiring speculation on which people had occupied which region first and which people were newcomers. His statistical-topographical works provided no collective characterizations of ethnic groups. Yet in his travel accounts of Galicia he remarked on the orderly farms and households of the industrious Lutheran German colonists there, with clover and fodder crops in the fields, well-bred cows in the cowsheds, tasty butter in the lard, and flower beds in front of the houses. He contrasted them with ignorant, lazy, nationalist Poles who ran about their fields on the night of Whitsuntide waving torches to protect their crops from evil, but never got as far as planting clover like the Germans.[41]

Behavior Patterns

The behavior of different peoples, especially their peacefulness or aggressiveness, attracted the attention of our authors. For example, the revolt of 1784 in Transylvania was above all a peasant uprising. It was, however, also a bloody crusade of Romanian speakers against the other status groups in society, including those of a different tongue (Hungarian). Schwartner enumerated the outstanding figures in the history of the Romanians, writing that the defenders of Christendom, Johann and Matthias von Hunyadi, were Romanians. The names of the most bloodthirsty rebels and the cruelest prince in Eastern European history, however, followed those of the guardians of the Christian lands. The implication is clear: the Romanians had some fine fellows, but they were bloodthirsty and cruel. It is unclear, however, whether the cruelty of the Romanians or the wild peoples is generalized, or whether it is specially directed against us, the observers, the civilized people.[42]

The authors noted the potential for conflict and behavior during a conflict. Demián's observations of the Croats' vengefulness, of their cruelty, even to their kin, have been cited above. Though Schwartner, Szirmay, and Marienburg provided only brief sketches of the less civilized peoples, with a few adjectives like "bloodthirsty" or "cruel," there was always the implication that things could improve. Sometimes, the authors were explicit: education and civilization would change the character of the wild people.

Economic Thinking, Work Roles, and Work Ethic

Especially the second generation of authors commented on three aspects of economic thinking, work roles, and work ethic. The first was the contrast between diligence/industriousness and laziness that had traditionally appeared in the image of Germans and Slovaks. After endless reiteration, the contrasting characterizations became the staple fare of ethnographic descriptions. The second aspect is the spendthrift or thrifty behavior of a particular ethnic group. There are repeated comments on large weddings or baptismal feasts. Whether the grain and food from one season would suffice until next harvest was a matter to be examined and judged against such factors as resource endowment and the character of a people. The writer often connected diligence and economy. What the highly valued diligence or industriousness of the peasants ensured, however, was self-sufficiency and absence of market dependence. The Benedictine friar Fábián Széder described the Hungarian subgroup of Palóc people as diligent farmers and cattle breeders, who were also good carpenters:

> In addition to building their own houses, they make their wagons, yokes, tubs, barrels, and wooden kitchen utensils themselves. Because a specialty of the women is linen making, one rarely sees a house without a weaving frame. At the fairs of Vác the Palóc women sell much yarn, linen and white clothing. They even spin and weave wool for their men. These are real signs of a people's diligence and economy. Thus it may be understood that these people have less occasion to part with their money.[43]

The third aspect of economic thinking and work roles that elicited comment is the division of labor among men and women. Invariably, the pastoral peoples or "wild peoples" were a source of wonder because the women carried so large a share of the burden and because the men held these women in such low esteem.

Common Themes–Criteria of Evaluation: Who Was Fit?

The stereotypes discussed here mirror not only the values of the authors, but also their vision, a program of social change. Stressed are the merits of self-control, the peaceful, regulated life of a community, which in turn rests on the rational behavior of the individual. The rational attitude enabled the participants in the project of building the future to agree upon mutually acceptable rules of conduct within a community. Another motivation for their striving for knowledge was their preference for higher standards of living in the dual sense of greater and more sophisticated consumption and their positive attitude toward accumulation of wealth. Restless striving after knowledge was just one useful activity reflecting a godly or at least morally commendable life. This implies a linear time perspective in which improvement makes sense.

This program of social change came to be the strongest drive for change in Habsburg Central Europe at the beginning of the nineteenth century. It is important to remember that the stereotypical characterizations of this first generation of writers sought both to separate, to filter the people who could and those who could not participate in the building of this new society, and, at the same time to recruit and train eventual participants in this program of social change. Judgment was passed as to who could or could not become "civilized." But the verdict on the ability to become civilized was tempered by reminders that through the raising of their *Geistescultur*, the failures could succeed, as well.

Summary and Outlook

Ethnic stereotypes changed little between the 1790s and the 1830s. The function and effect of creating and employing these stereotypes were relative. The stereotypes did not place various ethnic groups in rank order, but measured the groups against a number of characteristics that were considered to be the basis for a new type of society. This resulted in a better or worse fit between actual characteristics of particular groups and the ideal requirements of the project of building a civil society that our authors envisaged. The fit—or lack thereof—determined which group was capable of participating in the project of social and political reform. Membership in this civilization project was, however, open. Anyone who met the requirements—education and resoluteness—could join.

The concept of building a civil society assumed both that different peoples were capable to differing degrees of having a civil society and that they were capable of becoming more civilized. Together these statements come close to acknowledging that people had some competence and political responsibility for their own affairs. This concept did not fit well, however, with the political philosophy of monarchical élites. It was thus advisable for the authors engaging in *Staatenkunde* to limit the number and scope of such traits. Thus, the cultural traits that our authors dwelled upon were those that are both necessary for a civic society and conducive to the smooth running of the state administrative machine.

The concept of civic society was integrative. The kernel of the new concept was the regulation, according to universally and equally binding legal concepts, of the relationships of individuals and groups that were hitherto either unregulated or even prohibited. Of course, ethnic stereotypes did not constitute a legal system, but the norms of behavior they upheld matched such a system. The stereotypes introduced here and the significance attached to them were new, at least when stereotypes are expected to define images as vehicles of delineation, and distancing, as some theoreticians of nationalism expect stereotypes to do. A nationalist ideology came along at an appropriate stage of development and invoked "primordial loyalties" to make a nation/society culturally unified and distinctive. These stereotypes, however, have more to say on the correct, commendable way for different social segments to live together than on the strengthening of the border of a homogeneous community. At the end of the nineteenth century one could indeed find the "right," divisive, self-aggravating, and xenophobic stereotypes that Ernest Gellner or Benedict Anderson might have liked to see,[44] but what is the use of this discovery? With more-or-less developed national states and politically organized and represented nationalist movements at the end of the nineteenth century, the presence of divisive cultural images at these late stages is of little use in explaining the birth and development of these movements. That the movements produce their appropriate images is not surprising. The interesting question would have been, what facilitated the nationalist movements?

The stereotypes found in the Habsburg Monarchy at the beginning of the nineteenth century point in another direction. Already the early-nineteenth-century images depicted constituent parts of societies of orders, in a way that these images referred to a program of social change and development. The composition of the authors reflected the variegated nature of the societies they wrote on, but though stamped they were by their social background, the images they produced were no mere reflection of their class position. The authors wrote and influenced an educated public that was slowly accumulating political significance. The images were products and witnesses of a process of political exchange and should be analyzed accordingly. At least two concepts, those of a society of orders and of the enlightened, reforming state, are mostly absent from the anthropologic concepts of nationalism, usually conceived in non-European settings. To inquire into the causes and dynamics of nationalism and ethnic enmity in Habsburg Central Europe, one must reconstruct the stage with some precision by social-historical methods, listen to the political messages, and look at the products of political exchange. It is possible that the success or failure of these messages and the programs of social change to which they referred were at least as important in delineating the communities that developed into nations as the "primordial" factors of language and religion.

Notes

The research for this paper was supported by Országos Kiemelésű Társadalomtudományi Kutatások Közalapitvány (OKTK, or Public Foundation of National Research in Social Sciences), Hungary, project number A.1562/VIII.b, "Az etnikai sztereotípiák és a társadalmi-politikai programok változása 1800-1918."

1. Henri Tajfel, "Social Stereotypes and Social Groups," in *Intergroup Behaviour*, ed. John C. Turner and Howard Giles (Oxford: Blackwell, 1981), 144-67.
2. For example, the works of de Luca, Liechtenstern, Schwartner, and Demián.
3. See the works of Korabinszky, András Vályi, de Luca, and Samuel Bredetzky.
4. The birth dates and religion of the statisticians were as follows: Ignaz de Luca: 1746, Catholic; Antal Szirmay: 1747, Catholic; László Bartholomaeides: 1754, Lutheran; Michael Lebrecht: 1757, Lutheran; Franz Kratter: 1758, Catholic; Martin Schwartner: 1759, Lutheran; Joseph Max Liechtenstern: 1765, Catholic; Joseph Rohrer: 1769, Catholic; Johann Andreas Demián: 1770, Lutheran; Lucas Joseph Marienburg: 1770, Lutheran; Pál Magda: 1770, Lutheran.
5. Samuel Bredetzky: 1772, Lutheran; Johann von Csaplovics: Lutheran, 1780; Karl Georg Rumy: 1780, Lutheran-Catholic (convert); Dániel Ercsey: 1781, Calvinist; Jacob Melzer: 1782, Lutheran; Fábián Szeder: 1784, Catholic; Alajos Mednyánszki: 1784, Catholic; Pál Kis: 1793, Catholic; István Lassú: 1797, Calvinist.
6. On the significance of antecedents, see Anthony D. Smith, *The Ethnic Origins of Nations* (Oxford: Basil Blackwell, 1986).
7. This is the working definition of nationalism that informs the theoretical framework within which the present arguments have been developed. Compare John Breuilly, *Nationalism and the State* (Manchester: Manchester University Press, 1982). I believe Breuilly's concept and typology of nationalism is the one that lends itself best to description and analysis of multi-structured Central-European estate societies (*Ständegesellschaften*).
8. Matthias Bel, *Notitia Hungariae novae historico geographica divisa ...*, vol. 1-5 (Vienna, 1735-1742). Vol. 3 partially reprinted in Nándor Ikvai, ed., *Bél Mátyás Pest megyéről* (Szentendre, 1977), 34-36.
9. Michael Lebrecht, *Über den National-Charakter der in Siebenbürgen befindlichen Nationen* (Vienna: Johann David Hörling 1792), 54.
10. Martin Schwartner, *Statistik des Königreichs Ungarn, Ein Versuch* (Pest, 1798); 2nd ed.: *Statistik des Königreichs Ungarn*, parts I-II (Ofen: Gedruckt mit K. Universitätsschriften, 1809), part I, 142.
11. Lucas Joseph Marienburg, *Geographie des Großfürstenthums Siebenbürgen*, vols. 1-2 (Hermannstadt: Bey Martin Hochmeister, 1813), 2nd part (Main part), 94-95.
12. The civilizing mission of Germans among the culturally inferior Hungarians of earlier ages was a standard historical argument among the Saxons of Transylvania in struggles among estates and against the court. August Ludwig Schlözer forcefully reformulated it in *Kritische Sammlungen zur Geschichte der Deutschen in Siebenbürgen*, (Göttingen, 1795-1797).
13. Antal Szirmay, *Szathmár vármegye fekvése, történetei és polgári esmérete*, vol. 1 (Buda: M. kir. Universitas, 1809), 10.
14. Schwartner, *Statistik des Königreichs Ungarn* (1798), 121.
15. Lebrecht, *Über den National-Charakter der in Siebenbürgen befindlichen Nationen*, 15-25.
16. Ibid., 21-22.
17. Ibid.
18. Ibid.
19. Johann Andreas Demián, *Darstellung der österreichischen Monarchie nach den neuesten statistischen Beziehungen*, vol. 2, *Ostgalizien und Siebenbürgen* (Vienna: Camesianische Buchhandlung, 1804), 43-44.

20. Georg Hassel, *Statistischer Abriß des österreichischen Kaiserthumes nach seinen neuesten statistischen Beziehungen* (Nuremberg, 1807).

21. Marienburg, *Geographie des Großfürstenthums Siebenbürgen*, 2nd part, 94-95.

22. Pál Magda, *Magyarországnak és a határt örző katonaság vidékének legújabb statistikai és geographiai leirása* (Pest: Trattner János, 1819), 67.

23. Ibid., 69-70.

24. Demián, *Darstellung der österreichischen Monarchie nach den neuesten statistischen Beziehungen*, 51.

25. Ibid., 64.

26. Schwartner, *Statistik des Königreichs Ungarn* (1798),135-36.

27. Ibid.

28. Szirmay, *Szathmár vármegye fekvése*, vol. 1, 10. Similar depictions of Romanians can found in the travel diary of Vinzenz Batthyány, *Reise durch einen Teil Ungarns, Siebenbürgens, der Moldau und Buccovina im Jahre 1805* (Pest: C.A. Hartleben, 1811).

29. See the first Hungarian lexicon, *Közhasznú Esméretek Tára* (Budapest: Heckenast, 1844), entry "Oláhok."

30. See the example in Pál Kis, *Rövid Földírás a leg ujabb polgári változások szerint Tanuló Ifjak számára* (Vienna, 1818), 118.

31. Cf. Karl Gottlieb Windisch, *Geographie des Königreichs Ungarn*, vols. 1, 2 (Preßburg, 1780-81); *Topographie des Großfürstenthums Siebenbürgen oder Geographie von Ungarn*, part 3 (Preßburg, 1790). For Bel see note 8 above. Even de Luca and Bredetzky avoided stereotypes in a part of their work. See Ignaz de Luca, *Geographisches Handbuch von dem österreichischen Staate*, vols. 1-6 (Vienna: Degen, 1791-92, 1st ed. 1790) and *Staatsanzeigen von den kaiserlich-königlichen Landen* (Vienna: Degen, 1785). For Bredetzky, see note 41 below.

32. This also means that it is a fairly recent construction and not connected to the centuries-old discussion on the "wild men" in the parts of the world that were new to the Europeans.

33. An excerpt of Schwartner's work for use as a textbook, produced by the Calvinist University professor Dániel Ercsey, changes just one sentence in the set of stereotypes copied from Schwartner. It reads, in contrast to the quotation above, that the "Germans ... settled ... introduced mining and town industry, enlivened trade and formed the middle class of the nation, which was neither lord nor servant, but free 'bürger' [*Szabad Polgár*]." Italics in original. Dániel Ercsey, *Statistica* (Debrecen: Csáthy György, 1814), 113.

34. Joseph Rohrer, "Versuch über die Bewohner der österreichischen Monarchie," in *Archiv für Geographie und Statistik*, vol. 1, ed. Joseph Max Liechtenstern (Vienna, 1803), part 1, 6.

35. Jürgen Habermas, *Strukturwandel der Öffentlichkeit* (Neuwied-Berlin: Hermann Luchterhand Verlag, 1962).

36. See, for example, Károly Vörös, "A modern értelmiség kezdetei Magyarországon," *Valóság* 18 (1975): 1-20.

37. "G.", *Észrevételek tekintetes Schwartner Márton úr Magyarország Statisztikájában az Oláhokról tett jegyzésekre* (Pest, 1812).

38. The following authors were Lutheran: Karl Georg Rumy *1780, Johann von Csaplovics *1780, and Jacob Melzer *1782. Roman Catholics were Fábián Szeder *1784, Alajos Mednyánszki *1784, and Pál Kis *1793. Gábor Fábián *1795, István Lassú *1797, and Dániel Ercsey, *1781, were Calvinists.

39. J.A. Demián, *Darstellung der österreichischen Monarchie nach den neuesten statistischen Beziehungen*, part IV, vol. 1, *Die Militär-Grenze in Kroatien* (Vienna: Rötzl'sche Buchhandlung, 1806), 54.

40. Ladislaus Bartholomaides, *Gömörer Gespannschaft. Auszug aus dem Werke: Comitatus Gömöriensis notitia historico-geographico-statistica*, Typ. Jos. Caroli Mayer, Leutschau, 1804-1808. The excerpt is from Johann von Csaplovics, ed., *Archiv des Königreichs Ungern*, vol. 2 (Vienna: Anton Doll, 1821), 180.

41. Samuel Bredetzky, *Reisebemerkungen über Ungarn und Galizien*, vol. 2 (Vienna: Anton Doll, 1803), 116-18, 126, 128, 138-39. Compare this description with the sweeping condemnation of nationalism by the same author in *Beyträge zur Topographie des Königreichs Ungarn* (Vienna, 1803), Vorrede, V-VI.

42. Schwartner, op. Cit., 135-36.

43. Fábián Széder, "A palócokról," *Tudományos Gyűjtemény*, no. 6 (1819), 26-46. Reprinted in Attila Paládi-Kovács, *Magyar tájak néprajzi felfedezői* (Budapest, 1985), 137.

44. Cf. Ernest Gellner, *Nationalism* (London: Phoenix, 1998); Benedict Anderson, *Imagined Communities: Reflections on the Origin and Spread of Nationalism* (London and New York: Verso, 1983); Clifford Geertz, "Primordial Loyalties and Standing Entities: Anthropological Reflections on the Politics of Identity," public lecture, no. 7 (April 1997), Collegium Budapest.

Chapter 3

CZECHS, GERMANS, BOHEMIANS?
Images of Self and Other in Bohemia to 1848

Hugh LeCaine Agnew

Count Francis Joseph Kinsky (1739-1805) wrote himself into Czech history books in 1773 when, discussing teaching languages, he remarked that before learning Latin a pupil should be instructed in his mother tongue. He then explained,

> To the phrase "his mother tongue" I ought to add: namely, Czech. I confess that as a good descendant of the Slavs I have inherited the prejudice that if the mother tongue of a Frenchman is French and of a German, German, then the mother tongue of a Czech [*Böhmen*] must be Czech.[1]

Kinsky argued that learning Czech would be useful to a landowner whose peasants spoke only Czech or to an officer whose troopers spoke only Czech. Czech was more than useful, it was also beautiful. Kinsky compared it favorably with the classical languages, Greek and Latin, and argued that refined foreigners preferred it to German. He also credited the reputation his fellow countrymen *(Landsleute)* enjoyed as musicians to the fact that their ears were disciplined to distinguish long and short vowel sounds: "In the so-called German Bohemian [*sogenannten deutschböhmischen*] villages one finds incomparably fewer musical people than in the completely Czech [*ganz böhmischen*] areas."[2]

The fact that an Austrian general and Bohemian aristocrat would speak up publicly for the Czech language made Kinsky's *Erinnerung über einen wichtigen Gegenstand, von einem Böhmen* top of the list of "defenses of the language" that played an important part in the early phase of the Czech national renascence

---

Notes for this section begin on page 73.

(*národní obrození*). Yet Kinsky also exasperated later historians by defending German (calling it his own language) against French or English. As Arnošt Kraus exclaimed, "This Austrian General is a Slav, a Czech and a German at the same time!"[3] This exasperation comes from applying the yardstick of later nationalism to an earlier identity. The flexibility of Kinsky's sense of identity was in his own time—and for a long time to come—quite typical. Echoes of it sound at least to the mid-nineteenth century, as when Count Joseph Matthias Thun addressed the question of his own identity in 1845:

> To this I can only respond in all self-consciousness that I am neither a Czech nor a German, but only a Bohemian, that, filled with the glow of inner love for my Fatherland, I consider the intention to suppress either of these nationalities—it makes no difference which— as the most unhealthy calamity, and that I have spoken up for my Czech brethren, since I consider it my knightly duty to take the side of the weaker party.[4]

This "Bohemian" identity—usually equated with the aristocratic *Landespatriotismus* of the noble *natio*, but shared among broader social levels—included three elements that would have an effect on the self-images of Czechs and Germans in Bohemia in the era of modern nationalism. The first element was an assertion of Bohemia's uniqueness and loyalty to it as a political entity. Yet this "territorial patriotism" derived not merely from the administrative contours of Bohemia or its history as a separate political unit. It was also the Czechs and their history, language, and culture that made it unique. This element thus raised the question of the Czechs' relationship to Bohemia. However, Bohemia was also inhabited by Germans and associated with other German territories under Habsburg rule, and beyond them with the wider "Germany" of the Holy Roman Empire (after 1815, the *Bund*). Thus Bohemia's Germans and the sense in which they, too, "belonged" to Bohemia and Bohemia to them was a second element. A third element emerged in Kinsky's assumption that Czech would be used to communicate with subordinates or social inferiors, or in Thun's condescending *noblesse oblige*. These attitudes reflected the social relations in Bohemia, where for a long time language use was a far more reliable index of social status than of ethnic background or even personal identity.[5] In the following pages we will pursue the interplay of these elements of the Bohemian identity and its emerging Czech and German ethnic competitors through the revolutionary year 1848.

Already Kinsky's distinction among his *Landsleute* between the so-called German Bohemians (*Deutschböhmen*) and the Czechs (*Böhmen*) points out that contemporaries differentiated between Czechs and Germans in Bohemia, "both of them, the genuine Bohemian and the German Bohemian, by birth and country Bohemians to be sure, but otherwise in many respects quite different."[6] Not every author saw those differences as positively as Kinsky with his comments on Czech musicality. Johann Anton von Riegger claimed to see another difference, that a German Bohemian on his poor soil could produce much more than a Czech on the most fertile land, and he estimated that the Czechs were some fifty years behind the Germans in cultivation of reason and industry. One even had to address them differently: "The Slav must be moved with a somewhat peremptory, blustering, thunderous voice; the German demands advice, the Czech an order with a threat."[7] Such attitudes harked back to the famine of 1771-72 and the peasant revolt of 1775, confirming the suspicions of many local and higher officials that the Czech peasantry was not only inclined to rebelliousness, but was also cut off by its language from the benefits of civilization. Though some writers pointed to the consequences of serfdom, others ascribed this "backwardness" to character differences between Germans and Slavs.[8] Efforts to improve the situation naturally involved relying on German sources. The Bohemian provincial government published *Der Volkslehrer*, which František Jan Tomsa (1753-1814) translated into Czech as *Učitel lidu* as a means of spreading useful knowledge among the common people, stimulating other efforts at popular enlightenment through the translation of German models into Czech by Tomsa and many others.[9] The semiofficial Bohemian Patriotic-Economic Society (*Patriotisch-ökonomische Gesellschaft*) pursued similar goals, especially after 1838 when its monthly journal began to appear in a Czech version.[10]

Social realities and attitudes thus went some way to supporting the contemporary view that the Germans in Bohemia (and in Central Europe in general) brought knowledge and civilization. This view was reflected in much of the pamphlet literature of the *Vormärz*,[11] but one of its clearest expressions came from a figure whose other work ranked him among the leading Czech patriots of his day, the historian František Martin Pelcl (1734-1801). At the close of the 1780s, Pelcl wrote an article for the journal of the Royal Bohemian Society of Sciences on the Germans and their language in Bohemia, since "if it should someday be said, 'In Bohemia they used to speak Slavic,' it will not be unpleasant for the completely German Bohemian to understand how it transpired that the Czechs became Germans."[12] Starting from the first contacts with Christianity in the ninth century, Pelcl traced the German "influence on the cultivation [*Bildung*] of these coarse Slavs [*so rohen Slawen*]" to his own day.[13] Pelcl considered that this influence was rooted in the court, the church, and the development of urban life and technological progress. Though it frequently provoked reactions from the Czech side, he dismissed even the efforts of the Czech patriots of his generation (including his own!) as "swimming against the current."

> From all this one can probably conclude that someday Bohemia will find itself in exactly the same situation as Meissen, Brandenburg, and Silesia, where nowadays they speak German throughout, and all that still remains of the Slavic language are the names of towns, villages, and streams.[14]

Later publicists and writers of German–Bohemian background, such as the native of České Budějovice/Budweis, Franz Schuselka, emphasized similar conclusions. In his brochure "Deutsche Worte eines Österreichers" (1843), Schuselka called the Czechs in Bohemia "the noblest Slavic tribe [*Stamm*] which alone among them all has a place of honor in the cultural history of the world." Now, however, Bohemia was "practically a completely German land," where only part of the peasantry and the small–town bourgeoisie were Czech. In spite of past glories, the "tiny number" of enthusiasts who were trying to create an original Slavic-Czech literature would almost certainly fail.[15] An article in the Augsburg *Allgemeine Zeitung* in 1844 (possibly also by Schuselka) stated even more categorically:

> Bohemia was a German Imperial province, its education, its public intercourse, its political and municipal constitutions developed in a German way, it is a part of German Austria, its King is a German.... Whoever wants to have a great Austria, a great Germany, cannot tolerate a Slavdom that rules or wants to rule in German lands; such a Slavdom would go a long way towards Pan–Slavdom."[16]

Under these conditions the best solution for the Czechs would be to accept assimilation into the higher civilization.[17]

Not everyone who recognized the social and economic differences between the Czechs and Germans in Bohemia drew the simple conclusion that the Czechs should become Germans, even in a purely political sense. One alternative model for national integration in Bohemia, sharing some elements with the traditional "Bohemian" identity, emerged from the sermons of Bernard Bolzano (1781-1848).[18] Bolzano lectured from 1805 to 1820 at the university in Prague before being forced into a retirement spent largely pursuing theoretical mathematics. While in Prague he tried to inculcate his students with his abhorrence of the hostility that he saw between Czechs and Germans. His vision of the "nation" was based on the community of all citizens of the country, who all belonged to the state, and among whom divisions and conflicts worked against the common good. In considering the reasons why "the Czech does not love the German, nor the latter the former, the way fellow-citizens of one and the same land necessarily must love one another,"[19] Bolzano pointed first to the two languages in use in Bohemia. He saw an additional contributing factor in the differences in levels of culture, though he rejected any explanation based on natural characteristics of either group. Most dramatically, Bolzano cited the socially and politically advantaged position the Germans enjoyed, alluding to the events of Czech history only obliquely, but not mincing his words when he asked,

> For is not the native German Bohemian and those who join him even now still preferred in hundreds of very significant ways? Is it not the German language in which all the higher branches of knowledge are taught in this land? That has also been elevated to the language of business in all public affairs? ... Are not the greatest and noblest in the land, are not the rich and the propertied, all from only one of the two [nationalities], either native Germans or even foreigners, or perhaps such people who, since they have long since put aside the Czech language and customs, must be counted as Germans? Does not the Czech-speaking part of the population throughout live in a lamentable state of poverty and oppression?[20]

Yet these considerations, though they explained why the hostility he so regretted existed between Czechs and Germans in Bohemia, did not justify it.

Far from justifying hostility, Bolzano claimed the diversity of Bohemia's citizens could be its greatest strength if they were melded together—but his vision of assimilation differed markedly from what Schuselka and other German liberals would imagine. Who knows what Bohemians could be, he asked, "if we tried as far as possible so to combine the two nationalities [*Volksstämme*] that in the end they become only one?"[21] More than that he thought that whoever could arrange it so that "only one language would be spoken by all the inhabitants of our land" would be making a tremendous contribution to the well–being of the nation (*Volk*), just as the one who could introduce a single world language would be for all humanity.[22] In the meantime, since this goal was not realistic, Bolzano called on Germans and Czechs to learn each other's languages.

Bolzano's vision of assimilation, the fusing of the two nationalities in Bohemia into a new and different one, was not shared by many of his listeners. Nevertheless, a firm belief in the German character of Bohemia did not necessarily mean a denial of Czech culture and history as part of the heritage of Bohemia. During the *Vormärz* many intellectuals were attracted to the figures and legends of the Czech past and wrote sympathetically about them, although active support for the cultural strivings of the Czech patriots was more rare.[23] Karel Sabina (1813-1877), a leading Czech radical in 1848, described the Prague literary scene during the 1830s and 1840s in his memoirs, noting that for many writers it would have been impossible to say whether they would finally opt for a German or Czech national identity.[24] One of the most striking examples of such an intellectual was Alfred Meissner (1822-1885), one of the members of a group of poets known as "Young Bohemia." Besides Meissner, "Young Bohemia" included such writers and poets as Moritz Hartmann (1821-1872), Siegfried Kapper (1821-1879), and Isidor Heller (1816-1879). Most of them were members of the first generation of Bohemian Jewish youth who were able to have a secular gymnasium and university education. Rudolf Glaser (1801-1868) gave them an outlet for much of their work in his journal *Ost und West*, which appeared in Prague between 1837 and 1848.[25]

Meissner wrote a dramatic epic celebrating the Hussite period, *Žiška, Gesänge* (1846), in which he depicted this period of Czech history as an example for later generations of how a great nation (*herrliches Volk*) struggled for light and freedom.[26] While praising the Czech Hussites as martyrs and stirring examples for the present, Meissner also lamented the position of the present-day Czechs, who stood as servants and orphans at the table usurped by foreigners, with even their right to their own language taken from them.[27] Yet in his conclusion, Meissner clearly agreed with Schuselka that the Czechs had already contributed to history what they could, and should now be content with having passed the torch to others, specifically the Germans.[28] Meissner doubted that they would be content; he foresaw a bloody struggle to decide whether Czech or German would be victorious in Bohemia—only by then he would fortunately be resting in his grave.[29]

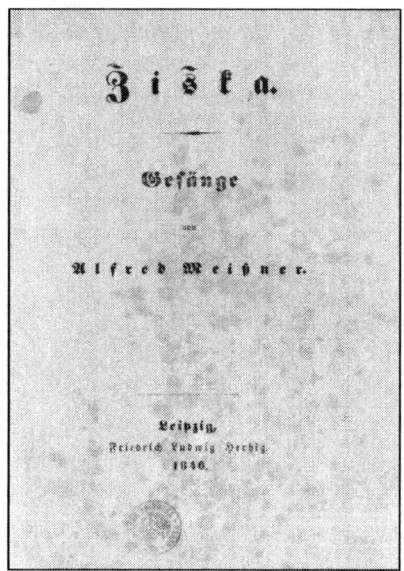

Figure 1 Title Page of Alfred Meissner's *Žiška*, which celebrates the Hussites as pioneers of freedom of conscience (1846). (Courtesy of the Národní knihovna České republiky)

Moritz Hartmann, another poet of "Young Bohemia," also turned to the Hussite period in his *Kelch und Schwert* of 1845. Hartmann linked Hussite Bohemia with the image of another holy, promised land, finding some common ground between his Jewish and Bohemian identities (an issue to which we will return). He addressed Bohemia as a "martyr among nations," who "in [its] own homeland, has become a foreigner without a homeland."[30]

However positive and sympathetic to Czech history German Bohemian intellectuals like Meissner and Hartmann were, their attitudes differed significantly from the views being articulated by some of their Czech contemporaries. The Czech intellectuals who were developing the ideas of modern Czech nationalism responded to the elements of the "Bohemian" identity that recognized the significance of the Czechs, raised the question of the position of the Germans, and expressed the socially disadvantaged status of Czech culture quite differently from either their most sympathetic German-Bohemian counterparts or Bolzano. In elaborating their sense of identity and reacting to these elements, the Czech patriots turned to language as well as history.

Unlike Bolzano, who viewed language instrumentally as a means of communication, the romantic intellectuals of the early nineteenth century—whether Czech or German Bohemian—saw it as something more. It was given by nature and birth, and was not something that could be changed like a pair of shoes. Citing Johann Gottfried von Herder, who greatly influenced romantic nationalism, especially among the Slavs, Karel Hynek Thám asked his listeners at the gymnasium in Prague's Old Town in 1803:

And does any nation [*Volk*], especially an uncultivated one, have anything dearer to it than the language of its fathers? Its entire intellectual treasury of traditions, history, religion, and principles lives in it, all its heart and soul. To take away or debase the language of such a nation means to take away its only undying possession, passing on from parents to children. Whoever suppresses my language also wants to rob me of my reason and way of life, the honor and rights of my nation. ... Even the very best culture of a nation is not a rapid growth, and does not come about the quicker for being forced in a foreign language; it thrives most beautifully, and I would say, only on the nation's [*Nazion*] own ground, in the dialect it has inherited and will bequeath to its heirs.[31]

Far from being only a feature of Bohemia that made up part of its uniqueness and could be the cultural property of both language groups in the country (as it was for Meissner or the other poets of "Young Bohemia"), the Czech language became identified increasingly with both the homeland and the nation to the exclusion of nonspeakers of Czech.

Building on attitudes in part already expressed in some of the "defenses of the language" of an earlier generation, Josef Jungmann (1773-1847) and his associates in the first decades of the nineteenth century clearly set out a linguistic concept of nation. Writing in the pages of his journal *Hlasatel Český* (The Czech Herald), Jungmann's colleague Jan Nejedlý (1776-1834) identified the nation with the language:

> Each nation is separated from another by *its mother tongue and customs*, and according to these two traits alone it is distinguishable from all other nations; if it should alter these two fundamental characteristics, then it would cease to be the nation that it is, merging with the one whose *language and customs* it has adopted.[32]

Thus the Czech nation, by implication, had to speak Czech or cease to be Czech. Nejedlý proceeded in the same article to extend the identification of language to include the homeland (*vlast*) as well as the nation. If a person is obliged, he wrote, "*sincerely and fervently to love his homeland, that is his mother tongue and the customs of his nation,*" then it is a transgression against patriotism and the fatherland to harm them.[33]

Josef Jungmann expressed this view of patriotism in his two "Conversations on the Czech Language," also published in *Hlasatel Český* in 1806. In the second of these articles, a discussion between a Czech patriot, Slavomil, and a self-described "cosmopolitan," Protiva, Jungmann developed Nejedlý's identification of language and homeland (*vlast*) further:

> I maintain, that if the Czech nation Germanized, or died out in any other way ... then the name Czechia would belong to this land as little as does that Bohemia, for there have been no more Boii in it for a long time.... For if it is impossible to conceive of a homeland without a nation, and a nation without its own language, then I assert once more that no one, except he who loves the language of his nation, can pride himself on genuine love for his homeland.[34]

Here we are light-years away from Bolzano's understanding of language mainly as an instrument of communication. Instead it is now the embodiment of the nation's customs, traditions, and heritage, and (so the linguistic nationalist asserts) identified with the homeland itself. Jungmann's attitude to the Czech language, then, "imagined" either a Czech homeland that was limited to the regions where Czech was spoken (not in fact the position he or his supporters held) or it implied that all of Bohemia was properly the homeland only of those who spoke Czech. These attitudes, with their exclusive identification of the Bohemian homeland with the Czech language and Czech nation, raised again the element of the traditional "Bohemian" identity represented by the Germans in Bohemia. As they fashioned their attitudes to the role of the Germans in Bohemia, these Czech patriots also fashioned their attitudes to their own past. In the process they further identified the essence of belonging to Bohemia in ways that excluded the Germans.

The dominant interpretation of Czech history among the patriots of the nineteenth century, as an eternal struggle with the German "hereditary enemy," is almost always traced back to František Palacký's monumental history of Bohemia, published in German as *Geschichte von Böhmen* (History of Bohemia) but in its Czech version as *Dějiny národu českého v Čechách a v Moravě* (History of the Czech nation in Bohemia and Moravia).[35] Yet already Pelcl sketched its basic outlines in the history of the Germans and the German language in Bohemia mentioned above. Pelcl's work has sometimes puzzled historians, who either attribute its pessimism to the influence of supporters of centralism and Germanization such as J.A. von Riegger, or attempt to reinterpret it in a positive light.[36] Certainly its conclusion, as we have seen, sounded pessimistic, but time and time again Pelcl presented the Czechs in Bohemia trying to protect and expand their language and drive out foreign influences. Thus he attributed the genesis of Dalimil's chronicle, with its well-known anti-German passages, to the fears of "certain Czech patriots [*böhmischen Patrioten*] that their national language [*Nationalsprache*] might be completely driven out by German now that the king himself (John of Luxemburg) was a German."[37] Pelcl made sure to mention that Pavel Ješín reprinted this chronicle at the time of the Estates' revolt in 1618, and that František Faustyn Procházka did so again in the 1780s.[38] He also mentioned Bohuslav Balbín's lament on the state of the Czech language after the defeat of the Bohemian Estates at the Battle of White Mountain in 1620, describing a time when "people so hated and despised the Czech language that one could not speak it in society" and attempts were even made "to root out a language that had for centuries been in use in the nation [*Nation*]."[39] But for Pelcl the greatest moment in the defense of the nation and language came during the Hussite era, when by about 1430 the completely German Bohemia had been made completely Czech again.[40]

Figure 2 Title Page of the Czech Version of F. M. Pelcl's Survey History of Bohemia, *Nová kronyka Česká* (1791). Note the symbol of the Bohemian double-tailed lion.(Courtesy of the Národní knihovna České republiky)

Whether the pessimistic conclusion cited above was intended to inspire Czech patriots to struggle to prevent it, or genuinely represented Pelcl's view at the time, his image of the Czech–German relationship in Bohemia was a powerful one. It was a story of constant struggle, on the Czech side to defend Bohemia's "national" language, customs, and ways of life, reaching a high point during Hussite times. On the other side it was a struggle to spread German influence and power, often in alliance with the rulers. In many respects these images resembled Palacký's view, especially as it was simplified and popularized during the nineteenth century. Even at the beginning of his literary career, the young Palacký expressed similar attitudes to the Germans and the Slavs, including the Czechs. Writing to Josef Jungmann in 1819, before his permanent move to Prague, Palacký lamented:

> Some ruinous Fate placed our good Slavs amidst the gaping maws of thieving nations. What the Germans are doing to us is what they recently did to the Poles, too, without having suffered any injury from them. It is a farce to make high-sounding proclamations about equilibrium in the political system of Europe, and tear apart countries, raise up robbers' hands against the holy rights, against the lives of glorious but unhappy nations. I ought not to write about the ruin of those countries: I would write flames into the tyrants' souls with every word.[41]

In the later formulations of the mature professional historian, Palacký sounded more dispassionate but no less influential when he wrote, "Czech history in general consists mainly of a struggle with Germandom, or of the acceptance and rejection of German ways and practices by the Czechs."[42]

This image of the Czech–German relationship no longer saw the German influence purely as a civilizing force among the uncultured Slavs. Czech patriots usually still recognized the virtues of German culture and enlightenment, but more frequently they called for emulation and competition rather than for assimilation. If the brothers Karel and Václav Thám, and their friend Václav Stach, recognized the German as the Czech's "teacher of enlightenment" and guide into the temple of the arts, they were quick to point out that the German had been "once your clever pupil."[43] Jungmann, too, admired the Germans for their education and recognized that the Czechs owed them at least as much as they did the French, but he also argued that a Czech could not be happy in Bohemia if the only way he could educate himself and advance would be through becoming a German.[44] "Let us learn German, Greek, Latin and other useful languages," called Jan Nejedlý, "but let us *especially speak and write in Czech.*"[45]

To call for the use of Czech was to run into the social question. Jungmann addressed this issue in the first of his conversations on the Czech language, when he imagined a conversation in the Elysian Fields between the shades of Daniel Adam of Veleslavín (an author and publisher from the sixteenth century), a modern Czech, and a passing German. When Veleslavín first speaks to the Czech, the reply is in such a caricature of German-pronounced Czech that he mistakes his counterpart for a German. When he is assured that he is speaking with a native Czech (*Ja Šek je, a v Šechy se narotil*), Veleslavín asks in horror how it comes about that he cannot speak his language. The Czech replies that he does speak his language, German, well because "he who has honor in his body and a good coat on his back should be ashamed to speak Czech."[46] The passing German confirms that Veleslavín's acquaintance represents a true picture of the contemporary Czechs, and in contrast praises the Germans, whose efforts to improve their language began not even sixty years earlier: "They should be an example for your [Czechs]."[47]

In the second conversation, when Protiva objects that Germanization has proceeded so far that all the higher educated strata of society are German and only the peasants (and not even all of them) are Czech, Slavomil retorts:

> The people are still Czech; as for the lords, let them speak French or Persian (the more rational will love the language of their people), what of it? The people will consider them what they proclaim themselves to be—foreigners, and will love them the less, the less they are loved by them.... Every language is a peasant's language where it is at home, and since the peasant is the foremost inhabitant of the land, he could rightfully say to them: What are you gibbering over my head for? I give you what you eat: if you are people like I am, speak so I can understand you![48]

This identification of the common people and the language took another step toward separating the Czech nationalism of the patriots from the Bohemian identity that was shared by the upper classes.

Since the nobility (representatives of the political Bohemian "nation") preserved social and to a lesser extent political prestige, many Czechs would have liked to have won them over to their vision of the nation and language. Karel Hynek Thám, in his fiery defense of the language published in 1783, attacked the nobility for neglecting their patriotic duty and their indifference to the fate of the Czech language that betrayed the examples set by their noble counterparts from the sixteenth century.[49] Noble initiative and participation in many "patriotic" institutions established toward the end of the eighteenth century and the beginning of the nineteenth century suggested that many of the nobility identified themselves at least as Bohemian. Direct involvement in the activities of Czech patriots was quite a bit more rare, making the handful of exceptions all the more valued. As Antonín Jaroslav Puchmajer wrote to Count Franz Sternberg (to whom he dedicated the fourth of his poetic almanacs in 1802), the Czechs had

> the not ungrounded opinion that the great and first men of the land, who should after all be representatives of the Czech nation [*Czechischen Nation*], did not want to do anything for the preservation, to say nothing of the enrichment, of the national language and literature. If only there were more patriotic–Czech feeling [*patriotisch-Czechischgesinnten*] great men as your Excellency, we would soon see our neglected, even despised Czech muse quickly bloom again.[50]

Few noblemen were prepared, however, to accept the exclusively Czech identity that Jungmann's generation propagated.

Thus one approach the Czech patriots could take was to participate where possible in the "patriotic" institutions that existed or were to be formed and use them as platforms for their ideas. The National Museum in Prague, founded in 1818, illustrates this tendency well. The impetus for creating a "national" museum for Bohemia came from the same circles of "Bohemian"-inclined nobility that had given Prague the Count Nostitz National Theater (dedicated to "The Fatherland and the Muses" but in Latin!), the Royal Bohemian Society of Sciences, the Patriotic-Economic Society, and the Patriotic Society of Friends of the Arts.[51] In fact, the original German text of the proclamation announcing the museum refers throughout to the "*vaterländisches Museum*" (Patriotic Museum or Museum of the Fatherland). The Czech version, translated by Josef Jungmann, consistently refers to the "*České národní museum*" (Czech National Museum), calls it an "institution of the nation," and describes its mission as "the preservation and improvement of the Czech language."[52]

When František Palacký presented proposals to establish a journal in both the Czech and German languages to the museum committee in December 1825 and May 1826, he did not go as far as Jungmann did in identifying the museum with the new concepts of Czech nationalism and homeland. He used the term "nation" (*Nation*) in contexts that identified it with the inhabitants of Bohemia (*die Böhmen*), but he recognized that this nation spoke two languages, Czech (*böhmische*, not *tschechische Sprache*) and German. Indeed, he warned that not using both languages equally in the museum could lead to the alienation of "one or the other part of the Nation [*Teil der Nation*]." Yet in spite of all these attitudes, which corresponded closely to the "Bohemian" identity, Palacký's ideas went beyond the traditional bounds of the "Bohemian" identity in two directions. Palacký insisted that even if German was commonly used among the educated, Czech was the genuine historical national language (*historische Nationalsprache*) as well as the language of the majority of the common people (*Sprache der grösseren Volksmasse*). This national language was the most precious gift of earlier generations to the present. Through it the Czechs constituted themselves a separate nation (*Nation*) and won for themselves their own history, a history that occupied a worthier position in world history than otherwise would have belonged to the people (*Volk*) and their land according to their size and numerical strength.[53] The other direction in which Palacký crossed the bounds of territorial patriotism was in his concern for Moravia and the Slovaks of northern Hungary. He included all the lands that once belonged to the Crown of Bohemia (Moravia, Silesia, Upper and Lower Lusatia, part of Brandenburg and Luxemburg) in the historical scope of his proposed journal. He also pointed out that the Czech journal should bear in mind the "Moravians and Slovaks who still hold true to Czech literature," suggesting in the second proposal that the journal could count on nearly six million readers by adding them to the potential readership in Bohemia.[54] This insistence on the Czechness, even if not entirely linguistically, of Bohemia, and the fact that Moravians and Slovaks belonged to it, too, transcended the traditional political limits of noble *Landespatriotismus*.

As Czech nationalists increasingly emphasized the Czech nation and its linguistic culture as attributes of belonging to Bohemia, attitudes toward German
and the Germans shifted further. German speakers were no longer seen neutral-
ly as representatives of the educated and propertied classes. Czech nationalists
now considered them in part Germanized Czechs or renegades (*odrodilci*) who
had turned their backs on their "natural language" and adopted a foreign one.
Patriots decried what they called the "senseless affectation of German manners
and language," so that even an artisan who had just a few words of German
picked up in his travels "inspired with arrogant stupidity, despising the language
of his fatherland, denigrating its customs, rites, and efforts, burns with the desire
to boast of his stupidity with a foreigner's words."[55] One goal of the new-style linguistic nationalists was to win back those Czechs who had fallen away from the
nation, so that they would, as Jan Nejedlý put it,

> recollecting that they come from Czech blood, be awakened to patriotic love, hold dear our
> Czech language, consider us as their brothers ... return to the bosom of their mother
> Bohemia, and ... will once more speak Czech, read Czech books, and increase and improve
> the welfare and honor of our homeland.[56]

The obverse of these efforts was to condemn the days when "enemies of our language, Germans and, alas! some treacherous Czechs," attempted to make German the sole language used anywhere in the Austrian monarchy.[57] In fact, some
Czech patriots turned the tables on the German language and its prestige, calling on Germans in Bohemia to learn Czech. The emphasis here was not, as it
was in Bolzano's case, on *each* nationality learning the *other's* language, since it
was assumed that Czechs would in the course of their education have learned
German anyway.[58]

If Czech nationalists considered the Germans in Bohemia partly as renegade
Czechs, for the rest they viewed them increasingly as guests who had usurped the
position of their erstwhile hosts. Puchmajer, in his ode "To the Czech Language,"
celebrating decrees in 1816 that promised to introduce Czech as a subject in the
gymnasia in Bohemia, harked back to images from a pamphlet of 1618 by Pavel
Stránský. In the poem, Puchmajer described how that "cruel foreigner, the German" lorded it over Bohemia, behaving like the hedgehog who wrangled his way
into the hare's hole only to drive the owner away with his spines. Just so the German had driven the Czech out of "offices, schools, councils, the theater," everywhere the "Swabian smothered and pursued you."[59] In 1845 Jakub Malý asked
ironically when exactly the Germans had made their contribution to Czech civilization and culture:

> Perhaps at the time that your half-savage ancestors invited Slavic settlers to till their fields
> while they were lying about on bearskins ... or at the time when the German masters who
> had emigrated from Prague arranged at the Council of Constance for the burning of Mas-
> ter Jan Hus out of personal spite? Possibly in the seventeenth century, when the dragoons
> returned our people to the Catholic faith and the Jesuits burned the treasures of our liter-

ature on pyres? Or possibly even later, when our nation was left without schools, given up entirely to ignorance, so that it would become obedient subjects?[60]

Malý's selection of historical events demonstrates clearly how the past could be used to overcome the feelings of Czech social and cultural inferiority embedded in the "Bohemian" identity.

This process of historical reinterpreting illustrates a paradox of Czech cultural development during the first generation of the nineteenth century that has been explored by Vladimír Macura, among others. Macura points out that as Czech culture attempted to liberate itself from German tutelage, it nevertheless did so in ways that were still dependent on German culture. We have already seen the attitudes that Macura terms "analogous relationship," in the calls by Czech patriots to imitate and equal the Germans in developing their language and culture. This tendency expressed itself in efforts to make Czech versions of everything of which the Germans could boast, by translating or creating the equivalent in Czech. The other way in which, more paradoxically, Czech culture depended on German, Macura calls "negative relationship." In its very effort to become free of German influence, Czech culture attempted not to develop simply differently from German, but specifically in the opposite direction. Thus its non-German qualities still derived, as in a mirror reflection, from the German model.[61]

Czech patriots' uses of historical arguments to separate themselves from the Germans in Bohemia and revalue their own self-image reflected elements of these analogous and especially negative relationships to German culture. Czech patriots sought to counter the traditional stereotypes about the Slavs in general and the Czechs in particular, drawn from foreign, especially German, sources. Many elements of these arguments had already appeared in the works of historians of the Enlightenment or sympathetic foreigners like Herder, such as the Czech role in creating the state traditions and rights of Bohemia or the image of peace-loving Slavs.[62] We have already seen how Pelcl in his history of the Germans articulated elements of the nineteenth century's dominant myth of the meaning of Czech history. His other works, such as the multiple editions of his *Kurzgefasste Geschichte der Böhmen* or the Czech-language *Nová kronyka Česká* (New Czech chronicle), also added to them. One very significant source of such historical materials, however, was not a work of professional history at all, but a literary monument. In fact, it was not a genuine literary monument; it was the famous forged manuscripts of old Czech poetry known as the Královédvorský/Königinhof and Zelenohorský/Grünberg manuscripts.

The manuscripts made a tremendous impact when their "discovery" was announced because they offered evidence for a very different picture of the early Slavs and Czechs than that given by German opponents of the renascence. Besides apparently predating the famous *Niebelungenlied*, they reflected a society quite different from the one depicted in German sources. If the Germans accused the Slavs of hereditary submissiveness (deriving the name Slav from *sclavus*, slave), the manuscripts (and many other works) celebrated their peace-loving qualities. If the *Niebelungenlied* depicted betrayal and lust, the manuscripts reflected a society that valued loyalty and fraternity and punished theft and betrayal. If the Germans claimed military prowess, the manuscripts showed them fighting for plunder and booty, while the Slavs defended their customs and moral values. If the Germans accused the Slavs of lacking the maturity necessary for political organization, the manuscripts celebrated their love of equality and set it off against the Germanic feudal system and its principle of subjection. In the manuscripts the Germans are presented as aggressive but cowardly invaders ("Beneš Heřmanóv" in the Královédvorský manuscript). The cultural level of the early Czechs, reflected, for instance, in "Libuše's Judgement" in the Zelenohorský manuscript, was so high that they had no need of German civilization.[63]

By the time Palacký's *Dějiny národu českého* discussed the ancient Czechs' civilization, it sounded remarkably like nineteenth-century liberalism:

> Not without feelings of pride will a descendant understand that his Slavic ancestors preserved and defended among themselves for ages those things for which even the greatest and most cultivated nations of our age strive and aspire, not always successfully: general liberty of all in the land, equality before the law and justice, the government both hereditary, and elected and responsible to the assembly, free elections of local offices and representatives of the nation, and other such institutions, even including that praiseworthy shield of all general liberties, trial by jury.[64]

Palacký's vision of Czech history, especially as his popularizers and imitators fixed it in Czech historical imagination, provided the Czech nationalists with a past that contributed something positive to all humanity. When they looked specifically at such episodes as the Hussite era, they could feel (with Meissner and Hartmann) that the Czechs then were struggling for more than territory or booty, but for positive values. What Czech intellectuals drew from the past, in particular the Hussite imagery, was evidence of their right to exist as a separate and equal nation among the other European nations. In this they went beyond the attitude of most German Bohemians, who generally considered Bohemia and the Czechs part of the wider German political nation. On this ground, then, German Bohemians such as the poets of "Young Bohemia" and the Czech nationalists parted company.

This parting of the ways affected another community within Bohemia, the Jews. The first half of the nineteenth century was marked, as we have seen, by the maturation of the first generation of Bohemian Jews to have the full benefits of the Josephine and post-Josephine reforms. As was probably natural, most of them had assimilated into the German cultural sphere. But in their gymnasium and university studies they were exposed to the "other" culture of Bohemia through such teachers as Václav Svoboda and fellow students like the poet Václav Bolemír Nebeský.[65] Inspired by Nebeský's belief that the Czechs could gain quite a lot from cooperation with and assimilation of the Jews, a number of Jewish writers connected to "Young Bohemia" attempted in the mid-1840s to win Bohemia's Jews over to the Czech national cause. Unfortunately, their newspaper campaign in 1844 began shortly before a major episode of worker unrest in Prague, when the textile printers, angered at the introduction of machinery in their (frequently Jewish-owned) factories, took to the streets, to be followed by the construction workers on the railway. Protests became riots and the violence was quickly directed against the Jews, requiring military intervention to restore calm. In the aftermath, this brief "Czech-Jewish courtship" came to an end.[66]

One writer who did not immediately abandon the idea of a Czech-Jewish symbiosis, however, was Siegfried Kapper. He had already made a significant contribution to Czech-German coexistence by translating many works of Czech poetry into German, thereby making them available to a wider world. In 1846 he published a volume of his own original poems, *České listy* (Czech leaves). This was the first modern work of literature in Czech by a Jewish writer and in it Kapper added to traditional themes of Jewish longing "an imaginative identification of the Jewish and the Czech nations, matching tragedy for historical tragedy and offering the vision of a common future."[67] Kapper's verses expressed a heartfelt love of the Czech homeland equal to that of any Czech romantic intellectual, but they also reflected his personal experience of rejection and "otherness." In a poem dedicated to Nebeský he lamented the anguish of loving the fatherland and yet being a foreigner in it, and the events of 1844 seemed to him like a rejection at the hands of the fatherland itself.[68] Still Kapper asserted his own identity as a Czech, warning those Czechs he wanted to claim as brothers not to call him a non-Czech.[69] Any hope the Czech side would accept this assertion of identity, however, was dashed by Karel Havlíček's review of *České listy* in November 1846.

Havlíček's criticism was not aimed at Kapper's poetic abilities, but rather at the idea that Jews could consider themselves Czechs. Havlíček (who had earlier been a close associate of Nebeský) focused not on whether the Jews spoke Czech, but on other factors:

> How can Israelites [*Israelité*] belong to the Czech nation when they are of Semitic origin? ... Undoubtedly all Jews—whatever country or part of the world they may live in—consider themselves as a nation, as brethren, and not solely as co-religionists. We hope that there is no need to prove the point that it is impossible to belong simultaneously to two fatherlands and two nations, or to serve two masters. Therefore anyone who wants to be a Czech must cease to be a Jew.[70]

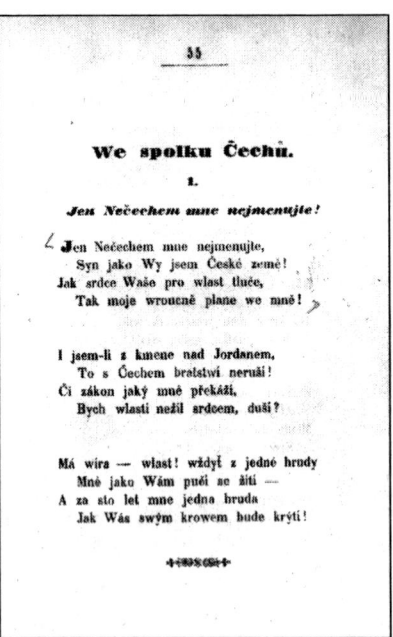

Figure 3 The poem, "Jen Nečechem mne nejmenujte!" (Just don't call me a non-Czech!) from Siegfried Kapper's *České listy*, 1846. (Courtesy of the Národní knihovna České republiky)

For Havlíček, the Jews were a separate nation with their own bonds of ancestry, religion, language, and history. Kapper looked with one eye to Jerusalem, the promised land, and with the other at Bohemia's fields, but "his poems clearly reveal that he loves still more what is truly his own—which is only natural and praiseworthy."[71] In conclusion, somewhat inconsistently, Havlíček said that if Jews must abandon their "natural" language, Hebrew, then they should "attach themselves to the Germans and their literature," since German had already become the second mother tongue of Central European Jews.[72]

The antisemitic violence of 1844, followed by similar outbursts during the 1848 revolutions, gradually ended hopes at this time for assimilation of Bohemia's Jews into the Czech nation. Siegfried Kapper was a notable exception to the trend, but even he did not write any more works in Czech, contenting himself with translations into German from Czech and other Slavic languages. More typical for most of these Bohemian Jewish intellectuals was Moritz Hartmann's reaction to the 1844 violence. Writing to Meissner in 1844, he said, "My friend, the time has come for us in Bohemia to stand as Germans; that will be our post in the future."[73]

Havlíček's thinking on what made up a nation and what elements contributed to national identity—the reasons that led him to deny Kapper's desire to identify himself as a Czech—informed his article "Slav and Czech," published in 1846. In it Havlíček attacked the fuzzy thinking that went into the popular Czech Slavism typical of many patriots during this phase of the renascence. Images of and identification with the Slavs had been, as we have seen, one important mechanism of defense and differentiation from the Germans. Slavism carried with it other dangers, however, since Tsarist Russia was identified, especially after the suppression of the Polish Uprising in 1830-31, with the darkest forces of reaction. Thus too much uncritical Slavic enthusiasm by the Czechs allowed their German opponents to see them as little more than a cat's paw for the Tsar.[74] Havlíček's article exploded some of the pretty bubbles of Slavic reciprocity, while maintaining that the Czechs could still logically find common ground with other Slavs within the Habsburg Monarchy.

More than to any other group, this Slavic common ground applied to the Moravians. During the first decades of the nineteenth century, developments in Moravia gradually led to the acceptance of a common national identity with the Czechs rather than taking the existing "Moravian" identity and building a modern Moravian nation out of it. The excursion into Slavism made in the struggle to define Czech identity and distinguish it from the Germans in Bohemia had enough space in it, even after Havlíček's article, to include not only Moravians but also the Slovaks—ironically just at a time when younger Slovak intellectuals led by Ľudovit Štúr were developing a distinct Slovak national identity.[75] As far as Moravia was concerned, however, the Czech identity could include it while preserving the concept of a single Czech nation. Palacký, as we have seen, considered the Slavs in Moravia an organic part of his idea of the Czech nation. As he wrote in his *Dějiny národu českého,*

My intention has been from the beginning not to put asunder what God has joined together, and not to create barriers where there are none from nature; I am firmly of the conviction that being born a Moravian, I am of the Czech nation [*Jsa rodem Moravan, jsem
národem Čech*].[76]

By the eve of the 1848 revolutions, then, the processes of national differentiation and integration in Bohemia had set the stage for the dramatic emergence
of political conflict between Czechs and Germans in Bohemia, conflict that eventually polarized the attitudes even of such former Czech sympathizers as Hartmann, Meissner, and others. Czechs and Germans would no longer seriously
consider themselves members of a common "Bohemian" nation, and even the
idea of a fruitful coexistence of two nations within Bohemia was getting lost in
the noise of struggle over Frankfurt, the Prague Slav Congress, and the shaping
of a new Austria.[77] One particularly sharply worded obituary for the "Bohemian"
identity, Vilém Dušan Lambl's "Fairy-tale about Unity between Czechs and Germans," appeared during 1848 in *Národní noviny:*

In the interest of Unity [*Svornost*] certain eccentric characters thought up a strange theory,
according to which the inhabitants of the Czech Lands are neither Czechs nor Germans,
but rather something that cannot even be expressed in Czech. ("Wir sind weder Deutsche
noch Čechen, wir sind Böhmen.") This is a doctrine of the kind of humanist who prefers
to sit on two stools and finally ends up sitting between them both on the bare ground. We
reject it pure and simple as a product of only about 5 or 6 years vintage. In Bohemia there
were always Czechs and Germans (or Czech-Germans [*Čechoněmci*]), which in German
always were called Böhmen und Deutschböhmen. With this newly imagined term (*Čechen,
čechisch*) either the Czechs as a Slavic nation are to be considered as simply one side (seem-
ingly the weaker one, dying out), or that difference in nationality, stamped by nature and
history, is to be effaced, which, however, in real life cannot be effaced in any way.[78]

In the course of the 1848 revolution and its aftermath, the Bohemian identity
gave way to Czech and German identities. The Jews for the time being sought
acculturation or assimilation rather with the Germans than the Czechs, while
most Moravians were content to make common cause culturally with the
Czechs. Later in the century, under changed social conditions, a movement
among the Jews to join the Czech nation reemerged, to be largely destroyed in
the Holocaust.[79] Moravia has retained enough of its own sense of regional patriotism to give rise to a (tiny, fringe) Moravian autonomy movement, but
Palacky's credo "*rodem Moravan, národem Čech*" still prevails today. As for the
Czechs and Germans in Bohemia, Meissner's foreboding of a day of reckoning
between them came to pass between 1938 and 1946, arguably to the detriment
of both nations.

Notes

1. Francis Joseph Kinsky, *Erinnerung über einen wichtigen Gegenstand, von einem Böhmen*, in *Des Grafen Kinskys, gesamelte Schriften*, vol. 3 (Vienna: Wappler, 1786), 57. Kinsky reorganized, and later directed, the military academy in Wiener Neustadt. See Anna M. Drabek, "Der Nationsbegriff in Böhmen an der Grenze von Aufklärung und 'nationaler Wiedergeburt,'" in *Vaterlandsliebe und Gesamtstaatsidee im Österreichischen 18. Jahrhundert*, Beihefte zum Jahrbuch der Österreichischen Gesellschaft zur Erforschung des 18. Jahrhunderts, vol. 1, ed. Moritz Csáky and Reinhard Hagelkrys (Vienna: VWGÖ, 1989), 50.

2. Kinsky, *Erinnerung*, 60. He claims that the French soldiers in Bohemia during the Seven Years' War (1756-1763) learned Czech more easily than German.

3. Walter Schamschula, *Die Anfänge der tschechischen Erneuerung und das deutsche Geistesleben, 1740-1800* (Munich: Wilhelm Fink, 1973), 119. On the "defenses of the language," see Hugh LeCaine Agnew, *Origins of the Czech National Renascence* (Pittsburgh: University of Pittsburgh Press, 1993), 53-70.

4. Joseph Matthias Graf von Thun-Hohenstein, *Der Slawismus in Böhmen* (Prague: J.G. Calve, 1845), 17.

5. Jan Křen, *Konfliktní společenství: Češi a Němci, 1780-1918* (Prague: Academia, 1990), 44-47.

6. Johann Anton Ritter von Riegger, *Skizze einer statistischen Landeskunde Böhmens* (Leipzig and Prague, 1795), 98-99.

7. Ibid., 98.

8. Milan Šmerda, "Zrušení nevolnictví a české obrození. K 200. výročí zrušení nevolnictví v českých zemích," *Slovanský přehled* 67, no. 1 (1982): 10. Smerda quotes J. J. Kausch in his *Ausführliche Nachrichten über Böhmen* (Gratz, 1794), 50-51: "Und doch glaube ich, dass man alle diese Fehler, so wie ich es von den beiden letztgenannten [Silesians and Czechs] bereits gezeigt habe, mehr noch auf Rechnung der Leibeigenschaft als des slawischen Herkommens schieben müsste."

9. *Der Volkslehrer* and its Czech counterpart were published by the Highest Burggrave, Karl Egon Fürstenburg. See Agnew, *Czech National Renascence*, 178-79; also Smerda, "Zrusení nevolnictví a české obrození," 9.

10. Published by Matthias Kalina von Jäthenstein, translated by Jan Nepomuk Štěpánek, *Ponaučné a zábavné listy pro polní hospodáře a řemeslníky v Čechách* began appearing in 1838. On the Patriotic-Economic Society see Miroslav Wolf, *Vlastenecko-hospodářská společnost 1767-1872* (Prague, 1956).

11. Jan Heidler, *Čechy a Rakousko v politických brožurách předbřeznových* (Prague: Matice Česká, 1920), 75, says this image appears in the earliest German brochure of the period, "Die österreichischen Länder und Völker" (1833), which presents Czechs as thieves and Bohemian Germans as bearers of culture.

12. František Martin Pelcl, "Geschichte der Deutschen und ihrer Sprache in Böhmen, wie auch von dem Einflusse, den sie auf Religion, Sitten, Regierung, Wissenschaften und Künste der Böhmen gehabt haben," *Abhandlungen der Böhmischen Gesellschaft der Wissenschaften zu Prag* 4 (Prague, 1788): 345.

13. Ibid., 355.

14. František Martin Pelcl, "Geschichte der Deutschen und ihrer Sprache in Böhmen," *Neuere Abhandlungen der königlichen Böhmischen Gesellschaft der Wissenschaften* 1 (1790): 310.

15. Franz Schuselka, *Deutsche Worte eines Österreichers* (Hamburg: Hoffman und Campe, 1843), 208-9. See also Křen, *Konfliktní společenství*, 73.

16. "Von den Sudeten," *Allgemeine Zeitung*, no. 283 (9 October 1844), cited (and authorship suggested) in Jiří Kořalka, *Tschechen im Habsburgerreich und in Europa, 1815-1914: Sozialgeschichtliche Zusammenhänge der neuzeitlichen Nationsbildung und der Nationalitätenfrage in den böhmischen Ländern*, Schriftenreihe der österreichischen Ost- und Südosteuropa-Instituts 18 (Vienna and Munich: Verlag für Geschichte und Politik and R. Oldenbourg,

1991), 39. The tone of this article is much more strongly anti-Czech than Schuselka's other brochures. See also Franz Schuselka, *Ist Österreich deutsch?* (Leipzig: Weidmann, 1843), 29, where he writes, "Bohemia is in and of itself [*an und für sich*] a German land."

17. Kořalka, *Tschechen im Habsburgerreich*, 41-42, and Franz Schuselka, *Das Revolutionsjahr, März 1848–März 1849* (Vienna: Jasper, Hügel und Manz, 1850), 107.

18. J.P. Stern, "Language Consciousness and Nationalism in the Age of Bernard Bolzano," *Journal of European Studies* 19 (1989): 169-89; and Derek Sayer, *The Coasts of Bohemia: A Czech History* (Princeton, N.J.: Princeton University Press, 1998), 57-62.

19. Bernard Bolzano, *Über das Verhältniss der beiden Volkstämme in Böhmen* (Vienna: Wilhelm Braumüller, 1849), 16.

20. Ibid., 25-26.

21. Ibid., 40.

22. Ibid., 44. It is interesting to note that Bolzano does not specify that this single language should be *either* Czech or German.

23. Josef Peřina, *Přehledné dějiny vztahů české a česko-nemecké literatury v 19. stoletî*, I (Ústí nad Labem: Universita J.E. Purkyně, 1996) discusses the symbiotic relationship between Bohemian-German and Czech literature during this period in detail. He has also published an anthology of works by authors from this period: *Dvoubarevný papršek Bohemie: Německy a česky psaná literatura na území Cech v letech 1780-1848* (Ústí nad Labem: Ústav slovansko-germánských studií, Universita J.E. Purkyně, 1997).

24. Karel Sabina, *Vzpomínky*, Paměti. Knihovna literárních vzpomínek a korespondence (Prague: František Borový, 1937), 25-64.

25. Alois Hofman, *Die Prager Zeitschrift "Ost und West": ein Beitrag zur Geschichte der deutsch-slawischen Verständigung im Vormärz* (Berlin: Akademie-Verlag, 1957); Eduard Goldstücker, "Jews between Czechs and Germans around 1848," *Yearbook of the Leo Baeck Institute* (London: Secker and Warburg, 1972), 67; Hillel J. Kieval, "The Social Vision of Bohemian Jews: Intellectuals and Community in the 1840s," in *Assimilation and Community: The Jews in Nineteenth-Century Europe*, ed. Jonathan Frankel and Steven J. Zipperstein (Cambridge: Cambridge University Press, 1992), 253.

26. Jiří Kořalka, "Evropský zájem o husitství a František Palacký (do roku 1848)," *Husitský Tábor* 8 (1985): 207-37.

27. Alfred Meissner, *Žiška. Gesänge* (Leipzig: F.L. Herbig, 1846), 198. "Indes die Fremden an den Tisch gekommen, / Lebt nun der Böhm' im eigen Haus als Knecht, / Ein armer Waise, dem die Zeit genommen / Sein letztes Erb': der Sprache heil'ges Recht."

28. Ibid., 187-88. "Tot bist du, Böhmen, und in Staub getreten, / Doch gleich der Bombe aus den Feuerschlünden, / Um einst mit wilden flammen, sturmverwehten, / Den Brand gen Rom in aller Welt zu zünden! / Zertreten bist du, Volk! Ja, doch wie Trauben / Vom Winzer totgekeltert unter Schmerzen, / Dass du dereinst als Feuerwein den Glauben, / Den Rausch der Freiheit tragst in alle Herzen.... / So zieht denn hin, verblutende Heroen,... / Sollt ihr noch andre Völker sterben lehren."

29. Ibid., 200. "Doch, weiss ich, kommt ein Tag noch, wo zum ringen, / Zum letzten ringen sich dies Land erhebt,... Ein Tag, an dem im Kampf sich soll entscheiden, / Ob Deutsch, ob Böhmisch endlich siegen soll. / Ich aber will nicht wissen, was ihm werde, / Für eine Lösung diesem Tag von Blut, / Ich freue mich, dass dann in kühler erde / Wohl lange schon mein müder Leichnam ruht." See also Sabina, *Vzpomínky*, 64.

30. Moritz Hartmann, *Kelch und Schwert. Dichtungen* (Leipzig: J.J. Weber, 1845), 289-90. See also Kořalka, "Evropský zájem o husitství," 222-23.

31. Karel Hynek Thám, *Über den Karakter der Slawen, dann über den Ursprung, die Schicksale, Vollkommenheiten, die Nützlichkeit und Wichtigkeit der böhmischen Sprache* (Prague, 1803), 36-37. Thám was taking up a position as Czech teacher at the gymnasium in Prague's Old Town. The lecture was largely a pastiche of other works defending the Czech language or the Slavs; the cited passage is from Herder's *Briefe zur Beförderung der Humanität* (Riga, 1793), 146.

32. Jan Nejedlý, "O lásce k vlasti," *Hlasatel Český* 1, no. 1 (1806): 15. Emphasis in original.

33. Ibid., 16. Emphasis in original.

34. Josef Jungmann, "O jazyku českém. Rozmlouvání druhé," *Hlasatel Český* 1, no. 3 (1806): 326.

35. Jiří Rak, *Byvali Čechové: České historické mýty a stereotypy* (Jinončany: H & H, 1994), 97-110; Rak, "Obraz Němce v české historiografii 19. Století," in *Obraz Němce Rakouska a Německa v české společnosti 19. a 20. století*, ed. Jan Křen and Eva Broklová (Prague: Karolinum, 1998), 49-57.

36. Rak, "Protiosvícenská reakce v pojetí husitství u F.M. Pelcla," *Husitský Tábor* 8 (1985): 195-204. See also Schamschula, *Die Anfänge der tschechischen Erneuerung*, 170, and Josef Johanides, *František Martin Pelcl* (Prague: Melantrich, 1981), 184-92.

37. Pelcl, "Geschichte der Deutschen," 282.

38. Ibid., 292-95. He was careful, however, to stress that Procházka's only motive was to protect this monument of Czech literature from extinction.

39. Ibid., 296-97. Once again Pelcl included a footnote mentioning a modern edition of this defensive work (one that he had printed himself in 1775), and again he stressed—if we take his words at face value—that his only goal was to gratify the antiquarian interests of lovers of the Czech language and its history.

40. Ibid., 291.

41. František Palacký to Josef Jungmann, 14 July 1819, Josef Jungmann collection, sign. I/14/2, Literarní archiv Památníku národního písemnictví, Prague (hereafter cited as LA PNP).

42. František Palacký, *Dějiny národu českého v Čechách a na Moravě* (Prague: B. Kočí, 1908), 8.

43. In their ode celebrating the first Czech performances at the Nostitz Theater in Prague in 1785. Printed flyer, "Svátek českého jazyka, na den druhého provozování Štefanového Odběhlce v Pražském vlastenském Dívadle od Bondynské společnosti Německých herců, dne 25 ledna 1785." Karel Hynek Thám collection, sign. I/12/29, LA PNP. "Plesej! Teuton jindy bystrý učedlník tvůj/Nyní, v tvé zastaralosti / Učitel osvícení / Jest vůdce tvůj, / Na důkaz vděčnosti/ By tvá řeč opět rozkvětla, / Zlatého věku ovotce přínesla / Přátelsky jest přihotovení / Den tvé skrz dívadla provésti / Až do svatyně moudrosti."

44. Jungmann, "O jazyku českém. Rozmlouvání druhé," 334.

45. Jan Nejedlý, "K vlastencům a milovníkům jazyka českého," *Hlasatel Český* 4, no. 1 (1818): 16.

46. Josef Jungmann, "O jazyku českém. Rozmlouvání první," *Hlasatel Český* 1, no. 1 (1806): 43.

47. Ibid., 46.

48. Jungmann, "O jazyka českém. Rozmlouvání druhém," 344.

49. Karel Hynek Thám, *Obrana jazyka českého proti zlobivým jeho utrháčům, též mnoha vlastencům v cvičení se v něm liknavým a nedbalým* (Prague: Schönfeld, 1783), especially the passage on 21.

50. Puchmajer to Franz Sternberg, n.d., Šternberk collection, no sign., LA PNP.

51. Marie Sklárová, "Musis et Patriae (Die sozialen Zusammenhänge des Patriotismus in Böhmen)," paper presented at the symposium "Patriotismus und Nationsbildung in der Spätphase des Alten Reiches," cosponsored by the Ústav světových dějin, Filosofická fakulta Univerzita Karlova, and the Historischer Seminar der Universität Köln, Prague, 5-6 May 1995. See also Sayer, *Coasts of Bohemia*, 53-57.

52. *List nepolitický novin Kraméryusových*, 25 April 1818, no. 17, 66-67.

53. All citations and the paraphrase taken from Jiří Kořalka, "K pojetí národa v české společnosti 19. století," in *Povědomí tradice v novodobé české kultuře (doba Bedřicha Smetany)* (Prague: Národní galerie, 1988), 34-35. The German original text of the two proposals is published in Franz Palacký, *Gedenkblätter: Auswahl von Denkschriften, Aufsätzen und Briefen aus den letzten fünfzig Jahren* (Prague: Tempsky, 1874), 47-64.

54. Kořalka, "K pojetí národa," 35.

55. Vojtěch Nejedlý to Šebastián Hněvkovský, 3 September 1792, in Jaroslav Šťastný, ed., "Korespondence Šeb. Hněvkosvkého, II," *Výroční zpráva cís. král. vyššího gymnasia českého na Novém městě v Praze v Truhlářské ulici za školní rok 1909-1910* (Prague: 1910), 5. Perhaps it is ironic that Nejedlý expresses these sentiments to his friend in Latin.

56. Nejedlý, "K vlastencům a milovníkům jazyka českého," 16.

57. Josef Rautenkranc, "Pročby se mělo v hlavních školách království Českého učiti také česky a češtinu," *Hlasatel Český* 4, no. 1 (1818): 73.

58. Examples of these suggestions come from inaugural lectures as professor of Czech language and literature at the Prague University by Pelcl (1793) and his successor Jan Nejedlý (1801). Pelcl indeed did not expect his suggestion (that the Germans learn Czech) to go down well, since Czechs had an advantage in competition for employment if they spoke both languages. Nejedlý hoped for better relations between the two communities: "a bond of friendship, as brothers, would encircle them the more the German communicated with the Czech [*Böhmen*] orally or in writing in the Czech language [*Czechensprache*]." See Pelcl, *Akademische Antrittsrede über den Nutzen und Wichtigkeit der Böhmischen Sprache* (Prague: Rokos, 1793), 18, and Nejedlý, *Akademische Antrittsrede gehalten den 16. November 1801* (Prague: Gerzabek, 1801), 21.

59. I do not know if Puchmajer intended a pun here, since in Czech *šváb* (Swabian, i.e., German) also means cockroach. I am citing the manuscript version in Puchmajer collection, sign. I/4/13, LA PNP. The manuscript is dated 5 November 1816. See also Rak, *Byvali Čechové*, 100-101.

60. Cited in Rak, *Bývali Čechové*, 102.

61. See Vladimír Macura, *Znamení zrodu. České národní obrození jako kulturní typ,* 2nd ed. (Jinočany: H & H, 1995), 31-41, especially 36. Macura's untimely death in 1998 was a great loss to Czech scholarship. See also Peřina, *Přehledné dějiny vztahů české a česko-nemecké literatury,* 53-55.

62. See Robert B. Pynsent, *Questions of Identity: Czech and Slovak Ideas of Nationality and Personality* (Budapest, London, New York: Central European University Press, 1994), 44-99; also Agnew, *Czech National Renascence,* 19-50.

63. "*Netřeba nám v Němcích iskati pravdu, u nás pravda po zákonu svatě*" (We do not need to take law from the Germans, we have our own holy laws), cited in Rak, *Bývali Čechové,* 101-2. On the manuscripts see the publication "Rukopisy Královédvorský a Zelenohorský. Dnešní stav poznání," *Sborník Národního muzea,* Řada C, 13 and 14 (Prague: Academia, 1969).

64. Palacký, *Dějiny národu českého,* 8.

65. Kieval, "Social Vision," 250-51. For more on the intellectual situation among Bohemian Jews during this period, see William O. McCagg, Jr., *A History of the Habsburg Jews, 1670-1918* (Bloomington: Indiana University Press, 1989), 66-71.

66. The phrase is Kieval's in "Social Vision," 263. See also McCagg, *Habsburg Jews,* 76-81.

67. Kieval, "Social Vision," 267.

68. "O Václave, ty neznáš boly rmutné: / Milovat vlast, a byt w ni cizincem!" (from "To V. B. Nebesky"), or addressing the Czech homeland: "Tys krásný sen mu sama zakalila, / Ranivši jej, když obejmout tě chtěl," in "August, 1844." Siegfried Kapper, *České listy* (Prague: Calve, 1846), 42 and 32.

69. Ibid., 55. See the pugnacious verse, "Jen Nečechem mne nejmenujte!" (Just don't call me a non-Czech!) in the cycle "Ve spolku Čechů" (In the society of Czechs).

70. Cited in Kieval, "Social Vision," 267-68. See also Goldstücker, "Between Czechs and Germans," 67-68.

71. Kieval, "Social Vision," 268.

72. Cited in Goldstücker, "Between Czechs and Germans," 68.

73. Kieval, "Social Vision," 270-71. Jewish reactions to events in 1848 are discussed in Bradley F. Abrams, "The Austro-Czech Jewish Intelligentsia of 1848 and the Österreichisches Central-Organ für Glaubensfreiheit, Cultur, Geschichte und Literatur der Juden," *Bohemia: Zeitschrift für Geschichte und Kultur der böhmischen Länder* 31 (1990): 1-20.

74. Rak, *Bývali Čechové,* 119-22, and Křen, *Konfliktní společenství,* 74-75.

75. See Macura, *Znamení zrodu,* 153-69, especially 168-69; a summary discussion of Slovak developments may be found in Hugh LeCaine Agnew, "Czechs, Slovaks, and the Slovak Linguistic

Separatism of the Mid-Nineteenth Century," in *The Czech and Slovak Experience*, ed. John Morison (New York: St. Martin's, 1992), 21-37.

76. Palacký, *Dějiny národu českého*, 4. For a discussion of developments in Moravia leading to this outcome, see Milan Řepa, *Moravané nebo Češi? Vývoj českého národního vědomí na Moravě v 19. století* (Brno: Doplněk, 2001), and Jiří Pernes, *Pod moravskou orlicí aneb dějiny moravanství* (Brno: Barrister and Principal, 1996), 81-102.

77. Among books on 1848 dealing with Bohemia, see Stanley Z. Pech, *The Czech Revolution of 1848* (Chapel Hill: University of North Carolina Press, 1969) and Arnošt Klima, *Češi a Němci v revoluci, 1848-1849* (Prague: Nebesa, 1994). See also Hugh LeCaine Agnew, "Dilemmas of Liberal Nationalism: Czechs and Germans in Bohemia and the Revolution of 1848," in *Nations and Nationalisms in East-Central Europe, 1806-1948: A Festschrift for Peter Sugar*, eds. Sabina P. Ramet, James R. Felak, and Herbert J. Ellison (Bloomington, IN, 2002), 51-70.

78. Vilém Dušan Lambl, "Pohádka o svornosti mezi Čechy a Němci," *Národní noviny*, no. 19 (27 April 1848): 73. Cited in Kořalka, "Pojetí národa," 37-38.

79. See Hillel Kieval, *The Making of Czech Jewry: National Conflict and Jewish Society in Bohemia, 1870-1918* (New York and Oxford: Oxford University Press, 1988), 10-63.

Part Two

AUSTRIA-HUNGARY IN THE AGE OF NATIONALISM

Chapter 4

THE IMAGE OF THE OTHER IN THE NINETEENTH CENTURY

Historical Scholarship in the Bohemian Lands

Jiří Štaif

The historiography of a nation has usually played an important part in the creation and consolidation of the basic concepts from which the self-image of that nation derives. These concepts involve not only straightforward images of the nation itself, but also images of other nations, especially those that are geographically most proximate or in various ways competitors. They have often suggestively described the ways in which "We" have developed historically in comparison to "Them." In Europe, the golden age of this kind of historiography was the "long" nineteenth century. During this time Czech historiography was primarily concerned with the question of the nature of "We—the Czechs" in contrast to "Them—the Germans." In wrestling with this question, Czech historiography, especially in Bohemia, was in line with general Central European trends, but it also displayed specific features, that were connected above all with František Palacký's concept of the Czech national past, as we will see in the following pages.

The Enlightenment conviction that history was not simply political history, but the history of civilization to be interpreted in terms of progress through particular developmental stages, strongly influenced Czech historiography. Another major influence was romanticism and its view of history as primarily the history of nations, with "nations" understood as unique ethnic wholes that had occupied a certain territory long enough for it to be regarded as "theirs." The German

Notes for this section begin on page 100.

legal-historical school and classical German philosophy, which regarded the state as the highest form of civilization, particularly if it boasted a long historical tradition, was a third influence.

Three ethnic groups have fundamentally molded the historical development of Bohemia: Czechs, Germans, and Jews. At mid-nineteenth century, the Czechs formed the largest group, making up about 60 percent of a population of almost 4.35 million. Germans represented nearly 39 percent, and Jews 1.6 percent. The relations among these ethnic groups have had a complex and frequently conflict-ridden history, with the major theme being the historical confrontations between Czechs and Germans.[1]

As far back as the Middle Ages, some chroniclers made the frequent difficulties in the coexistence of Czechs and Germans a key theme in their expositions of Czech history. The most famous example is the so-called *Chronicle of Dalimil* from the early fourteenth century. It presented Germans as the great enemies of the Czechs from the military, economic, and national (in modern terms "ethnic") point of view. The chronicle did not distinguish between Germans settled in Bohemia or Germans elsewhere, since "all Germans seek evil to Czechs." For Dalimil, the representative of ethnic Czechs was the Czech nobility in the both political and national sense.[2]

A later example of a strongly anti-German attitude can be found in the well-known *Respublica Bojema* (1643) by Pavel Stránský (1583-1657), who emigrated to Poland following the Battle of White Mountain. This is a passionate apologia for the Bohemian Estates monarchy as it had existed before 1620. Stránský, like Dalimil, believed that Germans threatened the ethnic "purity" of the Czech nation. In his view the Czechs, after settling in Bohemia, had not mingled their blood with other nations, and had equal status with them in terms of nationality and citizenship. He stressed that the Czechs had settled empty land and created their own state on its territory. Stránský, Dalimil, and other chroniclers asserted that the Germans had settled in Bohemia much later, and were therefore mere guests. Stránský's arguments about the Germans influenced the greatest historian of Bohemia of the Baroque era, the Jesuit Bohuslav Balbín (1621-1688).[3]

The historical argumentation Dalimil and Stransky employed would later attract the attention of Enlightenment and romantic historians in Bohemia. These older texts were not only republished, but became historical sources persuasive for their emotional content, which corresponded with the feelings of a number of historians in Bohemia at the end of the eighteenth century. The increased interest in Dalimil, Stránský, and other earlier historical authors who had emphasized the national (ethnic) element in Czech history was indirectly connected with the Enlightenment focus of scholarship on the historically "obscure" beginnings of Czech history. A crucial issue for historians of the time was the development of scholarly interest in Slavonic languages and culture. They were led by the founder of modern Slavistics, Josef Dobrovský (1753-1829). He was the author of *Geschichte der böhmischen Sprache und Literatur*

(1791), which provided the first modern overview of Czech cultural history. Also important was the experience of the period of the French Revolution and Napoleonic Wars, when not only rulers but also individual nations appeared on the stage of history.[4]

This kind of Czech cultural and political historiography left subsequent generations a historical legacy in the form of the following assumptions: the Czechs were the first people to settle permanently in the Bohemian Lands; these Czechs had claimed this territory through their concentrated efforts; the Czechs founded their own state in the Bohemian Lands and its tradition had survived; and during the thirteenth and fourteenth centuries, and after 1620, Czech culture had yielded ever more ground to German culture. This process of cultural and intellectual repression was considered Germanization. Historians' views on the positive or negative significance of Germanization varied. On the eve of the nineteenth century, however, almost every educated person recognized that Bohemia was home to both Czechs and Bohemian Germans (*Deutschböhmen*).

The Enlightenment historian František Martin Pelcl (1734-1801) launched the debate over the importance of the German ethnic group in Bohemia, in the sense that he was the first historian to draw attention to the important role of German culture, and especially German learning, in Czech history. Pelcl, however, regarded the Germanization of the Bohemian Lands as a historically negative process for both Czech inhabitants and Czech culture. He was one of the first generation of Czech "national revivalists" who attempted, within the framework of the provincial patriotism of the Czech nobility, to revive Czech language and literature and to press for a restoration of Czech social status. While tolerant in his view of the Bohemian Germans, Pelcl was critical of what he considered a state program of Germanization, especially during the reign of Habsburg Emperor Joseph II (1780-1790).

Pelcl believed that the Czechs had historically been the most advanced of the Slavic peoples, because

> they had settled almost in the midst of the German lands and held their own there. They had always defended their country from violent attacks, resisting the unfriendly incursions of nations from near and far, gaining many victories, annexing other countries to their realm, and founding a kingdom.[5]

In his account of Czech history Pelcl also emphasized the importance of the Hussite movement during the first half of the fifteenth century for the revival of ethnic Czech influence in the Bohemian Lands, although he condemned the Hussites for destroying many of the country's religious and cultural monuments.[6]

Enlightenment historiography in the Bohemian Lands did not deploy historical interpretation to construct an image of the national enemy. At most it developed a picture of Bohemian history in which Czechs and Germans were in competition. The Enlightenment historians in Bohemia simply assigned different social weight to the two ethnic groups at different periods. Pelcl's and

Dobrovský's versions of Czech history became the most influential accounts on this topic in Bohemia. The picture they painted was similar: the Czech element dominated up to the thirteenth century, again during the Hussite period, and to a degree in the sixteenth century, as well. The German element dominated the thirteenth and fourteenth centuries and above all after the defeat of the Czech Protestant nobility at the Battle of White Mountain in 1620. After White Mountain, the Germans provided significant support for the Habsburg's re-catholiciz-ing and later Germanizing project. Germanization culminated under Emperor Joseph II. At this time, a small group of Czech intellectuals decided to respond to what they perceived as Germanization by reviving Czech language and litera-ture. Their efforts, however, met with little success.

Neither romanticism nor the self-conscious nationalism of the Napoleonic period affected Pelcl's generation. His sympathies in Bohemia history were undoubtedly on the side of the ethnic Czechs, and in contrast to the romantic historians he attributed a high cultural level to the Czech Slavs in the pre-Chris-tian period. For Pelcl, but especially for Dobrovský, it was not simply the creation of their own state that made the Czechs a civilized people. More important was their conversion to Christianity. Both these processes started at the end of the ninth century. The influence of romanticism would fundamentally change this interpretative paradigm. This was partly because of the influence of Johann Got-tfried Herder's theories, but other factors also affected the development of a new interpretation of Czech history.[7]

One factor was the social and intellectual impact of the Napoleonic Wars on Czech intellectuals. During this period, the philologist and literary historian Josef Jungmann (1773-1847) emerged as a leading personality among the Czech revival-ists. He strongly believed that individual nations were becoming historical agents. In this context German popular resistance to Napoleon struck him as especially significant. He considered contemporary German nationalism to represent a major cultural and political threat to ethnic Czechs, since he was aware that the Czechs at the threshold of the nineteenth century had inferior cultural and social standing vis-à-vis the Germans among whom they lived. In contrast to Pelcl, he believed that the Czech revival movement ought not to seek support among the Czech nobility and gentry, but should rely on the young intelligentsia. Moreover, he con-sidered the Czech peasantry to be the heart of the Czech people as it then was.[8]

This conviction was related to his realization that in an era characterized by the rise of nationalism, Bohemian provincial patriotism had ceased to be an ade-quate ideological basis for revival. In this respect, too, he differed from Pelcl. Jungmann's new definition of the Czech nation was couched in essentially romantic terms. He considered a nation to be defined by the language of a cer-tain cultural and historical community and differing in this respect from any other communities. This community lived on its own territory, with its own par-ticular customs and mentalities, and members united by special sympathies.

In Jungmann's view, a Czech was not simply a person born in the Bohemian Lands, but rather someone whose mother tongue was Czech and who belonged to the community of those who also spoke Czech. Jungmann emphasized that this community was also united by its long-term historical fate. He believed that this fate had been extremely unhappy, since external and internal enemies had sought both to achieve material gains at Czech expense and to deprive the Czechs of their very identity. It was not only the enemies of the Czechs—by which he meant Germans—who were to blame for this historical misfortune, but also the Czechs themselves. The existing situation demanded that untiring efforts at cultural revival be made to change this historical fate:

> From the first moment the Czech set foot in Bohemia, he has been locked in an unending contest with the foreigners. So many enemies have waged war on his tongue that today it is surprising that after so much pressure even the weakest sound of the Slavonic [i.e., the Czech language] inherited from our forefathers can be heard. In this way the nation is dying in itself.[9]

Jungmann had already formulated these views in 1806 and developed them further in his subsequent work. He had little talent, however, for developing Czech history as an instrument of national emancipation, because he was more a philologist than a historian. His vision of Czech history concentrated on Czech literary achievements, leaving aside German language and culture. Thus he has not been associated with the adoption of romanticism as an interpretative model for Czech history as a whole. Much more important in this respect was the discovery of the forged Královédvorský/Königinhof (1817) and Zelenohorský/Grünberg (1818) manuscripts, which met with enthusiastic response from the Czech intelligentsia. Czech romantic historians also found inspiration in the publication of a new synthetic Czech history by Karl Ludwig Woltmann (1770-1817), a Prussian émigré who had found refuge in the Bohemian Lands during the Napoleonic Wars.[10]

The forged manuscripts had far-reaching impact on Czech historical thought, because they appeared to prove that ethnic Czechs had possessed a developed and unique linguistic culture and their own customary laws before their conversion to Christianity. The capacity to resist German enemies on the model of ancient heroes should make the Czechs a historically self-confident nation. The manuscripts thus served not only as a historical source, but also as a symbol of Czech historical identity. Here, history became quite unambiguously a way to reinforce national consciousness in the present. The crucial element in the national instrumentalization of the alleged or real past was the attempt to improve the terms of comparison, especially with Germans.

The manuscript forgery was not a uniquely Czech cultural phenomenon. Essentially, such forgeries were attempts to fill cultural gaps in the reconstruction of the beginnings of national histories, and similar forgeries had been produced in the context of romantic nationalism elsewhere in Europe. In the Czech environment, however, it was important that these manuscripts emotively completed the image of the German as the ancient enemy of the Czech. A feeling of inferiority and the specific geopolitical position of Czech science and culture, however, forced Czech intellectuals to work with a peculiar model of cultural emulation of the enemy, at least up to the mid-nineteenth century. They sought either to develop a particular literary genre or scientific field that would be as good as the German equivalent or to construct a genre or field in opposition to that which the Germans possessed.[11]

Romanticism therefore made a fundamental contribution to the situation in which the historical picture of the German as enemy became an important element of Czech nationalism. Henceforth, the proclaimed Czech relationship to German culture would be negative. This stereotype was often, of course, displaced by an implicit relationship of analogy, involving the attitude that "We Czechs are just as good as Germans," which in cultural practice frequently meant copying German science and culture. These attitudes had a logic, conditioned by the cultural and social position of a national group in an inferior position.[12]

Woltmann's romanticism was rather different. A foreigner in Bohemia, he formulated the relationship between ethnic Czechs and Germans in Bohemian history in an original and, in literary terms, absorbing way. He sought the long-term meaning of Bohemian history, and found it in what he considered the fruitful way that Czechs and Germans had influenced each other's national characters. In doing so, neither had lost anything essential to their individualism. Woltmann asserted that the cultural power of the Czechs consisted of creative fantasy, while that of the Germans was a certain untrammeled energy. Woltmann's description welcomed historical myths and legends as historical sources.

Thus, at the end of the Napoleonic Wars, we encounter a synthesis of Bohemian history that has already freed itself from the limitations of Enlightenment thought. Moreover, this synthesis presented a historical conception in which Czechs held a position of cultural level equal to the Germans in the terms of the romanticism of the time.[13]

Czech historiography began to change fundamentally from the early 1830s, above all with the appearance of the founding figure of Czech modern historiography and politics, František Palacký (1798-1876). Palacký became the historian of the Bohemian Estates. In this position he was able to publish a synthesis of Bohemian history, which first appeared in German as *Geschichte von Böhmen* (1836-1867). The later Czech-language version was titled *Dějiny národu českého v Čechách a v Moravě* (The history of the Czech people in Bohemia and Moravia) (1848-1876). Although the original Czech-language text was based on the German, this situation was later reversed. Nevertheless, there were important differences of national emphasis between the two versions. Both, however, ended in 1526, when the Habsburgs ascended to the throne of Bohemia.[14]

In the first German-language version of Palacký's history, the author showed considerable reserve on the question of nationality, likely in deference to his noble employers, who were Bohemian provincial patriots. This type of patriotism was basically neutral from the ethnic point of view, but gave precedence to German language and culture over Czech for reasons of prestige and practicality. The

Czech language, after all, was not attractive, nor did it offer long-term prospective benefits for most aristocrats in the Bohemian Lands. Thus, relatively few of them became convinced supporters of Czech revival. At this time, the nobility merely required history to justify its claims to be the political leaders of the province, because state absolutism had reduced the authority of the old political estates to no more than a few historical symbols. The most important of these was the politically impotent Bohemian Diet.

In his history Palacký was beginning to develop his conception of the nation. Initially he considered Bohemian history the coalescence, and finally the partial merger, of the Czech and German national characters. In practice, however, his *Geschichte von Böhmen* already presented a modern concept of Bohemian history. It was an original combination of Enlightenment criticism, romanticism, and Slavic liberalism. The latter involved Palacký's notion that since their arrival in the Bohemian Lands the Slavs had been capable of creating institutions that functioned on the same basic principles as the institutions of modern civic society.

What he had in mind was the supposed equality of all social groups before the law, allegedly guaranteed by original Slavic customary law, and the political power of independent courts with juries. He did not have sufficient historical proof for this theory and was forced to rely on the forged Zelenohorský manuscript and on a historical comparison with original legal systems, especially among the southern Slavs. In other cases his approach to his sources was one of Enlightenment skepticism, especially as regards the Czech tradition of chroniclers, starting with the priest Cosmas (1045?-1125).

Palacký asserted that the Czechs settled in the Bohemian basin in the mid-fifth century. They were a peace-loving people who defended themselves from outside aggression but did not threaten their neighbors. This fundamental conceptual shift in the interpretation of Czech national history involved a new stress on the theory that the Czechs had settled an empty land. For Palacký the assumption was important because it established the Czechs as the first people to have built a civilization and state in the territory. This was not a new claim; it can be found in the work of Stránský and others. What was crucial in Palacký's version, however, was the implication that in occupying an empty land the Czechs had neither enslaved nor subordinated other peoples. This meant that one of the attributes of the Czech national character, as with most Slavs, was the absence of lust for conquest.[15]

Unlike other Czech romantic historians such as Václav Hanka, Pavel Josef Šafařík, and Jan Erazim Vocel, Palacký presented his historical conception in the 1830s and 1840s with masterly skill. Indeed, German readers in the Habsburg Monarchy and elsewhere generally favorably received his view of Bohemian history. Almost right up to the Revolution of 1848, Palacký's colleagues in Germany regarded him as a Bohemian patriot who wrote his main work in German, one whose pro-Slav sympathies were only occasionally disturbing. Palacký's Czech-language journal articles, which were little known in Germany, were characterized by a much stronger Czech national interpretation of Bohemian history than was to be found in his *Geschichte von Böhmen*.[16]

According to Palacký, the Germans entered Bohemian history with what is known to modern historians as the German colonization in the thirteenth century. At the invitation of the Přemyslid rulers, they settled the Bohemian borderlands as farmers and founded economically efficient towns. With this development the original Slavic-democratic order of society in the Bohemian Lands began to disintegrate. By the beginning of the fourteenth century it had disappeared. In this way the Germans imported into Bohemia feudalism with its characteristic division of society into estates. Palacký, a Protestant, also argued that the Roman Catholic Church had been a source of pressure in this direction even before the Germans' arrival.

Palacký recognized that the historical development of feudalism had its logic in the Bohemian Lands, reflecting the efforts of the Czech monarchs to increase their income and find political support against the nobility. His sympathies, however, lay with the so-called Slav democracy. He considered German influence to have had bad effects in Bohemia, leading to legal inequality, the rise of patrimonial courts, and the Germanization of the towns and borderlands, and, to a certain extent, of the nobility itself. It also involved the emergence of tributary relations, which the feudal lords developed into serfdom. Palacký found the positive side of German colonization in the establishment of the estate of the towns in Bohemia, which perfected handicrafts, introduced lucrative silver mining, and developed trade. He also conceded that under certain conditions the German emphyteutic law brought peasants greater security than the original Czech customary law.

In *Geschichte von Böhmen*, Palacký had not yet fully developed his conception of Bohemian history as the "continuous encounter and struggle between Slavic and German culture ... as the supreme principle in this history prevailing from the beginning to this day."[17] On the basis of this theory he promised a more critical assessment of German influence on Bohemian history, but he did not develop the new conception until 1844-45. In fact, it was not presented to the reading public until the early days of the Revolution of 1848, when the first volume of *Dějiny národu českého v Čechách a v Moravě* was published with a new preface.

During the 1840s, it was already clear that the concentrated scholarly and publicizing efforts of the Czech revivalists had had a significant social influence on the Czech people. The Jungmann circle had won the support of residents of thousands in the larger and smaller towns in Bohemia. A group of town and rural Catholic clergy augmented the townspeople. Palacký now became the leading authority of the rising Czech national movement, coming to overshadow even Jungmann in importance. Czech national self-confidence was clearly increasing and was manifest in the entire public sphere.[18]

By this time national discussions had already begun throughout Central Europe on the question of whether the entire Habsburg Monarchy should be reorganized on the basis of liberal or democratic principles as part of a common German state in the future. Another proposal was its division into the two spheres of influence—liberal Germans (if necessary, Germany) and liberal Hungarians. Politically the most conservative idea in terms of state integrity was that of a Habsburg Monarchy reformed on the principle of national equality. In such a scheme Slavs would play the major role, since in Austria they constituted the most numerous ethnic grouping. This idea rapidly became known as "Austro-Slavism." Explicitly or implicitly, these conceptions involved images of other nations and nationalities as the Enemy. Nations and national groups that opposed the implementation of "our ideas" were enemies, or at least rivals. The Czech national movement was strongly oriented toward Austro-Slavism. It attempted to win the sympathy of the Habsburg dynasty and regarded the liberal Germans and the liberal Hungarian nationalists as its main enemies.[19]

National public polemics, growing Czech national self-confidence, and a certain sluggishness on the part of the authoritarian regime of Klemens von Metternich all had considerable effect on shifts in the opinions of Czech historians. Around 1845, Czech historiography began to focus more openly on the assessment of the role of Germans in Bohemia history. Palacký's younger colleague, Václav Vladivoj Tomek (1818-1905), explained the growth of German influence in medieval Bohemia in terms of Czech eagerness to take up fashionable Western models. He also stressed the importance of the Hussite movement for the Czechification of the towns, for which the capital city Prague served as example. Palacký concluded that from the seventh to the eleventh centuries Germans only resided in Bohemia as guests. The increase in their numbers and importance in the thirteenth century, and especially after the Thirty Years' War, was the result of shortcomings in the Czech national character. Czechs allegedly sought fashion and luxury, while in this respect the Germans were far more rational. Thus in the long term German frugality won out over Czech extravagance, and over the centuries the ethnic frontier advanced from the borderlands into the Czech interior. Only the Hussite movement represented a break in this trend.

The Czech national movement, then, interpreted history as a source of instruction on the strengths and weaknesses of the Czech national character. It was not simply an issue of scholarly acquisition of knowledge or information about ancestors, but an inspiration and a warning to their heirs. This was the model of historical science and its function that Palacký had in mind as he continued to develop his conception of Czech national history. He was morally and intellectually encouraged to find that some of his contemporaries in other countries took the same view of history. It is therefore not surprising that Palacký interpreted their texts in the light of his own concerns. For example, he favored their descriptions of German tribes in the early Middle Ages as coarse, conquest-loving ruffians.

Palacký now conceived Czech history as the story of the historical and cultural development of Czech Slavs not only in Bohemia, but also in Moravia. His definition of national past, meanwhile, was conditioned by assumptions that were common in contemporary European historiography. Like other national histories written in the nineteenth century, an explicit moral ethos characterized his work. In Western Europe this moral ethos was frequently directed against the forces of the *ancien régime*. Palacký, in contrast, expressed the moral resolve of a suppressed historical nation, which was renewing its claim to its rights, and accompanied this resolve with the conviction that the Czech people had contributed much to the development of European civilization. At the beginning of the Revolution of 1848, it seemed to him that nothing stood in the way of forming the Czechs into a free people. But he assumed they still needed moral support in the form of lessons learned from the mistakes of the past. They also needed conditions of fair play in competition with the more successful European nations, especially the Germans.

Both Palacký's construction of historical development in Bohemia and Moravia and his engagement in politics reflected these ideas. He came to consider Europea history as the history of contrasting poles of civilization embodied in individual historical nations. Bohemian and Moravian history became the stage for the confrontation between two civilizational principles. On the one side stood the peace-loving Slavs, and on the other Rome with its lust for conquest (whether imperial or papal), later replaced by equally aggressive *Germanii*. Thereafter, the character attributes of Slavs and Germans continually coexisted in peace or fought with one another. Both peaceful coexistence and struggle led to frequent positive mutual influence on each other's character.[20]

This mutual influence did not lead, however, in Palacký's view, to cultural coalescence as he had suggested earlier in his *Geschichte von Böhmen*. Now, on the contrary, he believed that the opposition between Czech and German character had been maintained throughout Bohemian history. The Germans had shown, on the one hand, a talent for enterprise, skill in crafts, and the successful organization of royal power. On the other, however, they had demonstrated an unattractive inclination toward aggression and religious intolerance. The Germans had also introduced the social inequality that Palacký identified with feudalism. The Czechs, in contrast, had distinguished themselves as the bearers of the principle of civil equality and the love of peace, but like all Slavs they had a tendency to anarchy, disrespect for authority, and unwillingness to subordinate themselves to common goals.

Palacký considered the principles of freedom and authority to be of equal importance, and principles that should be balanced in history, both philosophically and from the point of view of the development of civilization. His sympathies lay more with the Czechs than the Germans, who in his *Dějiny národu českého v Čechách a v Moravě* appear in times of peace as perpetual rivals and in times of war as direct enemies. It is clear that in his history of the Bohemian Lands Palacký idealized the role of the Czechs in line with his romantic assumptions. This idealization was most evident in the early 1860s when he was concerned with assessment of the importance of the Hussite movement for both Bohemian and European history.

In his description of Bohemia history Palacký was not, however, a nationalist utilitarian. He considered many factors besides hostility between Czechs and Germans. In the Hussite movement, for example, he saw far more than simply a

Czech national revolution that for a certain period made Czechs the ruling ethnic group in Bohemia. Indeed, he regarded the Hussite episode principally as the first serious attempt in history to install the modern age by undermining the two main pillars of the Middle Ages: unlimited papal authority in the religious sphere and the decisive role of the Holy Roman Emperor in the secular sphere. In his view the Czechs of the Hussite period sacrificed themselves as a nation to the higher goals of civilization. The defeat of the Hussites, therefore, meant the renewed strengthening of feudalism in Bohemian society. The Slavic-liberal principle in Bohemian history was progressively suppressed until, after 1620, it was reduced to almost two centuries of bondage.

Hussitism represented for Palacký the peak of Czech history:

> It was in a certain sense the zenith of the Czech role in history, when they [the Hussites], acting in the name of the pure gospel and the nation, introduced the first principle of reform into European life against the two main institutions of medieval society—hierarchy and the feudal order. But contending not only with the whole united West, but also with feudal elements at home, and unsupported by their kinsmen in the East, they succumbed at last, after a long and remarkable struggle, at the Battle of Lipany [1434].

Hussitism was given another chance to become a real social force in the reign of Jiří of Poděbrady (1458-1471), and Palacký believed that if the movement had relied on monarchic authority it could have created a new society. In his view, a great historical opportunity for the Czech people to provide Europe with a new model of civilization died with Jiří of Poděbrady.[21]

Palacký became a leading Czech politician in the Revolution of 1848. His political program was for the federalization of the Habsburg Monarchy on Austro-Slavic principles. The various nations were to be regarded as collective persons and to enjoy the same rights that Western European liberalism accorded to individual citizens. Palacký's program, which came to represent the generally accepted goal of Czech politics up to 1914 or 1918, was never implemented, but the combination of the roles of leading Czech historian and leading Czech politician brought Palacký great authority in Czech society, as well as the title of Father of the Nation. However, enthusiasm for his historical conception and political program was much greater in Bohemia than in Moravia, where Moravian provincial patriotism continued to enjoy considerable social influence at least until the 1860s.[22]

The Revolution of 1848 strengthened Czech and German nationalism in the Bohemian Lands to an unprecedented degree. The Czech national movement, in fact, entered the revolution with a relatively strong historical consciousness, a constitutive part of which was, as we have seen, the image of the Germans as rivals or enemies. The ethnic Germans in the Bohemian Lands had not developed such a strong historical consciousness before 1848. The main reason for this difference was that its intellectual leaders did not consider themselves to belong to an inferior nation that was threatened in some way by the Czech population.

Of course, even the first months of the Revolution of 1848 aroused strongly nationalist feelings among Germans in the Bohemian Lands, and especially in

Bohemia. Many of them became supporters of the Pan-German movement, which fixed its hopes on the German National Assembly in Frankfurt am Main. A number of Czechs, especially from Bohemia, considered the Pan-German ambitions of the Frankfurt Parliament a dangerous threat to Czech national identity, and looked to Palacký's Austro-Slavism for protection. The basic difference was that while nationalist Czechs in Bohemia had a strong feeling that they were pressured from outside, nationalist Germans had an equally strong feeling that they were threatened from within. At the beginning of the Revolution of 1848 the Pan-German movement was more self-confident than the Austro-Slav movement. The latter lacked political confidence and the courage to take fundamental revolutionary steps.[23]

The policies of the two sides for the solution of ethnic problems were mutually incompatible and therefore conducive to conflict. This inflammatory aspect was to survive as a strong element of thought on both sides, even when it became clear that neither the Pan-German nor the Austro-Slav program had great hope of success. Both sides employed historical arguments as ammunition. The Czechs assailed the Germans with the assertion that Germans were no more than emigrants to Bohemia who had always damaged the country. The Germans attempted to wound the Czech side with the argument that the Bohemian Lands owed all civilization and progress solely to German culture and that the territory had enjoyed a historic position in Europe only as part of the Holy Roman Empire. When these arguments became part of popular histories, polemics in the press, caricatures, and street songs, they took on a particularly uncompromising and offensive character.[24]

Most importantly, nationalists on both sides perceived the course of the Revolution of 1848 as confirmation of its image of the Other as historic enemy. Until the end of the 1860s, however, the German side could not underpin its nationalism with as refined a concept of national history as that which Palacký had given the Czech side. The social importance of the popularization of the historical picture of the enemy undoubtedly grew in the 1860s, once again mainly in Bohemia. At this point the Czech national movement achieved new cultural successes. Municipal control of some important towns, most importantly Prague, was transferred into the hands of the Czech politicians. A range of Czech national social organizations was founded. The most important was the gymnastics association Sokol (Falcon), which established branches throughout the Bohemian Lands. Even more important was the emergence of a network of Czech middle schools. In the political arena, however, the Czech national movement could boast few successes.[25]

This did not prevent the Czech national movement from developing into a broad Czech national society drawing its main support from the urban and rural middle classes. Various popular versions of Czech history, often simplified formulations of Palacký's account, were aimed at this audience. The most successful of these was the *Českomoravská kronika* (Czecho-Moravian Chronicle) published by the journalist Karel Vladislav Zap between 1862 and 1875. Like

Palacký, he stressed the pragmatic mission of national history both as a source of pride and as a warning to contemporaries.

Zap's description of Czech history was far more instrumental than Palacký's, and his Czech nationalism always took first place in his account of the past. This was evident in the much less ambiguous line that he took reassessing the relations between Czechs and Germans in Czech history. Zap made smaller intellectual demands on his reader, of course, since he was writing a popular account while Palacký produced scholarly books on Czech history. The difference can be seen in Zap's characteristic formulations such as the statement that the historic task of the Czech nation was to defend the Bohemian Lands "from the furious assaults of greedy and inhuman enemies." Czechs were, moreover, a bastion of Slavdom "which the Germans had sought to humble for a thousand years, but which with God's help would long survive, so long as the Slav spirit, dimmed but not destroyed by its thousand-year fight, retained its self-awareness."[26]

The versions of Czech national history published during the 1860s in Czech national society accepted the authenticity of the forged Královédvorský and Zelenohorský manuscripts. It appears to have been unimportant whether the Czech historians, or popularizers, concerned were generally politically conservative (Václav Vladivoj Tomek), liberal (Palacký and later Josef Kalousek) or democratic (Karel Sabina). From the conceptual point of view, the manuscripts were much more important for Czech national history than Palacký's assessment of Hussitism as the peak of Czech history. The latter idea was not unreservedly accepted; among those who rejected it were Tomek and a number of Catholic historians. What united all of them was the romantic vision of the role of Slavs in Czech history, and also the Czech political program based on Palacký's general ideological principles, albeit with successive different tactical emphases.[27]

The Germans thus appeared as the true enemies both in history and in the contemporary failures of Czech politics. For many years Czech publicists were able to adopt a relatively comfortable stereotype. In the gallery of antagonists they placed not only Germans, but also frequently Hungarians and German-Jewish writers and businessmen. In such cases history was instrumentalized without serious inhibition. The following is a typical formulation:

> Your style of rule has lasted twenty years [i.e. modern Viennese centralism], but our right has lasted a thousand years; it will survive and emerge the victor … because we [i.e., Czechs], the roots of Austria, are fixed deeper in the soil than you [i.e., Germans], the branches and leaves. Three centuries ago the agreement of our nation created this empire, and at the crucial time the continuance of this empire … will depend on our agreement.[28]

On the other side, German national society in the Bohemian Lands was also reaching for historical arguments to support its political ideas. The year 1862 saw the establishment of the *Verein für Geschichte der Deutschen in Böhmen* in Prague. Bohemian Germans had ceased to regard Palacký's *Geschichte von Böhmen* as a history also written for them, especially since after the Revolution of 1848 this work had become simply a German translation of the *Dějiny národu českého*. In

1869 the new association published its own *Geschichte Böhmen* for Bohemian Germans. The book was soon sold out and a second edition followed. Its author was the historian Ludwig Schlesinger (1838-1899), who in time became the leader of the German liberal party in the Bohemian Lands. Schlesinger's work was popular, but in no way amateur. From a technical point of view it was more professional than an earlier polemical attempt at a history of the Germans in the Bohemian Lands published in 1851.

In contrast to Palacký, Schlesinger replaced the Romantic idealization of history with an energetic German liberalism. He wrote at a time when romanticism was already an outdated source of conceptual inspiration for constructions of national history in Europe. From his point of view, a whole range of Palacký's ideas on Czech history was no longer adequate. Moreover, it was clear that the nationally oriented German liberals in Bohemia were now seeking legitimization in history in the same way that Palacký had sought justification for his romantic Slav liberalism. While Palacký had looked for support for his historical picture of Czechs and Germans in intellectual history and moralizing, Schlesinger took up the shield of cultural and social history. Palacký emphasized his sympathy for the Czechs as a Slavic people. Schlesinger, in contrast, sympathized with the Germans of the Bohemian Lands, whom he regarded as an integral spiritual and geographical part of the whole German people, both within and outside the Habsburg Monarchy.[29]

In their treatment of historical sources both historians observed high professional standards of historical scholarship for the time. The difference of more than a generation that separated Schlesinger from the now seventy-year-old Palacký gave Schlesinger and his contemporaries from the *Verein für Geschichte der Deutschen in Böhmen* an advantage in this respect. There is no doubt that for Schlesinger the Czechs in Bohemian history were either cultural followers, national competitors, or even direct political enemies of Germans in Bohemia. Unlike Palacký, however, he did not base his case on differences of national character but on differences in degree of civilization. According to Schlesinger and his associates, application of this criterion almost always testified to the superiority of Germans. In Schlesinger's book we encounter, in comprehensive form, the whole range of arguments that had gradually entered the historical consciousness of Germans in the Bohemian Lands over decades. Behind this achievement lay the solid organizational structure of the German historical association, which also published the influential historic-ethnographic journal, *Mitteilungen des Vereins für Geschichte der Deutschen in Böhmen*, and special book editions of historical sources.

Schlesinger emphasized the incorporation of the Bohemian Lands into the Holy Roman Empire. German culture expressed its superiority first of all, in his view, in the Christianizing of the Bohemian Lands, and only later in the colonization of the Czech borderlands. Still more important was the creation of an independent town estate, which had been lacking until the thirteenth century. Schlesinger believed that German achievement in science and arts was of fundamental importance, as was the leading German role in the industrialization of the Bohemian Lands. He conceded, however, that the modern development of national consciousness in the nineteenth century occurred earlier among the Czechs than among the Bohemian Germans. He did not regard the Hussite movement as the zenith of Czech history, but rather as no more than the destructive reaction of the feudal Czech nobility against the freethinking German townsfolk.

Schlesinger thus interpreted negatively some of the points Palacký had evaluated positively. Although both were concerned with processes and events that had unfolded in the Bohemian Lands, the accounts of national history produced by Palacký and Schlesinger established sophisticated versions of historical memory that were scarcely compatible. In the first case it was a question of the modern historical memory of Czechs in the Bohemian Lands and in the second case, the historical memory of Germans in the same place. In line with earlier Czech historiography, Palacký built on the tradition of the Czech state founded by Czech Slavs. Schlesinger, on the contrary, argued that after the end of the Holy Roman Empire in 1806, Bohemia and the other Bohemian Lands had become provinces of the Austrian Empire. The following quotation is a typical formulation of his view on the role of the Germans of the Bohemian Lands:

> Although the Bohemian Germans have thought of ways to defend against all of the dangers that threaten their nationality, in so doing they do not take nationality as their only standpoint. Truly inspired by the constitutional spirit they hold high, above all, the banner of freedom.... This is, of course, not the case with the Czechs. They fight only for their national idea and even sacrifice the people's freedom to that end. The course of Bohemia history is a vivid reminder of the difference. The Germans in Bohemia founded the Third Estate [i.e., the townspeople] and in the Middle Ages struggled for and won that estate a political position alongside the feudal nobility.[30]

In this scheme, the bearer of progress in Bohemia history was quite clearly the German townspeople forced to fight for such progress against the feudal Czech nobility. In this struggle the townspeople politically allied with wise rulers, since the reactionary feudal nobility infringed upon both their autonomy and the power of the Bohemian kings. Here it seems as if Schlesinger, like Palacký, drew on the French historian François Guizot, although from a different angle. He interpreted the Czech nobility as having sought political support for their intrigues by awakening the national idea in the Czech people, and exploiting it in the Hussite movement, above all. This view of Hussitism, however, did not undermine Schlesinger's insistence that Czech nationalism had never been progressive, since from his perspective Czech nationalism, in contrast to German nationalism, was always essentially reactionary:

> The Bohemian Germans, however, are resolved to remain faithful to the program that they have maintained for centuries, which is the advancement of the freedom of the townspeople, whatever changes the current development of social conditions may bring![31]

At the end of the 1860s and beginning of the 1870s a polemic developed between Palacký and Schlesinger and his associates over who was correct or more correct in his interpretation of Bohemian history. The strongest argument on the German side was the claim that Palacký's theory of the cultural superiority of the Czech Slavs before the arrival of the Germans was untenable, since it could not be properly supported by known historical sources. No less important was the argument of Schlesinger's contemporary Julius Lippert (1839-1909) that Palacký had not provided a persuasive explanation of why, during the Hussite period, property and national relations had undergone basic change in Bohemia to the benefit of the Czechs but the estate structure of society had remained essentially intact.[32]

Palacký, old and irritable, offered no substantial response to these or other arguments. He regarded the polemics as a typical expression of unjust German aggression toward Czechs and the intensification of malignant German hostility. In his arguments history now tended to coalesce with politics, and historical facts merged ever more overtly with desired ideological effects. Meanwhile, Czech politics under his patronage and led by his son-in-law František Ladislav Rieger (1818-1903) staggered from defeat to defeat. Only in the late 1880s and early 1890s could it record minor successes, but these scarcely satisfied Czech national society, which expected much more in the spirit of Palacký's national program.

In his last years, Palacký was unable to find any explanation for this situation other than blaming the failures of the Czech national movement on the traditional enemies of the Czech people. He regularly added new touches to the negative historical picture of these enemies. The arguments of Schlesinger and his associates made no headway in Czech society, which was as unprepared as German society was for dialogue on the theme of national tolerance in the Bohemian Lands. In any case, such dialogue was hampered by mutually incompatible interpretations of history as well as by different political and cultural experiences and identifications. Despite its declared self-confidence, Czech national society was still unable to rid itself of the feeling of inferiority, which was fed by new feelings of national and political injury. In German national society the fear that it was under threat from the large Czech majority in Bohemia gradually took firm root, although the ethnic ratio did not change dramatically up to the end of the nineteenth century.[33]

In nineteenth-century Czech society, the modern picture of national history and the modern political program was influenced much more deeply by a single personality—František Palacký—than was the case in German society in Bohemia. Neither Ludwig Schlesinger nor his successors were such commanding figures. In both cases—Czech and German—however, it seems that differing pictures of the past in Bohemia had fundamental effects on the modern mentality of both Czechs and Germans. The view of the Other as rival or enemy survived into the twentieth century. Very often, and without regard to progress in scholarship, this portrait of the Other has continued to be perceived via value constructs that emerged in the nineteenth century.

In Czech national society the negative image of the Germans was to have considerable long-term influence. It was frequently a simplified version of Palacký's theory of an aggressive nation basically hostile to Czech interests. This image survived in Czech mentality even after Czech scholarship had concluded in 1886 that the Královédvorský and Zelenohorský manuscripts were forgeries. Because of this discovery, Czech historiography abandoned Palacký's idea of the high level of civilization of the so-called original Slav democracy. Between the late nineteenth and early twentieth centuries, moreover, Jaroslav Goll's positivist school of historical scholarship rejected the theory that Hussitism represented the peak of Czech history, but the philosopher and future Czechoslovak president Tomáš Garrigue Masaryk (1850-1937) had nonetheless adopted the idea, in modified form, in the late 1880s.[34]

In Masaryk's case the idea was not linked to a historical image of the German as the enemy of the Czech, since Masaryk regarded Germans as an example of a positive cultural challenge. In his view, at the end of the nineteenth century the Czech national revival had achieved only relative successes, that is, to the point from which they had started. Other nations had also advanced, and it was necessary to compare Czech society with the most developed, that is, the German. Masaryk believed that Czech revivalist efforts should now be expanded and, above all, find moral inspiration in the example of the Bohemian Brethren, a movement that had developed out of Hussitism. He considered the Bohemian Brethren the bearers of the original Czech spirit, which should guide Czechs in their efforts to draw level with the Germans in all aspects of life:

> If the Czech word was sufficient for our fathers, then we must work to ensure that the word be carried out by a Czech spirit. It is not a paradox, but a conclusion drawn from thorough comparison of our current literature with the older, if I say that from 1848 and the era of constitutionalism [1861] Germanization has threatened us more internally, I would say, than in earlier times ... I am not at all afraid of this situation, but naturally regard it as my duty to point it out. We have no alternative to this internal, interior politics that Palacký again and again recommended to us.

Masaryk added, in a contemporary version of events, that Palacký expected salvation only from educational work, as if there had never been times in his life when he had expected salvation from politics (1848-1849, 1861-1871).[35]

Not even Masaryk's interpretation of Palacký, however, could prevent the historian's name from being associated in modern Czech historical consciousness with an anti-German attitude. In this context the social influence of the Goll historical school, significant as it was in Czech universities during the interwar period, was relatively limited. It was evident that Palacký's conception of Germans continued to be useful in both politics and ideology. This was the case on both the Czech and German sides, but from opposite points of view and with differing intensity. The crucial reality was a social situation in which the Czechs, on the one side, and the Germans, on the other, identified with two historically absolutely different wholes. In Czech national society it was that Palacký had constructed modern Czech identity in opposition to German identity, evidently because this was easily acceptable even to the non-élite, and remained so even at a period when the intellectual élite was more or less distancing itself from Palacký.

Palacký and his vision of Czech history constituted a challenge for German national society that had to be rejected more or less uncompromisingly. Schlesinger was followed by a number of German historians in the Bohemian Lands who took up the gauntlet. In the 1890s the most significant was Julius Lippert, whose views met with some approval from Goll's most important pupils Josef Pekař and Josef Šusta, who believed that Lippert's principal aim was a critical interpretation of Czech history. They were much less friendly to Adolf Bachmann (1849-1914), who at the turn of the century devoted great effort to refuting Palacký's account of Czech history. In doing so, however, Bachmann failed to take enough account of the fact the Palacký had ceased to be the main historiographical compass of the Goll school. Subsequently Bachmann inflamed the Czech public with his militant nationalism as one of the leading representatives of the German Progressive Party (*Fortschrittspartei*) in Bohemia.[36]

The interpretations of the German-Moravian historian Berthold Bretholz (1862-1936) produced an even greater wave of opposition on the Czech side. In 1912 he rejected Palacký's view that the German influence in the Bohemian Lands only started with the German colonization in the thirteenth century:

> It is particularly in the historical development of the Germans in the Bohemian Lands, that I [Bretholz] consider derives from different roots than Palacký and all other scholars. Believing as I do, I am bound to depart from the almost universally held view of the later German migration and colonization to these lands and all that is associated with it, since it does not have the slightest support in the data of any of our historical sources.[37]

Bretholz sought to demonstrate that Germans were the descendants not of medieval colonists, but of original Germanic tribes (*Marcomani*) who had survived in the Bohemian Lands even after the arrival of the Slavs. He thus raised once again the old question of the original inhabitants of the Bohemian Lands. He presented this opinion first in *Geschichte Böhmens und Mährens bis zum Aussterben der Přemysliden (1306)*, which he wrote at the suggestion of the *Verein für Geschichte der Deutschen in Böhmen* on the occasion of the fiftieth anniversary of the association. His ideas found little support even among German historians in Bohemia. Polemics with Bretholz, especially from Czech historians, continued after 1918. It does not appear, however, that they produced any basic change of direction in either Czech or German historical consciousness.[38]

The development of historiography in the Bohemian Lands in the nineteenth century confirmed that it was precisely this discipline that had a major impact on modern processes of nation creation, on the emergence of the modern "imagined community."[39] Historiography was, thus, a powerful tool in the transformation of the traditional into the modern mentality. Images of the Other undoubtedly played a fundamental role in the process; in this case, images of the

German/Germans in Czech historiography and images of the Czech/Czechs in German historiography. These images, of course, had a certain historical tradition discernible in medieval chronicles. Enlightenment historiography in the Bohemian Lands, however, did not sharpen their potential antagonisms, since its image of the Other was not an image of the Enemy, but rather of cultural otherness. It was with the rise of nationalism in the nineteenth century that the fundamental shifts in this direction occurred. In particular, there was a change in the values based on how such an image was constructed. The starting point now became an increasingly extreme nationalism first associated with romanticism and later with political liberalism.

In the case of historians, nationalism became ever more inseparable from their creations of images of the past. Nationalism increasingly became a defining factor in their approaches to historical sources and methods. In the historically unified and traditionally multiethnic territory of the Bohemian Lands, the creation of an image of the Other on these lines led to the confirmation of the group identity of one's "own" ethnic whole, that is, the group with which the historian personally identified. The ethnic group was thus becoming a modern nation in the sense of having its "own" version of "national" history, which had been researched and written to a respectable "academic" standard. This frequently involved the interpretation of the Other as a historically documented "national" rival or even enemy. In retrospect, one can therefore consider the Bohemian Lands in the nineteenth century a historical laboratory in which the past was gradually divided between two ethnic groups, the Czechs and the Germans, primarily through the production of mutually hostile images of the Other. The question remains how much we can attribute this development of a new type of modern social antagonism simply to the psychological need for national self-identification generated by overall social modernization, since at least two other factors should be considered. One is the role played by the leadership ambitions of historians in both national camps, some of whom were also major Czech (Palacký) and German (Schlesinger) politicians. The second is the underestimation of these historians and their successors of the social impact of mutually contradictory concepts that they used to interpret the past.

The historiographical images of the Other as Enemy are not just constructs produced by ambitious historians (in our case the Czech and German historians of the nineteenth century), but are the outcome of complex interaction between the capacity of historians to understand and present the past on the basis of professional methods, and what is known as "living historical memory." This type of memory is based on the experience of the past, personal or collective, that is stored in the continuously renewed generational memory. The investment of memory is a process governed more by emotion than by reason. It is not based on the sophisticated creation of a picture of the past that is typical for the history that has claimed in various social and cultural contexts to be scientific, but is founded on a sense of faith in authentic experience. Such interactive historical memory has a tendency to survive in society even when historiography itself has already gone beyond it. The fact that historiography today is trying retrospectively to analyze the constitutive elements of earlier constructed national historical memory may help to relativize it and open up new ways of understanding the past.

Notes

1. Moravia was approximately 70 percent Czech, 28 percent German, and 2 percent Jewish in a total population of 1.78 million. In Silesia the figures were approximately 48 percent German, 31 percent Polish, 20 percent Czech and 0.6 percent Jewish out of a population of 466,000. On increasing social interest in ethnic ratios in the Bohemian Lands, see, for example, Jiří Štaif, "Multietnicita a statistika v českých zemích, 1780-1880," in *Sborník k problematice multietnicity*, ed. Zdeněk Kárník (Prague: Desktop Publishing, 1997), 13-42.
2. Marie Bláhová, *Staročeská kronika tak řečeného Dalimila III* (Prague: Academia, 1995), 240-53.
3. See Eduard Maur, "Pojetí národa ve starší české historiografii jako východisko koncepce českého národa v první polovině 19. Století," in *Národní obrození a rok 1848 v evropském kontextu*, ed. Milan Skřivánek (Litomyšl: Město Litomyšl, 1998), 7-19.
4. See Josef Petráň et al., *Počátky českého národního obrození, 1770-1791*, (Prague: Academia, 1990) 233-318, and Milan Kudělka, *O pojetí slavistiky. Vývoj představ o jejím předmětu a podstatě* (Prague: Academia, 1984).
5. Jiří Štaif, *Historici, dějiny a společnost. Historiografie v českých zemích od Palackého u jeho předchůdců po Gollovu školu I*, vol. 1 (Prague: Desktop Publishing FF UK, 1997), 18.
6. See Josef Johanides, *František Martin Pelcl* (Prague: Melantrich, 1981); Jiří Štaif, *Historici, dějiny a společnost I*, 14-19.
7. See Štaif, *Historici, dějiny a společnost I*, 19-27.
8. See Josef Kočí, "Josef Jungmann a české národní obrození," *Slovanský přehled* 59 (1973): 112-30.
9. See Josef Jungmann, *Boj o obrození národa*, ed. Felix Vodička (Prague: F. Kosek, 1948), 34-44, and elsewhere.
10. Karl Ludwig Wolfmann's magnum opus was his *In Begriff der Geschichte Böhmens*, vols. 1-2 (Prague, 1875).
11. See Karel Krejčí, *Jazyk ve vývoji společnosti* (Prague: Jaroslav Podroužek, 1947), 47ff.
12. See Vladimír Macura, *Znamení rodu. České národní obrození jako kulturní typ* (Prague: Československý spisovatel, 1983), 45ff.
13. See Štaif, *Historici, dějiny a společnost I*, 27-30.
14. The scholarly literature on František Palacký is legion. See, for example, Josef Fischer, *Myšlenka a dílo Fr. Palackého I-II* (Prague: Čin, 1926-1927); Václav Chaloupecký, *Fr. Palacký* (Prague: Spolek výtvarných umělců "Mánes," 1912); Milena Jetmarová, *František Palacký* (Prague: Svobodné slovo, 1961); Jiří Kořalka, *František Palacký* (Prague: Argo, 1998); G.J. Morava, *Franz Palacký. Eine frühe Vision von Mitteleuropa* (Vienna: Österreichischer Bundesverlag, 1990); Josef Pekař, *Fr. Palacký* (Prague: Jan Otto, 1912); Georg Plaschka, *Von Palacký bis Pekař. Geschichtwissenschaft und Nationalbewusstsein bei den Tschechen* (Graz: Böhlau, 1955); Štaif, *Historici, dějiny a společnost I-II*; J.F. Zacek, *Palacký, The Historian as Scholar and Nationalist* (The Hague and Paris: Mouton, 1970).

15. Štaif, *Historici, dějiny a společnosti I*, 50-59.

16. See Jiří Kořalka, "Bavorská a saská korespondence Františka Palackého, 1836-1846," *Husitský Tábor* 5 (1982): 209-45.

17. Ladislav Kubík, "K české korespondenci adresované Lvu Thunovi," *Z minulosti Děčínska* 2 (1974): 174.

18. See Miroslav Hroch, *Die Vorkämpfer der nationalen Bewegung bei den kleinen Völkern Europas* (Prague: Universita Karlova, 1968), 41-61.

19. See Jan Heidler, *Čechy a Rakousko v politických brožurách předbřeznových* (Prague: František Řivnáč, 1920); Jan Křen, *Konfliktní společenství. Češi a Němci 1780-1918* (Prague: Academia, 1990), 68-86. On the same theme see Miroslav Šesták, "Der tschechische Austroslavismus bis zum österreichisch-ungarischen Ausgleich in der tschechischen Historiographie," in *Der Austroslavismus: ein verfrühtes Konzept zur politischen Neugestaltung Mitteleuropas*, ed. Andreas Moritsch et al. (Vienna: Böhlau, 1996), 24-36.

20. Štaif, *Historici, dějiny a společnost I*, 83-87, 92-96.

21. Ibid., 96, 135-42.

22. See Křen, *Konfliktní společenství*, 87-137, and Jiří Malíř, "Morava na předělu (K formování národního vědomí na Moravě v letech 1848-1871)," *Časopis Matice moravské* 109 (1990): 345-63.

23. See Arnošt Klíma, *Češi a Němci v revoluci 1848-1849* (Prague: Nebesa, 1994).

24. See Jiří Štaif, *Karikatura Němce v revoluci 1848-1849*, in *Obraz Němců, Rakouska a Německa v české společnosti 19. a 20. Století*, ed. Jan Křen and Eva Broklová (Prague: Karolinum, 1998), 33-48.

25. See Otto Urban, *Česká společnost 1848-1918* (Prague: Svoboda, 1982), 142-257.

26. Jiří Rak, "Obraz Němce v české historiografii 19. Století," in *Obraz Němců*, 64-69.

27. See Štaif, *Historici, dějiny a společnost I*, 142ff and 170ff.

28. See the anonymous leading article in the confiscated newspaper *Pokrok* [Progress] of 6 August 1869 from the estate of F. Palacký, inventory no. 633. Archives of the National Museum in Prague.

29. See F.A. Schmalfuss, *Die Deutschen in Böhmen: Geschildert in geographisch-statischer, staatswirthschaflicher, volksthümlicher und geschichtlicher Beziehung* (Prague: Verlag Friedrich Ehrlich, 1851), 135-218. Also cf. Štaif, *Historici, dějiny a společnost*, 113ff, 124ff, and 153ff.

30. Michael Neumüller, "Der Verein für Geschichte der Deutschen in Böhmen (von der Gründung bis zur Jahrhundertwende)," in *Vereinswesen und Geschichtspflege in den böhmischen Ländern*, ed. Ferdinand Seibt (Munich: R. Oldenbourg, 1986), 207.

31. Ibid.," 207.

32. See Julius Lippert, "Palackýs Angriff auf die Mitteilungen. Literarische Beilage zu den Mitteilungen des Vereins für Geschichte der Deutschen in Böhmen" (15 April 1868), 41-48; František Palacký, *Zur böhmischen Geschichtschreibung* (Prague: F. Tempsky, 1871), 161-216; Ludwig Schlesinger, "Würdigung der Angriffe des Herrn Franz Palacký auf die Mitteilungen. Mitteilungen des Vereins für Geschichte der Deutschen in Böhmen," vol. 9 (1871): 264-71; cf. Astrid Tönnies, *Julius Lippert. Sein Leben und Wirken in den Jahren 1839 bis 1885* (Ph.D. dissertation Universität, Hamburg, 1987), 75-78, and 84-89.

33. See František Palacký, *Spisy drobné I* (Prague: Bursík and Kohout, 1898), 295ff, 331ff, 334ff, and 390ff; Křen, *Konfliktní společenství*, 194-279.

34. See Jaroslav Marek, *Jaroslav Goll* (Prague: Melantrich, 1991), 158ff, 239ff; Milan Machovec, *Tomáš G. Masaryk* (Prague: Melantrich, 1968), 107ff.

35. T.G. Masaryk, *Palackého idea národa českého* (Prague: Čin, 1926), 47-48. This is a reprint of Masaryk's original article from 1898.

36. See Harald Bachmann, *Adolf Bachmann. Ein österreichischer Historiker und Politiker* (Munich: R. Lerche, 1962), 69ff, 80ff; Štaif, *Historici, dějiny a společnost II*, 318-23.

37. Berthold Bretholz, *Geschichte Böhmens und Mährens bis zum Aussterben der Přemysliden (1306)* (Munich: Dunker and Humbolt, 1912), VI-VII.

38. See J.W. Brügel, "Berthold Bretholz (1862-1936)," *Bohemia*, vol. 24 (1983): 369-79.
39. The term is Benedict Anderson's, *Imagined Communities: Reflections on the Origin and Spread of Nationalism*, Rev. ed. (London and New York: Verso, 1991), 6ff.

Chapter 5

GENTRY, JEWS, AND PEASANTS

Jews as Others in the Formation of the Modern Polish Nation in
Rural Galicia during the Second Half of the Nineteenth Century

Kai Struve

This essay examines changes in the relationship between peasants and Jews in Galicia during the formation of the modern Polish nation, a process that occurred simultaneously with the dissolution of the basic structures of estate society and the development of structures of modern civic society. The legal emancipation of peasants and Jews took place in parallel. The Galician Jews, like all Jews throughout Cisleithania, gained legal status equal to the Christian population during the Revolution of 1848. This status was partly revoked, however, with the suspension of the constitution in 1851. The constitution of 1867 finally brought equal rights for the Jews as citizens.[1] The most important step toward the peasants' legal emancipation took place in 1848 when serfdom, the *corvée*, and other rents were abolished and the peasants obtained full property rights to their land. During the constitutional reforms of the 1860s, peasants obtained ever more political rights at the communal, district, and provincial level. With enfranchisement at these levels, and in 1873 for the Viennese Reichsrat, the peasants became an increasingly important factor in the composition of the elected political bodies of the constitutional state. However, their influence remained restricted by the curial electoral system, which significantly reduced the weight of the peasant vote.[2]

Equal rights for peasants constituted an important precondition for the development of the modern Polish nation in Galicia. From the time of the Polish Commonwealth peasants had maintained the notion that Poles were identical with the *panowie* (landlords) and, in a wider sense, the upper classes. Due to the

---

sharp social tensions and cultural differences in feudal society, the peasants regarded the Polish landlords as the Other. Nationality played no role in the self-identification of the broad masses of peasants at least until the turn of the nineteenth century. Those collective identities with significance for the peasants were social (as peasants), religious, and territorial relating to locality and region. They provided the criteria for the peasants' distinction between "us" and "them."[3]

Peasants seldom mobilized for Polish national aims. They feared that the reestablishment of the Polish state would strengthen the power of the landlords and the latter would increase or, after 1848, reintroduce the *corvée*. The anti-Polish attitude of the peasants due to social tensions between peasants and landlords was exemplified by the bloody *rabacja* of 1846. That year the primarily gentry Polish national movement attempted to start an uprising in Galicia against Austria. Encouraged by Austrian officials, the peasants in central Galicia opposed that attempt to reestablish an independent Poland, and the Polish uprising broke down within hours. The peasants did not stop there, but attempted to remove serfdom and the hated landlords altogether. They plundered about four hundred estates in the area, killing some twelve hundred people. The Jews remained unmolested.[4]

Although serfdom was abolished in 1848 during the following two decades, tensions between the peasant communes and the estates remained high due to conflict over "servitudes," or rights to pastures and forests, which the peasants had used before 1848 and which were vitally important to them. This issue was not definitively resolved in 1848. State commissions, established in the second half of the 1850s to decide controversial cases, favored the landlords, who won 30,000 of 32,000 cases. There was violent conflict in many places as the peasants tried to claim traditional rights that the landlords now denied them.[5]

In the same period neo-absolutism paralyzed the political activities of the intelligentsia. Therefore, the formation of the modern Polish nation in Galicia started, for the most part, only during the constitutional phase of Austrian history after 1867, when Galicia gained far-reaching autonomy. Under the existing socioeconomic conditions in Galicia, where industrial development was limited and the industrial working and entrepreneurial classes remained small, the formation of the modern nation primarily referred to the processes leading to the integration of the peasantry.[6]

The rural population's greater political participation and the weight of their votes in elections made it increasingly important for the nationally engaged Polish intelligentsia to overcome peasant distrust of Polish national aims. The intelligentsia's motivation for work on behalf of the peasants often included a social concern for improving the peasant's miserable situation through education as well as better agricultural methods and management of communal affairs. In view of the ideas of positivism and "organic work," the intelligentsia regarded such activities as central to Polish national interest because they could strengthen the economic basis of the Polish nation.[7]

However, only a small number of the activist intelligentsia also sought to mobilize the peasants politically in pursuit of peasant social interests. More conservative forces feared a repetition of 1846 in any independent political peasant activity and thus attempted to maintain the dominance of the traditional élite. The Polish peasant movement developed out of the activity of the more radical intelligentsia, beginning in 1875 with the Roman Catholic priest Stanisław Stojałowski, and the aspirations of the peasants to improve their socioeconomic situation. Only at the end of the 1880s was Stojałowski joined by a group of left-wing democrats from Lemberg/L'viv/Lwów. They were led by the newspaper editor Bolesław Wysłouch, who in 1889 began publishing the peasant paper *Przyjaciel Ludu* (People's Friend). Though their relations were strained due to Stojałowski's Catholicism and Wysłouch's liberal views, both men encouraged peasants to organize independently from the landlords and to elect peasants for the Galician Sejm and the Viennese Reichsrat. As a result, peasant political parties were founded in the first half of the 1890s. The politicization of the rural population, which was reflected in a variety of political and social activities and later in the peasant political parties, was part of the modernization of the Galician countryside. New methods of communication reduced the isolation of the village communities: newspapers established links of communication beyond the locality, school attendance rose, and illiteracy declined. Toward the turn of the century, increasing migration for work primarily in Germany and North America began to play an important role in the changes in the villages and the peasants' mentalities.

The peasants' overall economic situation remained miserable, although there were some improvements at the end of the nineteenth and beginning of the twentieth centuries. In the decades after 1848, the average size of farms diminished due to population growth and the custom of partitioning land among the surviving peasant children. Hunger in the period before the harvests remained a threat for most peasants during the second half of the nineteenth century.[8]

Jews were the third important group besides peasants and landlords in rural Galicia. They were typical of a middleman minority: they had a dominant position as traders in the mediating functions in the economy. Although many of the Jewish peddlers wandering through the villages were extremely poor, Jews living in the villages as tavern-keepers held a traditionally middle-level social position between landlords and peasants. Because the taverns and the right to sell alcohol were usually owned by the landlords and rented to the tavern-keepers, these Jews were dependent on the landlords and served as their agents with the peasants. Many estate officials were also Jews, a tradition dating from the Polish Commonwealth.[9] After the end of serfdom, when peasants had become landowners, the importance of money increased because all economic exchange took place under conditions of a market economy. Paralleling the growing importance of money, the role of Jews in the rural economy increased. In contrast to the peasants, the Jews had the capital from which they earned their living, primarily in money or commodities, as well as knowledge of the money economy.[10]

In the decades before the First World War, Jews constituted some 11 percent of the Galician population. Living primarily in small and medium towns, they made up about 8 percent of the population in Western Galicia, while in Eastern Galicia they constituted some 13 percent.[11] Jews represented more than three-quarters of all those working in trade and in the tavern business before the First World War.[12]

The Traditional Peasant View of Jews

This section draws heavily upon anthropological studies that attempt to reconstruct the "traditional" mental world of the peasants and the place of Jews in it.[13] The approach of these studies and their use of ethnographic material collected in the second half of the nineteenth century might be in some respects problematic from the historian's point of view, because they present a static model of peasant culture and peasant consciousness on the basis of material from a time of deep changes within the peasant society nor does the model of culture that they construct include all possibilities for peasant behavior. But it is assumed here that that model does show an important aspect of the peasant-Jewish relationship and that its features considerably influenced the changes in the relationship between peasants and Jews.

A high degree of isolation and a lack of strong communication links beyond the locality, a certain resistance to change, a great importance of mythic and magical elements, and a strong distinction between "alien" and "own" characterized the traditional peasant world.[14] The cultural anthropologist Ludwik Stomma distinguishes between an *orbis interior* and an *orbis exterior* in the peasants' worldviews, between the world they experienced as their own and the other alien world. In the traditional peasant consciousness, Jews constituted the strongest personification of the "alien" because Jews were more part of peasants' daily lives than were other "aliens." Thus, Jews were ideal as mediators between the *orbis interior* and the *orbis exterior*. The *orbis exterior* was also the sphere of the devil and of death. Folktales, rituals, and customs show the figure of a Jew in a prominent place as mediator and representative of the devil and of the "other" world. In the Slavic mythologies the devil was not an unequivocally negative, but rather an ambivalent figure. He had a necessary role in the world's creation and its preservation. Therefore, Jews as representatives and mediators with the "other" world were a necessary part of its continuing existence. This is reflected in traditional plays at the end of the winter, which were intended to start the cycle of fertility anew.[15] Peasants very much appreciated visits by Jews at certain occasions during the Christmas/New Year period because they thought Jews brought luck, fertility, and wealth for the coming year.

Jews were well suited as mediators both because of their strong presence in the peasants' everyday life and because of their role in Christian mythology, which was firmly established in the peasants' worldview. Although Jews were represented as "Christ killers," they were also participants and witnesses in the mystery of God's passion and a living proof of the truth of the gospel.[16] These medieval or early modern views of Jews remained part of peasant culture in the nineteenth century and helped constitute the ambivalent peasant view of Jews as alien. Jews as aliens were at the same time better and worse than the peasant "we"; they were both holy and cursed.[17]

The peasants' relationship with "real" Jews, as reflected in ethnographic material, shows similar ambivalent features to those of the "mythical" Jew in peasant culture. Jews as aliens appeared, on the one hand, dangerous, and moral obligations toward them were reduced. On the other hand, peasants ascribed magical abilities to the Jews that could be both beneficial and threatening. Peasants often sought advice from tsaddiks, the Hasidic leaders, and rabbis. Reports from Eastern Galicia and Volhynia describe peasant women visiting the local markets, sometimes lighting candles in both the local church and the synagogue.[18]

Ethnographic sources indicate that peasants almost exclusively identified Jews with trade, taverns, and usury. Almost no proverbs and folktales show Jews in other professions, though many earned their living as craftsmen or workers. For peasants, the term "Jew" was virtually synonymous with "trader."[19] They viewed trade as "Jewish," thus morally suspicious and not suitable for themselves. The long-time village mayor of Dzików (near Tarnobrzeg), Jan Słomka, a peasant born in 1842, wrote in his memoirs about the peasants' attitude toward trade during his youth: "Peasants did not engage in trade at all. They regarded it as a Jewish occupation, which only a Jew—so they said—could manage. They were embarrassed by engaging in trade and made fun of a peasant who would have tried it."[20]

Despite the close contacts between Jews and peasants, there was a great distance between the two groups. The peasants' views of the Jews were strongly influenced by both beliefs in magic and stereotypes. Their knowledge of the real life of Jews was limited. For their part, Jews often regarded the peasants as primitive and uneducated, but as a latent threat.[21]

Father Stanisław Stojałowski and the Beginning of the Peasant Movement

The work that the Roman Catholic priest Stanisław Stojałowski began among the peasants when he took over two peasant newspapers, *Wieniec* and *Pszczółka*, in 1875 was a starting point for the development of the Polish peasant movement in Galicia. Stojałowski gave his papers a political character and increasingly pressed for the independent political mobilization and organization of the peasants. After the mid-1880s, this brought him into conflict with both state and church authorities, but in the 1870s Stojałowski was still moderate. However, new elements, that elicited positive response from the peasants were already visible in his papers. Stojałowski devoted much of each paper to political issues. He approached the peasants as equal citizens of the Austrian state and as equal members of the Polish nation. Other newspapers for the rural population were, however, written in a moralistic-paternalistic style that reflected the Polish upper classes' fear of social unrest and were intended to make the peasants accept the existing social order and the landlords' authority.[22] Stojałowski sought to mobilize the peasants to improve conditions in the villages, increase the level of education, and improve their economic situation through better management of village affairs and better agricultural techniques. He considered it in the interest of the Polish nation for the peasants to take active part in political affairs. Moreover, he was confident that the peasants as good citizens of the Austrian state, using their constitutional rights within the legal framework, would also strengthen the Polish nation.[23]

Stojałowski called upon his readers both to found reading rooms and savings and loan associations and to organize meetings to start this work.[24] Drawing upon the example of Poznań, he also helped found agrarian circles in Galicia. From 1882, the circles were organized in the Towarzystwo Kółek Rolniczych (TKR, Agrarian Circles Society). They spread rapidly and became an important organization promoting changes in the villages.[25] However, more conservative politicians who feared what they considered his social radicalism would later remove Stojałowski from the leadership of that organization.

When Stojałowski began his work among the peasants in 1875, one of his main aims was to expand national consciousness. He sought to convince the peasants that not only the *panowie*, but they, too, were Poles and that the peasants as Poles shared some common interests with the *panowie*. In this effort, Stojałowski relied on the peasants' Roman Catholic religious identity. He explained to them that being Catholic also meant belonging to the Polish nation. The suggestion that they belonged to the Polish nation was especially convincing to his readers when it was made in the context of demarcating the Other, both in terms of their religious and their national identity. Stojałowski described the Orthodox Russians and the Protestant Prussians or Germans as inimical not only to the Polish nation, but also to the peasants' Catholic faith. Demonstrating the Prussian and Russian suppression of Poles not only as Poles, but also as Catholics, was an especially useful way to spread knowledge of the Polish nation, its history, territory, and its striving for independence, as well as for strengthening the peasants' identification with the Polish nation.[26] The most important Others that the peasants came into daily contact with were Jews. And, while Prussia and Russia, like other states that suppressed the Poles, had to be made known to the peasants, it was not necessary to convince the peasants of the Otherness of Jews.

Antisemitic ideas, which were closely linked to his antiliberal and Christian-social convictions, strongly influenced Stojałowski. Typical of a growing number of antisemites elsewhere in Europe from the 1870s, he considered liberalism to be the work of and in the interest of Jews while harming Christian peasants, workers, and artisans. He also interpreted liberalism as an attack on the Roman Catholic Church.[27] Stojałowski already had racial concepts of Jewishness in mind and considered Polish assimilation of the Jews impossible.[28] However, Stojałowski's concrete anti-Jewish policy and agitation among the peasants was

primarily based on economic tensions between peasants and Jews. Racial ideology had no function in the Galician countryside during the nineteenth and early
twentieth century because it simply was not necessary to explain that the Jews
constituted the Other. Stojałowski represented Jews as a threat to both the peasants and the Polish nation. As a result of the Austrian liberal economic and cultural policy of the 1870s, he feared that Jewish preponderance over Christians
was increasingly emerging in Galician villages and towns.

Stojałowski considered three main issues involving Jews to threaten the peasants. The first was the role of Jewish tavern-keepers, as Stojałowski saw it, in fostering peasant alcoholism. The Galician public widely regarded alcoholism as the
most prominent reason why peasants fell into debt to Jewish moneylenders—
often identical with the tavern-keepers—and lost their land to Jews: "Only
through the tavern does every Jew come to preponderance over the whole village
or over a town. In the tavern he catches his victims and even those who are not
habitual drunkards, but drink often… fall easily into Jewish hands and traps."[29]
Stojałowski sought to warn his readers:

> The greatest plague of our country are the Jews who have already occupied our lords as well
> as our townsmen and peasants, exploit them with usury and destroy them all, make them
> drink, have taken over trade, and increasingly permeate everything with malice and fraud.
> Jews have driven already into land property—in one word: they use everything to their own
> advantage and to the destruction of the nation like a kind of bad ghost.[30]

Stojałowski called upon the peasants not to trust the Jews or to drink alcohol,
and to acquire a better education as defense against Jewish "preponderance."
Typically, nearly all of the intelligentsia's initiatives to improve the peasants' situation included both sobriety and better education as central preconditions to
prevent the peasants from falling into debt, for better village administration, and
for better agriculture. These aims of improving the peasants' lot usually included an anti-Jewish component. While Stojałowski was more antisemitic than
most of the contemporary Polish intelligentsia, there was a broad consensus
among the intelligentsia concerning the destructive role Jews played vis-à-vis the
peasants. The Jewish tavern-keepers and the peasants' drinking habits were
blamed for the peasants' misery. This permitted avoiding discussion of social
inequality and the privileged position of the landlords. But a closer look at the
relationships in the villages reveals that peasant-Jewish tensions emerged in several fields during the course of modernizing reforms in the villages, rather than
as a result of attempts to deflect responsibility for the peasants' misery from the
landlords' privileged position.

Fields of Tension between Peasants and Jews

Taverns and tavern-keepers played a central role in the social, political, and economic life of the villages. Weddings and other feasts took place here. Often the

tavern-keepers also ran a small trade and engaged in moneylending. Usually, taverns were sites of village council meetings, and the mayors held their "office hours" there and the members of the commune could settle their affairs with them.

The ownership of the taverns and the right of production and sale of alcohol, the *propinacja*, was a hereditary privilege of the landlords that dated from the Polish Commonwealth. In Galicia, the last remnants of the *propinacja* were abolished only in 1911. Beginning in the sixteenth century, the production and sale of alcohol primarily to the enserfed peasants played an increasing role in the economy of the estates, providing up to 40 percent of their revenue at the end of the eighteenth century. Already at that time, the taverns were usually rented out to Jews.[31]

At the end of the nineteenth century there were more than 17,000 taverns in Galicia, about one for every 420 inhabitants. From the 1850s to the 1870s there had been one tavern for every 200 to 300 inhabitants. High rents due to the landlord and fierce competition often made it difficult for tavern-keepers to earn their living from the taverns.[32] That was the background for the numerous accusations of the Jewish tavern-keepers of seducing the peasants to drink and driving them into poverty.[33]

The peasants' ambivalent attitude toward Jews showed itself most clearly toward the tavern-keeper. On the one hand, the tavern-keepers were often objects of mockery and crude jokes. On the other, peasants trusted many of them and appreciated their advice in difficult situations.[34]

From the end of the eighteenth century, accusations that Jewish tavern-keepers were seducing the peasants to drink and were "sucking them dry" figured prominently in debates on the improvement of the peasants' lot. Such accusations were one reason for the apparently unsuccessful attempts to drive the Jews of Galicia out of tavern keeping that had been undertaken already during the 1780s under the enlightened-absolutist rule of Emperor Joseph II.[35]

From the middle of the nineteenth century, the Roman Catholic Church actively engaged in an antialcohol campaign. Already during the 1840s there had been a strong movement for sobriety in Western Galicia. As quickly as it rose it disappeared after the *rabacja* of 1846 and the famine of 1847. A new movement with longer-lasting results emerged in the 1870s. When priests preached sobriety, they often employed the argument that the evilness of alcohol was due to its sale by Jews. The church helped found temperance brotherhoods in small towns and villages. Often these were the result of so-called missions, large religious gatherings, often with a thousand or more participants. At the end of these missions, those who wanted to give up alcohol took an oath. The foundation of a temperance brotherhood intended to spread sobriety and encourage adherence to the oath usually was part of the missions.[36] Moreover, during the 1870s when many village priests began more actively to fight alcohol, this was often a battle against the Jewish tavern-keeper.[37]

Secular initiatives for the improvement of village conditions also affected the battle against the taverns. The statutes of the TKR contained a paragraph limiting membership to Christians.[38] Parallel with the TKR struggle against alcoholism was the desire to create centers of social life in the villages outside the tavern. The aim was both to reduce the consumption of alcohol and to have a place from which changes and improvements in the village could be initiated. The proponents of village change considered taverns institutions that preserved bad habits and therefore deepened the crisis of villages. The TKR's statutes stated that in no case should the regular meetings of the village circles take place in a tavern.[39]

The battle against the tavern and alcohol was also a battle for social discipline. The statutes of the TKR described the organization's aim as the "moralization" (*umoralnienie*) of its members, meaning the avoidance of "alcoholism, prodigal feasts at weddings, baptisms and funerals."[40] In fact, it appears that by the turn of the century such traditional customs had already changed considerably. In contrast to earlier times, weddings now only lasted two or three days.[41]

Peasant newspaper discourse intended to encourage changes in the villages described the continuing importance of a Jewish role in a village as a sign that the bad "old order" still existed. Those changes meant to create a better "new order" were identified with the removal of the Jews. The changes were described as being in the national interest. For example, an article, "Three virtues of a peasant. Work, temperance, and economy," asserted that with

> work on working days, attending the divine service on Sundays and holidays, and useful reading or listening [to literate peasants, teachers, or priests who read newspapers, etc., to illiterate villagers] the country would regain its former glory and power. The Jews would no longer reside in the tavern, hundreds of lots would not go into their cheating hands; there would be less poverty, need, and mortality in our country. As the old Polish proverb says: work enriches, where there is work, there is bread and money; intemperance and laziness are the devil's company. In a word—if we do not want to remain serfs of the Jews, then let us love work and its company: temperance and economy.[42]

Thus, the battle against alcoholism and the tavern as a sign of striving for a better future was how Stojałowski presented this subject in his newspapers. A growing group of activists in the villages who wrote in Stojałowski's papers saw the battle in the same terms. For example, the teacher Karol Głowacki sent a letter from the village Majdan Kolbuszowa:

> Before [about ten years ago] there were permanent drinking-bouts and rows. Today the taverns where so many blasphemies took place stand empty. The wind howls through them because nearly the whole village joined the Brotherhood of Holy Temperance and from a thousand souls there are probably less than twenty who drink vodka, and they drink in a way that no one sees it.

Sobriety was accompanied by a strong religious movement in the village and attempts to improve the level of education.[43]

During the 1870s and 1880s, there had been accounts of the ruin of taverns and the removal of Jews from villages because most of the villagers no longer frequented the tavern.[44] However, statistical data points to Jewish immigration into villages because of better economic opportunities than in the cities in Western Galicia until 1880 and in Eastern Galicia until 1890.[45]

Many peasants broke their oath of sobriety. It appears, however, that at the end of the century a considerable part of the rural population did not drink alcohol at all or, at least, no spirits. Estimations for some regions of West Galicia place the abstainers at more than 50 percent.[46] This abstinence cannot be understood solely as the result of the missions. It reflected rather a fundamental change in the peasants' mentalities toward more social discipline, and was accompanied by the mobilization of peasants for self-help initiatives such as the agrarian circles, for the improvement of the village administration and, since the 1890s, also in peasant political parties.

The political mobilization of peasants for the improvement of their living conditions started on the village level. Here conflicts arose between reformers who wanted changes and a more conservative group among the peasants that often dominated village politics, had no interest in changes, and clung to the old habits.[47] In general, the Jews had little interest in change advocated by the reformers because one of the main aims of the reforms was to fight alcoholism and taverns. The next step was often the establishment of a so-called "Christian" shop that threatened the economic existence of Jewish shopkeepers and traders. The reformers in the villages sought to separate village politics from the tavern where the village affairs usually were managed with the aid of a larger or smaller quantity of alcohol.[48] Village mayors and councilors, who had considerable competence and, in principle, could do much to improve the living conditions in the villages, often did little because of their own lack of education. Corruption and fraud among the village functionaries also had a negative effect on village administration.[49] Stojałowski and the peasant movement aimed to change this situation and to make the village administration function more efficiently. Peasant newspapers also described the improvement of the village administration as a battle against Jewish influence. In 1876, the village teacher Tadeusz Kwiatkowski gave the following advice for the election of the village councils and the mayors:

> Before the elections, farmers should meet in an appropriate place, in no case in the tavern, the best would be in the school. There they should make up their minds under sober conditions into whose hands they want to place their property and the whole village administration. After such deliberation they should all come like one man on the chosen day and vote for those people who are distinguished by piety, scrupulousness, work, and temperance, and who also can read and write, especially the mayor, so that he will not later let himself be cheated and exploited by bad people. Such people should not be elected who at the smallest occasion steal money from the peasants, and use that money to spend whole days drinking in the tavern, enriching the Jews, and who drown many important things in that quarter and who, in the end, roll like nonhuman creatures under Jewish tables.[50]

The opposition of tavern-keepers to such a program probably was inevitable. If the mayor did not drink, then he posed the threat of causing problems for the tavern.[51] It appears that a tavern-keeper could suffer a considerable reduction of income if the mayor avoided the tavern and the village council did not hold meetings there, because then others also began to avoid the tavern.[52] An abstinent mayor could influence others by example and replace the role of the consumption of alcohol in peasant culture with the notion of the tavern as an evil place. (Such a notion was already present in peasant culture and had been reinforced by the sobriety movement.)[53] This is the background for conflicts between the local reformers and the Jews in village elections, in which Jewish tavern-keepers often used their considerable influence to oppose candidates who wanted change in the villages.[54]

Probably the issue that created the most Jewish-peasant tension was Jewish moneylending, often at usurious rates. The problem of peasant indebtedness rose quickly after 1867, when legal restrictions on the trade of land and land ownership by Jews, as well as the law against usury, had been abolished. As peasant indebtedness grew rapidly, becoming a major problem, new restrictions against usury were introduced, first in Galicia in 1877 and then throughout Cisleithania in 1881, when the conservative Iron Ring coalition of Count Eduard Taaffe replaced the liberal government.[55]

The peasants' most important source of credit was private moneylending, primarily from Jews. Borrowers often did not know how much they paid in interest because they gave a small sum every week or they paid in kind or in work. Often land also had to be given to the creditor, which he cultivated with the yield serving him as interest and the land itself as security. The overall picture painted by responses to an 1878 questionnaire that the Galician Provincial Statistical Bureau (*Krajowe Biuro Statystyczne*) sent the district authorities was a significant worsening of the peasants' economic situation during the 1870s.[56]

Between 1868 and 1880 there had been a rapid increase in the number of forced land sales from 164 to about 3,200 annually. For the most part the forced auctions were on behalf of Jewish creditors. In 1868 the crownland administration founded the *Bank włościański* (Peasant Bank) to improve the credit supply for the peasants. In fact, the bank had against its original purpose a rather negative influence on the economic situation of many peasants, demanding high interest rates of up to 40 percent and driving many peasants into ruin. Due to risky financial operations on the Vienna Bourse, it went bankrupt in 1884.[57] In contrast, the communal loan banks were institutions that actually improved the rural credit facilities. Their number rose from 1,246 in 1875 to 3,350 in 1893.[58] Beginning in the 1870s an increasing number of savings and loan associations on a modified model of the Schulze-Delitzsch associations were founded in Galicia. During the last fifteen years of the nineteenth century, they became the most important rural credit organizations. They offered considerably lower interest rates than the informal lenders and the *Bank włościański*, thus causing far fewer defaults, and representing a considerable improvement in the peasants' economic condition.[59]

After the turn of the century savings and loan associations based on the Raiffeisen system quickly appeared in Galicia. They provided even better credit opportunities than the Schulze-Delitzsch banks had. The aim of the Raiffeisen
associations was to liberate the peasants from usury, which they largely identified
with Jews. Their statutes contained paragraphs restricting membership to Christians and forbidding the holding of meetings of the members in taverns.[60] For the
peasant movement the foundation of communal loan banks, Schulze-Delitzsch,
Raiffeisen, and other credit institutions was a central aim for providing the peasants with better credit facilities and, simultaneously, for removing the private
Jewish moneylenders from the rural credit market.[61]

Jews began to acquire land from peasants and estates from landlords after the
abolition of restrictions on Jewish land ownership in 1867-1868. By 1889, 305
Jewish landlords owned estate land, and their number rose to 561 by 1912. Their
percentage of the total number of estate landowners increased from 13.1 percent
in 1889 to 22.1 percent in 1912, and their share in the estate land increased from
13.3 percent in 1889 to 16.0 percent in 1912. It is estimated that in 1902 some
15,000 Jews owned either peasant or estate land.[62] In the mid-1890s, Jews leased
more than 50 percent of all leased estates.[63]

The rapid increase of Jewish land ownership alarmed not only Stojałowski,
but also other Galician publicists.[64] Jewish acquisition of estates and the increase
in Jewish land ownership at the expense of peasants became an issue of Jewish-
peasant tension. During the second half of the nineteenth century, there was
peasant land hunger due to the prevailing system of partition. Especially in Western Galicia, middle-sized estates were often sold in total or in part by their own-
ers and then parceled out among peasants. Many of these transactions took place
through Jewish intermediaries who bought land from the estates and then sold
smaller parcels at higher prices to peasants.[65] Peasant interest in this case was the
exclusion of commercial intermediaries. The peasant parties later backed such
demands with national arguments that Polish land should be sold to Polish peasants and not to Jewish traders.[66]

The issue of land trade was also a starting point for peasants' critique of landlords acting unpatriotically by selling their land to Jews instead of Polish peasants.
The peasant claim of Polish identity thus became a means of condemning the
landlords for their close relationship with Jews.[67]

Part of the village reform effort was the founding of Christian shops as a means
of redirecting the profit from trade from Jews to "our" (the Polish peasants')
hands.[68] The center of activity for most agrarian circles in the villages was the shop.
In 1899, 437 of 529 agrarian circles owned a shop, or a shop was run by peasants
privately under the auspices of the agrarian circle. In 1912, 908 of 1,862 circles had
a shop.[69] The activities of the circles became increasingly independent from the
shops only in the last years before the First World War. It appears that the idea of
earning more money by taking over trade and not leaving the profit to the Jews had
considerable mobilizing power for many peasants. The foundation of a shop was
often the most important reason for peasants to organize an agrarian circle.[70]

By 1913, 3,150 shops connected with the agrarian circles had been opened. Only the above-mentioned number of shops survived as shops of the agrarian circles. The others separated from the agrarian circles and became the private property of individual peasants or dissolved due to their managers' lack of economic ability, quarrels among founders, and competition from Jewish shops.[71]

The peasants' opening of shops reflects a change in mentality, because they had traditionally regarded shops and trade as Jewish and, thus, alien to peasants. In the 1870s peasants began running shops and competing with the Jews for sources of additional income. Stojałowski, the TKR, and others supported this change because they considered it a bulwark against "Jewish preponderance," which they believed was a threat to the peasants and the Polish nation alike. Therefore, they considered founding the shops a patriotic enterprise.

The Galician Peasant Parties and their Relations to Jews

Due to the increasing political mobilization of the peasants, in the 1890s peasant parties were founded. Peasants had learned that the Austrian constitutional state provided them in principle with means of pursuing their interests within the political institutions if they organized properly.[72] A significant step in that direction was the election in 1889 and 1890 of five candidates of peasant electoral committees to the Galician Sejm. In 1889 Bolesław Wysłouch, a coeditor of the left-wing daily *Kuryer Lwowski,* began publishing the peasant paper *Przyjaciel Ludu,* which also backed peasant candidates in the Sejm elections that year. Wysłouch's aim was the active involvement of the peasants in politics, which he thought would encourage them also to support actively the endeavor for Polish independence.[73] The L'viv left-wing democrats' cooperation with groups of peasant activists around the *Przyjaciel Ludu* was the basis for the creation of the *Stronnictwo Ludowe* (SL) in 1895 (from 1903 *Polskie Stronnictwo Ludowe* [PSL], Polish People's Party). Already in 1893 the *Związek Stronnictwa Chłopskiego* (ZSCh, Union of Peasants' Party) had been founded by relatively wealthy peasants around Nowy Sącz/Neu-Sandez. A regional party, harassed from both left and right, it disbanded in 1908.[74]

Since the mid-1880s, when Stojałowski had started to propagate independent peasant political organization, he had come under increasing pressure from the church and the state hierarchies. This resulted in his further radicalization, making him more popular among the peasants, and culminated in his excommunication in 1896. That same year, following failed attempts to cooperate with the ZSCh and the SL, he founded his own political party, *Stronnictwo Chrześcijańsko-Ludowe* (Christian People's Party). Despite competition from the other parties, Stojałowski maintained a large following among the peasants. Only after the turn of the century did the SL become the dominant political group among the peasants, while Stojałowski's party merged with other Christian-social, antisemitic groups and lost influence among the peasants.[75]

The anti-Jewish unrest in Central Galicia during June and July 1898 was, in part, the result of competition between Stojałowski and the SL.[76] After the first riots in Wieliczka in mid-March 1898, there was greater unrest beginning the second week of June in the Jasło district, where by-elections for the fifth curia of the Reichsrat were to take place on June 23. Jan Stapiński, the leading SL-politician who was most influential among the peasants, was competing with a candidate of Stojałowski's party. While allegations that Stojałowski deliberately started the riots to delay the elections and avoid the defeat of his candidate have not been proven,[77] there is little doubt that conflict over the election contributed to the tense atmosphere. These by-elections had been preceded by intense election campaigns to the Galician Sejm in 1895, to the Reichsrat in 1897, and by-elections in the neighboring district of Łańcut-Nisko in February 1898. Stojałowski had employed increasingly antisemitic slogans against the SL after the 1895 campaigns and attacked Stapiński as having been "bought" by the Jews.[78]

The unrest soon spread to other parts of Central Galicia. It was worst between Nowy Sącz and Jarosław. The government reacted strongly against the riots, which it perceived as a threat to social order.[79] On 16 June gendarmes shot and killed twelve rioters in Frysztak.[80] On 28 June martial law was imposed in thirty-three districts. More than 1,800 people were taken in preventive custody, and criminal proceedings were opened against 5,166 people.[81]

Rumors that the Emperor Francis Joseph had permitted violence against Jews and the plundering of their property was the immediate cause of the mid-June unrest. Two versions of this rumor appear to have circulated. The first was that crown Prince Rudolf (who had committed suicide in 1889) was still alive but living in hiding because the Jews had tried to kill him. The second version was that Jews had tried to kill the Emperor himself. Both versions said that the Emperor had permitted, in revenge and for a limited period, the plundering of Jewish property, but not the killing of Jews.[82] In fact, the level of anti-Jewish violence during the riots was relatively low. It remained mostly restricted to damaging taverns or the shops of Jews.

Stojałowski party deputies denied any responsibility for the riots. Indeed, they blamed them on the Jews themselves, asserting that the unrest was a result of "Jewish exploitation" of the peasants, and suggested that the Jews had their own political aims in provoking the riots.[83] The conservative peasant party from Nowy Sącz, the ZSCh, condemned the unrest more clearly, but called for legal actions against exploitation by Jews. However, in previous years the rhetoric of that party's paper, *Związek Chłopski* (Peasant Union), had been rather more antisemitic than Stojałowski's papers.[84]

Although the SL newspaper, the *Przyjaciel Ludu*, was less antisemitic than those of Stojałowski and the ZSCh, it also encouraged boycotting the Jews to drive them from the villages:

> It is well known that also the *ludowcy* [the followers of the SL] did not like the Jews and that we try hard to stop their abuses. But we are doing so in a proper, responsible, and legal

manner. We call for boycotting the tavern: then the tavern-keeper will leave without force if he no longer has anything to do in the village. Do not buy from a Jew, do not sell him anything, and do not borrow from him. Let us take the trade in our own hands, found banks and let us organize the wage work ourselves. Then even the worst Jew will no longer be able to harm us, and we will get rid of him without violence and misery.[85]

Przyjaciel Ludu attacked Stojałowski as responsible for the unrest, but showed no sympathy for Jewish suffering during the riots. It considered the riots disastrous for the peasants because gendarmes and soldiers had killed and wounded peasants. Thousands more had been arrested, separating them from their families and farms.

Three features of the peasants' and the peasant parties' relationship with the Jews, which would be typical for the next decades, can be distinguished in the riots of 1898. First, there was spontaneous social-revolutionary peasant violence. In its last large-scale outbreak—the *rabacja* of 1846—this violence had been directed against the landlords. In both 1846 and 1898 the point of positive reference for the peasants' actions was the mythical figure of the good Emperor who had to be defended against the onslaught of the landlords or the Jews. In contrast to 1846, the main social tensions in 1898 were with the Jews, and it was rumored that their property could be plundered without punishment.

The second feature was the instrumentalization of the Jewish subject against competing political groups in the countryside as Stojałowski had done against the SL. This would be repeated in the following decades by right-wing or centrist parties against more leftist competitors.

Third, the *Przyjaciel Ludu*'s comments on the riots clearly reflect the SL's attitude toward Jews. The party rejected violence, but called upon the peasants to boycott Jewish tavern-keepers and traders as a legal part of political and economic work for the improvement of the peasants' situation. Also, this leftist peasant party did not seek to include Jews in their efforts to improve the village conditions, but considered the removal of the Jews from their positions in the rural economy and the villages part of a strategy to improve the peasants' material situation.[86]

From the side of the intelligentsia, Wysłouch had formulated the basic political ideas of the SL in an 1886 article, *Szkice programowe* (Programmatic Sketches). His aim was both social and national. He was convinced that the future Polish national politics could only rest on the peasants and would only be successful if it was taken over by the peasantry. A necessary precondition was thus the improvement of the peasants' education and economic situation. The basis of his political program was an ethnic conception of the nation. Wysłouch believed the peasants, the *lud*, rather than the nobility, the *szlachta*, constituted the real core of the nation.[87] Thus he argued that the peasants should replace the *szlachta* as carriers of the Polish national aspirations. The ethnic concept of the nation provided both an ideological basis for the program of the peasants' political emancipation and had the aim of a homogeneous nation with no room for national minorities or unassimilated Jews. These positions became also part of the PSL's basic program of 1903. Concerning Jews, it read:

> Within the Jewish element we distinguish that part which has a feeling of national belonging to the Polish society and wants to be different only in its belief.… The Jewish question in any case only starts beyond those, that is, as the question of a tribe that usually tends toward the German culture and considers itself alien to Polish culture and whom we also consider as such. Thus we hope that the most important point of the Zionists' program, that is, emigration to Palestine, will be achieved.[88]

The intelligentsia active in the Galician SL did not adopt the radical antisemitic ideas contained in both Stojałowski's writings and the ZSCh newspapers. However, the intelligentsia, as Wysłouch's writings clearly demonstrate, did regard at least the unassimilated Jews, who constituted the overwhelming majority in Galicia, as the Other. Wysłouch considered it impossible if not undesirable for these Jews to become a part of the Polish nation.

The removal of Jews from Polish soil advocated in the PSL party program of 1903 on the basis of an ethnic concept of the Polish nation paralleled the aim of removing Jews from the rural economy to assure additional income for the peasants by acquiring trade for them. In fact, the Jews were offered only one alternative: emigration. The idea of resolving Poland's economic problems through Jewish emigration and opening their places in the economy for peasants would become a central theme of antisemitism in the 1930s.[89]

At that point the aims of the intelligentsia linked with the interests of peasants who also sought solutions to their economic misery and for whom trade provided possible additional income. When the right of *propinacja* was abolished and state concessions introduced in 1911, the Galician authorities denied concessions to many Jewish tavern-keepers, giving them to peasants instead. At that time, the PSL already had considerable influence on the Galician administration and used it to help its followers obtain them.[90]

Conclusion

For the peasants the Otherness of the Jews was a matter of course. The peasants' perception of Jews was, however, ambivalent. They traditionally considered Jews a necessary part of the world. It appears that through the mid-1800s they had no strong desire to remove the Jews, in contrast to the landlords, as the *rabacja* of 1846 clearly demonstrates.

Following the abolition of serfdom, the Jews became the peasants' most important economic antagonists. Private moneylending primarily by Jews became an increasingly important factor in the rural economy. Many peasants fell into debt to Jewish moneylenders or lost their land—in part or wholly—after the liberal economic reforms of the 1860s. The result was increasing tension between peasants and Jews. Even if an individual peasant did not lose his land, he saw that many of "us," the peasants, lost land to "them," the Jews.

Jews were also the Other for those members of the Polish intelligentsia who worked to improve the peasants' situation. This was true for Stojałowski, with his Catholic, Christian-social and antisemitic convictions, as well as for Bolesław Wysłouch and his more leftist group, which initiated the foundation of the SL. The common goal was the removal of Jews from the villages.

This was due both to the concept of Jews as Other and to the fact that the economic, social, and political aims of the peasant movement conflicted with those of Jews in their roles as village tavern-keepers, traders, or moneylenders. Peasants began to establish Christian shops, thus entering those parts of the rural economy that had hitherto been restricted primarily to Jews and that they had heretofore regarded as "Jewish" and therefore alien. In large part, the conflict was not over the abolition of real grievances such as the high rates of interest charged by private moneylenders, but about resources, namely if the profit from the trade got into "our" or into "their" hands. Peasants attempted to improve their economic situation by acquiring a larger part of the economic resources through removal of the Jews. This was not a strategy of individual peasants to improve their situation, but rather it occurred within the framework of a movement for improving the peasants' living conditions, which backed the endeavors in the individual villages. It not only propagated the foundation of Christian shops, communal or cooperative savings and loan banks, and other organizations to improve the peasants' lot, but understood these undertakings as a national task for the preservation and strengthening of the Polish nation. Part of that strengthening included the removal of the Jews from their economic position. Here there was a link between the intelligentsia's national aims and the economic interests of peasants. The latter were articulated in the national discourse of the Polish peasant movement, and peasant and national interests were presented as identical. In the last decades of the nineteenth century, the removal of the Jews became an aim of the Polish peasant parties, which was pursued with the means of political and economic organization that the Austrian constitutional state provided. The removal of Jews from the villages was a part of an overall strategy of peasant political and social emancipation. Outbursts of violence like that in 1898 could upset rather than help to achieve that aim.

The political peasant movement was both an expression and an engine of modernization of rural society, of the transgression of the peasants' communicative and mental isolation as well as of their continuous interregional organization for articulating their interests. Peasant mobilization to work for change in the villages, for the improvement of living conditions, and for political organization took place in a large part against Jews. This was true of the mobilization discourse, which attempted to activate the peasants through emphasizing the negative role of Jews in villages, as well as the concrete work of the organizations and institutions that resulted from the mobilization.

Thus, an ambivalent picture of the peasant movements' strategies of change emerges. They worked successfully for the peasants' political and social emancipation. However, a part of that was the removal of Jews from the villages and the rural economy.

Notes

1. Piotr Wróbel, "The Jews of Galicia under Austrian-Polish Rule, 1869-1918," *Austrian History Yearbook* 25 (1994), 99-104; Filip Friedmann, *Die galizischen Juden im Kampfe um ihre Gleichberechtigung (1848-1868)* (Frankfurt am Main: Kauffmann, 1929).

2. Krzysztof Groniowski, *Uwłaszczenie chłopów w Polsce. Geneza-realizacja-skutki* (Warsaw: Wiedza Powszechna, 1976), 71-115; Stefan Inglot, "Historia społeczno-gospodarcza chłopów polskich w zaborze austriackim," in *Historia chłopów polskich*, vol. 2: *Okres zaborów* [Period of the partition], ed. Stefan Inglot (Warsaw: Ludowa Spółdzielnia Wydawnicza, 1972), 229-44.

3. Ludwik Stomma, *Antropologia kultury wsi polskiej XIX w.* (Warsaw: Pax, 1986), 56-63. On the peasants' identification with the Polish nation, see Keely Stauter-Halsted, *The Nation in the Village. The Genesis of Peasant National Identity in Austrian Poland, 1848-1914* (Ithaca, N.Y.: Cornell University Press, 2001), and Jan Molenda, *Chłopi–naród–niepodległość* (Warsaw: Neriton, 1999). For a comparison of the Polish and the Ukrainian case in Galicia, see Kai Struve, "Bauern und Nation in Ostmitteleuropa. Soziale Emanzipation und nationale Identität der galizischen Bauern im 19. Jahrhundert," in *Nationalismen in Europa. West- und Osteuropa im Vergleich*, ed. Ulrike von Hirschhausen and Jörn Leonhard (Göttingen: Wallstein, 2001), 347-71. On the peasants as a problem of Polish national politics in the nineteenth century, see Stefan Kieniewicz, *The Emancipation of the Polish Peasantry* (Chicago: University of Chicago Press, 1969).

4. A survey of the literature on 1846 can be found in Thomas W. Simons, Jr., "The Peasant Revolt of 1846 in Galicia: Recent Polish Historiography," *Slavic Review* 30 (1971): 795-817. See also Arnon Gill, *Die polnische Revolution von 1846. Zwischen nationalem Befreiungskampf des Landadels und antifeudaler Bauernerhebung* (Munich: Oldenbourg, 1974).

5. Inglot, "Historia społeczno-gospodarcza," 245-46; for Eastern Galicia, see John-Paul Himka, *Galician Villagers and the Ukrainian National Movement in the Nineteenth Century* (Houndmills: Macmillan, 1988), 48-56; M.M. Kravets, *Selianstvo Skhidnoi Halychyny i Pivnichnoi Bukovyny u druhii polovyni XIX st.* (L'viv, 1964), 143-72.

6. On the social structure of the Galician society, see Józef Buszko, *Zum Wandel der Gesellschaftsstruktur in Galizien und in der Bukowina* (Vienna: Verlag der Österreichischen Akademie der Wissenschaften, 1978) (Österreichische Akademie der Wissenschaften. Philosophisch-historische Klasse. Sitzungsberichte, vol. 343); on the Galician bourgeoisie and intelligentsia, see Claudia Kraft, "Das Galizische Bürgertum in der Autonomen Ära (1866-1914). Ein Literaturüberblick," *Polen und die böhmischen Länder im 19. und 20. Jahrhundert. Politik und Gesellschaft im Vergleich*, ed. Peter Heumos (Munich: Oldenbourg, 1997), 81-110.

7. A good survey on the little-researched Polish intelligentsia's work among the peasants in the 1860s and 1870s can be found in Ryszard Terlecki, *Oświata dorosłych i popularyzacja nauki w Galicji w okresu autonomii* (Wrocław: Ossolineum, 1990). On positivism in Galicia, see Halina Kozłowska-Sabatowska, *Ideologia pozytywizmu galicyjskiego 1864-1881* (Wrocław: Ossolineum, 1978).

8. Inglot, "Historia społeczno-gospodarcza," 248-86; Franciszek Bujak, "Wieś zachodnio-galicyjska u schyłku XIX wieku," in Franciszek Bujak, *Wybór pism*, vol. 2 (Warsaw: PWN, , 1976), 279-341; for a fairly positive picture on the situation of peasants in some Eastern Gali-

cian districts, see Stella Hryniuk, *Peasants with Promise: Ukrainians in Southeastern Galicia, 1880-1900* (Edmonton: Canadian Institute of Ukrainian Studies Press, 1991).

9. On the position of Jews in the society of the Polish Commonwealth, see M.J. Rosman, *The Lord's Jews: Magnate-Jewish Relations in the Polish-Lithuanian Commonwealth during the Eighteenth Century* (Cambridge, Mass.: Harvard University Press, 1990); Hillel Levine, *Economic Origins of Antisemitism: Poland and Its Jews in the Early Modern Period* (New Haven, Conn.: Yale University Press, 1991); Antoni Podraza, "The Jews and the Village in the Polish Commonwealth," in *The Jews in Old Poland 1000-1795*, ed. Anthony Polonsky (London: Tauris, 1993), 299-321.

10. So is the thesis of John-Paul Himka's excellent study on Eastern Galicia, "Ukrainian-Jewish Antagonism in the Galician Countryside during the Late Nineteenth Century," in *Ukrainian-Jewish Relations in Historical Perspective*, ed. Peter J. Potichnyj and Howard Aster (Edmonton: Canadian Institute of Ukrainian Studies, 1988), 111-58; see also Himka, *Galician Villagers*, 158-75.

11. Wróbel, "The Jews of Galicia," 105-8.

12. Statistics for 1889 show that Jews constituted 84.5 percent of those who made their living from trade and tavern- keeping in Galicia, i.e., 338,000 out of 400,000 people. The statistics for 1900 show a further increase in the share of Jews, up to 88 percent of all people working in trade. See Ignacy Schiper, *Dzieje handlu żydowskiego na ziemiach polskich* (Warsaw: Nakładem Centrali Związku Kupców w Warszawie, 1937), 444-47; or slightly different numbers in Wróbel, "The Jews of Galicia," 117-21. The occupational structure of the Galician Jews is also the subject of Teresa Andlauer, *Die jüdische Bevölkerung im Modernisierungsprozess Galiziens (1867-1914)* (Frankfurt am Main: Lang, 2001).

13. Władysław T. Bartoszewski, *Ethnocentrism: Beliefs and Stereotypes. A Study of Polish-Jewish Relations in the Early Twentieth Century* (Ph.D. dissertation, University of Cambridge, 1984). Alina Cała used some of the same materials, but relied more on interviews with older villagers recorded between the mid-1970s and mid-1980s, in *Wizerunek Żyda w polskiej kulturze ludowej* (Warsaw: Wydawnictwo Uniwersytetu Warszawskiego, 1992) (English version, *The Image of the Jew in Polish Folk Culture* [Jerusalem: Magness Press, 1995]).

14. Kazimierz Dobrowolski, "Chłopska kultura tradycyjna," *Etnografia polska* 1 (1958): 19-52 (a shorter English-language version is: "Peasant Traditional Culture," in *Peasant and Peasant Societies: Selected Readings*, ed. Teodor Shanin [Harmondsworth: Penguin, 1971], 277-98); William I. Thomas and Florian Znaniecki, *The Polish Peasant in Europe and America: Monograph of an Immigrant Group*, 5 vols. (Boston, 1918-1920), esp. vols. 1 and 4; Joseph Obrębski, *The Changing Peasantry of Eastern Europe*, ed. Barbara and Joel Halpern (Cambridge, Mass.: Schenkman, 1976), 21-77; Stomma, *Antropologia*.

15. Bartoszewski, *Ethnocentrism*, 181-205; Cała, *Wizerunek*, 121-30.

16. Cała, *Wizerunek*, 11-12; Stomma, *Antropologia*, 219-21.

17. Alina Cała writes about Jews as "holy strangers" in peasant culture (*Wizerunek*, 178); on the ambivalent character of the "alien," see also Bartoszewski, *Ethnocentrism*, 275-76, 290-92.

18. Ch. Chajes, "Baal-Szem-Tow u chrześcijan" in *Miesięcznik żydowski* (1934), 440-59, 550-65. In Leżajsk and Sieniawa the graves of former local tsaddiks were still revered by local peasants in the 1970s. See Bartoszewski, *Ethnocentrism*, 243-50; Cała, *Wizerunek*, 109-20, 147-8.

19. "No Jew, no merchant-no merchant, no money," went a Polish proverb. See Piotr Kraszewski, "The Image of the Jew in Polish Proverbs," *Polish Western Affairs*, no. 1 (1993): 32-33.

20. Jan Słomka, *Pamiętniki włościanina. Od dni pańszczyzny do dni dzisiejszych* (Warsaw: Ludowa Spółdzielnia Wydawnicza, 1983), 86 (English edition: *From Serfdom to Self-Government: Memoirs of a Polish Village Mayor, 1842-1927* [London: Minerva, 1941]).

21. Aleksander Hertz, *The Jews in Polish Culture* (Evanston, Ill.: Northwestern University Press, 1988), 76-78; see also Israel Bartal, "On Top of a Volcano: Jewish-Ukrainian Co-Existence as Depicted in Modern East European Jewish Literature," in *Ukrainian-Jewish Relations*, 310.

22. On the peasant papers in Galicia, see Krzysztof Dunin-Wąsowicz, *Czasopiśmiennictwo ludowe w Galicji* (Wrocław: Ossolineum, 1952); Stanisław Lato, "Galicyjska prasa 'dla ludu' 1848-1913," *Rocznik historii czasopiśmiennictwa polskiego* 2, no. 2 (1963): 57-74.

23. According to Stojałowski, a journal for peasants also had to address the "affairs of the country and the world," because "little tales and stories from history and interesting things like that which have heretofore been published in peasant papers do not teach people to be good citizens or to deal with their own affairs and those of the country. To read about what happens in the world, in the parliament, and in the Galician Sejm as well as what the simple people are doing elsewhere ... will teach our people what they can and shall do for the good of the nation and the country." See "Odezwa do wszystkich, zwłaszcza do pp. Marszałków, nauczycieli i wójtów," *Pszczółka* 1, 1 January 1876, 1; see also "Odezwa dwu redakcyi do Prześwietnych Rad powiatowych i gminnych," *Pszczółka* 4, 20 February 1878, 1.

24. See calls to organize meetings in *Wieniec* 8, 26 November 1875, 4; *Wieniec* 10, 24 December 1875, 5; *Pszczółka* 3, 4 February 1876, 3; *Pszczółka* 16, 28 July 1876, 1; *Pszczółka* 15, 25 July 1878, 2.

25. Antoni Gurnicz, *Kółka rolnicze w Galicji* (Warsaw: Ludowa Spółdzielnia Wydawnicza, 1967); Stauter-Halsted, *The Nation in the Village,* 115-42.

26. See, for example, "O wzajemnem zaufaniu i wspólnem działaniu," *Wieniec* 1, 7 January 1876, 2. *Wieniec* and *Pszczółka* contained a column "Wiadomości ze świata" in which the papers regularly also reported about the suppression of the Poles and Catholics in Prussian and Russian Poland.

27. "Gdzie korzeń złego," *Pszczółka* 2, 22 January 1880, 9; on Stojałowski's anti-liberal attitude, see also Franciszek Kącki, *Ks. Stanisław Stojałowski i jego działalność społeczno-polityczna,* vol. 1 (1845-1890) (Lwów, 1937), 57-60; on his position regarding the "Jewish question" with a palliating tendency, ibid., 88-90. On the growing antisemitism in Galicia at the end of the 1870s, see Andrzej Żbikowski, "Rozwój ideologii antysemickiej w Galicji w II poł. XIX w. Teofila Merunowicza atak na żydowskie kahały (cz. 2)," *Biuletyn Żydowskiego Instytutu Historycznego,* nos. 1-3 (1994): 21-39. On the attitude of the Galician peasant movement toward the Jews, see also Claudia Kraft, "Die jüdische Frage im Spiegel der Presseorgane und Parteiprogramme der galizischen Bauernbewegung im letzten Viertel des 19. Jahrhunderts," *Zeitschrift für Ostmitteleuropaforschung* 45 (1996): 381-409.

28. See his article written under the impact of the rise of antisemitism in Germany and Austria, "Sprawa żydowska," *Wieniec* 5, 24 February 1881, 34.

29. "Jak się bronić żydom," *Wieniec* 6, 10 March 1881, 41-42.

30. "Dwa obozy," *Wieniec* 4, 1 October 1875, 3-4.

31. Hillel Levine, "Gentry, Jews, and Serfs: The Rise of Polish Vodka," *Review: A Journal of the Fernand Braudel Center for the Study of Economies* 4, no. 2 (1980): 223-50.

32. Himka, "Ukrainian-Jewish Antagonism," 137.

33. The exceptionally high level of alcohol consumption in Galicia asserted by some contemporary authors and suggested by the numerous complaints about the *pijaństwo* of the rural population remains an issue of contention. Stella Hryniuk argues that the alcohol consumption of the Galicians at the end of the nineteenth century probably did not exceed the usual levels in other regions of Europe; see *Peasants with Promise,* 185-86; "The Peasant and Alcohol in East Galicia in the Late Nineteenth Century: a Note," *Journal of Ukrainian Studies* 11 (1986): 75-85. There is much evidence that drinking on credit was an important factor in the impoverishment of peasants. In view of the poverty of many peasants, even relatively small expenditures on alcohol might have been able to ruin them.

34. Józef Burszta, *Społeczeństwo i karczma* [Society and tavern] (Warsaw: Ludowa Spółdzielnia Wydawnicza, 1951), 170-93; Słomka, *Pamiętniki włościanina,* 83-102; see also Magdalena Opalski, *The Jewish Tavern-Keeper and His Tavern in Nineteenth-Century Polish Literature* (Jerusalem: Daf-Chen Press, 1986).

35. Between 1782 and 1809, seventy-six decrees were issued with the aim of removing the Jews from the villages. An 1840 document from the Viennese Hofkanzlei admitted that those attempts had been unsuccessful. See Roman Rozdolski, *Stosunki poddańcze w dawniej Galicji* [Subject conditions in former Galicia], vol. 1 (Warsaw: Państwowe Wydawnictwo Naukowe, 1962), 99f, 154. For similar, more "successful" attempts to drive Jews from the villages in Russian Poland, see Jürgen Hensel, "Polnische Adelsnation und jüdische Vermittler 1815-1830. Über den vergeblichen Versuch einer Judenemanzipation in einer nicht emanzipierten Gesellschaft," *Forschungen zur osteuropäischen Geschichte* 32 (1983): 71-84.

36. Burszta, *Społeczeństwo i karczma*, 98-110. On the sobriety movement of the 1840s, see Stefan Kieniewicz, *Ruch chłopski w Galicji w 1846 roku* (Wrocław: Wydawnictwo zakładu narodowego im. Ossolińskich, 1951), 69-81.

37. See, for example, the relations from the village of Tuszów, *Pszczółka* 16, 28 July 1876, and from Barzyczka near Niebylec, *Pszczółka* 10, 15 May 1884, 76.

38. Gurnicz, *Kółka rolnicze*, 61. In a debate at a convention of the TKR in March 1884, Stojałowski called the relevant paragraph the "soul" of the TKR, *Wieniec* 6, 13 March 1884, 44; see also *Wieniec* 8, 10 April 1884, 59-60; *Wieniec* 9, 24 April 1884, 69.

39. *Instrukcya dla kółek rolniczych* (Lwów, 1883), 2.

40. Ibid. This was also an often discussed subject in the newspapers. See, for example, "O weselach po wsiach," *Wieniec* 4, 14 February 1884, 31. A letter "Z pod Mielca," contains a description of two modest weddings that are presented as models, *Pszczółka* 7, 3 April 1884, 53; another letter reports that "more educated peasants" no longer had their wedding feasts in the tavern, "Z Barzyczki pod Niebylcem," *Pszczółka* 10, 15 May 1884, 76. A critique of excessive wedding feasts still taking place can be found in a letter from Lubocza, *Wieniec* 1, 4 January 1884, 5.

41. For a description of earlier wedding customs, see Słomka, *Pamiętniki włościanina*, 107-14; on the shortening of weddings at the end of the nineteenth century, see also Jan Madejczyk, *Wspomnienia* (Warsaw: Ludowa Spółdzielnia Wydawnicza, 1965), 26.

42. *Pszczółka* 12, 13 June 1878, 1-2.

43. *Wieniec* 10, 24 December 1875, 7. A correspondent from Lubatówka describes the improvement of the peasants' economic situation after the reduction of the alcohol consumption in his village, *Pszczółka* 4, 17 February 1876, 2.

44. On the village of Tuligłowy, *Wieniec* 6, 10 March 1876, 3; on Zazdrość/Zazdrist' in the district of Trembowla/Terebovlja, *Pszczółka* 2, 10 January 1884, 3; on Barzyczka near Niebylec, *Pszczółka* 10, 15 May 1885, 76; on Radawa near Jarosław, *Wieniec Polski* 4, 19 April 1885, 30; on Łozów/Lozova in the district of Tarnopol/Ternopil', *Pszczółka* 26, 23 December 1884, 222-23; and on Borek Szlachecki, *Wieniec* 10, 8 May 1884, 78.

45. Until these years the proportion of Jews residing in the countryside grew at the expense of the Jewish urban population. After 1889, some rural areas in Western Galicia also had an immigration of Jews when the average urbanization rate rose. See Sławomir Tokarski, *Ethnic Conflict and Economic Development: Jews in Galician Agriculture 1868-1914* (Ph.D. dissertation, European University Institute, Florence, 1995), 69, 324. See also the letter from Cerekiew, *Pszczółka* 16, 28 July 1876, 3; for Eastern Galicia, see Himka, "Ukrainian-Jewish Antagonism," 124-31.

46. Zofia Daszyńska-Golińska, "Alkoholismus und soziale Verhältnisse in einigen galizischen Bezirken," *Separatabdruck aus der Internationalen Monatsschrift*, no. 4 (April 1901): 6. See also the memoirs of the peasant activists Słomka and Magryś, both of whom were abstinent. Słomka, *Pamiętniki włościanina*, 118; Franciszek Magryś, *Żywot chłopa działacza* (Warsaw: Ludowa Spółdzielnia Wydawnicza, 1987), 43.

47. This has been shown for the Ruthenian villages by Himka, *Galician Villagers*, 175-89. Among the Polish peasants this was quite similar. See Stauter-Halsted, *The Nation in the Village*, 78-91.

48. Zofia Daszyńska-Golińska called alcoholism a kind of "occupational disease" of the village mayors ("Alkoholismus," 7).

49. Józef Kleczyński, "Życie gminne w Galicyi," *Wiadomości o stosunkach krajowych* 4 (1878): 97-279.

50. *Wieniec* 7, 24 March 1876, 5.

51. See, for example, the letter from Ujście Solne where, although the election had taken place in the tavern, the new abstinent mayor forbade music in the tavern on Sundays and holidays, *Pszczółka* 4, 17 February 1876, 5; see also M.D., "Z pod Baranowa," *Pszczółka* 2, 14 January 1876, 4.

52. See the letter from the village Kopki, *Pszczółka* 18, 24 August 1876, 3.

53. In a letter from the village Baczków, the anonymous correspondent S.B. described the reaction when he spoke against the election of a drinking mayor: "I stood up and asked: 'What are you doing, he will sell the whole village for a glass of vodka.' On that immediately rose voices: 'What kind of mayor would it be who would not drink vodka, and what kind of deal could one make with him—if he would not drink, neither would the whole village.'" *Pszczółka* 5, 4 March 1876, 4. This letter describes a mayor who regularly organized parties and dances in the tavern.

54. For such conflicts and complaints about the influence of Jews on the elections see, for example, *Pszczółka* 8 i 9, 14 April 1876, 4; F.K. from Jazłowiec, *Wieniec* 7, 24 March 1876, 5; Himka, "Ukrainian-Jewish Antagonism," 139.

55. Tokarski, *Ethnic Conflict*, 114-20; Himka, "Ukrainian-Jewish Antagonism," 121.

56. Leopold Caro, "Lichwa na wsi w Galicyi w latach 1875-1891," *Wiadomości statystyczne o stosunkach krajowych* 14, no. 2 (1893): 1-50. See also, for example, Słomka's account of the credit conditions in his village Dzików where many peasants lost land to Jewish moneylenders, *Pamiętniki włościanina*, 89-95.

57. The data on forced land sales have been analyzed in detail by Tokarski, *Ethnic Conflict*, 123-85. They were regularly published in the journal of the Statistical Biuro, the *Wiadomości Statystyczne o Stosunkach Krajowych*. On the *Bank włościański*, see Leopold Caro, "Bank wtościański w Galicyi (1868-1884)," in Leopold Caro, *Studya społeczne* (Cracow: Czas, 1908), 52-124.

58. Caro, "Lichwa na wsi," 26. Few worked very well. But after 1887 a new law allowed a tighter control of the district authorities, which was to secure a better administration and prevent fraud.

59. Tokarski, *Ethnic Conflict*, 142-47.

60. Ibid., 149-53, 166. These cooperatives usually were called *kasy Stefczyka* after Franciszek Stefczyk, who introduced and promoted them in Galicia.

61. See, for example, the campaign for the foundation of savings and loan associations, which Stojałowski began in 1878, "O wydobywaniu się z biedy. Tani kredyt, czyli tania i korzystna pożyczka," *Pszczółka* 12, 13 June 1878, 3-4; "Kasy zaliczkowe oparte na 'własnej pomocy,'" *Pszczółka* 13, 27 June 1878, 2-3.

62. Tomasz Gąsowski, "From *Austeria* to the Manor: Jewish Landowners in Autonomous Galicia," *Polin* 12 (1999), 125; Himka, "Ukrainian-Jewish Antagonism," 126.

63. Franciszek Morawski, "Dzierżawy w obrębie własności tabularnej w Galicyi. Na podstawie sprawozdań Wydziałów powiatowych," *Wiadomości statystyczne o stosunkach krajowych* 15. zesz. 2 (1895), 19.

64. Gąsowski, "From *Austeria* to the Manor," 131-35.

65. Caro, "Lichwa na wsi," 42-43.

66. In 1899, for example, peasant deputies in the Galician diet proposed a bill meant both to help peasants acquire estate land and was directed against Jewish intermediaries. See Antoni Gurnicz, *O "równą miarkę" dla chłopów. Poglądy i działalność pierwszej chłopskiej organizacji politycznej w Polsce Związku Stronnictwa Chłopskiego 1893-1908* (Warsaw: Ludowa Spółdzielnia Wydawnicza, 1963), 173-74. That same year, under the influence of the *Stronnictwo Ludowe*, the *Bank parcelacyjny* was founded. It helped Polish peasants buy land.

67. The peasant writer Franciszek Magryś commented on the Jewish purchase of estates: "It is very strange for us that the *panowie* sell the soil which their ancestors paid with blood in that way. It is true that also peasants sell a lot of their patrimony, but they do so because they are uneducated and many of them even do not know what patronal land is [*ojczysta ziemia*, probably it is impossible to translate that term accurately. It means the land inherited from the forefathers and contains an obligation to preserve that land. It is close to the term *ojczyzna* = fatherland]. If it continues this way, I do not know what will happen to us-the *panowie* should provide us, their little brothers, a good example and defend their patrimony." Magryś, "Z Handzlówki w pow. Łańcuckim," *Wieniec Polski* 2, 15 March 1885, 14. Similarly, on the sale of land to Jews, see "Z Morawska koło Jarosławia," *Pszczółka* 3, 7 February 1884, 19; "Z powiatu Brzeskiego," *Pszczółka* 13, 26 June 1884, 102; *Wieniec* 10, 8 May 1884, 78; Michał Tworek, "Trwoniciele," *Przyjaciel Ludu* 43, 25 October 1903, 3-4, and 45, 8 November 1903, 5-6f.; Słomka, *Pamiętnik włościanina*, 92-94; see also Wincenty Witos, *Moje Wspomnienia*, część I (Warsaw: Ludowa Spółdzielnia Wydawnicza, 1988), 182.

68. For example, see "Zakładanie sklepików wiejskich," *Wieniec* 1, 1 January 1881, 2-3.

69. Gurnicz, *Kółka rolnicze*, 251. From Jan Madejczyk's memoirs: "When agrarian circles were first founded, the intelligentsia's aim was to improve agriculture; the peasants predominantly thought it to be a shop where they could purchase certain goods" (*Wspomnienia*, 56).

70. In the village of Żmiąca an agrarian circle founded in 1885 soon showed few signs of life. It was revived only in 1899 when the peasants wanted to have their own shop. See Franciszek Bujak, *Żmiąca. Wieś powiatu limanowskiego* (Cracow: Gebethner i Spółka, 1903), 105.

71. Gurnicz, *Kółka rolnicze*, 244-51; for the opposition of Jewish competitors to the foundation of "Christian" shops, see Jadwiga Dawidowa, *Kółka rolnicze w Galicyi* (Warsaw, 1890), 25-28.

72. On these processes, see Stauter-Halsted, *The Nation in the Village*, 216-42.

73. Andrzej Kudłaszyk, *Myśl społeczno-polityczna Bolesława Wysłoucha 1855-1937* (Warsaw, Wrocław, 1978); Peter Brock, "Pioneer of Polish Populism," in Peter Brock, *Nationalism and Populism in Partitioned Poland. Selected Essays* (London: Orbis Books, 1973), 181-211.

74. Gurnicz, *O "równą miarkę" dla chłopów.*

75. Wilhelm Feldman, *Stronnictwa i programy polityczne w Galicyi 1846-1906*, vol. 2 (Cracow, 1907), 235-64.

76. Frank Golczewski, *Polnisch-jüdische Beziehungen 1881-1922. Eine Studie zur Geschichte des Antisemitismus in Osteuropa* (Wiesbaden: Steiner, 1981), 60-84; idem, "Rural Anti-Semitism in Galicia before World War I," in *The Jews in Poland*, ed. Chimen Abramsky, et. al. (Oxford: Blackwell, 1986), 97-105.

77. Golczewski, *Polnisch-jüdische Beziehungen*, 70-71; Jan Stapiński, *Pamiętnik*, ed. Krzysztof Dunin-Wąsowicz (Warsaw: Ludowa Spóldzielnia Wydawnicza, 1959), 141.

78. "Do Braci Wyborców z 7-miu powiatów Sanok, Krosno, Jasło, Brzożów, Lisko, Dobromil, Staremiasto, do naszych przyjaciół, zwolenników i wszystkich ludzi dobrej woli," *Wieniec Polski* 18, 20 June 1898, 285-86; "Stapiński i jego przyjaciele," Ibid., 286-87. In general, the frequency of anti-Jewish subjects in Stojałowski's papers had increased compared to the preceding years. See also Golczewski, "Rural antisemitism," 102-3.

79. See, for example, the letter of the Galician viceroy to the *Starosts* from 1 July 1898, Centralnyi derzhavnyi istorychnyi arkhiv Ukrajiny u Lvovi fond 146, op. 6, od. zb. 106/3, pp. 366aff. One aim of the Viceroy's office was also to use the unrest to crush radical political groups, including Stojałowski's party. That probably explains the large area put under martial law, exceeding the actual territory of the unrest as well as the long duration of martial law.

80. Golczewski, *Polnisch-jüdische Beziehungen*, 73-74; see also the quite antisemitic Karol Marcinkowski, *Krwawe nieszpory we Frysztaku w 1898 r.* (Philadelphia: Tow. im. Romana Dmowskiego, 1983).

81. See the statistical survey of the Ministery of Justice from 17 November 1898, Archiwum Główne Akt Dawnych we Warszawie, C.k. ministerstwo sprawiedliwości, sygn. 307, act no. 93. On arrests and criminal proceedings, see *Przyjaciel Ludu* 21, 20 July 1898, 305.

82. The statements of the defendants at the trials on the length varied between six days and three month. See Golczewski, *Polnisch-jüdische Beziehungen*, 76-78.

83. "Głos chrześcijańsko-ludowego Koła pols. w sprawie zaburzeń w Galicyi," *Wieniec Polski* 19, 1 July 1898, 305-08.

84. "'Ktoś' i 'coś,'" *Związek Chłopski* 20, 6 July 1898, 153; see also the declaration of the editors in "Nadzwyczajny dodatek do Nru 19 'Związku Chłópskiego' z dnia 1. lipca 1898,"; on the antisemitism of the *Związek Chłopski*, the paper of the ZSCh, see Kraft, "Die jüdische Frage," 397-400; Golczewski, *Polnisch-jüdische Beziehungen*, 66-70.

85. "Skutki nędzy i ciemnoty," *Przyjaciel Ludu* 19, 1 July 1898, 283.

86. See also Kai Struve, "Die Juden in der Sicht der polnischen Bauernparteien bis 1939," *Zeitschrift für Ostmitteleuropaforschung* 48, no. 2 (1999): 184-225.

87. The "Szkice programowe" of 1886 can be found in *Programy stronnictw ludowych*, ed. Stanisław Lato and Witold Stankiewicz (Warsaw: Państwowe Wydawnictwo Naukowe, 1969), 27-48; on the Jews, 47-48. The term *lud* is insufficiently translated as "people." In fact, in the political discourse of the end of the nineteenth century it meant the peasants, at least when the urban *lud*, the workers and other "uneducated" inhabitants of the cities, were not mentioned explicitly, although there were more sophisticated definitions in theoretical discussion. On the *lud*, see also Brian Porter, *When Nationalism Began to Hate: Imagining Modern Politics in Nineteenth-Century Poland* (New York: Oxford University Press, 2000), 104-17. Porter analyzes this term in the political language of the Polish National Democrats in the Russian partition. In the 1880s, that group's ideas were similar to those Wysłouch voiced in Galicia, but later the National Democrats became increasingly nationalistic and forgot their social concerns.

88. *Programy stronnictw ludowych*, 73.

89. Emanuel Melzer, "Antisemitism in the Last Years of the Second Polish Republic," in *The Jews of Poland Between Two World Wars*, ed. Yisrael Gutman et al. (Hanover, N.H.: University Press of New England, 1989), 127-37; Anna Landau-Czajka, "Koncepcje rozwiązania kwestii żydowskiej w programach polskich stronnictw politycznych lat 1933-1939," *Przegląd historyczny* 87 (1996): 549-62; for the peasant parties in this period, see Struve, "Die Juden in der Sicht der polnischen Bauernparteien," 218-25.

90. Stanisław Kowalczyk et al., *Zarys historii ruchu ludowego*, vol. 1, 1864-1918 (Warsaw: Ludowa Spółdzielnia Wydawnicza, 1963), 73. The governor at that time was Michał Bobrzyński, whose memoirs mention the attempts of Stapiński and the other peasant deputies to promote the granting of concessions for their supporters, but deny that this lobbying influenced the procedure. Michał Bobrzyński, *Z moich pamiętników* (Wrocław: Ossolineum, 1957), 63, 72. Schiper writes that in 1911 only 8,000 of 20,000 Jewish families that had lived before from the trade with alcohol remained in that business, (*Dzieje handlu żydowskiego*, 451).

Chapter 6

NATIONALIZING RURAL LANDSCAPES IN CISLEITHANIA, 1880-1914[1]

Pieter M. Judson

"German Festival Participants Attacked and Beaten Bloody"[2]

What actually happened at Bergreichenstein/Kašperské Hory on the night of 7 September 1908 was never clearly established. That week, members of the *Deutscher Böhmerwaldbund* (German Union for the Bohemian Woods) converged on this small southern Bohemian village for their association's annual convention.[3] The two-day annual ritual, a combination of hortatory speeches and celebratory festival, spilled out of the local inn and onto the flag bedecked village streets, where late at night, some of the more aggressive members demonstrated their German solidarity in front of the *beseda*, the building that accommodated the local Czech cultural and nationalist center. Did the drunken revelers force their way into the *beseda*, smash furniture and threaten the few terrified men and women they found cowering upstairs? Or did the brazen occupants of the house hurl stones provocatively from the upper floor windows, wounding several of the harmless revelers below? Was the *beseda* vandalized? Were several students below actually wounded by the stones? Rumors of all kinds quickly spread to the surrounding hamlets and villages.[4]

The next day, a hostile crowd of Czech nationalists eager to revenge the real or imagined attack of the night before ambushed some departing *Böhmerwaldbund* members as they passed through Schüttenhofen/Sušice, the nearest town with a regional railway connection. Yelling nationalist slogans, the angry demonstrators pelted the surprised travelers with stones, injuring several of them, and forcing them to take refuge in a local inn. When news of this latest attack reached

Notes for this section begin on page 146.

Bergreichenstein, angry German nationalist demonstrators gathered in the village square, protesting the violence in Schüttenhofen and calling for prompt police action against the Czech nationalists. The local district administrators, portrayed in German nationalist accounts as Czech sympathizers, feared violence. They called in both district gendarmes and military reinforcements, and the former used their bayonets to drive back the crowd. During this brief action they wounded several German activists, one of whom later died. Some time later the demonstrators heard the cavalry approach. Believing the soldiers had arrived to aid them against imagined Czech nationalist attacks, the German nationalist demonstrators greeted them with shouts of "Heil." In a flash, however, a cavalry charge cleared the square and nearby streets, throwing several surprised bystanders to the ground. When another group of *Böhmerwaldbünd* members made its way to Schüttenhofen the next day, this time under heavy military guard, it too was attacked with stones, and once again several association members took refuge in a local hotel until the enraged crowds had dispersed.[5]

In the wake of the violence at Bergreichenstein, Schüttenhofen, and some surrounding villages, all sides demanded justice from the state, calling upon their political leaders to investigate the matter thoroughly. This set of incidents provided nationalist activists on both sides with new ammunition for their respective propaganda arsenals. Newspapers kept Bergreichenstein before the public, reporting horrific new details of atrocities perpetrated by one side against the other as they emerged from eyewitness interviews. Bergreichenstein remained front-page news in Bohemia for more than a week until far more destructive street rioting by Slovene nationalists against German-owned property in Laibach/Ljubljana, capital of Carniola, stole the headlines from the Bohemians. By late September, German nationalist newspapers could speak of a coordinated Slav attack on Germans and their property throughout the Monarchy. They used this opportunity to urge Germans of all social classes to form a united political front. Czech and Slovene nationalists, meanwhile, called for Slav unity against German arrogance in all linguistically mixed regions of the Monarchy.

In their respective editorials, Czech and German nationalist newspapers agreed on one crucial element of this story, namely its underlying nationalist significance. A conflict had broken out in Bergreichenstein among people highly sensitized to the importance of nationalist issues. No matter who was at fault, the rural inhabitants of Bergreichenstein and Schüttenhofen clearly took their nationalist identity as seriously as did their urban counterparts who frequently fought each other in the streets of Prague. And while both sides may have claimed to deplore the violent incident, both saw the incident as proof that the rural peasant masses cared deeply about nationalist goals.

Vandalism, name-calling, stone throwing, and brawling had long-established traditions in rural Austria, but the attachment of nationalist significance to such incidents around 1900 was relatively new.[6] Bergreichenstein also seemed exceptional because one of its inhabitants had been killed. In other respects, however, the Bergreichenstein incident typified a striking development in rural areas of multilanguage use such as the Bohemian Woods, South Styria, and the South Tirol between 1880 and 1914: the rise of violent incidents that could be traced directly to nationalist causes. Nationalist conflict appeared increasingly to permeate every aspect of public life in these crownlands, even in rural areas. The reader of any one of several village newspapers from these areas in 1908 would be easily forgiven for imagining that a war raged, a war for national territory, for ownership of squares, markets, and country paths, a war for control of the very sidewalks themselves. Villages such as Bergreichenstein brought to mind tiny tinderboxes: capable at any moment of bursting into flame when one side might find it necessary to defend itself against the apparent incursions of the nationalist Other. Contemporary observers (and later historians) concluded from such incidents that the nationalities' conflict dominating political life in Austria's cities and legislative institutions had now swallowed up the countryside, as well.[7]

The skeptical historian can interrogate the nationalist reading of these events from at least two perspectives. The first focuses on the journalistic portrayals of the incident: to what degree did the way the local press recounted these events create the unquestioned nationalist significance they were assigned? Did nationalist newspapers and local politicians portray such incidents in terms that those who had experienced them would actually have recognized? Did village stone throwers in Bergreichenstein connect their own interests to the abstract concept of an embattled nation? Or were they perhaps striking a blow for their village against the perceived incursions of a diverse array of outsiders? The latter view might seem reasonable, given traditional rural suspicions directed against outsiders of all kinds, but it needs further interrogation. It is too convenient to presume that embattled villagers simply conflated the category outsider with a particular nationalist group of others. We also know from several local studies of rural Europeans during this period that peasants as often as not welcomed connections to the outside world brought by outsiders, if those connections were perceived to generate greater social mobility or access to new resources.[8] A second way to interrogate the nationalist quality of these events is to question not their nationalist significance but rather the claim that they incited the active participation of socially near-universal categories like "the peasants." A careful examination of events might suggest that despite the best efforts of newspapers to depict rural nationalist violence as a socially universal phenomenon, in fact their accounts too easily elided the activism of a rural nationalist minority with the notion of a nationalized peasantry.[9]

In this essay I investigate changing constructions of the national Other propagated by German nationalist associations who struggled to gain a foothold in rural villages such as Bergreichenstein. I argue that these constructions aimed to nationalize German-speaking peasants, but that ultimately their failure to do so adequately, coupled with the transformation of the rural world around 1900, produced an attempt to nationalize the idea of the rural landscape instead. An analysis of nationalist depictions of rural life from 1880 until 1914, along with evidence culled from associational records and newspapers, suggests that while nationalist activism did indeed take root in the Austrian countryside after 1900, it did not necessarily involve a mobilization of the traditional rural or peasant population.

For two decades urban German nationalist activists could report frustratingly few successes in their efforts to mobilize rural Austrians. In the 1880s, as German nationalism took off in the cities, activists regularly bemoaned peasant indifference to the nationalist cause. Early German nationalist campaigns directed at the peasantry clearly derived from liberal cultural strategies of the 1860s and 1870s. Liberal politicians had defined a broad mission that sought to enlighten the supposedly ignorant rural masses, to weaken their religious ties, and to make model citizens of them. Liberals had built libraries, founded newspapers, organized economic self-help institutions, and legislated a school system in order to bring peasants the benefits of modernity. The early nationalists, too, adopted this one-dimensional liberal attitude toward rural life in concocting their appeals. Their publications for country readers, for example, focused on defining appropriate German behavior for their rough audience and avoided any mention of the nationalist enemy. Articles entitled "Useful hints for the Home," "The Golden Rules of Business," and "The Ten Commandments of the German Farmer," all stressed the importance of thrift, sobriety, punctuality, and technical proficiency to their rural audience.[10]

Activists' attempts to help rural Austrians understand their world in nationalist terms went hand in hand with continued efforts to build up nationalist organizations in the countryside. Yet nationalist associations experienced some difficulty establishing branches in the linguistically mixed rural areas where they hoped to recruit peasants. Their condescending didactic propaganda had little impact on the rural communities they sought to win for their operations. Membership in these organizations grew slowly and unevenly. At the time of the 1897 Badeni crisis, for example, a considerable wave of new members signed up to join several of the nationalist associations. Yet within a year or two, leaders complained bitterly that the level of commitment displayed by the new rural activists left much to be desired, and membership numbers soon declined. A series of political reforms around the turn of the century, culminating in universal manhood suffrage in 1907, did give more and more peasants a vote in Reichsrat elections, bringing them into closer contact with regional and national party organizations at election time. Yet peasant voting behavior itself conveyed an ambivalent picture where nationalist issues were concerned. German-speaking peasants in the Bohemian Woods, for example, voted overwhelmingly for a German Agrarian Party that acknowledged the abstract importance of nationalism, but defined itself as often according to peasant economic needs.[11]

At first glance most rural nationalist violence does seem to have been sparked by the kind of local self-defense issues traditionally associated with a peasant milieu, issues primarily understood in territorial terms. Already in the 1880s, but far more frequently after 1900, violent incidents attended nationalist festivals held in so-called threatened regions. Celebrations by one group were increasingly met with carefully planned protests by another group. And this makes sense, for most such celebrations were designed to assert the national identity of a disputed place. When violence broke out, observers on both sides interpreted it as an organic reaction. They stressed the strong nationalist identity of the peasant inhabitants, driven by outside provocation to defend their archaic national identity. Yet despite the insistent logic of such journalistic portrayals, further investigation suggests that such incidents had little to do with a local peasant defense of national identity. Given the overwhelming evidence of increasing rural nationalist violence after the turn of the century, we must still ask: who rioted and why?

Whose Violence?

In the decade after 1900, the rural nationalist situation seemed to change qualitatively as more and more villages reported both the establishment of nationalist organization branches and an increased intensity of regional activism. Urban nationalists, too, seemed to pay closer attention to the peculiarities of rural experience in order to convey their own worldview more convincingly to the locals. But by this point, rural experience itself had changed dramatically. Nationalist successes did not take place in a social vacuum, nor did they necessarily involve the traditional rural peasant population as much as the organizations themselves liked to claim. During the late nineteenth century, expanding networks of state administration, transportation, communications, and commercial markets increasingly brought an influx of teachers, civil servants, railroad employees, telegraph operators, credit officers, and tourists to rural areas. The growing nationalist success in rural Austria after 1900 depended in large part on the influence, activism, and loyalties of these new figures in the local landscape.

Those who organized nationalist incidents or provoked counterattacks, as well as their opponents, often turned out to have been more recently arrived white-collar workers, teachers, civil servants, railway workers, and innkeepers. These recent arrivals did not simply provide the catalyst that sparked organic peasant violence. Often the brawlers themselves were urban outsiders or students, brought in for the occasion with promises of money and free beer. Far from an archaic local peasant response to outside intrusion, nationalist violence engaged relatively new social groups in the countryside. And yet newspaper accounts inevitably tried to characterize the brawlers as authentic fixtures in the rural landscape.

An early nationalist incident in the South Styrian village of St. Georgen an der Südbahn/Sv. Jurij na juzni zeleznici (population ca. 500) in 1884 provides an early example of these dynamics. An attempt by local German speakers to found a branch of the German School Association (*Deutscher Schulverein*) there produced a brawl that eventually brought police intervention. Both German and Slovene nationalist newspapers agreed upon the bare facts of the story: German nationalists from nearby villages had been invited to help inaugurate the new association, among them over a hundred outsiders who arrived in St. Georgen that morning by train from the city of Cilli/Celje. When the German nationalists tried to hold their meeting in a local inn, they claimed to have been heckled and then physically attacked by Slovene nationalist peasants. While the women took refuge in the kitchen (and, it was claimed by one newspaper, held a Slovene kitchen boy captive, threatening to roast him on the stove), the men fought off the Slovene nationalist attack. When the police arrived, they arrested three Slovene nationalist activists and escorted the German nationalists back to the train for the return trip to Cilli.

As more details of the incident emerged, it turned out that many of those who had fought for the Germans had been promised money and free beer to make the trip from Cilli. Similarly, Slovene nationalist leaders had gathered their own outsiders from the surrounding villages beforehand and instructed them to disrupt the meeting. The Slovene papers ridiculed the contention that St. Georgen needed a branch of the German School Association, claiming that only three or four German-speaking families lived there in the first place. To the Slovene nationalists, the only apparent purpose of founding a local association in St. Georgen was to Germanize the local population. German newspapers claimed, in turn, that the hard-pressed local German minority had requested help in founding a local branch of the School Association from the influential Cilli branch. Both sides asserted their right to organize locally, and each accused the other of being the tool of outsiders who did not belong in the area.[12]

Far from signifying an organic response by defensive peasants, nationalist violence reflected some powerful concerns created by what we might call "white-collar invaders." Their growing presence in rural villages and towns, as well as their nationalist activism, is suggested by an examination of regional associational records. In the years after 1900, urban-based associations like the *Böhmerwaldbund*, the German School Association, and the *Bund der Deutschen in Böhmen* (League of Germans in Bohemia) started taking root in more rural parts of Bohemia. An 1896 survey of local branches of the League of Germans in Bohemia, for example, showed that only four villages in the primarily rural Bohemian Woods region could boast local branches of the organization (total membership: 426). In a 1909 survey, however, the Bohemian Woods region alone (leaving aside the predominantly urban Budweis and Linz branches) counted 35 branches of the Bund with a total of 2,362 members. Among these was Bergreichenstein's with 139 members.[13]

The annual published lists of local branch secretaries for the two years yields further suggestive evidence for an "invasion of the countryside." Whereas in 1896 close to 40 percent of local club secretaries had belonged to what we might call the traditional rural *Mittelstand*—independent craftsmen and small retail merchants—by 1909 that figure had shrunk by more than half to just 18 percent. Instead, school employees who in 1896 had made up only 5 percent of the total now predominated among the secretaries with 30 percent. In fact, white-collar workers as a whole, who had constituted about a quarter of the officers in 1896, now made up over 50 percent of the total. Since membership statistics by occupation are only available for associational officers and not for the membership at large, we cannot place too much significance on these statistics alone. Neverthe-less, when considered in the context of local newspaper accounts, associational reports, and associational publications like almanacs, these statistics give us a sense of how the nationalist growth in the countryside proceeded and how its for-tunes were linked to the increased presence of schools, railroads, regional market opportunities, and tourists.

A look at *Deutsch Böhmerwald*, a Prachatitz/Prachatice weekly that served Bergreichenstein and its neighboring villages (and whose monthly supplement was entitled *Der Bauer*) confirms the leading role that educators and other new arrivals played in shaping programs and directing the nationalist movements at the local level. To the local nationalists the challenge was not simply to broaden participation in village associational life but to reorient its perceived tasks, and ultimately to redefine for Bergreichensteiners their very sense of community identity. Thus in 1908, during the fateful months leading up to the bloody acts of September, we find weekly articles addressing all manner of local economic and cultural concerns expressed in a highly nationalist rhetoric. This rhetoric, in turn, equated nationalist positions with progress and modernity. And this nationalism was no backward-looking ideology designed to revive a rural past utopia, but a vibrantly progressive creed that embraced change for the sake of national improvement. The *Deutsch Böhmerwald* consistently equated the village community's interests with increased education, communications and trans-portation infrastructure, commerce, and tourism. Each of these fields offered unlimited possibilities for increased social mobility and prosperity. The success or failure of these important local initiatives, however, was bound up with the abil-ity of the German national community to determine its own future.[14]

The fact that Bergreichenstein, with a majority of German speakers, was attached to a predominantly Czech-speaking district that exercised considerable political power over its fate was a constant theme in the *Deutsch Böhmerwald*'s pages. The paper consistently blamed what it labeled hostile Czech administra-tors for supposedly ignoring village roads in dire need of repair. The paper claimed that Czech nationalist bureaucrats consistently thwarted Bergreichen-stein's efforts to gain a rail link to the Southern Bohemian rail system, a factor that would improve tourism and winter sport possibilities significantly. The same administrators imposed bilingual signs on Bergreichenstein, despite the fact that only 5 percent of its inhabitants reported Czech as their language of daily use in the census. The paper constantly reiterated the "fact" that the only Czech speak-ers in town were the hand-full of district civil servants. Countless articles extolled the civic, and by extension the nationalist, activism of the local German teachers, administrators, and white-collar workers. Their efforts brought a new vocation-al school, adult agricultural classes, a successful town beautification campaign, a swimming pond with summer swim classes, the renovation of a local castle ruin, and the promotion of winter sport to Bergreichenstein.

Virtually no one at the time remarked on the fact that through their civic activism, the new white-collar arrivals to town had swiftly come to define themselves as authentic insiders with the right to set the local agenda. This is suggested by the equally voluminous stream of self-critical newspaper articles that found fault with traditional Bergreichensteiners' insularity. How could the village attract tourists, for example, if local Germans failed to provide the proper amenities? How could villagers hope to compete with crafty Czechs in shops or on market day when the latter behaved with a higher degree of courtesy and deference towards tourists? Why did short-sighted Germans close their shops earlier in the afternoon than did their Czech counterparts? The local German community would have to hone its competitive edge if it hoped to vanquish the Czechs. Only through a consistent policy of modernization could the German community actually come to embody the higher cultural qualities that (ironically) by definition made it superior to all other peoples.

Earlier Constructions of the Rural Other: Peasant against Peasant

The growing importance of these white-collar invaders to the rise of a local nationalist politics is reflected in the changing ways the nationalist associations constructed national others in their publications. In what follows I use examples of fiction aimed specifically at rural audiences culled from German nationalist almanacs (*Volkskalender*) to illustrate this transformation. The almanac served as a source of important annual information: it included a lunar calendar, weather predictions, and postal rates, and it listed the dates and locations for annual regional markets and fairs. It published informational pieces on farming technology and short works of fiction or poetry. After 1880 the almanacs increasingly carried illustrations, advertisements, and mail order offers.

Starting in the 1860s, some liberal political associations had begun issuing such almanacs as alternatives to the religious ones purveyed by the Catholic Church. In the 1880s, early nationalist self-help organizations like the German School Association, itself a product of the liberal political milieu, began publishing their own annual almanacs, as well. Continuing the pedagogical approach of the liberals, the School Association published educational pieces, but very little specifically nationalist material, and nothing that directly mentioned the enemy. Other organizations soon followed suit. Given their regional organizational biases, the nationalist associations frequently used the early almanacs as a vehicle both to teach local Germans about their region's heritage, and to introduce them to other territories within the Monarchy where German-speaking populations lived. They also published articles that attempted to define the content of a German national identity and the particular qualities of Germanness for their readers. But as mentioned above, these early nationalist almanacs said almost nothing about a nationalist Other. They made few references to the qualities embodied by rival peoples, and this makes sense if we consider that the immediate task confronting the early nationalist associations was to imbue rural populations with a rudimentary sense of their own nationality, to convince German speakers to become in fact Germans.

The few examples of almanac fiction that raise the issue of the Other did so in terms both highly localized and intimate. They recounted private tragedies that resulted from dangerous social interaction between peoples. The narratives did incorporate some telling details that skillfully conveyed an implicit portrait of the nationalist Other. They also managed to weave in a bare minimum of contextual material explaining why there was a national problem in the first place. This historical background, however, was always incidental to the story. Neither the state nor politics is ever mentioned. It is the tragic personal outcome alone that conveyed the necessity of taking a strong stand on abstract nationalist issues.

"Eine Mischheirat" ("A Mixed Marriage") by German radical nationalist Karl Türk appeared (among other places) in the *Deutscher Volks-Kalender für Schlesien* published by the nationalist organization *Nordmark* for Moravia and Austrian Silesia in 1898. The story takes place in rural Moravia. Josef, the only son of a wealthy German-speaking peasant family in Feldsbach, loves Boženka, daughter of a wealthy family in the nearby Czech village of Velka. Josef's parents are dead set against the match. The only context with which Türk provides the reader is the parents' observation that the Czech-German relationship had not always been a hostile one. As a child, for example, his parents had sent Josef to live with Boženka's family for two years, as part of an exchange, so that he might learn the other language.[15] This relatively cordial relationship changed as the local Czechs had fallen under the sway of political nationalism. This development had negated their potentially positive characteristics and brought out the bad elements of the Slavic character, many of which were enumerated during the course of the story. When Josef points out that Boženka has a dowry of 6,000 gulden, his father answers that in earlier times, when the Czechs were harmless, he might have welcomed the match. Nowadays, however, the Czech nationalists are always looking for ways to insinuate themselves into purely German communities. "It would be a scandal for me as town councilor and for the entire village," he exclaims, "if I were responsible for helping these new Czechs to gain a foothold here!"

Josef answers that his personal affairs are none of the council's or the village's business, a statement that directly contradicts nationalist teachings that the personal is in fact political when it comes to national defense. Josef continues his visits heedless of his father's frequent warnings that "Boženka is an obstinate Slav through and through who will do her best to Czechify the family; she knows nothing about viticulture, she will bring ruin upon the family." At the climax of the story a fateful encounter helps seal Josef's destiny. One Sunday he meets the town Jew, a trader on his way to Velka for business. The "always talkative and inquisitive Jew" soon elicits the whole story from young Josef, and offers him this advice:

Don't pay any attention to your father. Germans are always telling me I'm not a real German and the Czechs are always saying I'm not a real Czech, *although I speak both languages perfectly* [emphasis added].... Learn a lesson from me—I don't pay any attention to national status of any kind. You should marry wherever you find it advantageous to do so. And once you're married, your father will forget about the whole thing.[16]

Josef and Boženka are married, although Josef's father refuses to attend the wedding. His mother, who makes the trip, is treated as an outsider at the wedding since she cannot speak Czech, and Boženka's family makes little effort to befriend her. Josef's parents generously give their son the estate and move to a small outbuilding. Boženka, indeed, brings a 6,000-gulden dowry, but to obtain it, Josef has to sign a contract making her co-owner of the farm. From this moment Josef's fortunes decline dramatically. Boženka does not get along with the servants and the farmhands, so she fires them all and replaces them with Czechs from her own village. The farm is rapidly transformed into a tiny Czech colony where both German language and customs are quickly forgotten. Worse, the German sense for order and cleanliness are forgotten, as well. And they are not replaced with a traditional Slavic simplicity, Türk tells us, but with the lazy, arrogant qualities that reflect the shadow side of the Slavic character. Josef, for all of his good German efforts, cannot keep the estate from financial deterioration. His children have trouble at school, because they never speak German at home. They grow up hating German and the other German-speaking village children. Josef dies at the age of thirty-three, exhausted and depressed. Boženka soon remarries a young Czech. The story ends with the stoic German grandparents, silent witnesses to the tragedy, doing their best to raise the children and inculcate them with something of their German heritage.

More than anything else, Türk's picture of the Other conveys a sense that nationalist developments have perverted the normal Slavic character, bringing out a shadow side: Boženka's and her people's lazy indifference, as opposed to their former simplicity and diligence. It is not that Czechs are congenitally bad, Türk seems to be telling his reader, but that they have been led by nationalists to believe that they can acquire something for nothing. After all, Boženka's family is prosperous, and her dowry of 6,000 gulden is not inconsiderable. However, her generation is unwilling to work the way her parents have. Instead she and her kind focus their parasitic efforts on obtaining the fruits of the Germans' labor. If the Germans want to maintain the prosperous position they have built up over the centuries for themselves, they must be careful not to allow the Other to mix with them. For the Other, formerly culturally docile, has become devious. This much is clear from Türk's narration of what takes place after the marriage. The fact that Boženka brings Czech workers with her to a German village and that she steadfastly maintains a Czech identity instead of assimilating into the German ways reflect the standard claim of German nationalists that the Czechs actively sought to establish a breach in the German territorial front. Once a Czech colony had been established in a German area, it would then be easier for the Czechs to demand their own language instruction for their children, their own schools, their own administrators and lawyers conversant in Czech, and bilingual street signs for the village. Before the Germans had realized what was going on, their German village would be reclassified as a bilingual one, and perhaps later as a Czech one.[17]

Türk's story attempts to translate the specific political worries of German nationalists into a language that peasants far away from Prague, Brünn/Brno, or Vienna will recognize. It reflects the German nationalist politicians' goal to win some kind of administrative separation of the German-inhabited regions of Bohemia from the Czech regions. For this to work, however, all Germans would have to practice a rigorous personal separation in every aspect of life. Otherwise the Czech nationalist politicians who vigorously opposed such autonomy could claim that in fact some Czechs at least inhabited every part of Bohemia. The story does little to define the nationalist Other. Instead, it translates a political issue of key importance to German nationalists into language imagined to be comprehensible to people who up until now have demonstrated little interest in the political battles of the day.

Another such tragic fiction told in a different region altogether, the South Tirol, suggests how malleable images of the rural Other could be, and just how localized, how cut off from any sense of national politics these images still remained. The story "Heimweh" ("Homesickness") by the German nationalist deputy Karl Hermann Wolf appeared in an almanac published by the *Tiroler Volksbund* in 1908. Superficially, at least, it deals with the same theme as Türk's "Mischheirat": a tragic love between children of two nationalities. But where Türk's story painted a deteriorating situation against a devious foe, one that required vigilance and action, Wolf's story suggests the possibility of reconciliation and assimilation. The affluent *Burgerbauer* (owner of the Burghof farm) is a widower with a young daughter, Lenerl, and a strong prejudice against the Italian or *Welsch* Tiroleans who are his new neighbors. Wolf makes it clear from the outset that this prejudice, which may at first appear unreasonable when applied to individuals, grew out of legitimate fears about important social problems besetting the region. The *Burgerbauer's* real objection to the Other relates to the use of cheap Italian labor brought from the south to work in the Tirol by his new neighbor, an irresponsible noble outsider. The latter has recently bought up several local farms in order to create a large estate with a luxury villa. The hired Italians naturally find working conditions in the Tirol much better than those they are used to across the border to the south.

When the *Burgerbauer* discovers that his daughter Lenerl loves Giuseppe Dellapiazza, son of the foreman in charge of building his neighbor's villa, he rages that no Italian will ever inherit his farm. He does interrupt his rage long enough to notice that

> the young Giuseppe, with a carnation behind his ear, actually didn't look like an Italian [*sah eigentlich gar nicht einem Welschen gleich*]. Thick blonde hair framed his fresh face with healthy color, in fact his figure was dashing; one could tell from the way he held his arms, from his calloused hands and slightly stooped posture that he must be used to hard work.[18]

The *Burgerbauer* also notices that "the Italian worker had a remarkable self-assurance about him, a manly pride shone from his eyes, the pride of a man who imagines he has worked his way out of poverty." Still, the *Burgerbauer* will not countenance an Italian, however manly, inheriting his farm. Lenerl and Giuseppe run away together. Months later the two are married at a church in a nearby village. As a condition for granting his permission for the union, the *Burgerbauer* insists that his daughter never return to her homeland or *Heimat*. He then becomes a recluse. Years pass, and employers in the region discontinue the practice of hiring Italians from the south. The village is rife with new rumors that young Giuseppe has died, leaving a poverty-stricken widow and son in an Italian village to the south. The scene changes to a dirty unpaved street in a small Italian village on a Sunday. After mass and a visit to Giuseppe's grave, the blonde six-year-old child complains to his careworn mother about the uncouth Italian village children and begs her (in good German Tirolean dialect) to return "to the German *Heimat* that you are always telling me stories about. Since father died I don't want to stay here, I don't!" His mother surveys the sterile fields, the treeless hills, the sunburned soil and remembers the green fields and fruit trees of her homeland. Together they return to the farm, where her father welcomes them. While they never speak of the past, the grandfather observes the blue eyes of his grandson, strokes his blonde hair, and whispers, "God, let him become a good German" so that he may inherit the farm one day.

In this story the national Other acknowledges German cultural superiority. After all, the Italians are deferential, and they all try to speak German, although with a noticeable accent. Victims of circumstance, they are ignorant pawns in the hands of the scheming developers who display no concern for the consequences of bringing Italian laborers into a German region. The Italian lot is poverty, but the example of the blonde Giuseppe shows the possibility of raising oneself up and perhaps fathering a German (if not becoming one oneself). If there is a nationalist lesson to be learned, it has more to do with the dangers of so-called "guestworkers" than with the badly intentioned schemes of the Other. And, in fact, this message fits well with German nationalist efforts in the South Tirol, which were very different from those of their counterparts in Bohemia and Moravia. In the Tirol German nationalists had to tread carefully in order not to alienate a strongly Catholic population and to win over Ladino-speakers to the German nationalist cause. Although German nationalists fought their Italian counterparts (who were less well organized than the Czech nationalists), they also worked hard to maintain a hegemonic position, not to partition the region into German and Italian units. Assimilation (or at least acculturation) remained an imagined (if by 1900 an unrealistic) option for the region's poor Italian peasants, if not for the region's well-established Italian speaking urban bourgeoisie.

Both these stories, however they differ in their presentation of the Other, share the following key elements: (1) the localization of the conflict in the rural village world, (2) the absence of a larger context, whether political or theoretical, and (3) the prominence of peasants as actors in the stories.

Later Constructions of the Rural Other: The Vanishing Peasant

After 1910, however, the image of the Other and, more importantly, the fictional context for nationalist conflict, took on a decidedly different look. If earlier fiction had focused on the rural Other as peasant, they now focused on the rural Other as municipal councilor, local administrator, or local school board director. And the situations had changed, as well. The earlier stories had taken place in a rural village context that celebrated the local and had focused its fears and hopes on strictly local relationships. No more. Now the nationalist struggle was increasingly linked to the infrastructure of the state itself, most often through the agency of the local bureaucracy. The German community was no longer figured in terms of the local either. Now the villain was as often as not a regional administrator, and the hero was more likely to be an outsider in some way, someone who worked to connect the embattled inhabitants of a given village more productively to the larger German community. The new stories stressed the importance of what they presented as a tangible thing (a thing that was in fact a highly abstract notion): namely, the interregional German national community. The stories work hard to make this abstract community appear real, usually by embodying that community in the figure of the nationalist activist.

Rudolf Fiedler's "Wie der Schneiderflori wieder deutsch geworden ist" ("How the Tailor Florian Became German Again") and the anonymous "Ein wackeres deutsches Mädchen" ("A Valiant German Maid") reflect both a new rural situation and an altogether different construction of the rural Other. The protagonists of these stories are not peasants, but rather a tailor and the daughter of an innkeeper. Although the setting is rural, peasants as such play no role. Outsiders, however, are critical to both plots. Both stories mention the government, civil servants, schools, and the census. The "Schneiderflori" tells the story of a poor German tailor in a village on the *Sprachgrenze* (language frontier). Already in the first paragraph the national conflict is introduced in ways that immediately link the village to events in the outside world. Florian is poor because most of the village folk, figured as Czech nationalists, take their work to a "Czech" in the next town who (ironically) advertises himself as a Viennese tailor. The few German speakers in the village have gradually submitted over time to Czech rule: "Czech was preached from the pulpit, Czech was taught in the school, business at the town hall took place in Czech, and at the local inn they played cards in Czech." There is no one among the villagers who might lead the German speakers to a stronger sense of German nationalism. Florian and his wife, for example, depend so heavily on the kindness of their Czech customers that they send their children to Czech schools. Worst of all, in the most recent Imperial census, Florian had reported his language of daily use as Czech.

All of this changes when Josef Reimer, a wealthy German outsider with the "imposing look of the ancient Teutons about him" arrives in the village and buys a piece of hitherto Czech-owned property. Reimer brazenly speaks German to the local priest and the mayor. He visits every family that might potentially have a

German background, and he invites the men to join a German association. Soon, with the help of the German School Association, Reimer builds a German language school in the town, and hires a teacher to live there with his wife and children. Although angry Czech vandals occasionally break the school windows and paint graffiti on its whitewashed walls, Reimer succeeds in attracting several German children to the school. But not those of the *Schneiderflori*. He and his wife still fear the loss of their Czech customers. Their children are even forced by Czech pupils to take part in an ambush of children from the German school.

Florian's nationalist guilt tears him apart internally. Christmas Eve finds him standing in the snow outside the little German schoolhouse, his tearful face pressed against the window, watching the Christmas party inside. Candles light the room and the strains of "Silent Night" reach the outside as happy children survey the Christmas tree and the presents provided for them by the generosity of Reimer and the German School Association. Speaking to the children, the teacher admonishes them to help bring the spirit of the Christ child to the German people by always remaining loyal to their language and their people. Suddenly the idyllic scene is shattered as a stone smashes the window and hits a young girl in the forehead. Florian gives chase and manages to catch the culprit, who turns out to be the son of the Czech mayor. After this incident Florian decides to join his fellow Germans and bring his family to the Christmas party, even though, as his wife points out, it will mean almost certain loss of his business. "God and Reimer will provide for us," Florian tells her, as Reimer welcomes the family back "to the German *Umgangssprache*."[19]

"Ein wackeres deutsches Mädchen" tells the story of a brave young woman whose quick wits and commitment to the nationalist cause save the local German-language school. It takes place in a German-language enclave, S—, in Moravia that is surrounded by a Czech administrative district. The villagers are poor, most of them peasants or workers in a nearby factory, and their children attend school in a town one hour's distance away by foot. Under normal conditions the roads to the school are bad; in winter they are virtually impassable. So, the villagers decide to petition the state to erect a school in their village. The Czechs in the neighboring town of G—, and particularly the teachers at the local Gymnasium, do their best to convince the villagers to erect a Czech-language school. Although their sense of national identity is weak, the villagers do at least decide that they want a German- language school. Still, as the author points out, a Czech school would probably have been built anyway, if it hadn't been for the quick-witted efforts of the local innkeeper's daughter.

The young woman in question has learned a trade (*Gastwirtschaft*) in a nearby German town. Her frequent contact with German guests at her father's inn has helped her to develop a strong nationalist attitude that she now hopes to impart to her fellow villagers. She urges them to speak more German, to break off commercial relations with Czechs, and to do their shopping in German-owned stores. At Christmas, with the help of some regional nationalist associations, she organizes a gift-giving program for the children of the poor. Everyone in the village is invited to the party, and even some regional representatives of German national-ist associations make the long trip to attend. At this Christmas party the decision is officially taken to build a German-language school and to invite the help of the German School Association, which has offered to pay for the building.

The neighboring Czechs try to turn the village against the School Association, spreading rumors that the villagers would eventually have to repay the costs of the building as well as the salary and housing of the teacher. When these tactics fail, the Czechs turn to outright bribery. On Christmas Eve the postman delivers a registered letter to the innkeeper, explaining that he has three more such letters to deliver to other influential citizens. The letters are postmarked from the Czech town G——. The young woman watches as her father turns pale. Greatly agitated, he hands her the letter and asks what she thinks. In it she reads a proposal by a local Czech contractor who was already building a school in G——, asking the innkeeper to exert his considerable influence over his fellow villagers to help him get the contract to build a Czech school in S——. The Czechs offer to build a brand new schoolhouse, fully furnished, and to endow a fund to pay for instructional materials. The German language could even be a part of the curriculum. In return for his aid, the Czechs offer the innkeeper 750 crowns for himself, 50 crowns to pay for free beer for the villagers, and all the new business for his inn that the building of the school would bring.

The young woman falls to her knees and begs her father not to take the money and betray his German *Heimat*. But even as she speaks, the town crier arrives, announcing a council meeting for the next morning, "so quickly did the Czech letters influence things." She rushes from the house into the night, mak-ing her way through waist-high snowdrifts to bring this news to her nationalist friends in the nearest German town. Early Christmas morning the School Asso-ciation's district chairman, along with an Association teacher, return with her by sled to the village, just in time for the village meeting. Perhaps it is the magic of the Christmas tree and the shining eyes of the children, opines the author, or perhaps it is the effect of their collective conscience, but the villagers decide then and there to give the contract to the School Association, and the village council proclaims: "The language of instruction in the new school will be German." Over the entrance to the new school a plaque reads: "Founded on the Loyalty of a German Maid."[20]

If the earlier stories (the "Mischheirat" and "Heimweh") warn against unguarded contact between Germans and their non-German neighbors, the later stories depict a Hobbesian world where only vigilant activism might guard against the wiles of a persistent enemy. This enemy has the most sophisticated of methods at his disposal to gain his desperate ends: the economic boycott, munic-ipal or state administrative power, the power to assign contracts, the means to influence the young. This latter world, despite its innocent rural setting, is bureaucratic, technical, and modern. The German nationalists, too, stand squarely on the side of bringing progress to the countryside. And inevitably that progress is closely associated with Germanness.

It is almost ironic, if not downright surprising, that the most common rural object of nationalist violence in such nationalist depictions is not the German peasant but that intrusive instrument of state modernization itself, the school—ironic because ever since its establishment by the liberals in 1868, Austria's system of eight-year compulsory education for boys and girls had raised strong opposition among rural Austrians. Peasants resented the loss of much of their seasonal workforce to the schools. After the fall of the Liberal ministry in 1879, conservative Catholic politicians had worked hard, if unsuccessfully, to overturn the school laws. In the 1880s, however, both German and Slav urban nationalist organizations began to make the national school the centerpiece of their activist efforts. They raised and spent hundreds of thousands of florins to fund minority language schools in districts where not enough minority children of school age lived to qualify for a state-funded school. Nationalist activists established kindergartens, built school buildings, hired school instructors and rural traveling teachers (*Wanderlehrer*), created adult agricultural education courses, organized teacher retirement and insurance funds, and outfitted poor children with school supplies. To accomplish these aims they forged networks of voluntary and paid activists, networks that linked rural areas more effectively to urban ones. From a hated symbol of state intrusion, the rural German or Czech or Slovene school became a venerated symbol of nationalist pride, a symbol of what ordinary Austrians might accomplish working in association with each other and without the help of the officially supranational state.

The transcendent importance of the minority school in nationalist politics made it an obvious target of nationalist violence, as well. German and Slav violence against such schools soon became a common way for people to vent their frustration against the nationalist enemy in both urban and rural settings. Newspapers at the turn of the century frequently carried brief reports of broken school windows and graffitied walls. In 1909, however, *Der getreue Eckart*, the German School Association's monthly, raised the stakes considerably. The journal published a bloodcurdling account with illustrations of a nocturnal siege by 300 (supposedly Czech nationalist) rioters against a German-language school in the Bohemian town of Stickau. This report, and several that followed, went well beyond the simple destruction of property to stress the physical danger to which the brave nationalist teacher and his terrified family had been subjected. Images like broken windows were no longer enough to fuel local outrage; now stories required defenseless women and bloodied children:

> As the raging crowd approached the house the schoolmaster retreated with his wife and four children, all under ten years of age, to a room inside the schoolhouse. They barricaded the windows and door against the invasion as well as they could in the dark and in such haste, using wardrobes. There, deathly afraid, the family awaited its fate.[21]

The new importance accorded to the local rural schoolhouse may or may not have been shared by peasants. There is plenty of evidence to suggest that initial

Vandalized interior of the German School Association schoolhouse at Stickau.
Source: Getreue Eckart (1909).

Vandalized exterior of the German School Association schoolhouse at Stickau.
Source: Getreue Eckart (1909).

opposition to compulsory schooling for peasant boys and girls had waned after 1900, particularly since sons and daughters of peasants seem to have made growing use of agricultural and home economic classes periodically offered by nationalist organizations. However, what is important is not peasant attitudes toward the schools, attitudes that were undoubtedly diverse depending on local circumstances, but rather the heroic importance accorded the school by local rural nationalists.

Whose Activism? Whose Violence?

The rise of the schoolhouse siege narrative demonstrates the extent to which people like teachers and their families, themselves relative newcomers to the countryside, had in fact become the authentic subjects of didactic fiction about the rural world. As urban Austrian nationalists examined the situation in the countryside, they clearly placed these relative newcomers at the center of their thinking about mobilizing rural populations for their purposes. And just as these white-collar invaders had become the rural heroes of German nationalist fiction, the image of the Other propagated by nationalist associations now focused almost entirely on white-collar outsiders, as well. Ironically, these newer narratives about rural Austria barely mentioned peasants of either nationality. When they did appear, peasants never played a role integral to the story but served only as part of a static rural backdrop. They existed literally outside history as far as nationalist authors were concerned. Villains like the Czech district administrator, local contractor, or bureaucrat were all people with connections to the outside urban world, just as the German heroes were themselves outsiders who make good use of activist networks to rally their German comrades.

Does this transformation belong within the traditional didactic framework that structured urban nationalist activists' appeals to the rural peasantry? In other words, did nationalists after 1900 still seek to teach a deeper understanding of the broader world to the supposedly narrow-minded provincial peasants they aimed to convert to nationalist positions? I suggest far different readings, both of these fictions and of their intended audiences. Even if they took every opportunity to teach the reader about the importance of nationalist solidarity, these stories were no longer didactic in the liberal tradition. They no longer aimed seriously to convert the peasantry into a nationally conscious and enlightened citizenry. Like their liberal predecessors, nationalist authors and activists directed their fiction, whether consciously or not, toward those who might see their own experience reflected in the stories. If earlier stories like the "Mischheirat" and "Heimweh" reproduced the rural world in order to make nationalism relevant to peasants, the later stories, along with the schoolhouse dramas, targeted different subjects and different readers. The latter extolled the activism of those relatively recent arrivals in rural areas, the teachers, bureaucrats, technicians, and even in some cases the German tourists. In the same way that local newspapers discussed rural problems in terms consistently recognizable to the educated white-collar workers who had invaded the countryside, so these new nationalist activists themselves became both heroes and consumers of their own rural tales.

This recognition should make us wary of arguments that view the rise of nationalist violence in rural Austria as somehow comparable in meaning to the nationalist violence that plagued much of urban Austria at the turn of the century, as reflecting the authentic nationalist sentiments of a peasantry. It also should encourage us to question contemporary accounts that too easily read the actions of the few as the actions of the majority. If we accept the notion that violence in Bergreichenstein simply reflected the spread of already-existing forms of nationalism to the peasantry, that is, the nationalization of the masses (in both senses of the word nationalization), we must still specify exactly whose nationalism we are witnessing. Did such incidents prove that by 1900 all rural inhabitants, understood collectively as the "peasantry," had become drawn into the vortex of nationalist politics that so vexed politicians in Vienna or Prague? I have suggested that peasants may well have participated in nationalist violence, but they may equally have held themselves aloof, depending on the specific context of an incident. The larger phenomenon seen in Bergreichenstein does indeed indicate that the nationalization of the countryside was proceeding apace, yet the process was highly uneven. Above all, this mobilization does not seem in fact to have always included every or even most segments of the rural populace.

Historian Jeremy King has noted perceptively that the decade leading to the First World War saw the gradual erasure of the social possibility of choosing to be not nationalist in Austria and particularly in Bohemia.[22] Accepting this point does not require us, however, to conclude that by 1914 Austrians had in fact become nationalists, whether Czech, German, Italian, or Slovene. Nor does it imply that those who came to see themselves as part of a larger nation necessarily ranked this aspect of their lives ahead of more pressing local concerns when deciding on a particular course of action. The final step in this process could only occur after 1918, when these populations often found themselves living under regimes that called themselves nation-states and acted accordingly. In some cases the moment when new borders were being determined in places like Styria and Carinthia even illustrates the degree to which nonnationalist concerns could shape the choices of a rural population about which state it preferred to join.

It would be easy to adopt a simple teleological view that interprets the spread of nationalist conflict in the countryside as an inevitable result of modernization, a set of transformations that necessarily brought urban nationalist politics to the innocent Austrian countryside. Surely increased transportation and communications infrastructures, new market opportunities, and schools did change the countryside, but not necessarily in such a transparent fashion. Urban nationalist politics did not simply become rooted in the countryside without themselves undergoing some transformations. Furthermore, not every rural region experienced nationalist violence on the same scale. Even in regions that saw such violence, other factors such as rural voters' electoral or economic behavior suggests that they did not simply adopt the worldview presented to them by their nationalist city cousins without modifying it themselves. They certainly did not always elect candidates who made nationalist concerns their most important ones. And even when they did elect nationalists, it seems misleading to speak of an authentic traditional peasantry when the social profile of rural regions had changed so much in the years since 1870.

It is therefore all the more important to examine those individuals and organizations that carried out the challenging, often tedious work of making their neighbors into nationalists. If Austrians became nationalists, it was due in large measure to the tireless efforts of these men and women, and not to the inevitable results of an impersonal process of modernization. And if this is the case, then we should also listen carefully to what those activists tell us regarding the nationalization of the rural masses. Their accounts betray a consistent disappointment with the apparent failure of their rural compatriots to become nationalist or nationalist enough. If nationalists in Cisleithania succeeded largely against the best efforts of the state and those social forces that opposed the growing influence of nationalism in public life, they rarely convey a sense of victory. On the contrary, they consistently despair of integrating rural populations successfully into the national community. Those groups that I have called "white-collar invaders" in particular celebrate their local victories, but they look to the future with a pronounced pessimism regarding their ability to transform rural conditions according to their nationalist vision. The dynamics of nationalist politics in a multinational Monarchy of course required a continual raising of the stakes. Yet it is instructive that German nationalists in the end seem to have focused more of their efforts on nationalizing conceptual landscapes than on nationalizing the people who actually inhabited those landscapes.

Notes

I would like to thank Timothy Burke, Laura L. Downs, Robert S. Duplessis, Peter Haslinger, Jeremy King, Douglas McKeown, Heidemarie Uhl, and Tara Zahra for their extremely helpful comments on this work.

1. The term, Cisleithania, refers to the lands encompassed by the non-Hungarian half of the Dual Monarchy. In this essay I use it interchangeably with the unofficial term, "Austria." The latter should not be confused with present-day Austria. For place names in multi-lingual regions I use both the German and the Czech or Slovene name in the first reference and the German name in subsequent references. This simplified usage should in no way be understood to imply a political preference for the German language name.

2. "Die deutschen Festteilnehmer überfallen und blutig geschlagen," *Deutsch Böhmerwald*, 13 September 1908, 1.

3. The largely bourgeois membership of the *Böhmerwaldbund* worked to promote German nationalism among a broad social spectrum of German speakers in rural southern Bohemia by organizing local educational and economic self-help projects. On the work of the *Böhmerwaldbund*, see Pieter M. Judson, "Frontiers, Islands, Forests, Stones: Mapping the Geography of a German Identity in the Habsburg Monarchy, 1848-1900," in *The Geography of Identity*, ed. Patricia Yeager (Ann Arbor: University of Michigan Press, 1996).

4. *Deutsch Böhmerwald*, 13 September 1908, 1-3; and "Paměti spis o utrpeni Čechů a nasilnostech německých, spachaných na české menšine v Horach Kasperských ve dnech 6. Az 12. Zaři 1908,", Státní ústřední archiv, Prague, PM 1901-1910 (3641); also reprinted in *Budivoj*, October 15, 1908, 4.

5. See the exhaustive accounts in the *Deutsch Böhmerwald* and the *Deutsche Volkszeitung* (Reichenberg) as well as "Paměti spis." In fact, the mayor of Schüttenhofen had attempted without success to prevent the *Böhmerwaldbund* meeting in Bergreichenstein from taking place, claiming that German nationalists traveling through Schüttenhofen would provoke violence. *Deutsche Volkszeitung*, (Reichenberg), 9 September 1908, 2.

6. The central government had only recently recognized such nationalist incidents as constituting a separate category from more traditional and local forms of violence. Their larger and interregional significance meant that these incidents warranted the attention of the provincial government rather than simply the local authorities.

7. For an account of a comparable violent incident in the Trentino area of South Tirol that attracted even more attention Monarchy-wide than did events in Bergreichenstein, see Hans Kramer, "Der 'Argonautenzug' der Deutschen nach Pergine oder die 'zweite Schlacht von Calliano' 1907," in *Mitteilungen des Oberösterreichischen Landesarchiv*, vol. 8 (Graz: Hermann Böhlaus Nachf., 1964), 330-41. The Italian nationalist "attack" on Edgar Meyer's hiking party gained enormous publicity in German nationalist newspapers across the Monarchy, and was viewed as comparable to events the following year in Bergreichenstein, Laibach, and Pettau/Ptui.

8. See, for example, two highly suggestive works on France, Michael Burns, *Rural Society and French Politics. Boulangism and the Dreyfus Affair 1886-1900* (Princeton, N.J.: Princeton University Press, 1984), and Tony Judt, *Socialism in Provence, 1871-1914: A Study in the Origins of the French Left* (Cambridge: Cambridge University Press, 1979). On Germany, see David Blackbourn, "Peasants and Politics in Germany, 1871-1914," in *Populists and Patricians: Essays in Modern German History* (London: Allen & Unwin, 1987) and *Marpingen: Apparitions of the Virgin Mary in Nineteenth-Century Germany* (New York: Knopf, 1994); the essays in Robert Moeller, ed., *Peasants and Lords in Modern Germany: Recent Studies in Agricultural History* (London: Allen & Unwin, 1986); and Richard J. Evans and W.R. Lee, eds., *The German Peasantry: Conflict and Community in Rural Society from the Eighteenth to the Twentieth Centuries* (London: Palgrave, 1986). On Austria and Bohemia, see the work of Peter Heumos, particularly "Interessensolidarität gegen Nationalgemeinschaft. Deutsche und tschecheische Bauern in Böhmen 1848-1918," in *Die Chance der Verständigung. Ansichten und Absätze zu übernationaler Zusammenarbeit in den böhmischen Ländern 1848-1918*, ed. Ferdinand Seibt (Munich: Oldenbourg Verlag, 1987), 87-99.

9. For important arguments about the unevenness of the process of nationalization in Bohemia, see Jeremy King, "The Nationalization of East Central Europe: Ethnicism, Ethnicity and Beyond," in *Staging the Past: The Politics of Commemoration in Habsburg Central Europe, 1848 to the Present*, ed. Maria Bucur and Nancy M. Wingfield (West Lafayette, Ind.: Purdue University Press, 2001), 112-52.

10. See examples from the *Deutsche Volkskalender für das Jahr 1889* (Olmütz 1888), 100.

11. For lack of viable alternatives at election time, nationalist associations and newspapers celebrated a party like the German Agrarian Party as integral to the German nationalist movement, despite the fact that the party itself rarely made a virtue out of taking strongly nationalist positions. On the German Agrarian Party's, see Lothar Höbelt, *Kornblume und Kaiseradler. Die deutschfreiheitlichen Parteien Altösterreichs 1882-1918* (Vienna: Verlag für Geschichte und Politik, 1993), 229-42. For examples of the Party's ambivalence about nationalism, see *Tätigkeitsbericht über das 9. Jahr des Deutsch-österreichischen Bauernbundes* (Budweis, 1908); *Der Dorfbote. Ein Wochenblatt zur Belehrung und Unterhaltung für das deutsche Landvolk*, #37, 1908, 11, #39, 11-12. The latter was edited in Budweis by Franz X. Reitterer. Reitterer was one of the region's German Agrarian deputies to both the Bohemian Landtag and the Vienna

Reichsrat. Although German nationalists regularly endorsed his candidacy at election time, and he himself seems to have behaved like a German nationalist in the Diet and Reichsrat, a glance at Reitterer's newspaper in the fall of 1908 (like the *Tätigkeitsbericht*) suggests that the Serbian trade treaty raised far more interest than the Bergreichenstein events, although the latter were duly reported and elicited critical comment.

12. See *Deutsche Wacht*, 22 May 1884, 1-2, 4-5; *Südsteierische Post*, 21 May 1884, 1-2. The *Südsteierische Post* was a politically moderate Slovene nationalist newspaper published in German in Marburg/Maribor.

13. *Bericht Über die Thätigkeit des Bundes der Deutschen in Böhmen* (Prague, 1896), 52-81; "Die Bezirksverbände und Ortsgruppen," in *Bericht Über die Thätigkeit des Bundes der Deutschen in Böhmen* (Prague, 1909). I am grateful to Tara Zahra for compiling these statistics for me.

14. See Pieter M. Judson, "'Every German visitor has a *völkisch* obligation he must fulfill.' Nationalist Tourism in the Austrian Empire, 1880-1918" in *Histories of Leisure*, ed. Rudy Koshar (London: Berg, 2001). This kind of nationalist rhetoric was a far cry from that in other local publications like *Der Dorfbote*, the weekly published by Franz X. Reitterer (note 10), Bohemian leader of the German Agrarian Party. The articles in *Der Dorfbote* focused on narrowly conceived issues of economic interest and rarely made the presumed connection between progress and nationalist activism that can be found in the pages of the *Deutsch Böhmerwald*.

15. On the tradition of such exchanges among German- and Czech-speaking families, which continued in some regions well into the twentieth century, see Helmut Fielhauer, "Kinder 'Wechsel' und 'Böhmisch-Lernen.' Sitte, Wirtschaft und Kulturvermittlung im früheren niederösterreichisch-tschechoslowakischen Grenzbereich," in *Österreichische Zeitschrift für Volkskunde* 81 (1978): 115-48.

16. Karl Türk, "Eine Mischheirat," in *Deutscher Volks-Kalender für Schlesien*, Verlag des Deutschen Schutzvereines "Nordmark," Troppau, 1898, 92-96. The significance of the Jew's speech goes well beyond the small citation here. In the course of the speech he gives a history of the region, its various inhabitants, and concludes that the very concept of national identity is unimportant.

17. For an excellent example of this kind of thinking, see the article "Zur Volkszählung," in *Mitteilungen des Deutschen Böhmerwaldbundes*, 23, December 1890, 241-42.

18. Karl Wolf, "Heimweh," in *Tiroler Volksbund-Kalender*, Verlag der Wagner'schen Universitäts-Buchhandlung, 1908 (no page numbers).

19. [Rudolf Fiedler], "Wie der Schneiderflori wieder deutsche geworden ist," in *Der Kampf ums Deutschtum. Zeitschrift des Deutschen Schulvereines*, vol. 3, no. 3 (1913): 42-44. Several German nationalist associations both in Bohemia as well as in other provinces raised money annually for the specific purpose of providing poor German-speaking children with gifts at Christmas.

20. "Ein wackeres deutsches Mädchen," in *Der Kampf ums Deutschtum. Zeitschrift des Deutschen Schulvereines*, vol. 3, no. 1 (1913): 4.

21. "Die tschechische Kulturtat von Stickau (mit 2 Bildern)," in *Der getreue Eckart*, January 1909, 1-3. German nationalists saw the event strictly in terms of national conflict and characterized the attackers as Czech nationalists. However, we should be careful about following the German nationalists in attributing a specifically Czech nationalist intent to the rioters, although this reading is possibly correct.

22. See King, "The Nationalization of East Central Europe." I am grateful to Professor King for furnishing me with a pre-publication copy of the manuscript for his book, *Budweisers into Czechs and Germans. A Local History of Bohemian Politics, 1848-1948* (Princeton, N.J.: 2002).

Chapter 7

ETHNOLOGY, CULTURAL REIFICATION, AND THE DYNAMICS OF DIFFERENCE IN THE *KRONPRINZENWERK* [1]

Regina Bendix

In March 1884, Crown Prince Rudolf von Habsburg presented a "promemoriam" to his father Francis Joseph I, requesting license to undertake a truly imperial, encyclopedic endeavor:

> Your Majesty,
> Despite many good initial attempts, the Austro-Hungarian Monarchy still lacks a great ethnographic work which would communicate in both stimulating and educational fashion a comprehensive image of our fatherland and its peoples [*Volksstämme*], building on the best of current scholarly research and supported by the perfected means of artistic reproduction. [2]

A highly educated man, Rudolf put all his energy and prestige behind this proposal. He regarded ethnography and related disciplines as "far from all immature theories and all passions of parties" and thus particularly capable of bringing forth a work that would foster collective patriotism. His plan called for collaboration between scholars and artists from the entire realm, with "well-known names enhancing the attractiveness of the work and lesser-known contributors receiving an opportunity to gain recognition." Joined in the task of describing the richness of the Monarchy's cultures and histories, these scholars and artists would "overcome the difficult beginnings and ... struggle to emerge from their meager existence and join the ranks of the esteemed world of scholars and artists." [3]

Notes for this section begin on page 162.

Francis Joseph granted the request, and production of the Crown Prince's Work (*Kronprinzenwerk*, hereafter KPW) began immediately. Published between 1886 and 1902, the twenty-four volumes of *Die österreichisch-ungarische Monarchie in Wort und Bild* constituted an astonishing array of personnel and accomplishment: 432 scholars and authors wrote a total of 587 texts and 264 artists created 529 paintings that, for purposes of publication, were turned into woodcuts (*Xylographien*) and chromo-zincographs (*Chromozynkographien*), using the latest in available print technology.[4] Savoring the anticipation of this encyclopedic work, spanning the Monarchy from Dalmatia to Galicia, Rudolf reiterated his vision in an introductory article in the KPW. He believed that it would generate a collective sense of love for the fatherland based on the recognition of the power and strength of cultural diversity. Completed, the work would constitute a "monument for all the future: 'Austria-Hungary in Word and Image.'"[5] Rudolf acted within the tradition of royal forebears and relations. His great uncle Archduke Johann had enacted his "love for the people," not least in statistical-ethnographic writing. Rudolf's cousin Johann Salvator was similarly committed to a Josephine patriotism, characterized by an empathy for "the people" and a virtuous desire to achieve a governmental structure within which a humane existence would be legally secured.[6] Rudolf's political writings invoke this legacy, though it was at odds with Francis Joseph's governmental style in the Dual Monarchy. In January 1889, Rudolf committed suicide. He was seriously ill, despairing of ever gaining his father's trust and access to real political power, and saw a Monarchy shaken by increasing ethnic strife rather than the harmony he hoped for.[7]

Despite Rudolf's death, the KPW was completed. His widow Stephanie became its patron; Francis Joseph granted continued use of imperial funds, but most of all it was the editorial committee, with the support of a tenacious and dedicated secretary named Joseph Böck, that carried on the monumental task of coordinating authors and artists, and oversaw the printing, subscription, and distribution process. The German-language version sold reasonably well, not least because in addition to the bourgeois subscribers, regional and local offices (libraries, schools, etc.) were encouraged to subscribe.[8] The Hungarian version, by contrast, was a financial flop.

But what exactly *was* the KPW? What was the nature of its content? How and by whom was it shaped and how was it received? In this essay I will argue that the work was very successful in confirming, if not essentializing cultural differences, both aesthetically and conceptually. This very effectiveness, however, contributed to the growing nationalist tendencies in numerous parts of the Monarchy's extremely diverse population, rather than fostering the holistically patriotic goal envisioned by the Crown Prince. Ethnography, contrary to Rudolf's claim, was riddled with "immature theories" and open to all kinds of "passions of parties."

Ethnography as a scholarly endeavor has a tradition not only of "Creating the Other" but also of boosting cultural self-conceptions, which in turn fuel (ethno-) nationalist thought and movements.[9] The KPW texts and the realistic illustrations fueled rather than inhibited separatist sentiment and ethnic animosity within the crumbling Monarchy. Conceptualized as an illustrated historical and ethnographic encyclopedia, the KPW helped to popularize ethnological assumptions. In support of my argument, I will thus first discuss the state of Central European ethnography and ethnology in the fin-de-siècle and then consider the ways in which these fields informed the KPW. Second, I will draw attention to how the work itself was produced by documenting the infrastructure created to generate the texts and the artwork. The extensive correspondence between (and among) editors and authors as well as artists demonstrates how the contents were continually negotiated, though the Viennese editorial committees maintained intellectual and artistic control. There was little opportunity for a more equal, collaborative scholarly vision to emerge on such central issues as linguistic diversity, translation, or indigenous political organization, as the table of contents was created in Vienna, and the vision remained hegemonic.

Guided by the tenets of scholarly standards, KPW authors built on the intellectual tradition of ethnic or national specificity, and wrote in the evaluative and at times cultural evolutionist vein typical of their era. Their work thus fostered a sense of separateness and difference, for celebrations of cultural uniqueness ultimately undermine a sense of joint purpose and common humanity.

Studying and Representing Peoples:
Central European Ethnography in the Late Nineteenth Century

The Crown Prince was quite accurate in observing the dearth of ethnographic documentation about many if not most peoples living within the Austro-Hungarian Monarchy. However, the KPW innovated neither ethnography nor cultural representation. Rather, the work built on existing ideas and practices of how to understand and represent culture. Exhibitions, long-standing pictorial traditions, and belletristic as well as governmentally sponsored efforts to account for cultural peculiarities were part of the rich discourse, both popular and scholarly, into which the KPW must be placed.

National and international exhibitions celebrating industrial achievement were frequently held following the Great International Exposition in London's Crystal Palace in 1851. Exhibitions in New York, Paris, and other cities with "regional, national or international pretensions" also inspired Vienna to hold such a mammoth event in 1873.[10] In this case the exhibition also built on an extant tradition of craft and technology exhibitions, but enthusiasm extended far into the periphery of the Austro-Hungarian Monarchy. The Galician city of Lemberg/L'viv/Lwów thus held a craft and technology fair already in 1877 and again in the 1890s, and Cracow followed suit in 1887.[11] Exhibiting people as representatives of "living cultures" became an increasingly popular aspect of such events, similar to the showing of "natives" in Western zoos. Unlike technological demonstrations, displaying living cultural groups built on more recent ethnographic exploration, whereby the agency of display informing such exhibitions rested soundly on the power inherent in Western categories and aesthetics.[12]

For Western viewers, gazing upon groups of Native Americans or Africans within the display setting must have resonated with familiar ways of conceptualizing differences. In the Austrian context, the parallel familiarity was with the tableau of peoples (*Völkertafel*), which offered in tabular form words and images typifying national or ethnic types from the Hessian to the Turk.[13] Ethnic and national stereotyping (or *blason populaire*) naturally reaches back through centuries, just as observing "difference" is as old as humankind's travels for purposes of commerce, war, and pleasure. Thinking about the significance of difference has been a Western preoccupation since the Renaissance, arising from the dual impetus of colonial expansion and Enlightenment thought.[14] Yet "difference" within the European setting was perceived or projected not only onto distant colonial territories but also onto the peasantry.[15] In addition to the ideological texts from the romantic-nationalist tradition, there is a good deal of other data available that attests to the ways in which peasants were reified. Collections of folk songs and narratives were published, peasant customs and costumes were imitated by the nobility, and by the mid-nineteenth century, an extensive tradition of pictures of peasants and peasant couples in regional costume—gouaches, woodcuts, water colors, and etchings—existed.[16]

The Central European exhibitions also began to include representations of the peasantry within their realm, expanding from a focus on craft and industry to traditional handicrafts, folk architecture, and other elements of native arts and livelihood subsumed under the label of home industry (*Hausindustrie*). Striving for comprehensive and accurate representation of diverse peasant cultures within the realm, exhibit organizers (as well as public institutions and private individuals) sponsored ethnographic collecting expeditions, which resulted in complete replicas of peasant dwellings and chapels, and displays of costumes, agricultural tools, and handicrafts.[17] Though inspired by a desire for "scientific accuracy," exhibitions ultimately idealized and aestheticized the folk cultures they represented. The same process is in evidence in the KPW, not least because many of the researchers involved, for instance, in the Lemberg exhibitions were also called on to write for the KPW.

Emerging as fields of documentation and inquiry, ethnography and ethnology were intertwined with this growing public discourse—be this in word or image—on cultural distinctiveness.[18] Within scholarship itself, the romantic-nationalist enthusiasm for the folk intermeshed with the already existing, governmentally inspired effort to inventory "land and peoples" so as to govern them more successfully.[19] Carried out under the label of "statistics," this systematic and often questionnaire-based documentation resulted in enormous reservoirs of detailed information. Guided by the principle "knowledge is power," Austria-Hungary's major mid-nineteenth-century statistician, Karl Freiherr von Czoernig, had as his ultimate goal the creation of a map that would accurately depict the geographic location of ethnicities within the realm.[20] Czoernig's three-volume work and its map, executed with the newest mapmaking technology by the Vienna Military-Geography Institute, was sent to the Paris Industrial Fair of 1855, and was clearly a source of pride for its scholarly as well as technological sophistication. Czoernig's introduction shows the ideology that guided his efforts very clearly. Austria-Hungary's strength and peculiarity were asserted to be attributable to the fact that

> All of the major European tribes encounter each other within the parameters of the Monarchy; in some places they constitute compact masses, elsewhere the most diverse national colorations interpenetrate each other and form ethnographic islands ... which express the peculiarity of the stock of peoples [*Völkerbestand*] within Austria, not to be found anywhere else.[21]

Czoernig opted for an ethnographic rather than a linguistic map for historical and political reasons. A linguistic map might have obscured the diversity of languages spoken within a given area, as the administrative languages of German and Hungarian slowly made their way into colonized regions (Czoernig does use the term "colonies" persistently). The ethnographic map would demonstrate the "circumstances as they are."[22] Czoernig undertook the work as a result of the same kind of patriotism that would later be expressed by Crown Prince Rudolf. Sound knowledge of the diverse peoples within the realm was needed in order to "devise measures to rule them to their greatest well-being."[23] Research for this map was carried out right through the Revolution of 1848, and Czoernig, faced with the question of whether or not he should cover the deep transformations wrought by 1848 in his work or whether he should report on the *status quo ante*, opted for including the revolutionary period. Witnessing the ethnic bloodshed during this turbulent time convinced him that the "national principle" as advocated by other states was not suitable for Austria-Hungary, where "racial fighting" and attempts at mutual suppression amongst tribes within the same territory would result in raw violence and anarchy. Instead, Czoernig saw in the Monarchy the possibility of continued peaceful coexistence of the most diverse "tribes," based on rights to land and property granted by the crown.[24] His three-volume work thus includes not only new survey data, but also a record of the most important historical treaty documents that detail the privileges and duties for any given colony.[25]

Next to this governmentally sponsored and benevolently paternalistic statistical ethnography, another model of comprehending emerging nation-states ethnographically also blossomed. This might best be called the "land and peoples" model, propagated in particular by the German Wilhelm Heinrich Riehl. He had authored a work by this title not least in an attempt to create a unified sense within (politically segmented) peoples in what would grow to be the German state.[26] Riehl advocated that the "real" ethnographic researcher should set out alone and on foot, because only this way would he come to know "the people" closely and thus be competent to report on them. The approach was thus individualistic and idealistic, and stood in contrast to the bureaucratically launched and executed statistical ethnographic data gathering by many trained hands.[27] Riehl's volumes were a prominent part of bourgeois German households, much like the encyclopedic *Bavaria* volumes sponsored by the Bavarian monarch Maximilian II beginning in the 1850s.[28] Aside from Riehl and the *Bavaria*—initiated by Maximilian's related and competing Wittelsbach dynasty—there were "land and peoples" publication efforts in Vienna itself, which clearly influenced the Crown Prince and his circle, particularly the series *Die Völker Oesterreich-Ungarns: ethnographische und culturhistorische Schilderungen* published by Prochaska since 1881.[29] Prochaska's circular sought subscribers for his projected twelve-volume series, which ranged from the Germans in Tyrol to the Romanians in Hungary, the Serbs, the Slovenes, the Jews, and the Gypsies.[30] Prochaska's volumes were not illustrated, and each was authored by an individual scholar.[31] All of these volumes, furthermore, focused on a specific people or a tribe, and thus were diametrically opposed to the goals of the KPW whose aim was to represent cultural diversity within regions and colonies. At least symbolically, the KPW wanted to undermine the idea of territorial exclusivity for individual ethnicities.

The KPW, in the Crown Prince's own terms, was to offer the reader an ersatz-journey through the Monarchy, facilitated through word and image.[32] Growing from this mélange of efforts to comprehend, contain, and represent diverse cultures, the work was clearly built on problematic underpinnings. The KPW's goal was to emulate the belletristic style of the "land and peoples" model, but the KPW was also heavily informed by the paternalistic and controlling impetus of statistical inquiry. The potentially liberating impulse inherent in an invitation to cultural self-representation found itself at cross-purposes with the heavy hand of scholarly and editorial control exercised by the committee in charge of preparing the work for publication.

Crafting Die österreichisch-ungarische Monarchie in Wort und Bild: Ethnicity and Class in the KPW Organization

The first months of 1884 saw feverish and slightly clandestine efforts on the part of the Crown Prince and his friends and advisors to craft the initial scope of the work and secure Francis Joseph's approval. The journalist and dramatist Josef von Weilen was appointed head of the editorial committee, and it was he who crafted the final outline (*Disposition*) of the work. By the end of March, *Das Neue Wiener Tagblatt*, run by Rudolf's loyal friend Moritz Szeps, could print a lead article on the planned work and its promise and potential to bring peace.[33] Yet this peaceful intent was continually faced with questions about ethnicity, language, and representation, not just in terms of content, but also in terms of organization, audience, and distribution.

Szeps was a Jew, as were von Weilen and a great many more of Rudolf's friends, and so were some of both the participants in the editorial committees and the authors who would write for the work. In the intensely antisemitic climate of fin-de-siècle Vienna, the ethnicity of those involved in crafting an ency-clopedia of Austria-Hungary's "state of many peoples" (*Vielvölkerstaat)* must be taken in account. Within the Monarchy, crumbling under the onslaught of eth-nonationalist demands in its farthest corners, Jewish intellectuals were perhaps the only ethnic interest group loyal to Austria-Hungary. Marginalized and ghet-toized by majority ethnics in all parts of the realm, Jews had every reason to fear nationalist sentiment and to hope for continued rights and protection within the moderately parliamentary Dual Monarchy.[34] Though it is almost impossible to trace antisemitic reactions against the KPW (almost all newspaper reviews were censored or else written by the editorial staff itself),[35] antisemitic critique or car-icature leveled against committee members certainly did occur.[36] The Crown Prince was a personage revered and loved by the population—in death even more so than in life—and the KPW, bearing his name, could not be publicly besmirched. But given the thick evidence of antisemitic practice in everyday life at the time, there is no doubt that latent and complex feelings about the KPW endeavor existed, not least based on the Jewish ethnicity of many of those who contributed to its completion.[37]

By June 1884, the KPW had its own letterhead and occupied an office in Vienna's Stallburggasse, immediately adjoining the imperial residence. Four com-mittees had been formed to undertake the monumental task, and they began meeting in early summer 1884 as well. An editorial committee determined the organization of the materials, the amount of space allotted to each, and the choice and tasks of collaborators. The artists' committee met most often: 118 ses-sions were held between 1884 and 1901 to choose the artists, assign the themes of illustrations in consultation with the authors, and oversee the reproduction of the paintings for publication. The finance committee met just once a year to maintain and supervise the contracts with the printer. A directorial council, final-ly, was entrusted with establishing conformity between the German and Hun-garian editions of the work.

The organization of the KPW was thus firmly entrenched in Vienna and Budapest, respectively.[38] Scholars and university professors (some of whom, like the economist Karl Menger, were former tutors of the Crown Prince), well-known art sponsors and bankers (for example, Nikolaus Dumba), and writers (for example, the music critic Eduard Hanslick) constituted the core of the enter-prise. While the Crown Prince presided over initial committee meetings, it was this prestigious collective that conceptualized the scope of the work, and it was their networks of artists and regional scholars who were enlisted into contribut-ing to the work.

In addition to the ideological orientation the Crown Prince had set for the KPW, the work was primarily driven by a grueling production schedule. Sub-scribers were promised regularly appearing self-contained installments that then could be bound once all installments for a given volume had arrived. The pres-sure to find authors and get them to adhere to the production schedule and the length (or brevity) of their assignment gave the effort the feel of an industrial endeavor, and the shorthand for the KPW used among members of the editorial board was indeed "the enterprise" (*das Unternehmen*).

Language and Its Representation

By the time of Szeps' newspaper announcement, Rudolf had already had to make a major concession, namely to appoint both a German and a Hungarian editorial committee and to produce the encyclopedia in both languages, with the content of the six volumes devoted to the Hungarian kingdom being entirely in the control of the Hungarian editors.[39] The equal status of the two administrative languages was thus inscribed into the work, opening the door to questions on the part of other language groups regarding a print version of this major endeavor in their language. Ludwig Hevesi served as translator of the six Hungarian volumes into German, and a whole series of individuals translated the German volumes into Hungarian.[40]

The repercussions of publishing the work in two languages were not just financial. Following Benedict Anderson's argument that, among other things, shared language expressed in commonly embraced literary works fuels the national imagination, we can understand why the Vienna contingent felt undermined in its political goal.[41] Having two rather than one language edition of the KPW not only undermined a common imperial imagination, but it also opened the door to questions from other language groups seeking at least partial translations of the KPW into their language—preferably, of course, the volume (or excerpts from different volumes) devoted to their particular language group. Such initiatives were recognized as problematic. It was the whole of the KPW that was meant to reach the population, in order to leave its unifying mark, and requests for permission to translate individual volumes were treated slowly and with caution.[42]

Language and translation were also an issue in generating the volumes themselves. For many authors, neither German nor Hungarian was their native language. Some simply chose to write in their native tongue and rely on the KPW's staff to organize a translation. Thus, for instance, the contributor entrusted with the task to write about the "physical characteristics of the population of Galicia" wrote in June 1891 that

> [he] wrote [his] article in Polish, following the instructions of Minister Zaleski. Thus the formal instructions concerning the format and external nature of the manuscript fall away for now, as the translation will be arranged by the editors and then returned to the author for revision.[43]

Implied here is that writing in a language other than German permitted the author to diverge from the formal aspects laid out by the editors; expression even of scholarly knowledge could not conform to the guidelines set out by the center. Johann Galtung has demonstrated in this century how strongly intellectual styles diverge along national lines.[44] KPW author-scholars experienced this acute-

ly, as well, through the comments, editorial cuts, and revisions they faced shortly after they sent their contributions to Vienna. Drastic revisions were not only
demanded in order to conform to the space needs and the popular style of the
encyclopedia format, they often also concerned the very ways in which the material was conceptualized and organized.[45]

Some authors experienced the language dilemma far more acutely. A Polish
contributor, Constantin Maria Ritter von Gorski, wrote (in German) on 17
December 1895 to Heinrich Zeissberg, the main editor during the 1890s:

> I shall attempt to write the essay in German. Linguistic errors could then be corrected by
> German friends who reside here.

Some three months later he reports:

> I had the brave plan to write the article in German; this pretension has ruined me. The dif-
> ficulty of being able to express oneself in a foreign language, the feeling to want to play on
> a little-known instrument and groping for the keys in vain, without being able to invoke
> the sounds one would like to make audible—all this has discouraged me and made me
> await a better hour.[46]

Similar sentiments were voiced by some of the Italian-speaking authors. The
process of writing in the foreign language thus drove home the power and beauty of one's own language, bolstering one's linguistic identity and increasing the
sense of alienation from the administrative language. Yet throughout such testimony, there is a tone of subservience to the language of the center, and ample
self-accusation for not having a better command of German.

Language and literature were also a component of the KPW's content, either
as separate articles or covered in articles on folklife (*Volksleben*). Authors struggled
to balance sincere interest in depicting linguistic diversity, giving due to each language present in the region—and thus creating evidence for lasting linguistic
(and hence cultural) difference while also covering linguistic or dialectal mixes. A
group of German settlers (from the time of Maria Theresa's rule) in otherwise
Slovene-speaking territory is first described as follows: "Aside from the exclusively German last names nothing reminds one of the origin of these inhabitants."[47]
Yet a few sentences later, we are told that said inhabitants "continue to label certain objects of daily use with German expressions and their pronunciation of
Slovene makes them differ considerably from the original Slovenes of the area
whom they themselves call "pravi Slovenci"—real Slovenes." Elsewhere one finds
an author asserting the fluid boundary between Slovene and Croat, based on ethnic similarity as well as continual and close commerce. He states that Slovenes
tend to hear the "sounds of their homeland" when they are already far in Croat
territory, while "the Croat is gladly inclined to count Slovene villages to the Croat
language area, because he encounters Croat terms and proverbs."[48] Given such
potential territorial claims, it does not come as a surprise that the author suggests
the river Dragnoja as a possible linguistic boundary.

Behind the printed efforts are negotiations and occasional outbursts concerning accurate language representation in correspondence. Thus, Ferdinand Lehner complained about the Germanification of village names in his article on early Bohemian history:

> I use historical sources concerning village names of the Romanesque period, of which the Bohemian villages have remained unchanged till this day. In the galley proofs, [some of these were] renamed [with German names]. I have to protest energetically to protect my literary reputation.[49]

Johann Danilo, having seen the galleys of one of his contributions on Dalmatia, requests in a polite if firm Italian epistle that the term Serbo-Croatian not be used as an adjective, but solely as a noun to refer to a somewhat shared language. "A person can only be Serbian or Croatian, but not both," he states, and furthermore he admonishes,

> If this appellation Serbo-Croatian should appear ... in a work of such importance of which your Highness directs the editorship and in which I have the honor to collaborate, I am sure that there would arise a scandal in the country in which I do not want to figure in any way at all.[50]

Questions of Maps and Political Representation

Already in its first session, the editorial committee hotly debated whether an ethnographic map ought to be part of the first volume. Maurus Jokai (one of Hungary's foremost nineteenth-century literary figures and the editor of the Hungarian edition who attended many of the early Viennese editorial meetings, as well) advised against such a supplement "because such a map might create ill-feeling in Hungary." A final decision was delayed in favor of soliciting the opinion of another Hungarian collaborator, and the cost of such a map had to be discussed, as well.[51] By the time the committee met for the second time, the Crown Prince decided to drop the maps, citing pragmatic reasons: "The size of the maps ... would preclude their purpose, namely the elucidation of the text."[52] Although the secretary writing the protocols refrained from offering further explicit detail, the mere usage of the expression "hotly debated" indicates how aware the participants were of a map's potential. Offering a visualization of the realm's territory within a work intended for popular consumption could result in all kinds of reactions, including the bolstering of claims for independence based on suddenly available maps of linguistic and cultural terrain.[53]

Similar political caution must have been at work in the suppression of three complete manuscripts that were intended for the first volume. Karl Freiherr von Lemayer wrote an extensive manuscript on the administration of the Austro-Hungarian Monarchy, and two manuscripts on the constitution of Austria and Hungary, respectively, also exist. Böck, the enterprise's secretary, wrote on the brown wrapping paper around all three of them that "concerns" had arisen and the printing was "saved" for the last volume instead, at which point neither resources nor time permitted inclusion.[54] As with the maps, the nature of these concerns can only be surmised from the historical context. While none of the three documents appears particularly liberal from a present-day perspective, the Crown Prince, who lived under continued secret service scrutiny due to his liberal leanings, may not have wanted to jeopardize imperial support for the venture. While the goal of the KPW was surely political, its content was to avoid political confrontation. Thus Rudolf asked one of his closest friends, Ladislaus von Szögenyi-Maarich (who would also become his executor), to carefully read the essay on constitutional history:

> One must not lose sight of the fact that a work such as this one requires the constitutional history; it may not be left out. But on the other hand one does have to think of all the confused and unclear times we had to work through to arrive at the present position, and all the still existing frictions and the barely healed wounds of the earlier battles, as well as the sensitive view of the emperor.[55]

The vision behind the KPW aimed for a precarious balance: there was to be the celebration of economic and technological progress as well as of historical and artistic achievement. There also was to be recognition of individual cultures, yet an emphasis on the good fortune of all remaining within one Monarchy rather than embarking on the path of separate nation-states. In Rudolf's most optimistic visions he could foresee a liberalized state in which he would serve as president. What the KPW ignored was the close connection between nationalism and essentialized cultural representation.

Physical, Cultural, and Artistic Essentializing

In the tradition of nineteenth-century anthropology or ethnology, most KPW volumes contain articles devoted to the "physical make-up of the population." They tend to contain a wild mixture of "scientific" evidence and character speculation, and waver between strings of laudatory adjectives and more derogatory, upper-class character assassinations of the common people. The emerging stereotypes, be they endearing or harsh, solidified images of self and other and clearly drew on long-standing *blason populaire* traditions. Given the tremendously mixed populations in most parts of the realm, the effort to sort out the differences draws on early genetic or "breeding" knowledge as much as on uncertain information about people's migrations.

To choose one among many possible examples, the article on "physical traits" in volume 10, devoted to the Coastal Lands (*Küstenland*),[56] begins by asserting that the region assembles no fewer than eight types of peoples from the three broader categories of Slavs, Romans, and Germans. Cranial descriptions, physical stature, and statistical data concerning eye and hair color are used first to disentangle the possible tribal components. This is followed by a more unifying character trait: a diversity of occupational opportunities, which is said to have brought about a vigorous people, steeled by its continual struggle with nature.[57] The Italianate branches are distinguished by their "glowing brown eyes," and the adjective 'glowing' remains reserved for this race, though other brown-eyed people are described, as well. The facial structures of men of Trieste bring about a "noble expression" while for women it is "generally beautiful ones." By contrast, the facial features of the in-migrated Cici might "make one suspect heartlessness and roughness where in reality there is only indolence."[58]

Articles on body types are usually illustrated with portraits of a given man or woman. Yet each such portrait shows the individual wearing costume; thus, the textual description of skulls, cheekbones, and prevalent eye and hair color is fused with a representation of ethnicity. Working from within a nineteenth-century scholarly paradigm, a close connection between physical traits and cultural or ethnic elements such as costume and custom was taken for granted and expressed itself in these illustration choices. Artists appear to have known precisely what kind of picture was requested, for there is no evidence within the ample correspondence from artists asking for clarification. Whether the request was for a "type of Slovene woman" or "type of Jews from Cracow," the illustration invariably featured culturally characteristic dress and hairstyles.

Throughout, the illustrations showing people enhanced clichéd perceptions of self and other. The ethnological descriptions of each area follow more or less the same pattern, addressing occupational culture, food ways, religiosity, superstition, and year and life cycle ritual. Illustrations for these articles are most frequently drawn from the ritual repertoire: weddings, dances, or winter and summer festivities featuring people in "typical" costume that show the particulars of a given place. Adumbrated with evaluative vocabulary attesting to the good-naturedness, joviality, bravery, or sullenness of the group in question, the KPW truly did essentialize, as its title promised, in "word and image" the peoples within the Dual Monarchy.[59] The KPW's artwork shows its lineage to earlier visualizations and displays of ethnicity or culture most clearly. While most of the paintings reproduced in the KPW are originals, the scope of what was to be captured visually was familiar to the artists—some of whom undoubtedly were chosen precisely because they had training or a reputation in this particular genre of painting, a genre that had aestheticized folk cultures and costumes for at least a century. Zygmunt Ajdukiewicz's illustration of a Lyra player provides an acute testimony to this influence. Ajdukiewicz found his Lyra player not in the most remote valley of Galicia but instead painted the man seated in front of a replica of a Greek Orthodox church at the Lemberg exhibition of 1894. One may assume that the subject was enacting his tribe and musical skill for the benefit of visitors to the exhibition.[60]

Conclusion

The words and images of the KPW assemble an amazing array of information coupled with an equally amazing array of judgmental hyperbole.[61] Contrary to the Crown Prince's assumption, "ethnology" was hardly a field of knowledge free of political leanings. Wavering in style between travelogue, cultural self-assessment, and depiction of the cultural Other, the KPW's innovations—a multi-authored, illustrated encyclopedic scope—was also burdened by traditions of cultural and class stereotyping.

While it is difficult to document the role the KPW might have had in strengthening ethnonationalist tendencies, it certainly did not achieve the goal of greater collective patriotism and interethnic peace the Crown Prince had aimed for. Native readers back then, and perhaps even now,[62] appear to be interested foremost in the volumes wherein they can find themselves—hence also the efforts to get permission to translate "one's own" volume. In this role the KPW might have fueled nationalist fervor, but it clearly also served as a source book for groups inclined to cherish "their" traditional culture. With full description of year cycle rituals, music, and narrative traditions perhaps already declining during the time of initial writing, the KPW as a reifier of cultural practices could also be the source of cultural revitalization.

Die ungarisch-österreichische Monarchie in Wort und Bild was completed despite its leading spirit's suicide, and one may recognize in the nature of its completion another reason for its failure to fulfill Crown Prince Rudolf's dreams. For as forward- looking and even democratic as Rudolf conceived the KPW's production as being—with indigenous scholars and artists speaking for their own lands in harmonious collaboration—the actual execution of the plan employed a centralized, highly bureaucratic pattern, especially once the Crown Prince was dead and no longer providing the aura of opportunity and auspiciousness to the editorial meetings. A new idea, developed along familiar patterns of organization, is easily and unawares co-opted. With the organizational structures of committees, the central secretariat from whence everything ultimately had to be sanctioned, the rigorous schedule of production, and last but not least the style of communication between the central committees and the contributors residing in the Monarchy's peripheries, the KPW grew into a mirror of any other task undertaken in the Dual Monarchy's enormous bureaucratic apparatus.

Notes

1. The research for this paper was supported by a fellowship for university teachers from the National Endowment for the Humanities (1998), as well as a Type A grant from the University of Pennsylvania Research Foundation. The primary materials from which this paper draws were found in the Stadt- und Landarchiv Wien (hereafter SLW), and to a much lesser extent the Oesterreichisches Haus-, Hof- und Staatsarchiv (hereafter HHSt). The originals of the illustrations for the work are in the Österreichisches Portrait- und Bildarchiv (hereafter PB). Thanks go to Heinrich Berg at the SLW and Gerda Mraz at the PB. Particular thanks go furthermore to Reinhard Johler, Vienna, for helping me with establishing contacts with other researchers working on the Kronprinzenwerk (hereafter KPW) and to John Bendix for comments on this paper. All translations from German as well as Italian are my own.

2. Renate Basch-Ritter, *Österreich-Ungarn in Wort und Bild. Menschen und Länder* (Graz: Styria, 1995), 6. The original is available in the HHSt, Nachlass Kronprinz Rudolf 15, as well as in Nachlass Arneth, K. 20.

3. Basch-Ritter, *Österreich-Ungarn*, 6.

4. See Robert Wagner, "Das Kronprinzenwerk," in *Rudolf—Ein Leben im Schatten von Mayerling.* 119. Sonderausstellung des Historischen Museums der Stadt Wien (Vienna: Eigenverlag der Museen der Stadt Wien, 1990), 59-70. While photography was already practiced extensively at this time, combining the printing of photographs and text on the same page only became possible during the time that the KPW was already in production, and it was considered aesthetically preferable to keep the work uniform in the style chosen.

5. Crown Prince Rudolf, "Einleitung," in *Die österreichisch-ungarische Monarchie in Wort und Bild*, vol. 1 (Vienna: k.& k. Hofdruckerei, 1887), 17.

6. See Justin Stagl, "Vom Menschenfreud zum Sozialforscher. Der 'Patriotic Traveller' des Grafen Leopold Berchtold," in *Kulturwissenschaft im Vielvölkerstaat*, ed. J. B. Rupp-Eisenreich and J. Stagl (Vienna: Böhlau, 1995), 49-63.

7. See Brigitte Hamann, *Rudolf. Kronprinz und Rebell* (1978; reprint, Munich: Piper, 1997) for a well-contextualized biography of Rudolf, and Brigitte Hamann, ed., *"Majestät, ich warne sie ..." Geheime und private Schriften* (1979; reprint, Munich: Piper, 1998) for a selected, commented edition of Rudolf's political and scholarly writings.

8. KPW, Box 9, at SLW, contains a copy of Circular 270/5 of 22 November 1902, sent from the Ministry of the Exterior to consulates abroad. It describes *Die österreichisch-ungarische Monarchie in Wort und Bild* and requests that the work be made known to libraries as well as German and Hungarian voluntary associations in colonial territories.

9. The literature on the relationship between folklore, ethnology, and the rise of nationalism is extensive and the issue does not require further development here. For useful summaries see Roger D. Abrahams, "Phantoms of Romantic Nationalism in Folkloristics," *Journal of American Folklore* 106 (1993): 3-37, and Richard Handler, *Nationalism and the Politics of Culture in Quebec* (Madison: University of Wisconsin Press, 1988).

10. Curtis Hinsley, "The World as Marketplace: Commodification of the Exotic at the World's Columbian Exposition, Chicago, 1893," in *Exhibiting Cultures*, ed. I. Karp and S. Lavine (Washington, D.C.: Smithsonian Institution Press, 1991), 344. Allan Pred, *Recognizing European Modernities: A Montage of the Present* (London: Routledge, 1995), 31-95, offers a stimulating account of the Stockholm exhibition of 1897; at the time it was, in many ways, a "peripheral" city like those competing for attention in the Austro-Hungarian Monarchy.

11. Franz Grieshofer, "Die Bedeutung des Ausstellungswesen für die Entwicklung der Ethnographie in Galizien und Wien," in *Galizien. Ethnographische Erkundungen bei den Bojken und Huzulen*, ed. Klaus Beitl (Vienna: Oesterreichisches Museum für Volkskunde, 1998), 22-31.

12. Barbara Kirshenblatt-Gimblett, *Destination Culture: Tourism, Museums and Heritage* (Berkeley: University of California Press, 1998), 34-56.

13. For a brief discussion of the *Völkertafel* now exhibited in the Austrian Museum of Folk Culture (and hence one familiar to the society that produced the KPW), see Wolfgang Brückner, "Die Wiener Völkertafel in Berlin," *Bayrische Blätter für Volkskunde* 21 (1994): 202-4; idem, "Von Welschen und Itakern. Oberschichtliche Vorurteile und volkstümliche Stereotypenbildung im deutschsprachigen Mitteleuropa," *Bayrische Blätter für Volkskunde* 21 (1994): 204-16. In this article he offers a more comprehensive assessment of ethnic or national stereotypes that can be reconstructed from linguistic and pictorial sources. The most recent and comparative study of *Völkertafeln* is Franz K. Stanzel, ed., *Imagologisch-ethnographische Studien zu den Völkertafeln des frühen 18. Jahrhunderts* (Heidelberg: Universitätsverlag C. Winter, 1999).

14. Tzvetan Todorov, *On Human Diversity: Nationalism, Racism, and Exoticism in French Thought* (Cambridge, Mass.: Harvard University Press, 1993).

15. The history of European nationalism is closely connected to this process. The peasantry was an object of curiosity for the nobility, and in the process of democratization and the corresponding emergence of a class structure, peasant culture took on new ideological significance as the "culture foundation" of the new nation-state form. The history of this transformation has been amply documented and theorized within folkloristics and European ethnology. For a recent example, see Abrahams, "Phantoms of Romantic Nationalism," 3-37.

16. Regina Bendix, "Moral Integrity in Costumed Identity: Negotiating 'National Costume' in Nineteenth-Century Bavaria," *Journal of American Folklore* 111 (1998): 133-45. The article summarizes some of this history.

17. Grieshofer, "Die Bedeutung des Ausstellungswesen," 19-42, especially 34-37.

18. It is impossible to do justice to the complex issues involved in the ideology and emergence of ethnology or anthropology within Central Europe, particularly the Habsburg Monarchy. Among the most thorough works are those of Justin Stagl, including *Kulturanthropologie und Gesellschaft. Eine wissenschaftssoziologische Darstellung der Kulturanthropologie und Ethnologie* (Berlin, 1981); *Apodemiken: eine räsonnierte Bibliographie der reisetheoretischen Literatur des 16., 17., und 18. Jahrhunderts* (Paderborn: F. Schöningh, 1983); *A History of Curiosity: The Theory of Travel, 1550-1800* (Chur, Switzerland: Harwood Academic Publishers, 1995); and "Vom Menschenfreud zum Sozialforscher," 49-63.

19. Mohammed Rassem, *Die Volkstumswissenschaft und der Etatismus*, 2nd enlarged edition (1951; reprint, Mittenwald: Mäander Kunstverlag, 1979), discusses the earlier linkages between etatism and cultural scholarship. See also Uli Linke, "Folklore, Anthropology, and the Government of Social Life," *Comparative Studies in Society and History* 32 (1990): 117-48 for a discussion of the ideological split within eighteenth- and nineteenth-century German scholarship.

20. See Britta Rupp-Eisenrich, "Trois ethnographies," in *Kulturwissenschaft im Vielvölkerstaat*, 81-99, and Karl Freiherr von Czoernig, *Ethnographie der oesterreichisch-ungarischen Monarchie*, 3 vols. (Vienna: K. & K. Hof- und Staatsdruckerei, 1857). Benedict Anderson's insight in *Imagined Communities: Reflections on the Origin and Spread of Nationalism*, 2nd enlarged edition (London and New York: Verso, 1991) of how maps assisted in imagining the community is further substantiated here. What was different in the Austro-Hungarian configuration was that the community was to remain overtly multi-ethnic; diversity was to be stressed.

21. Czoernig, *Ethnographie*, vol. 1, v. Czoernig's use of the term "coloration" (*Färbung*) avoids what after 1848 was an embattled idea of "nation," and also indicates the surface nature of difference. A term like "local color" (*Lokalkolorit*) for cultural specificity is used even today, and invokes a similar emphasis on the visually or aesthetically striking, while avoiding reference to deep-seated differences in social structure or in the dynamics of interaction.

22. Ibid., x-xi. Czoernig's term is *bleibende Verhältnisse*.

23. Ibid., v.

24. Ibid., xv.

25. Ibid., xiii.

26. Wilhelm H. Riehl, *Land und Leute* (Stuttgart: Cotta, 1854).

27. Wilhelm H. Riehl, *Wanderbuch* (Stuttgart: Cotta, 1869).

28. See Konrad Köstlin, "Die Vielfalt als Einfalt. Ethnographie als ästhetischer Kitt," in *Volkskultur zwischen Staat und Nation. Volkskunden zur Jahrhundertwende in Zentraleuropa und "Die österreichisch-ungarische Monarchie in Wort und Bild*," ed. Jurij Fikfak and Reinhard Johler (Vienna: Selbstverlag des Instituts für Europäische Ethnologie, forthcoming), and Joseph F. Lentner, *Bavaria—Land und Leute im 19. Jahrhundert* (München: Süddeutscher Verlag, 1988).

29. Empress Elizabeth or "Sisi" was a Bavarian Wittelsbach princess, and relations with that dynasty patterned Rudolf's life throughout—including inducing constant anxiety to have inherited the madness diagnosed among members of the Wittelsbach house. The first draft for what would become the KPW was created by Archduke Johann Salvator, Rudolf's Bavarian cousin, with whom he competed intellectually, militarily, and socially. However, Johann's draft for an "Ethnography of Austria-Hungary," dated 24 December 1883, followed the Prochaska "land and peoples" model that did not focus on territories (cf. Nachlass Habsburger Hausarchiv, KR Rudolf, 15, HHSt).

30. Alfred von Arneth, imperial archivist and one of the most prominent KPW committee members, kept one of Prochaska's circulars in his folder of KPW draft materials (HHSt, Nachlass Arneth, K20).

31. For example, Paul Hunfalvy, *Die Ungarn oder Magyaren* (Vienna: Prochaska, 1881), and Jaroslav Vlach, *Die Czecho-Slaven* (Vienna: Prochaska, 1883).

32. Reinhard Johler, "… Die Lesewelt auffordern zu einer Wanderung durch weite weite Lande," in *Galizien. Ethnographische Erkundungen bei den Bojken und Huzulen* (Vienna: Oesterreichisches Museum für Volkskunde, 1998), 43-55, and Georg Schmid, "Die Reise auf dem Papier," in *Kulturwissenschaft im Vielvölkerstaat*, 100-12. There are ample precedents for this notion of the traveling scholar-author within the European scientific travelogue literature. See Marie L. Pratt, "Alexander von Humboldt and the Reinvention of America," in Marie L. Pratt, *Imperial Eyes: Travel Writing and Transculturation* (New York: Routledge, 1992), 111-43.

33. Hamann, *Rudolf: Kronprinz*, 228-29.

34. Ernest Gellner, *Language and Solitude: Wittgenstein, Malinowski and the Habsburg Dilemma* (Cambridge: Cambridge University Press, 1998), 82-83. Gellner drew a poignant picture of the dilemma faced by the Jewish *deraciné* intellectual in the Austro-Hungarian center and periphery.

35. This is evident from the boxes of KPW materials at the SLW, for example Box 2, and especially Box 9, "Direktionsakten" in which a small selection of reviews published in German-speaking magazines is preserved. A number of these reviews were written by Carl von Lützow, director of the Academy of Arts and member of the editorial committee. The secretary of the enterprise, Josef Böck, is likely to have authored some press releases, as well.

36. Hamann, *Rudolf: Kronprinz*, 234-35.

37. See Brigitte Hamann, *Hitler's Vienna: A Dictator's Apprenticeship*, trans. Thomas Thornton (New York: Oxford University Press, 1999). Also consider the cartoon-filled popular weekly *Kikeriki. Humoristisches Volksblatt*, published from 1860. Even a cursory glance through it reveals continuous, and apparently fully acceptable, antisemitism.

38. A first visit to Budapest in July 1999 in search of the Hungarian editorial committee's records turned up comparatively little material, as there was apparently no individual entrusted with keeping all correspondence together, and thus materials can only be found by tracing individual committee members' and contributors' personal archives. Professor Tamas Hofer, Budapest, has begun to look at some of these sources, but thus far nothing has been published on them.

39. Toward the end some of the Hungarian work, in particular the completion of the volume "Croatia," was taken over by the German editors as the Hungarians were facing numerous delays and would not have been able to complete the deliveries by 1902, the scheduled date the publication was to have been finished. See the Sitzungsprotokoll des Aufsichts-Comités, 18. Sitzung, 3 April 1900 (KPW, BD2, at SLW).

40. For an accounting of the names, see the KPW's *Schlusswort*, printed in 1902, and usually bound into the last volume of the KPW.

41. Anderson, *Imagined Communities*.

42. For a case study on one such volume see Jasna Z. Capo, "'Dalmatia'—its Authors and Translators," in *Volkskultur zwischen Staat und Nation*. It is hard to judge how many such efforts were undertaken. In addition to the well-documented Dalmatian case discussed by Capo, a Slovak volume may have appeared (Gabriela Kiljanova, personal communication). A possible Bohemian translation was discussed in the thirteenth session of the editorial committee on 23 October 1894; a request from a bookseller named R. Promberger in Olmütz/Olomouc was to be more closely considered and a draft agreement to be drawn up (KPW, BD3, at SLW). It is less likely that an Italian translation for the Tyrolian volume was undertaken, as some of the authors chosen for this volume were not highly regarded by their Italian-speaking peers (Reinhard Johler, personal communication).

43. Letter from Mayer, KPW, Box 5, at SLW. Unfortunately, the KPW materials preserved in SLW do not contain the original letters sent out by the editors, nor are there copies of subsequent letters sent to individual authors. The extant materials only permit one to guess the nature of the correspondence that was sent out and how authors and artists reacted to it. The letters themselves are organized more or less by last name, and often show blue pencil marks in those places where editorial action was required.

44. Johann Galtung, "Structure, Culture, and Intellectual Style. An Essay Comparing Saxonic, Teutonic, Gallic, and Nipponic Approaches," *Social Science Information* 20, no. 6 (1981): 17-56.

45. For a discussion of this issue, see Regina Bendix, "Zwischen Weltsicht und Druckbogenpedanterie," in *Volkskultur zwischen Staat und Nation*.

46. Letters from Constantin Maria Ritter von Gorski in KPW, B1 Box 7, at SLW.

47. Franz Graf Coronini-Cronberg, "Volksleben in Görz und Gradiska," in *Die österreichisch-ungarische Monarchie in Wort und Bild*, vol. 10 (Vienna: K. & K. Hofdruckerei, 1891), 162.

48. Anton Klodic von Sabladoski, "Slavische Sprache und Literatur," in *Die österreichisch-ungarische Monarchie in Wort und Bild*, vol. 10 (Vienna: K. & K. Hofdruckerei, 1891), 232.

49. Ferdinand Lehner to the Editorial Board of the KPW, K. Weinberge, 27 March 1895, KPW, B1 Box 7, at SLW.

50. Johann Danilo to the Editorial Board of the KPW, Zara, 20 September 1891, KPW, Box 4, at SLW.

51. Protocols of the editorial committee, meeting of 7 June 1884, KPW, BD1, at SLW.

52. Ibid., session of 25 October 1884.

53. Benedict Anderson's revision of *Imagined Communities* (London: Verso, 1991) adds maps as tools of forging national cohesion. In the Habsburg case, maps were a means of rule generated through military, commercial, and finally statistical recognizance; once generated as tools of domination, they could, however, also empower factions among the ruled.

54. The manuscripts remain with the KPW materials at SLW. Böck's note dates from 29 June 1931.

55. Hamann, *Rudolf: Kronprinz*, 232.

56. These included Görz, now called Gorizia, Gradiska, Trieste, and Istria. The entire region is today part of Italy.

57. Emil Zuckerkandl and Karl Vipanz, "Zur physischen Beschaffenheit der Bevölkerung des Köstenlandes," in *Die österreichisch-ungarische Monarchie in Wort und Bild*, vol. 10 (Vienna: K. & K. Hofdruckerei, 1891), 155.

58. Ibid., 159-60.

59. The scope of this essay does not permit differentiating between divergent authorial postures, but it must be pointed out that the tone of the ethnological articles does differ, depending on the ethnicity and class of the author.

60. Franz Grieshofer, "Die Bedeutung des Ausstellungswesen," 37.

61. This essay purposely excludes the nonethnological and nonlinguistic components of the KPW from consideration. However, there are descriptions of economy, prehistory, history, and art history as well as descriptions of geography, flora, and fauna.

62. Facsimile editions of some of the volumes featuring the provinces of present-day Austria have been advertised in the late 1990s, though they do not appear on listings of books in print. A volume of excerpts from all twenty-four volumes with an intelligent introduction is Christiane Zintzen, ed., *Die österreichisch-ungarische Monarchie in Wort und Bild: Aus dem Kronprinzenwerk des Erzherzog Rudolf* (Vienna: Böhlau, 1999).

Also in the 1990s, the Archiv Verlag in Vienna undertook a reprint edition of Friedrich Umlauft's fifteen-volume work, *Die Länder Österreich-Ungarns* (originally published between 1881 and 1883), as well as Umlauft's geographic-statistical handbook of the Monarchy. Otto von Habsburg endorses this Umlauft reprint on the publisher's home page with the words, "It is good to show especially to our contemporaries how things once were, and what an enormous role Austria played. Knowledge of history is here not only a basis for patriotism, but also for an attitude toward the unified Europe. For if one looks at European efforts closely, one will recognize that European unification is to a great extent the realization of an Austrian idea in the shape of our present century" (http://www.archiv-verlag.at/).

Part Three

**"THE LEGACY:
WHERE IMAGES COLLIDE"**

Chapter 8

HUNGARIAN MOTIFS IN THE EMERGENCE AND THE DECLINE OF A CZECHOSLOVAK NATIONAL NARRATIVE, 1890-1930

Peter Haslinger

Most authorities on Czech nationalism have argued that despite some signs of radicalization during the 1890s, the Czech movement for national emancipation was well embedded in the political framework of Imperial Austria.[1] Until 1914, the political activities of Czech nationalists aimed at a solution designed to achieve self-government and regional rule for the Czechs of the Bohemian Lands. In most national concerns, the Slovaks thus remained outside of the perspective of Czech society well into the 1890s. Political cooperation with Slovene and other South Slav politicians took priority over establishing close contacts with Slovak politicians. Although a notion of closeness had long existed,[2] the Slovak élites did not appear to be potential allies in the battle for Czech political supremacy over the Germans in the Bohemian Lands.

In the 1890s Czech knowledge of Slovak society was limited and the image of a linguistically related but culturally isolated and stagnant people prevailed. Indeed, following the Austro-Hungarian *Ausgleich* of 1867, communication between the political and cultural representatives of Czechs and Slovaks had decreased. Direct contacts were limited and in general were dependent on the regular activities of individuals and cultural associations, such as the *Československanská Jednota* (the Czechoslav League). Only a small segment of the Czech political spectrum consistently devoted energy to the Slovak question. Some of these activists shared the perspective that the Slovaks were archaic and bucolic Slavic noble savages.[3] After the turn of the twentieth century, political initiative was increasingly restricted to Czech realist politicians, together with a comparatively isolated but dynamic Slovak movement grouped around the journals *Hlas* (Voice) and *Prúdy* (Streams). These nationally conscious Slovaks hoped to have found a neighboring brotherly nation that would help them to overcome national oppression and to achieve a national emancipation process of their own.

Overall, the reemergence of isolated contacts at the turn of the century could not make up for their overall decrease since the 1860s. As a result, there was even a lack of terminological clarity in referring to the Slovaks. Czech publications referred to them as Slované or Slováci interchangeably.[4] Popular works on Czech national identity, such as Václav Štech's 1897 *Národní katechismus aneb Co má věděti každý Čech!* (National catechism or what every Czech needs to know!) contained contradictory interpretations of the Czech-Slovak relationship. In some sections of the book, the Slovaks formed part of the Czech national collective, while in others, primarily in politico-historical contexts, they did not.[5]

At the same time, Czech perceptions of Hungary and its position within the Monarchy had become increasingly ambivalent. Hungary still served as an example of how to obtain historic state rights in the form of unfettered internal autonomy, enabling successive Hungarian governments to institute an independent national policy of stimulating economic development. The Czech national élite sought similar treatment based on the traditional state rights (*státní právo/ Staatsrecht*) of the Bohemian crown, but Hungarian governments intervened against these attempts on several occasions. Thus, Czech politicians increasingly considered the Magyars rivals, who joined the Germans of the Monarchy in their attempt to prevent all Slavic emancipation processes. Within this framework, one of the main reasons that the Czechs distrusted Magyar politicians was their treatment of the Slovaks, who had been confronted with increasingly forceful Magyar nation-building efforts since the 1870s.

As late as 1903, the influential Czech journal *Naše doba* (Our time) still complained about the lack of involvement of Czech society in the Slovak question. According to this journal, it could not be only a matter of ignorance that a small nation of six million was not able to develop a program to support two million conationals suffering under foreign rule. The Slovak question had been subordinated to the dogma of Bohemian state rights.[6] After the events at the village of Černová on 27 October 1907, when Hungarian gendarmes fired on demonstrating local Slovaks, leaving fourteen dead, the Slovak question made its way into Czech media.[7] There were several months of anti-Hungarian demonstrations throughout the Bohemian Lands, and a number of brochures with an explicitly political message were published.[8] Support and sympathy among Czech organizations, however, proved unpredictable. The journal *Naše Slovensko* (Our Slovakia) issued its final number after just three years, due, according to the editor Antonín Reis, to lack of interest among Czechs.[9]

There was no serious consideration on either side of creating a single Czech and Slovak state prior to 1914.[10] This changed after the outbreak of the First World War, which made a Czech political life outside the framework of the

Monarchy thinkable and, for some, even a necessity for achieving national liberation. The change is clearly reflected in one of the most important publications
of the wartime Czech exile movement, *La nation tchèque*, which first appeared in
April 1915. Its editor was Ernest Denis, professor of history at the Sorbonne and
one of the prominent critics of Hungarian minority policy before the war.

During its first year *La nation tchèque* focused on the problems of Bohemia,
Moravia, and Silesia, rarely mentioning Slovak topics. Indeed, the Slovaks first
appeared as an independent category in November 1915 in a short article
describing the banning of the *Slovenský Denník* (Slovak Daily).[11] By 1916, however, we find descriptions of a future Czech national territory, which was to
include Slovakia.[12] Parallel to this, the "Magyars" were increasingly depicted as a
hostile nation.[13] Indeed, the journal rejected notions of a liberal Hungary and
noble Magyars.[14] If, however, the Magyars would renounce their sympathies for
the Central Powers, the whole of Europe "would secure a place [for them] in a
revived and free Europe, at the side of the united and independent Czechoslovaks, Yugoslavs, and Romanians."[15]

Despite Denis's criticism of what he labeled "Magyar terror" after the *Ausgleich*, his comments did not meet the expectations of Czech wartime exile circles. He argued that after 1867, relations between the Slovaks and Prague
"became less regular and more uncertain" and that there were "striking contrasts
between the two countries" (Moravia and Slovakia).[16] Denis's analysis presented Slovak identities as being far more hybrid and fluid than suited the Czech-
exile politicians who were elaborating the new Czecho-Slovak national narrative.
In April 1917 important changes occurred in the journal. Denis resigned as editor, and the journal was reorganized under the future foreign minister and second president of Czechoslovakia, Edvard Beneš, who gave it a more explicitly
propagandistic character.[17]

Beneš's publications in support of Czech independence were not, however,
limited to the journal. In *Bohemia: A Case for Independence* (1917), a translation
of his book, *Détruisez l'Autrich-Hongrie* (1916),[18] Beneš described the Czech-
Slovak relationship as follows:

> The term Czecho-Slovaks, or simply the Czechs, includes two branches of the same nation:
> seven millions of Czechs living in Bohemia, Moravia, Silesia, and three millions of Slovaks
> inhabiting the north of Hungary.... These two peoples have the same civilization, the
> same language and history ... The only obstacle of their complete union is one of a polit-
> ical character, the Czechs being under the yoke of Austria, while the Slovaks are under that
> of Hungary and the Magyars.[19]

In order to squelch any doubt about the national affiliation of the Slovaks,
Beneš elaborated on the inimical nature of the Magyars, an argument that would
set narrow limits to Slovak national self-articulation as well as to the establishment of friendly relations with whatever would remain as a Hungarian state. In
the chapter "The Czecho-Slovaks and the Magyars. A legend to be destroyed,"
Beneš wrote that a division of the "two branches of the Czecho-Slovak nation"

had in fact existed only since the second half of the nineteenth century, and thus the differences between the two peoples were insignificant. He also questioned the degree of both integration of the Slovak territory into the Hungarian state and contacts between Slovak and Magyar societies, which he asserted had been marginal, primarily due to the Orientalness of the Magyars. Their national character was, according to Beneš, incompatible with European norms as well as with the needs of the Slovak population.[20]

The looming demise of Austro-Hungarian dualism and the geopolitical thinking that had developed during the war made Czecho-Slovak unity seem an ideal basis for all possible options. The first publications describing the territory of a future Czech-Slovak state without considering any longer the problem of the constitutional framework of the Austro-Hungarian Monarchy appeared in early 1918.[21] Although most Slovak politicians favored independence from Hungary by the end of the war,[22] there were no declarations from within Slovakia proclaiming the Czechoslovak concept before spring 1918. In their first declaration after years of silence, the leaders of the Slovak National Party claimed the right of self-determination and declared themselves in favor of the formation of an independent state of Czechs and Slovaks on 24 May 1918. Two weeks earlier, a declaration of Czech writers had spoken of the "Czechoslovak nation," a formula that Czech members of the Viennese Reichsrat employed only three weeks later, on 30 May.[23]

In this context, however, it was a serious drawback that at the end of the war both the Czechs and Slovaks were limited in their ability to conceptualize their new *imagined community*. Slovak elements in and contributions to it were mainly minor additions to the already well-established Czech national narrative. Only a few academics attempted to apply scholarly rigor to a shared definition of the term Czechoslovak. The Czechs Victor Dvorský[24] and Jan Kapras,[25] both members of the Czechoslovak delegation at the Paris Peace Conference, attempted to create a normative Czechoslovak geography or states right concept. Emanuel Chalupný, a Czech sociologist and author of works on the Czech nation, displayed conceptual helplessness when he tried to construct an overlapping national character for both Czechs and Slovaks in *Český stát s hlediska sociologie* (The Czech state from a sociological perspective)(1918).[26] Chalupný dwelled upon the incompatibility of various national characters, for example, "The Magyar character is the opposite of the Czech one" or "The Magyar and the Slovak character go together like fire and water." Some of his main arguments, however, referred to the location of the Magyars in space and natural environment. In contrast to the Magyars, who occupied the Hungarian plain, the other nations within Hungary stayed in the mountainous areas, where they found protection against Magyar attacks. "One of these nations was the Slovaks," Chalupný wrote; "Slovakia is mountainous, more mountainous than Bohemia or Moravia." The character of the region "differs therefore more from the character of the Magyar areas than from those of the lands of the Bohemian crown…. The character of the Slovaks is a typical mountainous one, like the Czech one, as well."[27]

Not only Czech authors became active in claiming the Slovaks as part of their nation. Confronting defeat and facing the disintegration of the multinational Hungarian state, a vivid Hungarian propaganda campaign emerged with the end of the war.[28] In this context, the Hungarian leadership partially reinterpreted the Hungarian national concept. Before the war, national rhetoric seemed to have accepted linguistic diversity within the country, but had also aimed at the assimilation of the middle stratum of the national minorities into Magyar society in the course of modernization. The prewar and wartime rhetorical aggressiveness of newspapers and scholars toward the minorities virtually disappeared. While multiethnicity had clearly been a negative construct before 1918, the existence of ethnic minorities now served as proof of Hungarian national tolerance. Needless to say, in this context self-critical approaches to the strategies of assimilation that applied before 1918 remained in the minority.[29]

In their publications, Magyar authors referred to the newly created Czechoslovak Republic as a national state with a contradictory territorial and thus cultural legacy,[30] and Slovakia as a territory only provisionally occupied by the "Czechs" (or, as one author noted, "occupied by the Masaryk crowd").[31] They depicted Czechoslovakia as the product of arbitrary border changes with a highly artificial state concept—they even compared the notion of the "Czecho-Slovak people" to "ethnographical curiosities such as the Austro-Hungarian or the Swedish-Norwegian people."[32] Under the oppressive rule of the Czechs, they argued, the Slovaks would automatically return to Hungarian rule as soon as a free expression of collective will—in the form of a plebiscite—made it possible.[33]

Hungarian propaganda was designed to get the attention of two groups: the international community and élite in Slovakia, whom they assumed remained overwhelmingly patriotic toward Hungary as a mother nation. The signs coming from the Slovak political élite, however, were not encouraging. In the Declaration of Turčiansky Svätý Martin on 30 October 1918, an assembly of Slovak politicians and intellectuals demanded self-determination and expressed a desire to join the Czechs in a common state. At the meeting, however, two camps emerged on the question of how to organize Slovakia within the new Republic. A clear majority favored full-scale national emancipation in the frame of territorial autonomy. This cleavage among Slovak politicians was poorly hidden in the text of the declaration, however, which referred to the Slovaks in contradictory terms ("The Slovak branch of a united Czecho-Slovak nation," "the Czecho-Slovak nation living in Hungary," and "the Slovak nation").[34]

As the proclamation of an independent Czecho-Slovakia became known in Slovakia, it met with nothing like the enthusiasm it had met in part of the Bohemian Lands.[35] Whereas the Czech national movement had strong support from political parties and national protective organizations, Slovak national structures were at best decentralized.[36] In 1919, general instability mounted due to clashes between Czechoslovak forces and troops of Béla Kun's Hungarian Soviet in southern and eastern Slovakia. Moreover, the Slovak share in the political leadership of the new state suffered a substantial blow with the death in an airplane crash on 4 May 1919 of the designated Minister of War, Milan Rastislav Štefánik, who might have served as an overarching integrative figure.

Those Slovaks who supported the Czechoslovak concept (for example, Ivan Dérer and Vavro Šrobár) perceived any institutional framework of Slovak self-government as endangering Czechoslovak national emancipation. In 1924, Dérer, a leading Slovak Social Democrat, Minister of Unification from 1920 to 1921, and later Minister of Education, would describe the situation in Slovakia during 1918-19 as follows:

> [Slovakia] was in one respect totally different from that in Bohemia, Moravia, or Silesia, where the war had roused the spirit of the whole Czech nation. Almost everyone considered it an offense of national feeling, national pride, and the holiest ideals of the nation ... In Slovakia conditions were much different. The brutal Magyarizing regime, which made even the smallest free movement impossible, led so far that with the outbreak of the World War there was almost no national consciousness in the broad masses of the people.[37]

The Czechoslovakists therefore harbored suspicions from the beginning that Slovak autonomy would function as a retreat for pro-Hungarian loyalties and sentiments. They were convinced that Hungarian propaganda influenced the pro-autonomist statements of politicians like Andrej Hlinka and Vojtech Tuka.[38] That Hlinka's former collaborator, František Jehlička, had joined the ranks of revisionist authors in Hungary only increased their suspicions.[39] The way Slovak autonomy was implemented with the help of Hlinka's Slovak People's Party in 1927-1928—the *Slovenská krajina* (Slovak land) formed one of four administrative units with only limited autonomy—failed to meet the expectations of Slovak autonomists. Soon after Slovakia was granted limited autonomy, Tuka was convicted of high treason, on the grounds of an article in which he proclaimed the existence of a legal vacuum in Slovakia, and sentenced to fifteen years in prison. On 5 October 1929, the Slovak People's Party returned to pro-autonomist rhetoric.[40] Their plan for autonomy, submitted to the Czechoslovak National Assembly in 1930, was not, however, debated in the parliament.[41]

In 1929, Albert Pražák, professor of Czech literature at Comenius University in Bratislava, published the pamphlet *Maďarská propaganda proti Československu* (Hungarian propaganda against Czechoslovakia), with which he must have poured oil into the flame of Slovak autonomy. Pražák took what he called the "intensified psychosis [of] the Magyars in neighboring Hungary" as a basis for reenforcing the official narrative of Czechoslovakia. Responding to what he considered the aggressive tone of some Hungarian propaganda, Pražák asserted that Slovak autonomy would be "the last phase of their [Hungary's] work undermining Czechoslovakia."[42]

It is difficult to estimate the level of influence of the Hungarian revisionist propaganda, but we can be quite sure that the Czechoslovakists overestimated the danger it posed to the integrity of the First Republic.[43] What is perhaps more important is that the constant flow of Hungarian revisionist propaganda into Slovakia also stimulated suspicion of political forces like the People's Party, whose majority was definitely not pro-Hungarian. Throughout the 1920s, various publications of an explicit Czechoslovak character reflected this suspicion. For example, in *Zehn Jahre tschechoslowakischer Politik* (1929), Josef Borovička commented that among the Slovak clerics under the leadership of parliamentary deputy Hlinka who were "agitating with the catchword of a Slovak autonomy and turning it against the Czechs … remarkable influences of Magyar culture and Magyar milieu and of purely irredentist elements that are hostile to the state" had not yet been overcome.[44]

This perspective encouraged the inclusion of anti-Hungarian elements in the Czechoslovak national narrative. To explain the passive behavior of Slovak society in autumn 1918, the authors pointed to the legacy of Magyar domination in Transleithania: The policy of Magyarization resulted in subservient behavior on the part of the majority of ethnic Slovaks. The authors further elaborated upon the anti-Magyar elements that had been developed in exile during the First World War. In a semiofficial Czechoslovak publication published in 1919, *Magyars and the Czecho-Slovak Republic. Their Past and Their Present Relations*, Karel Kadlec, one of the few Czech experts on Hungarian affairs before 1918, described the Magyar-Czech relationship as one of intimate enmity. He asserted a pattern similar to that of the Czech-German *Konfliktgemeinschaft* when depicting the "brutal Magyar egoism." Like the Germans, the Magyars "are fanatical enemies of the Czecho-Slovak nation." The real Magyar

> has a different mentality than other Europeans, and it is useless to debate with him even the most elementary political questions…. Like the Huns and Avars of earlier times they are settled in the center of Hungary and hold by terror, or rather did before the monarchy was broken up, the nations living around them.[45]

In the early 1920s, only a handful of Czechs—Karel Kálal, Karel Kadlec, Alois Kolísek, Albert Pražák, and Stanislav Klíma—elaborated on the suppressive character of the pre-1918 Hungarian system and the alleged Orientalism of the Magyars.[46] Nevertheless, the majority of those Czech politicians who commented on the problem believed that Slovak national-political individuality was a legacy of the Hungarian period. As they did with the Moravians, most Czech politicians considered the differences between Czechs and Slovaks to be of an ethnographic quality only. They believed that these differences would disappear virtually automatically over the course of time. Therefore, the differences should have no consequences for the administrative structure of Czechoslovakia, not least because of the need to stress Czecho-Slovak national unity. From that perspective, the Moravian-Slovak divide appeared artificial and reversible. Most markers of ethnic difference—which obviously existed between the Czechs and the Slovaks—would disappear under the impact of modernization, which was to be patterned upon the successful Czech model. This attitude was reflected in the chapter on folk culture in *Die Tschechoslowakische Republik. Jahrbuch 1928*, one of the official publications of the tenth anniversary of the Czechoslovak Republic in 1928:

Thus far, there are great differences between the West and the East of our republic. These are likely to disappear within a couple of years, however, through the hard work of the intelligentsia and the people. But, as a result, the original folk culture and art that are so characteristic for these territories will slowly die out.[47]

Clearly, those publications that attempted to inform Czech society about the eastern part of the Republic reproduced prewar images of Slovakia as home to a neglected but authentic Slavic people.[48] The Czech writer František Xaver Šalda's critical remarks, in a review of Alois Mrštík's description of his journey through Slovakia (1919), pointed to the lack of political dimension in most such descriptions. Šalda wrote:

What does the author, one of the most outstanding of this time, tell us about the Slovak soul? … In Mrštík's book we find hardly any human beings. And if we do, they mostly appear as decoration…. The author maintains a purely tourist perspective when taking a look at the soul of the people…. What we need today is twenty or thirty years of work on Slovakia.[49]

During the 1920s, Slovakia evoked less and less interest among political and intellectual circles in Prague. Some influential works on "national essence," such as, Ferdinand Peroutka's *Jáci jsme* (What we are like), made little reference to the Slovaks at all.[50] It was, however, Peroutka, one of the central figures in the political life of the First Czechoslovak Republic, who came up with the terse but telling formula for dissolving Slovakia "like sugar in a glass of water."[51] This left Czechoslovak President Tomáš Garrigue Masaryk complaining about the ignorance of Czech politicians, who were bound to their own clientele in Czech-speaking territories.[52] As professor of philosophy at the Czech University in Prague, Masaryk had tried to establish cordial relations between Czech and Slovak intellectuals before 1914.[53] Masaryk, however, consistently rejected the notion that the Slovaks formed an independent nation, declaring that they were Czechs, "although they use their dialect as a written language."[54] He paid little attention to the development of the Czechoslovak national concept, but rather considered Czech-Slovak unity natural.[55]

The first encounters between Czech state officials and the Slovak population at the local level resulted in mutual frustration. As the historian Yeshayahu Jelinek has written, "the industrious, free-thinking, social-minded, somewhat jovial Czech found himself in a deeply religious, rather old-fashioned, conservative country with a high appreciation for the ethos of the aristocracy."[56] Moreover, the Czech political élite found it difficult to understand why Slovak politicians from across the spectrum, Hlinka and Šrobár alike, employed antisemitic rhetoric after the Bolshevik interlude of summer 1919.[57] Such rhetoric contradicted the confessional tolerance promoted in official Czechoslovakism, which recognized the Jews of Czechoslovakia as a national minority. On the local level in Slovakia, social unrest contributed to a large extent to the stigmatization of Jews. The victims of riots and plundering in Slovakia in the wake of the First World War had been almost exclusively Magyars and Jews.[58]

By the early 1920s, the Hungarian motif began to function as a formula to explain the political performance of many Slovak politicians. For example, *Přítomnost*, edited by Peroutka and one of the most influential political-intellectual publications of the First Republic, often contained ambivalent reports on the political situation in Slovakia. Although the articles contained self-critical remarks about Czech behavior and attitudes from 1918 to 1919, they at the same time promoted a very negative picture of Slovak political culture. Typical of remarks on politics in Slovakia, which still assumed the superiority of the Czech element in Czech-Slovak relations, is the following:

> We, the Czechs in Slovakia, are fighters in a historical battle, which is not to be won within a mere ten years, but which can be lost with only one tactical mistake. We are creators of the Slovakia of the future and with that also the future of the Czechoslovak Republic.[59]

The Czech journalist Bohumil Müller, chief editor of *Slovenský východ* (Slovak East) in Košice during the early 1920s, who had also worked as a correspondent in Budapest, believed that the actions of many Slovak politicians were due to the value system they had adopted under Hungarian rule. In his arguments, Müller transferred Magyar "Orientalism" to the Slovaks, which enabled him to clearly distinguish between two nations, the Czech and the Slovak, by 1926.[60]

The inability of Czech politicians, publicists, and scholars to conceptualize the new national community of the Czechoslovaks left the task of constructing the narrative of unity mainly to the Slovak representatives of the Czechoslovak concept. To emphasize unity with the Czechs, some of their contributions argued along "Czech" patterns, which originated in a different social and political context, namely that of Czech-German relations in Bohemia, and were not always fully understood on the Slovak local level. It is therefore not surprising that even the Czechoslovakists among the Slovaks referred to "the Slovaks" (and not to the "Czechoslovaks") in certain contexts, and to the "Slovak" nation when confronting the "Magyars" (not the "Hungarians"). The half-hearted implementation of the new Czechoslovak state concept on the Slovak side sometimes resulted in ambiguity in the rhetoric, which was thought to be pro-Czechoslovakist.[61] There are indications that most Slovak politicians, who viewed themselves as advocates of the new state, adopted a double rhetoric similar to tactics employed in the 1930s by Sudeten German activist politicians. When addressing their political grass roots, they adopted language that seemed to contradict the rhetoric they applied in an official, Czechoslovak context.[62]

In this respect Šrobár, first plenipotentiary minister for Slovakia and one of the most important proponents of Czechoslovak interests in Slovakia, provides a good example of this. Šrobár often delivered statements that were compatible with Slovak style and argumentative patterns of that time: "We still have to work today, in order to bring the city dwellers, who had become unfaithful to their nation, back to the bosom of the Slovak nation."[63] Such rhetoric differed substantially from his performance when expressing adherence to the principles of the First Czechoslovak Republic:

The Czechoslovak Republic wants to develop into a modern, progressive state—in the spirit of its traditions and the most noble and humanitarian principles of its president. Into a state in which there will be the shield of freedom, civil equality, nationality, and social justice.[64]

It is likely that Šrobár's use of the term "Slovak" in this context ought not to be interpreted as a subtle revolt against a patronizing Czech perspective. Rather, it should be understood as a means of bringing the Slovak intelligentsia closer to the abstract Czechoslovak concept. The outcome, however, must have been contrary to the intentions of the Czechoslovak élite. During the 1920s, Slovak autonomists transferred a rhetoric of dependency from the Magyars to the Czechs by expressing political frustration over the fact that they, at one time or another, seemed to be dominated by benevolent yet ignorant Others (first the Magyars, then the Czechs). As the debate over the reform of Slovak orthography in 1931 clearly demonstrated,[65] by the early 1930s two varieties of a Czechoslovak national narrative had been developing, one Czech, one Slovak. Neither was any longer compatible with the other. Indeed, in 1937, Czechoslovak Prime Minister Milan Hodža, himself a Slovak, spoke in favor of accepting the fact "that in the Czechoslovak people there exist two nationalisms, one Czech and one Slovak." On the issue of whether "there will develop an artificial dualism where we do not need any," however, Hodža's position still reflected the need of a disintegrating state to balance its centrifugal forces. Despite the two languages, he asserted, "I am convinced that there must be only one national spirit."[66]

The effectiveness of the Czechoslovak national narrative was therefore diminished not only by the serious problems that occurred in the administrative field. The ambiguity and incoherence of the official reading of Czechoslovakism, which failed to meet the demands of the majority of the nationally conscious Slovak intelligentsia who wished the Czechoslovak state to develop as a binational entity, also reduced it. This enabled the Slovaks to consolidate as a national community according to their political traditions, which differed from those of the Czechs.

In the end, the incorporation of "Hungarian" elements into the national narrative first served as a means of establishing "Czechoslovakism," then as a means of destabilizing it. Hungarian claims to Slovakia did not result in a strengthening of the Czecho-Slovak axis, primarily because neither Czechs nor Slovaks had the capacity to conceptualize the new national community. A division of labor between Czech and Slovak politicians and publicists was needed to make Czecho-Slovak unity plausible. In this context, the claims put forth in Hungarian political literature provided an independent Slovak intelligentsia additional room to maneuver. The inclusion of Hungarian motifs fueled discussion over "Slovakness," while those arguments that should have been promoting Czechoslovak national unity by creating a sharp division with the Magyars stressed the divide with the Czechs, as well. Unintended by either Czech or Hungarian leaders, the overlapping claims on both sides supported Slovak efforts to preserve and develop an independent national narrative within the new Czechoslovak context.

Notes

1. The following studies survey the social and cultural development of Czech society within the framework of the Habsburg Monarchy. See Peter Bugge, *Czech Nation-Building: National Self-Perception and Politics, 1780-1914* (Ph.D. dissertation, Aarhus Universitet, 1994); Jiří Kořalka, *Tschechen im Habsburgerreich und in Europa 1815-1914. Sozialgeschichtliche Zusammenhänge der neuzeitlichen Nationsbildung und der Nationalitätenfrage in den böhmischen Ländern* (Munich: Oldenbourg, 1991); Jan Křen, *Die Konfliktgemeinschaft. Tschechen und Deutsche 1780-1918* (Munich: Oldenbourg, 1996); Otto Urban, *Die tschechische Gesellschaft 1848 bis 1918* (Vienna: Böhlau, 1994), 2 vol.

2. Jan Rychlík, *Češi a Slováci v 20. století. Česko-slovenské vztahy 1914-1945* (Bratislava: Academia Electronic Press, 1998), 23. For the Czech-Slovak relationship in the First Republic, see also Elisabeth Bakke, *Doomed to Failure? The Czechoslovak Nation Project and the Slovak Autonomist Reaction, 1918-38* (Oslo: Unipub forlag Akademia, 1999).

3. David W. Paul, "Slovak Nationalism and the Hungarian State, 1870-1910," in *Ethnic Groups and the State*, ed. Paul Brass (Totowa, N.J.: Barnes & Noble, 1985), 117. For examples of this perspective see Karel Kálal, *Jdete na Slovensko!* (Královské Vinohrady: Svoboda, 1904); Karel Kálal, *Na krásném Slovensku* (Prague: Vilímek, 1910); *Slovensko. Sborník statí věnovaných kraji a lidu slovenskému* (Prague: Umělecká beseda, 1900).

4. Josef Harna and Ivan Kamenec, *Česká a slovenská kultura mezi dvěma válkami* (Prague: Horizont, 1988), 13.

5. Václav Štech, *Národní katechismus aneb Co má věděti každý Čech!* (Prague, 1897).

6. *Naše doba* 9 (1903): 1-2.

7. On the events at Černová and their role in Slovak national emancipation, see Roman Holec, *Tragédia v Černovej a slovenská spoločnost* (Martin: Matica Slovenská, 1997).

8. Karel Kálal, *Slovensko a Slováci* (Prague: Šimáček, 1905); Karel Kálal, *Proč se o Slováky staráme?* (Prague: Československá jednota, 1906); Stanislav Klíma, *O národních poměrech na Slovensku* (Prague: F. Hoblík, 1902); *Naše Slovensko. Časová úvaha agitační* (Prague: Náklad. Antonín Reis, 1907).

9. *Naše Slovensko*, June/July 1910, 329-30.

10. James Ramon Felak, "*At the Price of the Republic*," *Hlinka's Slovak People's Party, 1929-1938* (Pittsburgh: University of Pittsburgh Press, 1994), 13.

11. *La nation tchèque* 1, 1 November 1915, 209-10.

12. *La nation tchèque* 1, 1 June 1915, 35.

13. First in *La nation tchèque* 1, 15 January 1916, 280-83.

14. *La nation tchèque* 2, 1 July 1916, 70.

15. Ibid., 2, 1 July 1916, 72. In this number, the "Czecho-Slovaks" as a national collective—and not "Czecho-Slovakia" as a state—appeared in an article describing education, economy, and arts of both groups separately (69-83). Articles appearing in July and August still referred to the "Czech lands without Slovakia" or "the Czech people" only. *La nation tchèque* 1, 15 July 1916, 89; *La nation tchèque* 1, 15 August 1915, 125.

16. *La nation tchèque* 2, 15 September 1916, 150.

17. Frank Hadler, ed., *Weg von Österreich! Das Weltkriegsexil von Masaryk und Beneš im Spiegel ihrer Briefe und Aufzeichnungen aus den Jahren 1914 bis 1918* (Berlin: Akademie-Verlag, 1995), 376-77, 434; on the political history of the Czech exiles, see H.L. Rees, *The Czechs during World War I: The Path to Independence* (New York: Columbia University Press, 1992).

18. Edvard Beneš, *Détruisez l'Autrich-Hongrie! Le martyre des Tchéco-Slovaques a travers l'histoire* (Paris: Delagrave, 1916). On the life and work of Edvard Beneš, see among recent publications, Z.A. Zeman and Antonín Klímek, *The Life of Edvard Beneš, 1884–1948: Czechoslovakia in Peace and War* (Oxford: Clarendon Press, 1997); F. Havlíček, *Edvard Beneš. Čověk, sociolog, politik* (Prague: Prospektrum, 1991).

19. Edvard Beneš, *Bohemia: A Case for Independence* (London: Allen & Unwin, 1917), 1.

20. Beneš, *Bohemia*, 39. For Beneš's views on Slovakia during the First Czechoslovak Republic, see Valerián Bystrický, "Eduard Beneš a Slovensko, 1918-1938," *Historický časopis* 43 (1995): 246-62; Valerián Bystrický, "Dokumenty o postoji Eduarda Beneša k česko-slovenský vztähom koncom tridsiatych a začiatkom štyridsiatych rokov," *Historický časopis* 43 (1995): 317-27.

21. For example, Karel Kálal, *Slovanské pohledy* (Praha: Vilímek, 1917); Alois Kolísek, *Slováci do státu československého* (Hodonín, 1918). At the end of the war, Viktor Dvorský, one of the main representatives of the Czech delegation to the peace conference, also attempted to provide a detailed description of the future borders of Czechoslovakia. Viktor Dvorský, *Území českého národa* (Prague: Český Čtenář, 1918).

22. László Szarka, *Szlovák nemzeti fejlődés—magyar nemzetiségi politika 1867-1918* (Bratislava: Kalligram Könyvkiadó, 1995), 199.

23. Harna and Kamenec, *Česká a slovenská kultura*, 24; J. Šolc, *Slovensko v českej politike* (Banská Bystrica: Enterprise, 1993), 44.

24. Viktor Dvorský, *Území českého národa.*

25. Jan Kapras, *Český stát v historickém vývoji a v dnešní podobě dle ustanovení kongresu pařížského* (Prague: Národa, 1920).

26. Emanuel Chalupný, *Národní povaha česká* (Prague, 1907); Emanuel Chalupný, *Úkol českého národa* (Prague: Přehled, 1910).

27. Emanuel Chalupný, *Český stát s hlediska sociologie* (Prague: Borový, 1918), 29-30.

28. The following foreign-language publications on the Slovak question appeared: Ferenc Fodor, *The Geographical Impossibility of the Czech State* (Budapest: Ferdinand Pfeiffer, 1920); L. Steier and J. Makoldy, *There Is No Czech Culture in Upper Hungary* (Budapest: Ph. Wodianer & Sons, 1920); Zoltán Gerevich, *La Slovaquie, Terre de l'avenir* (Budapest: Viktor Hornyánszky, 1920).

29. Peter Haslinger, "Spannungsfelder zwischen Ethnikum, Nation und Territorium in ungarisch-sprachigen Monographien 1890-1919," in *Ethnikum und Territorium*, ed. H. Förster (forthcoming). For the institutional background of the Hungarian revisionist movement, see Anikó Kovács-Bertrand, *Der ungarische Revisionismus nach dem Ersten Weltkrieg. Der publizistische Kampf gegen den Friedensvertrag von Trianon (1918-1931)* (Munich: Oldenbourg, 1997). For emphasis on Slovakia see F. Ruttkay, *Maďarská irredenta a Slovensko (1918-1920)* (Bratislava: Kubko Goral, 1997). For political background of the late 1930s, see Magda Ádám, *The Little Entente and Europe (1920-1929)* (Budapest: Akadémiai Kiadó, 1993); Ladislav Deák, *Hra o Slovensko. Slovensko v politike maďarská a polská v rokoch 1933–1939* (Bratislava: VEDA, 1991); Jörg K. Hoensch, *Der ungarische Revisionismus und die Zerschlagung der Tsche-choslowakei* (Tübingen: Mohr, 1967). On the Czechoslovak aspects of the Trianon Peace Treaty, see also Ignác Romsics, *Trianon és a magyar politikai gondolkodás* (Budapest: Osiris, 1998).

30. Analysis of the use of arguments on historical and natural rights in the border-drawing process can be found in O. Krejcí, *Czechoslovak National Interest: A Historical Survey of Czechoslovak National Interests and Reflections on the Demise of Czechoslovak Communism* (Boulder, Colo: East European Monographs, 1996), 104-32.

31. B. Iványi, *Felső-Magyarországról* (Szeged: Városi nyomda és könyvkiadó, 1930), 5.

32. Ibid.

33. Peter Haslinger, "Im Schatten von Trianon: Konstruktionsversuche eines nationalen Territoriums und einer nationalen Wir-Gruppe in der ungarischen politischen Publizistik 1919-1939," in *Bilder vom Eigenen und Feinden aus den Donau-Balkan-Raum*, ed. Gabriela Schubert and Wolfgang Dahmen (Munich: Südosteuropa-Gesellschaft, 2003), 281-301. The most influential work in this respect is Lajos Steier's massive *Ungarns Vergewaltigung. Oberungarn unter tschechischer Herrschaft* (Vienna: Amalthea-Verlag, 1929).

34. Felak, *"At the Price of the Republic,"* 15. The most comprehensive study on the administrative and constitutional law of Czechoslovakia remains Ladislav Lipscher, *Verfassung und politische Verwaltung in der Tschechoslowakei 1918–1939* (Munich: Oldenbourg, 1979).

35. Robert B. Pynsent, *Questions of Identity: Czech and Slovak Ideas of Nationality and Personality* (Budapest, London, New York: Central European University Press, 1994), 151.

36. Several examples of local implications of the struggle over national identity can be found in Ismo Nurmi, *Slovakia–a Playground for Nationalism and National Identity: Manifestations of the National Identity of the Slovaks, 1918-1920* (Helsinki: Suomen Historiallinen Seura, 1999).

37. Ivan Dérer, *Slovensko v prevrate a po ňom* (Bratislava: Graf. knihař. a nakl. družstvo, 1924), 1-2.

38. On Andrej Hlinka, see A. Bartlová, *Andrej Hlinka* (Bratislava: Obzor, 1991).

39. His publications include František Jehlička, *Naš program* (McKeesport, Pa.: Samostatnost, 1932); Ferenc Jehlicka, *A revízió és a szlovákok* (Budapest: Erdély férfiak egyesülete, 1933); Francis Jehlicka, *Reply to Mr. R.W. Seton Watson's Book "Slovakia Then and Now"* (Vienna, 1932).

40. Vojtech Tuka, *V desiatom roku Martinskej Deklarácie. Štátofilozofická úvaha* (Bratislava, 1928).

41. Bakke, *Doomed to Failure*, 512. For a detailed analysis of Slovak plans for autonomy see ibid., 454-510.

42. Albert Pražák, *Maďárská propaganda proti Československu* (Bratislava, 1929), 3-4, 9.

43. On the activities of Hungarian revisionists, see also Stanislav Klíma, *Maďárská propaganda. Jak pracuje k odstranění trianonského míru* (Prague: Orbis, 1923); Ivan Dérer, *K revisi trianonského míru* (Prague: Svaz Národního Osvobození, 1928); Karel Stloukal, *Československá jednota a Rothermerova akce* (Prague: Politický klub československé národní demokracie, 1928).

44. Josef Borovička, *Zehn Jahre tschechoslowakischer Politik* (Prague: Orbis, 1929), 5.

45. Karel Kadlec, *Magyars and the Czecho-Slovak Republic. Their Past and Their Present Relations* (Prague: Czecho-Slovak Foreigners' Office, 1919), 16, 5, 15; in Hungarian translation, *A magyarok és a Cseh-szlovák köztársaság. Múlt és jelenkori érintkezések* (Prague: Czecho-Slovak Foreigners' Office, 1919).

46. On the predominantly Slovak contributions to the scholarly debate over Czechoslovakism, see Bakke, *Doomed to Failure*, 239-62.

47. Bohumil Horák, *Die Tschechoslowakische Republik. Jahrbuch 1928* (Prague: Orbis, 1928), 210.

48. For example, Stanislav Klíma, *Slovenská vlasť* (Prague: Náklad. Českej grafickej unie, 1921); Stanislav Klíma, ed., *Z českej spisby o Slovensku* (Prague: Unie, 1921); Karel Kálal, *Češi na Slovansku* (Prague: Kočí, 1919); Václav Chaloupecký, *Staré Slovensko* (Bratislava: Filosofická fakulta univ. Komensk., 1923); František Kretz, *Informace o Slovensku* (Uherské Hradiště: Kiesswetter, 1918). Stanislav Klíma published a textbook for Czechs, who thereby became familiar with the basics of Slovak grammar and simpler texts. Stanislav Klíma, *Jak se naučím slovansky?* (Prague: Topic, 1919).

49. Cited in Josef Harna, "Nationalkulturen und Koexistenz der Tschechen und Slowaken in den Jahren der Ersten Tschechoslowakischen Republik," *Bohemia* 32 (1991): 42.

50. Peroutka, author of *Budování státu,* asserted: "All in all, as a nation we still do not know well enough what we are like…. It seems to us that the existence of the Czech nation becomes more certain and our national character more clear." Ferdinand Peroutka, *Jací jsme* (Prague: Borový, 1934), 8-9. On the absence of Slovak elements in works on the national cause, see František Joklík, *Naše dějinné poslání. Časová úvaha politicko-ethická* (Prague: Hejda & Tuček, 1920); Antonín Hajn, *Naše poslání. Šest kapitolek o minulosti a budoucnosti* (Prague, 1918); Kapras, *Český stát v historickém vývoji;* Václav Sobotka, *Masarykův realismus a dnešní problémy českého nacionalismu* (Beroun: Šefl, 1925).

51. Owen W. Johnson, *Slovakia, 1918-1938: Education and the Making of the Nation* (Boulder, Colo.: East European Monographs, 1985), 68.

52. Friedrich Prinz, "Die tschechische Literatur zwischen Staatsbejahung, Gesellschaftskritik und Internationalismus," in *Die demokratisch-parlamentarische Struktur der Ersten Tschechoslowakischen Republik,* ed. Karl Bosl (Munich: Oldenbourg, 1975): 159-69.

53. Masaryk's attitudes towards Slovakia are documented in Jaroslav Opat, Miloš Tomčík, and Zdeněk Urban, *T.G. Masaryk a Slovensko* (Prague: Masarykova Společnost, 1992).

54. Cited in Jaroslav Šolc, *Slovensko v českej politike* (Banská Bystrica: Enterprise, 1993), 40.

55. Vladimír Bakoš, "Nation, Nationalism, and Culture in Slovakia," in *Formen des nationalen Bewußtseins im Lichte zeitgenössischer Nationalismustheorien*, ed. Eva Schmidt-Hartmann (Munich: Oldenbourg, 1994), 311.

56. Yeshayahu Jelinek, *The Parish Republic: Hlinka's Slovak People's Party, 1939-1945* (Boulder, Colo.: East European Monographs, 1976), 5-6.

57. This can be found in most of the following works, which dealt with the inclusion of Slovakia into the new state primarily from the perspective of a decade: Václav Chaloupecky, *Zápas o Slovensko 1918* (Prague: Čin, 1930); Fedor Houdek, *Osvobodenie Slovenska(1918-1919)* (Bratislava, 1929); Milan Janota, *10 rokov oslobodeného Slovenska* (Bratislava: Typografie, 1928); Stanislav Klíma, *Osvobozené Slovensko* (Prague: J. Otto, 1926); Vavro Šrobár, *Osvobodené Slovensko. Pamäti z rokov 1918-1920* (Prague: Čin, 1928), 2 vol.

58. Nurmi, *Slovakia–A Playground for Nationalism*, 186-87.

59. *Přítomnost*, 21 July 1927, 433.

60. "Národ Československý," *Přítomnost*, 16 October 1926, 568. Müller's statements were also paternalistic. The Slovaks, unfit for a full-fledged national development, had to rely on help from others: "We understand why the Slovaks dislike the Czechs: because of their westernness. This is only a cultural conflict of a sort that … we already have been confronted with in Moravia." In spiritual terms the Slovaks were the "better Slavs" than the Czechs. "It is [however] certain that without the help of the Czechs the Slovaks would not have been able to rely on an independent national and cultural life in the future. Proof of this is the striking advance of Magyarization." Bohumil Müller, "Česko-slovenské rozpory a protiklady," *Přítomnost*, 1 April 1926, 179-81.

61. One version read: With the declaration of Turčiansky Sväty Martin "the whole of Slovakia was taken by the initiative of her leaders. The Czechoslovak idea was winning all along the line, and it made its way into the hearts of every Slovak." Houdek, *Osvobodenie Slovenska*, 11.

62. Ronald M. Smelser, "Die Henleinpartei. Eine Deutung," in *Die Erste Tschechoslowakische Republik als multinationaler Parteienstaat*, ed. Karl Bosl (Munich: Oldenbourg, 1979), 200.

63. Vavro Šrobár, "Slovensko a prevrat," in Cyril Merhout and Bohumil Němec, eds. *Československá národní čitanka* (Prague: Státní nakladatelství, 1928, 16.

64. Vavro Šrobár, *Československo na mapě Evropy* (Prague, 1928), 19.

65. On the conflict over the new Slovak orthography see Bakke, *Doomed to Failure*, 352-55.

66. Milan Hodža, *Moderní nacionalismus* (Prague: Legie, 1936), 6. Recent publications on Hodža include: K. Kollár, *Milan Hodža. Moderní teoretik, pragmatický politik* (Bratislava: STIMUL, 1994); J. Juríček, *Milan Hodža. Kapitola z dejín slovenskej, československanskej a európskej politiky* (Bratislava: Obzor, 1994); Miroslav Pekník *Milan Hodža. Štátnik a politik* (Bratislava: Veda, 1994).

Chapter 9

THE SOUTH SLAVS
IN THE AUSTRIAN IMAGINATION

Serbs and Slovenes in the Changing View
from German Nationalism to National Socialism

Christian Promitzer

In 1819 the Austrian poet Franz Grillparzer journeyed to Italy, visiting the crownland of Styria, whose southern part was populated by Slovenes. Leaving the German-speaking part of the country, he wrote in his journal:

> The landscape is changing here. The beautiful, cheerful region of the German Styrians ends and that of the Slovenes begins…. The landscape is increasingly barren and unpleasant, the cottages throughout Slovene Styria are filthy; the people look poor, the children ran some one-half mile along with the coach begging for money.[1]

Grillparzer, who is known as a fierce opponent of all forms of nationalism, German or non-German, reveals here a different side of his personality. His aversion to the Slovenes was, however, couched in terms of backwardness and lack of culture. These were not Grillparzer's only anti-Slavic remarks. Moreover, his is only one of many voices of this era that reflected such prejudices against the Slavs both inside and outside the Habsburg Monarchy. And what seems to be still more symptomatic: anti-Slavic attitudes in Austria can be traced from the period of Grillparzer through the Third Reich. Perhaps this question should be posed: Was there a connection or even a continuity between the anti-Slavic attitudes of Austrians like Grillparzer in the early nineteenth century and the racist policy of the National Socialists, especially the Austrian National Socialists, more than a century later?

This essay addresses the anti-Slavic intellectual tradition in Austria. The first part provides insights into this tradition from the early nineteenth century to the end of the First World War. A recurring theme in German discourse on the Slavs from that time is the attempt to demonstrate the superiority of German culture in the Habsburg Monarchy in order to legitimate the leading role of the German élite in politics and culture. The second part of the essay describes some fundamental aspects of the anti-Slavic paradigm developed by Austrian scholars in the wake of the First World War. It also focuses on developments that resulted in the employment of this anti-Slavic paradigm as the core of a new interdisciplinary orientation: German *Südostforschung*, which was increasingly racist. Austrian Nazis participated in the transition of *Südostforschung* from a discipline of Austro-German national revisionism into a tool of National Socialist geopolitics.

Anti-Slavic paradigms are not restricted to the last two centuries, and hostile attitudes are not the only ones Germans expressed toward the Slavs,[2] but they would characterize the relations between Austrians (Austro-Germans) and Slavic peoples from the late nineteenth century until the end of the Second World War. These negative discourses did not unfold within a contextual vacuum; they were dependent on a variety of factors. The internal composition of the Habsburg Monarchy was the framework that fostered or restrained the emergence of possible Austro-German discourses on the Slavs. Social and cultural power relations, the course of politics, state-building and nation-building, and lastly the internal grammar of different discursive forms of German nationalism regulated this composition. Anti-Slavic discourse finally merged with a second discourse on imagined boundaries and borders between Western and Central Europe on the one hand, and Eastern and Southeastern Europe on the other. The latter discourse can be characterized by a "saturation of the geographical appellation with political, social, cultural, and ideological overtones," as the historian Maria Todorova has argued.[3]

In addition to external factors, discourses must also be considered within the general context of the relation between language and reality. As the philosopher Elisabeth List has remarked:

> Contrary to the received philosophies of language one of the most important features of language and meaning is not so much reference, the fact that allows it to refer to reality, to reality thought of as independently pregiven [sic; developed]. It is much more important to understand its performative power, the ways in which our use of language contributes to the very construction and formation of what we call reality, be it the reality of ourselves, our natural or social environment.[4]

So anti-Slavic discourse can seldom be understood as an exchange of communication between Slavs (the Other) and Germans (the Self). Contact was mostly realized within the collective self, that is, the German élite of the Habsburg Monarchy. The representation of the Other was reduced to its role as an object.

This essay concentrates on two Slavic nations, which can be considered para-
digmatic to Austrian Germans: the Slovenes in the Habsburg Monarchy and the
Serbs of the Kingdom of Serbia. Focus on the Slovenes and Serbs permits clear
understanding of the rise of German *Südostforschung*. Since the late nineteenth
century, the perception of internal and external boundaries has played a decisive
role in German discourse on these two nations. The Slovenes have long been situated on the cultural frontier marking the German "core lands" of "Central
Europe," while Serbia, a neighbor of the Habsburg Monarchy, has been part of
the Balkans. Serbia thus lay outside the national, but not the imperial, interests
of the German élite. Austro-German discourse on the Slavs, like its discourse on
the Balkans, "is present primarily in journalistic and quasi-journalistic literary
forms (travelogue, political essay, and especially that unfortunate hybrid—academic journalism)."[5] No exhaustive analysis of the respective discursive elements
in the daily press and in the political sphere is intended here. Rather I mainly
concentrate on prominent representations of the academic discourse, which pose
the question of moral responsibility in social science and the humanities.

Widespread Anti-Slavism?: The Habsburg Period

Even before the rise of national movements, the German élite had become
uneasily aware of the presence of other ethnic groups within the Habsburg
Monarchy. The historian Larry Wolff has described an episode from Wolfgang
Amadeus Mozart's first trip to Prague in 1787, in which Mozart, a cosmopolitan
European who spoke German, French, and Italian, was confronted with the
Czech language, which he did not understand. His reaction to this representation
of otherness was one of imaginative liberation. He attempted to assimilate the
other through employing elements of pseudo-Slavic and pseudo-Oriental sounds
in a comical conversation.[6] Unlike Grillparzer a generation later, Mozart perceived Slavic otherness positively, and, after having grown familiar with Bohemia,
he subsequently incorporated elements of Bohemian folk songs into his work.
This episode reveals that the otherness of non-German people living in the Habsburg Lands had transgressed the threshold of awareness of German intellectuals.
This new awareness, attained by intellectuals of bourgeois descent and from the
ranks of state bureaucracy, was not accidental. It occurred at a point when the
Habsburg Monarchy underwent the process of state building and modernization.
Indeed, the development of a uniform central state could be observed from
the middle of the eighteenth century. It subjected the various peoples of the
Monarchy to a "social division of labor" into agricultural producers, the bourgeoisie, soldiers, bureaucrats, and nobles. The intention was to incorporate and
to homogenize the laterally separated small communities of the ordinary members of this society.[7] Because Vienna was the center of political and cultural power
and the bureaucratic élite used German as the official language, this process of
standardization had a German flavor. First, a standardized German administra-

tive and cultural language was developed. The course of this development, conveyed by German language, fostered nation-building, because the various nations and nationalities took shape in both confirmation and opposition to these tendencies toward homogenization and standardization.[8]

The new awareness of peoples with another mother tongue can also be found in Anton Thomas Linhart's *Versuch einer Geschichte von Krain,* published in 1796. Linhart argued that Austria, like Russia, should actually be called a Slavic state. Believing there were more Slavs than any other people in the Monarchy, he wondered why they were so underrepresented in public life.[9] In 1801 the traveler Balthasar Hacquet published *Beschreibung der südöstlichen und östlichen Wenden.* It was hailed in Viennese journals because it treated the Slavs, "a nation, of which we know and appreciate so little, but which constitutes more than half, almost two-thirds, of the population of the Austrian Monarchy."[10] Similarly, Joseph Rohrer focused the public's attention on the Slavs in his *Versuch über die slawischen Bewohner der österreichischen Monarchie* (1804).[11]

These works represent only the beginning of a variety of statistical, topographic, and ethnographic publications on the different regions and peoples of the Habsburg Monarchy. While German-speaking authors produced the first monographs, this changed by the early 1880s. Experts, including Friedrich Umlauft, Karl Prochaska, and the editors of the *Kronprinzenwerk,* assembled intellectuals from other national groups to publish encyclopedic works on the peoples and the lands of the Monarchy. The use of collaborators demonstrated that no single author could master the rapidly increasing ethnographic and geographic knowledge. The inclusion of non-German authors reflected the recent development of their nations within the Monarchy. But, since the individual texts could be only superficially homogenized by "terms of reference," this procedure was a step away from an imagined overall homogeneity toward the notion of "unity within diversity."

This synoptic tradition, which focused on statistics, geography, and ethnography, contributed to an ideologically defined collective self-portrait of the Dual Monarchy which, at least in the second half of the nineteenth century, was increasingly sinking into a national trench war. The synoptic approach, however, represented a harmonic image of the Monarchy that corresponded less and less with reality. In 1868, the statistician Adolph Ficker could still draw attention to the so-called *sujets mixtes* on the linguistic frontiers. They neither belonged to the two nations nor formed a third one: "How often are children from a German family in such regions given to a Slav household and vice versa, so the second language will also become a mother tongue for them, instead of an acquired language second to the mother tongue."[12] This practice was first of all an economic survival strategy for common people. But Ficker, a representative of the synoptic tradition, interpreted it as an idealized example of "unity within diversity" against developing nationalisms. Similarly, the bureaucrats of the educational system, who determined which academic books should be funded, promoted publications that conveyed such idealistic and harmonic images.[13]

This policy was closely tied to the ruling dynasty, and thus paternalistic. It is true that this ideology was directed at German and non-German national sentiments alike, but it was nonetheless implicitly hierarchical. Later, when non-German authors participated in joint academic projects like the *Kronprinzenwerk*, they employed a more moderate discourse concerning their own nations in German-language publications than they did in those publications produced in their mother tongues. Such was the case with Josip Šuman, whose *Slovenski Štajer* (Slovene Styria, 1868) was a standard work promoting the Slovene national movement. Šuman also was coauthor of Prochaska's series and a contributor to the *Kronprinzenwerk*, from which he omitted nationalist notions that could harm the purposefully created synoptic tradition of homogeneity.

At least before the Revolution of 1848, Grillparzer's views also had a place within the hegemonic synoptic scheme, since his anti-Slavism did not affect the principled rejection of any nationalism. Shortly after the revolution, Grillparzer wrote on Czech nationalism:

> Where is the noise about nationality coming from ... than from the German professorial chairs, where learned fools have driven the mind of a calm and reasonable nation toward madness and crime? There is the cradle of your Slavomania, and when the Bohemian is agitating against the German, then he is nothing other than a German, transformed into a Bohemian.[14]

In a remote Slovenian region on the linguistic frontier in Styria, a Slovenian contemporary of Grillparzer portrayed the hegemonic view in his own way:

> The relations, as they were—German in the offices and in the school and as the only common language between the learned ones of both nationalities—seemed to have been created by God at the same time as the world.... Although there was no tension due to nationalist feelings, as there were no greater conflicts and frictions, one could certainly assume that something like that would have been the case, if someone on the Slovene side had undertaken the smallest attempt to change those humiliating relations in favor of the Slovenes.[15]

This bias against national emancipation of the Slavs could also be found in a review on Slovene literature that appeared in the *Österreichische Blätter für Literatur und Kunst* in 1844: "In the sciences, like mathematics, jurisprudence, medicine, philosophy, and so on, we cannot soon expect Slavic works, or even translations [into Slavic languages], for who needs them, if one has known German for a long time?"[16]

The Upsurge of Nationalism(s)

There was unity of state power as long as the regime was based on the dynastic principle. The dynasty was German by descent and a considerable part of the imperial élite considered itself part of the German *Kulturnation*. Thus, disparities between the German center and the non-German periphery of the Monarchy would have serious consequences in the age of nationalism. The Revolution of 1848 had already demonstrated that the national programs of the representatives of non-German nations differed from those of the liberal German national revolutionaries. The nationalist endeavor to unite all Germans failed, and the Germans blamed the Slavs for betraying the revolution. Still, among the heterogeneous populations of the Habsburg Lands, the German élite enjoyed a privileged position due to the central location of the German hereditary lands. In the 1860s, when the autocratic regime had to accommodate the constitutional laws, national struggles again became one of the main issues in the unfolding political field. The new situation revealed the non-German politicians' aim of shifting traditional national relations of power in their favor. Following the exclusion of Austria from the German *Bund* in 1866, the Monarchy's Germans became a minority in a multinational state. The *Ausgleich* with the Magyar oligarchy was, according to Solomon Wank, a limited response to nationalism ... but at a price of alienating most of the Slavs."[17] Czech and South Slav politicians called in vain for a compromise, while Austro-German politicians obstinately tried to preserve their *Besitzstand*, that is, the leading role of Germans in cultural, political, and economic affairs, especially in the predominantly non-German territories of the monarchy, first in Bohemia, but also in southern Carinthia and Lower Styria, where the Germans were a urban minority with the Slavs dominating the countryside. To defend its *Besitzstand*, the German national movement, which had emerged from the former German liberals, attempted to establish a virtual boundary between their own nation and the Slavs. This boundary was not only determined by national affiliation, but also by the perception of backwardness and underdevelopment that supposedly characterized the Slavs.[18]

In contrast to the political sphere, where German nationalists had to cope with the Slovene national movement, an explicit German national discourse on the Slovenes appeared rather late in the scholarly literature. The *Zeitschrift des Historischen Vereins für Steiermark*, for example, published only three articles on the Slovenes before 1892. For a long time official policy prevented open nationalist discourses in academic publications. This was especially the case in German-language publications, since it was the most widely used language of Cisleithania, employed by German and non-German scholars alike. The situation changed, however, in the 1890s, when the success of Slovene political parties in Lower Styria resulted in the demand for parallel Slovene classes in the German secondary school at Cilli/Celje. This demand led to solidarity between Slovene and Czech political organizations, the notion "this far and no further," developed on the German side, which experienced a profound feeling of insecurity.[19] In response to the show of Slavic solidarity, the attorney and German Reichsrat deputy from Cilli, Richard Foregger, who was already known for the dictum "Fiat justitia Slavica, pereat Austria!" (If Slavic law predominates, Austria will perish!),[20] wrote a popular pamphlet in which he asserted that the Slovenes lacked their own culture and history. The missionary role of the Germans as propagators of civilization and the cynical invitation to the Slovenes to abandon their "artificial" national conscience and to participate in the German nation-building constituted its ideological basis.[21] Foregger's pamphlet was only one symptom of the profound internal political rift in the Austrian half of the Monarchy, which in 1893, 1895, and again in 1897 would topple the government in Vienna. Hybrid in its political aim and "academic" argumentation, this pamphlet was also a step toward the implementation of German national views in official academic discourse.

Some ten years later the statistician Richard Pfaundler published a series of articles presenting a new interpretation of the national power relations in Styria that appeared in the official *Statistische Monatsschrift* as well as in other journals. While also a German national, Pfaundler applied a different language than Foregger: by his endeavor to apply an objective, academic style, his articles could not be dismissed as mere political pamphlets. Pfaundler laconically wrote that compared with the German part "in the Slovene part of Styria, in southern Styria, industrial development lags." He presented statistical documentation that "the industrial companies are not only mainly located in the German part of the country, but also the population, employed in industries, is overwhelmingly German." Pfaundler further argued that the higher fertility rate in the Slovene part of Styria ought not to be considered the result of racial characteristics, but rather the consequence of unfortunate social circumstances and great poverty due to lack of education and culture. The "lower cultural level" of the Slovenes resulted in a higher marriage rate than among the Germans. While it might be assumed that the number of Slovenes would have increased in the last decades, "the economic power of the Germans" and "their higher industrial development" had led to rapid immigration, assimilation, and consequently the augmentation of the German element.[22]

The sources and the language that Pfaundler employed appear objective. It is only a matter of the arrangement and of another point of view that excludes cultural, national, and moral biases that leads to another, more contemporary reading of the phenomena, as described and interpreted by Pfaundler. According to Miroslav Hroch, the development of national identity can take at least two different paths. The path taken depends on the size and power of a nation. An individual in the ethnically rather homogenous core of a nation—like most Germans in the hereditary lands—has no other option than to become a participant in that nation's evolution. Nation-building was consequently a linear process of diffusion. In the case of smaller nations, however, which—like the Slovene—developed in the neighborhood of greater ones, the individual had two options: he might join either the greater or the smaller nation. Hroch argues that processes of national differentiation always reflect the power relations between the two nations in question. This differentiation is expressed particularly if one of the two developing nations (the German) is politically and economically dominant while the other (the Slovene) is inferior, perhaps because it did not have the opportunity to develop its own aristocracy or influential bourgeoisie.[23]

At the same time as Pfaundler was writing, the historian Martin Wutte evaluated the censuses of Carinthia with focus on the Slovene population. He found development similar to that which Pfaundler had noted for Styria.[24] Another statistician, Wilhelm Hecke, concentrated on the Slavic minorities who had migrated to the developing urban areas in the German-speaking part of the Habsburg Monarchy. Although he warned against the wholesale increase of the Slavic population in the Monarchy, he could still comfort his readers with reference to the ongoing rapid linguistic assimilation of the "Slavic masses."[25]

Statisticians were thus the first to make accurate observations of real or imagined Slavic demographic threats to the German nation in the Habsburg Monarchy. In the decade before the First World War, similar articles also appeared in official periodicals, reflecting a gradual change in official educational politics in the last decades of the Monarchy. The national struggles and the demands of Czech and South Slav politicians for an *Ausgleich* with the Slavs of the Monarchy led the bureaucracy to be increasingly lenient regarding the anxieties of German authors and to treat its own synoptic tradition less carefully.

Moreover, a new approach concentrating on the construction of cultural frontiers between Central and Southeastern Europe became popular in the discipline of geography. The Viennese geographer Erwin Hanslik opened this discourse by postulating that the German-Slavic linguistic frontier, which passed through the Habsburg Monarchy, was a cultural border between "civilization" and "backwardness." He employed various statistical data concerning different economic and educational developments to support this thesis.[26]

The authors cited above considered their German national attitude both modern and liberal. They considered the Slav élite of the Monarchy both their political adversaries and their national enemies and consequently rejected Slavic culture, arguing for the assimilation of the peoples they represented. Aware of the fragility of the Habsburg Monarchy, they wanted to preserve the privileged position of their nation within a new framework, more biased than the synoptic one. They finally succeeded in influencing the hegemonic discourse in the academic field, as well. This constituted a victory over the patriarchal bureaucrats who, while primarily German, remained adherents of the earlier tradition. But this new generation of scholars could only symbolically remove the insecurity of the German élite. In reality the German national option was marginalized as a result of the first elections following the introduction of universal, equal, male suffrage in January 1907. This generation had been acting in a sphere of divided, even schizophrenic, loyalty to the old synoptic tradition (and the dynasty) that had left its mark on them and their newer, stronger affiliation with the German nation. The latter would be historically decisive in confirming the arguments for the new tradition they had founded. This tradition would be radicalized during the First World War, opening a path to National Socialism.

In this context a further important development must be addressed. Beginning in the last quarter of the nineteenth century, scholars were attracted to a new discipline—physical anthropology, which also dealt with "racial" differences of the population. By 1878 the Anthropologische Gesellschaft zu Graz had examined more than 10,000 Styrian pupils to ascertain the color of their eyes, hair, and skin. This study attempted to establish a connection between mother tongue and certain somatic characteristics. But the results showed only minor differences between Germans and Slovenes: 64.2 percent of the Slovene pupils and 61.5 percent of the Germans had light (blue or gray) eyes. These similarities led researchers to conclude that a considerable part of the German population was of Slavic descent.[27] The results of the study demonstrated the difficulties of employing somatic characteristics as ethnic markers. Other investigations revealed similar results.[28] These primarily academic studies adumbrated the appearance of a number of pamphlets on racial difference, which reinforced cultural arguments with the argument of "blood." In this argument, the notion of the "Slavic race" was only a metaphor for cultural inferiority vis-à-vis the hegemonic "German race."[29]

Serbia and the Serbs

In contrast to the large-scale academic production of studies on Slavs by Austrian Germans in the Habsburg Monarchy, the output of academic works dealing with Serbia was relatively small and their authors primarily from Germany. Following two insurrections against the Ottoman Empire in the first two decades of the nineteenth century, a Serbian state was formed on the border of the Habsburg Monarchy. Because the insurrections were directed against the Ottoman Empire, the ancient adversary of the Habsburg Monarchy, the Austrian public sympathized with the insurgents who "had suffered and are still suffering for liberation."[30] From the first Serbian rebellion until the Congress of Berlin in 1878, a variety of actions aimed at strengthening and modernizing of the principality of Serbia were observed.[31] The Austrian point of view was paternalistic: it was one of a "civilized" people observing how hard another people was working to abandon its traditional "barbarian" behavior in order to meet European standards. This attitude is reflected in an anonymous German author's description from 1811 of Serbs as

> A well-shaped, sharp-witted and brave people, naturally interested in all arts and sciences like any other European nation, but having so long endured the Ottoman yoke, they had become ignorant and superstitious, and appear to lag behind other, luckier European nations and to be halfway degenerated by the blood of their fathers.[32]

Among the travelers to Serbia during the mid-nineteenth century, Felix Philipp Kanitz, the son of a Jewish manufacturer in Budapest, was most notable. Kanitz first came to Serbia in 1859 and stayed until 1876. An admirer of the Serbian people rather than a scholar, his descriptions became the most important source for geography, ethnography, and history of Serbia during the second half of the nineteenth century. He opposed the Austro Hungarian *Ausgleich* of 1867, since it reduced the autonomy of the South Slavs.[33]

Austrian sympathy for Serbia decreased following the Congress of Berlin, when Austria occupied the former Ottoman province of Bosnia-Herzegovina, which Serbia also claimed. So, analogous to the internal boundary between Germans and Slavs within the Monarchy, the external border of the state became a second line of confrontation with the Slavic peoples. Serbia, which was, after 1878, formally an independent kingdom and gained additional territory at the expense of the Ottoman Empire, became dependent on Austria-Hungary. In this period, several journalistic publications on Serbia began to reflect the arrogance and sense of power that would dominate Austrian journalism before the First World War.[34]

This confrontational attitude was not yet apparent in the social sciences and the humanities, where the traditional sympathy, mixed with paternalism and the missionary spirit of propagating culture from the West to the East still predominated. In 1887 the statistician Hugo Bach spent several months in Serbia, which he found a "pleasant disappointment" to his expectations. He explained the Austrian underestimation of the intellectual life in Serbia due to lack of command of the language. He ascribed the high level in science in Serbia to the fact that most Serbian experts had studied abroad. Moreover, he considered the underdeveloped educational system, the widespread illiteracy, and the low social position of women in the Serbian regions gained in 1878 the consequence of long-time Ottoman rule. Although Serbia was on the "borderline between Occident and Orient," he observed a "move toward Western culture." Bach noted that

> the cited data leave little doubt that the promotion of national education in Serbia has to be ascribed primarily to the influence of the adjacent [Habsburg] Monarchy. According to the 1874 Serbian census a number of Serbian citizens had been born in Austria-Hungary. This demonstrates that the historical mission to carry culture into the East has been fully accomplished on Serbian soil.[35]

Bach apparently thought that the Habsburg Monarchy had been indirectly responsible for improving the level of civilization, because he believed the Serbs who had migrated from the Monarchy spread Western attitudes in Serbia.

Increased official interest in the Balkans resulted in the establishment of a special academic *Balkankommission* at the turn of the century. The Commission, which operated within the framework of the Austrian Academy of Sciences, published a number of books on archeology and linguistics. Serbia was underrepresented in the series *Zur Kunde der Balkanhalbinsel*, edited by Carl Patsch, the archeologist who directed the Institut für Balkanforschung in Sarajevo. Just one book on Serbia, *Die Wiedergeburt des serbischen Staates*,[36] by the Serbian author Stojan Novaković,[37] was part of the series. After the turn of the century, Austro-Serbian relations steadily deteriorated. Following the regicide and the dynastic change of 1903, Serbia freed itself from Austrian tutelage. By annexing Bosnia-Herzegovina in 1908, Austria-Hungary confronted Serbia and most of the European great powers with a fait accompli. Also, the Serbs in Croatia and Dalmatia had become more self-confident. Slovenian, Croatian, and Serbian politicians called for a South Slav Crownland within the Monarchy, but only small radical groups of South Slav intellectuals really dreamed of possible unification of their territories with Serbia within a Yugoslav state.

At this time, the Viennese historian Heinrich Friedjung published documents alleging conspiratorial activities by Serbian politicians in Croatia-Slavonia against the Monarchy in collaboration with the Belgrade government.[38] As a result, dozens of Serbian politicians were convicted of treason at a trial in the Croatian capital, Zagreb. But Friedjung's documents proved forgeries and the Emperor pardoned the convicted.

The Viennese press also propagated a radical anti-Serbism that dominated the years prior to 1914. The books by the journalist Leopold Mandl on Austro-Serbian relations are an example of this kind of discourse. After the First Balkan War, Mandl again warned Austrians that the goal of the Serbian kingdom was "the liberation and reunification of all lands that are inhabited by Serbs." In addition to delineating the backwardness of the Serbian state, he described some characteristics of the Serbs, emphasizing the "Austro-phobic putrefaction in the nation," which was the foundation of Serbian foreign policy. Mandl also noted that far from flourishing, the towns in Serbia were degenerating. He argued that "the state-run expansionism of Serbia is neither conditioned by the increase of population nor by lack of space, and therefore is without a stable national foundation." Concerning the national myth of Kosovo polje, where the Ottoman Empire defeated the medieval Serbian state in 1389 and which the Serbs reconquered in 1912, he wrote: "There is no other European people where imagination is of such a great importance as the Serbian nation." The Serbs of Kosovo polje had not fled the Turks in 1389 but rather the Albanians later on. Now the Albanians feared being exterminated "with fire and sword."[39] Mandl's explanation of the Serbian-Albanian enmity was racial:

> One can clearly discern that an enormous racial process is taking place here. It started under [the medieval Serbian dynasty of] the Nemanjići and will, since it is necessarily carried out at the cost of the one or the other of the peoples involved, make the nations mortal enemies. The Albanians are the racially more potent, the Serbs the softer element.[40]

Had Serbia remained under Austrian tutelage, Mandl concluded, its cities would now be flourishing. But the turn to Russia had made it dependent on the Tsarist ambassador: "Thus small Serbia became a laboratory where in the last years all kinds of poison have been produced that are directed against the South Slav lands of the Monarchy."[41] These remarks demonstrate that the plausibility of specific facts was not at issue, but rather the arrangement of the facts was what counted, in other words, the performance of the discourse, not its reference. This discourse was radicalized in the wake of the declaration of war in August 1914. Scholars like Friedrich Salomon Krauss, who had done ethnographic work on South Slavic sexuality, were involved in this radicalization.[42] These images and stereotypes were partly revised by the reports of Austrian writers and officers who were in Serbia following its occupation by Austria-Hungary in late 1915.[43] In addition, ethnographers, geographers, statisticians, and other scholars went to the occupied lands to conduct research. They included the ethnographer Arthur Haberland, who did extensive research in Montenegro, Kosovo, and Albania. He asserted that in the desolate highlands the Slavs had gained cultural supremacy over the Albanians, due to the cultural power of the Orthodox Church, which was actually a Byzantine legacy, and to their adaptation to the Western influence that radiated from the Austrian regions north of the Danube.[44]

The "Guilt" of Pan-Slavism—Instead of a Résumé

The demise of the Habsburg Monarchy was traumatic for many Austro-German intellectuals, especially those who found themselves in nascent Slav-dominated states like Czechoslovakia and Yugoslavia. They sought the reasons for the decline of the Monarchy in the face of the united Slav assault, even if Russia, the ideological leader of Pan-Slavism, had been neutralized by revolution in 1917. The Bohemian-German Alfred Fischel, lawyer, historiographer, and politician, attempted to provide this approach historical legitimization in an historical overview of Pan-Slavism, published in 1919. He sought to demonstrate that the fusion of different Slavic peoples was in fact a nineteenth-century construction of German authors like August Ludwig von Schlözer and Johann Gottfried Herder. According to Fischel their labor, like the missionary propagating of Western culture to the Slavs by various German intellectuals, went unrewarded. During the Revolution of 1848 the Slovenes, who in the early nineteenth century had no standardized language until a national council of scholars "constructed" it, responded to the German engagement on behalf of the Slavs with a call for separation. Fischel used the same paradigm—the imparting of culture, the ingratitude of the Slavic "novices," their turn to Pan-Slavism and Russia—to describe the relationship of the Serbs in the Kingdom of Serbia toward the Monarchy. He repeated Mandl's earlier arguments, although in more academic terms. Fischel criticized the official reactions of the Monarchy to its Slavic population. In general, his overview was a comprehensive expression of the predominant Austro-German image of the Slavs.[45]

German *Südostforschung* and the Slavs:
Border and Race—Two Paths toward *Südostforschung*

In fall 1918, the Republic of Austria, the Kingdom of the Serbs, Croats, and Slovenes (hereafter Yugoslavia), and other new states emerged on the territory of the former Habsburg Monarchy. Austria was conceived as a German state, while Yugoslavia, although under Serbian hegemony until its collapse in 1941, was based on the theory that Serbs, Slovenes, and Croats were only different names for members of the same South Slav nation, which consequently named itself Yugoslavia (i.e., South Slavia) in 1929. One important difference between the two states was that Austria belonged to the losers of the war, while Yugoslavia was among the victors.

Because the provinces of Styria and Carinthia had ethnically mixed populations with Slovenes in the south and Germans in the north, these two provinces were sites of contestation after 1918. Austrian and Yugoslav experts made various suggestions for the drawing of new state borders, since no clear linguistic boundaries separated homogeneous ethnic territories. Although three cities in predominantly Slovene Lower Styria had had German majorities, the Paris Peace Conference awarded all of Lower Styria to Yugoslavia. It implemented a plebiscite in southern Carinthia to permit the population to decide whether to become part of Austria or Yugoslavia. Although southern Carinthia was ethnically Slovene, at the plebiscite, held in 1920, residents favored incorporation into Austria.

Especially in Austrian Styria, Germans perceived the drawing of the border as *Die Zerreißung der Steiermark* (the rending asunder of Styria). Indeed, this was the title of a popular pamphlet on the topic by the Styrian historian Arnold Luschin-Ebengreuth. The border was tearing the Styrian mainland away from the German minority under South Slavic rule in Lower Styria. Luschin-Ebengreuth repeated the myth of the Germans teaching the Slovenes culture and the Slovenes' subsequent ingratitude reflected in leaving the common state. But three circumstances were new: The setting was no longer the Habsburg Monarchy; therefore, imagining the Slovenes had become a matter of foreign policy, of national territories, of border drawing, and of ethnic separation. The purpose was no longer to legitimize the subordinate role of the Slovene population, but to disprove the Yugoslav claims that had been accepted at the peace conference. No one could better do this than historians. So—and this is the second important circumstance—historiography joined geography, ethnography, and statistics as the fourth discipline engaged in imagining the Slavs. The historical approach seemed appropriate, since the situation represented the end of a long period of living together. The historian could go further back and demonstrate that the Slovenes had never had a state of their own, nor an upper class nor towns, but had been peasants, dependent on German nobles and German towns. The third circumstance concerns a classification of the Slovene people that had already been used in politics, but was now embedded in the social sciences and humanities. The Styrian Slovenes, as "Windisch" and historically oriented toward the Germans, were separated from the "real" Slovenes who were from Carniolia, which was considered the Slovene heartland.[46] Luschin's pamphlet was the academic expression of the political mood of the defeated German élite of Styria. They considered the Slovenes of Lower Styria rebellious "brothers" who had joined the other South Slavs, thereby rising against their own "blood," their elder German "brothers."[47]

If most Slavs had become a matter of "foreign policy," what was to be done with the Slovenes who remained in southern Carinthia after the plebiscite? The classification of the Slovenes, already employed by Luschin, guaranteed that the existence of this minority would be neglected in the long term. The historian Martin Wutte elaborated upon this approach, which sought to marginalize the more nationally conscious Slovenes, in his popular pamphlet *Deutsch-Windisch-Slowenisch*.[48] Wutte argued that the Carinthian Slovenian language differed from the Slovenian standard language and other Slovenian dialects. Thus, the Carinthian Slovene minority would barely understand either the standard language or the other dialects. Due to their geographic separation from Slovenia and the peculiarities of Carinthian history and culture, a "natural" assimilation was underway. Like Luschin, Wutte designated the German-oriented Slovenes (in contrast to the anti-German "Slovenes") "Windisch." This term was meant as an honor, since it referred to those persons who were ready to be incorporated into the German majority of Carinthia. Wutte and his successors consequently treated the "Windisch" language as a mixed German-Slav idiom and claimed common bloodlines for the "Windisch" people and the German Carinthians.[49]

Luschin and Wutte employed the same ideological approach but to different targets, due to the differing political situations in their respective provinces. While Luschin was concerned with the fate of the German minority in Lower Styria now living in Yugoslavia, Wutte attempted to deal with a Slavic minority that was endangering national unity in southern Austria. Both concerns were addressed in the publications of the *Deutscher Schulverein Südmark,* a society for the cultural protection of the German nation in Austria and the German minorities in the successor states. This society's publications represented the Slavs (Czechs, Slovaks, Slovenes, Serbs, and to a lesser extent Croats) either as suppressers of the autonomy of the German diaspora in their countries or as protagonists of a national infiltration of Austria. The organization investigated and publicized the activities of the cultural associations of the Czech, Slovak, and Yugoslav migrants and of the Croatian and Slovenian minorities in Austria.[50]

In this climate, physical anthropology and "racial science" grew closer together and the latter was increasingly accepted in academic circles. Gustav Kraitschek's *Rassenkunde* (1923) characterized the new orientation of physical anthropology in Austria. Atop his racial hierarchy was the much-discussed dolichocephal (long-headed) Nordic and Germanic master race. The brachycephal (short-headed) Dinaric race, in which he placed the South Slavs, ranked next to it. Kraitschek connected the physical characteristics with the mental characteristics of the respective "races." Thus he characterized the Dinaric race as "superior" to all the other European races (except the Nordic race), even if "we cannot prove evidence of an original culture." Kraitschek distinguished the Dinaric race by its "energy and uprightness," "courage, sense of heroism and reliability, earthy humor, and biting wit." Its mixture with the Nordic race in Austria produced "a fine, efficient, and talented stock." Compared to the Slovenes, who also displayed traits of the culturally inferior "Eastern race," the Croats and Serbs were more authentic representatives of the Dinaric race.[51]

In *Die rassische Zusammensetzung der Bevölkerung der Steiermark*, Rudolf Polland adopted Kraitschek's derogatory views of the Slovenes. In Styria, due to a "mixture of races," the "brachycephals" had become dominant: "At the border of the Slovene territory we can find the Eastern [eastern Baltic] type, which in everyday usage also is named the 'Slavic' type." Hence the assumption that "the culture of our German people is endangered in its survival" and "that the cultural values of the German people in general and the Styrian homeland in particular have to be protected against decay and degeneration."[52] Robert Routil, of the Institute for Anthropology of the University of Vienna, was more cautious, however, in *Völker und Rassen auf dem Boden Kärntens*. Proceeding from an examination of two hundred individuals, Routil attempted to establish the somatic differences of the Carinthian population based on national characteristics: While Germans and Slovenes possessed equal Dinaric characteristics, the Germans more often had Nordic features, while Eastern (eastern Baltic) characteristics were found more often among the Slovenes. Routil attempted to connect the somatic attributes of Germans and Slovenes with different mental characteristics, but documentary evidence failed to support these mental differences: "Carinthia's German is honest, simple-minded, warm-hearted, and partly sensuous. The Slovene, on the other hand, particularly stands out for his modesty, diffidence, and good-naturedness."[53]

Most interwar investigations of the South Slavs were oriented toward the border or remained within the borders of the Republic of Austria. In comparison with the Monarchy, the focus was on smaller regions and the setting more provincial. Only in the publications of the *Deutscher Schulverein Südmark* a younger generation of intellectuals transgressed Austria's borders. They had a clear political goal in mind—the re-conquest of "lost German territory"—and would come to the fore after the *Anschluß*. But the decisive academic initiative to focus on vast regions of Southeastern Europe would come from Germany.

The Institutionalization of German *Südostforschung*

The basis for a new academic approach, *Südostforschung*, was laid in 1928 when the German government allocated money for an institute in Munich for investigation of the ethnic-cultural territory on the southeastern border of the German nation. The Institut zur Erforschung des deutschen Volkstums im Süden und Südosten, founded in 1930, was but one link in a chain of similar institutions to investigate the "damage" caused by the revisions of the eastern border of the German Reich following the First World War. The new institution was the first, however, to focus on Southeastern Europe.[54]

From 1930 to 1936, the Munich institute was exclusively concerned with the Germans of Austria, Hungary, and Yugoslavia. This orientation reflected the perception that the Paris Peace Treaties had separated Austria, a second "German state," and the German minorities of East Central and Southeastern Europe, which had come under non-German rule, from their fatherland. The Southeastern German territories, *Volksboden,* comprised Austria, the northern part of Lower Styria (in Slovenia), some enclaves in central and southern Hungary, and the Banat (part of Serbia and Romania). German *Volksboden* could also be found in Transylvania. The *Kulturboden* imagined borders of German cultural influence and constituted "a great frontier of civilization" between East and West. This cultural frontier comprised the whole of Slovenia and the areas around the German enclaves in Southeastern Europe.[55]

From 1933, the Munich institute began publishing a series of books on the topic. The first volumes were almost exclusively devoted to Austria. In 1935, the German geographer Doris Kraft published her dissertation on part of the German *Volksboden* immediately south of the Austrian border in Yugoslavia. She described the local Slovene population as German settlers who had been "Slavicized" during the Middle Ages, while the real Slovenes had been "slaves" of the early medieval Avars. Kraft considered the region a "German borderland" and sharply criticized its forced incorporation into Yugoslavia. With respect to the Slovenes, she took the view that "national feelings are awakened only among a small leading stratum, the common people still follow their own instinct of attachment to the German *Volksboden* and *Kulturboden.*"[56]

In his doctoral dissertation, published in 1936, Hugo Suette took a different view on the national struggles in Lower Styria during the late nineteenth century, which he described as a "battle between Germandom and Slavdom, the latter pressing forward with all its might." The Slovene slogans had been "far more electrifying, sweeping, and pugnacious" than those of the Germans, which were only defensive. The German bourgeoisie had failed to recognize that its adversary's success was the result of Slovene "attachment to territory and blood." If the German bourgeoisie had behaved similarly it could have won the German lower classes, Suette concluded. He concluded with an appeal: "May the German bourgeoisie in Lower Styria and in the whole world give way to the German *Volksgemeinschaft* to prevent our great nation from again losing German people and German territory."[57]

Two new elements had entered Suette's narrative: mention of the National Socialist *Volksgemeinschaft,* which indicated adaptation to the ruling ideology of the Third Reich in terms of discourse and a respect for the enemy's methods that rendered him more dangerous. Suette's case study imagined the power of the Slavs in order to legitimize the Nazi approach by which the Germans would finally defeat them. Both elements were constitutive for a discourse of German hegemony that was to be realized within future Nazi geopolitics. This discourse reached far beyond the older discourse of "mourning" the disloyalty of former "brothers."

Also in 1936, the historian Fritz Valjavec, a member of the institute in Munich who hailed from the German minority in Hungary, founded the journal *Südostdeutsche Forschungen.* This led to a broadening of the concept of German

Südostforschung. In the first issue of the journal, Valjavec outlined the purpose of *Südostforschung*: it was to address the cultural influence of the Germans in South-eastern Europe. He argued that the "intellectual and economic superiority of the German settlers influenced the surrounding peoples not only by their culture, but also in the national sense. Therefore, the interaction of *Volksboden* and *Kulturboden* was extremely powerful, particularly in Southeastern Europe." Valjavec wrote that the Southeastern European peoples possessed "inalienable values of their own,"[58] but this notion has to be seen in the same light as the respect Suette showed for the Slovenes as a national adversary. The interdisciplinary approach of *Südostforschung* reflected an academic orientation, but it acted on behalf of national policy, which emphasized cultural concern for the German diaspora. The institute in Munich and the Südosteuropa-Institut of the University of Leipzig (founded in 1936) represent steps toward closer cooperation in politics and science.

The next step was taken in Austria following the *Anschluß* in March 1938. On 8 April, the Nazi provincial government of Styria founded the Südostdeutsches Institut in Graz. Part of the government rather than the university, the institute was supposed to undertake "practical work", that is, the investigation of Germandom in Southeastern Europe for political purposes, providing the political authorities with knowledge of the situation of German minorities in Southeastern Europe.[59] In reality, the Institute concentrated mainly on Lower Styria, since the political and ideological reconquest of this region was its true motive.

Helmut Carstanjen, who had been responsible for Lower Styria in the *Volksbund für das Deutschtum im Ausland*, directed the institute. He was a leading Nazi among the German minority in Slovenia. Already in 1928, he both organized ideological courses in Graz for German youth activists from Yugoslavia and traveled under an assumed name through Slovenia to recruit agents for subversive activity throughout Lower Styria.[60] His doctoral dissertation, *Sprache und Volkstum in der Untersteiermark* (published in Germany in 1935), became an important part of Nazi discourse on the Slovenes. In the historical part, Carstanjen proceeded from Luschin, while in the statistical part he attempted to provide detail on the example of Pfaundler. He, however, employed dubious statistical methods to increase the number of Germans in Lower Styria. The decisive part of his thesis was the application of Wutte's theory on the Windisch people in Lower Styria. He argued that the majority of the Slovenes, by their racial and cultural affiliation, were pro-German (*deutschfreundlich*, in contrast to the so-called "national Slovenes"), even if they spoke another language. This policy of *divide et impera* in the Nazi context took on a new meaning after 1940, when SS policy would be to recognize as many nationalities, the so-called *Volkssplitter*, as possible in Eastern Europe in order to weaken adversaries, be they Poles, Slovenes, or Russians.[61] Carstanjen claimed that all of Lower Styria was German *Volksboden* and a German borderland.[62] This new arrangement of several parts of the German discursive archive on the Slovenes is captivating, indeed. It is the Mephistophelian character of "sophisticated" Nazi writing, which generates a "modern" style—whereby merciless insensitivity masquerades as objectivity—while providing the ideological foundations for genocide at the same time.

"The research of the German *Volksboden* beyond the borders ought to serve for the improvement and reinforcement of the relationships between peoples."[63] What did the cynical principle of the Südostdeutsches Institut mean in practice? In 1938 the institute spent some 30,000 Reichsmarks to finance pilot studies of regions at the German (formerly Austrian) side of the Styrian border with Yugoslavia, where remnants of a Slovenian minority could be identified.[64] In summer 1938, eighteen students conducted a detailed investigation in one of these regions. The outcome, published as "Lebensfragen der Grenzbevölkerung," was distributed to all relevant offices of the Nazi Party. The students sought a "scholarly" based separation of ethnic entities. They argued that the physical attributes were the decisive identifying factors. On the one hand, they unveiled the "stronger" German blood in cases of "blood mixture" even if the original language was lost. On the other, they permitted the discovery of the "falseness" of German attitudes in cases of clear Slavic descent. Otherwise there would be the danger of recognizing as Germans those who were not such in biological terms. The students determined hair color, eye color, and the shape of the cranium of several hundred pupils in order to define their "racial composition."[65] Characteristics of the racial "Slovene" type included:

> conspicuous dark hair, dark eyes, thus dark appearance in general, slightly prominent cheekbones, sometimes small stature. Characteristics which need not be present altogether.... Among the observations made among that group, which is strange to the German people in racial respect, are: passiveness, an impression of filth, home and farmstead untidy and neglected, lack of hygiene, double-dealing, slyness (tendency to lie).[66]

It is unsurprising that the statistical analysis reflected the desired results: Mother tongue and somatic appearance coincided in most cases, and German children, of course, performed better in school. Crime among the Slovenes was also higher. But it has to be kept in mind that these "results" were already anticipated during data collection as the categories of German and Slovenian "race" were constructed out of the *a priori* presumption of a connection between somatic and mental attributes. For the authors of the study, the presence of a small Slovenian population on the border seemed to threaten the new order in one of the most sensitive regions of the state. The Nazi-students wanted to separate inferior, disposable individuals from the German "race," who should be removed in the long run. In light of the planned conquest of Lower Styria, they sought individuals with a trustworthy "appearance" on the German side of the border.[67]

In 1940, the Südostdeutsches Institut ordered a secret study of the Reich's southern border in Styria, which was based on the literature on Lower Styria from Luschin to Carstanjen and was meant to serve as ideological foundation for the military reconquest of this region.[68] That same year the institute produced a catalogue of German place names in Lower Styria. These names would be reintroduced at the time of reconquest.[69]

Between 1941 and 1943 the activities of the Institut peaked. Following the German defeat of Yugoslavia during the *Blitzkrieg* in April 1941, Lower Styria was incorporated into the Reich. The SS organized the deportation of some ten thousand Slovenes from Lower Styria and other parts of Slovenia, which came under Nazi rule. These people, initially intellectuals, "agents of the campaign against the Germans," than those elements that after 1918 had been settled by the first group in order to "Slovenize" the region and finally also the whole population of the southern margin of the conquered region, were deported to Serbia, Croatia, and Germany proper.[70] Throughout Lower Styria, Slovenian organizations were dissolved and Slovenian place names replaced by German ones, following the suggestion of the Südostdeutsches Institut. Use of the Slovene language was forbidden in public, even in church, and Slovenian children had to attend German schools. The situation was similar to that in the *Generalgouvernement* of Poland, but on a smaller scale.[71]

A statement by a commission of the *Reichskommissar für die Festigung des deutschen Volkstums,* the central SS authority for deportations, which was ordered to make an inventory of the regions of Lower Styria and southern Carinthia in summer 1941, clarifies the reasons for these actions:

> When we take measures of any kind, under no circumstances must we be seduced to put the Slovenes on the same level with the Poles, the Slovaks, or the Serbs. The Slovene is not a proper Slav—either by his external appearance or by his cultural or civilized achievements.
>
> First of all it is necessary to thin the Slovene population by removing the inferior elements. Furthermore, an additional indispensable culling can take place by transferring one part of the rural proletariat into urban occupations in the *Altreich* [Germany proper]. But a large portion of the Slovenes will withstand a rigorous process of selection. They have to be left in the new areas and to be Germanized by a careful policy in the long run that does not allow for brutal solutions.[72]

This "evaluation" of the Slovenes was an economical one; the Reich leadership had realized the need for additional manpower for its far-reaching imperialistic projects, which its own population could not meet. The Germanization of colonized peoples who were willing to fulfill the needs of the Nazis was a consequence of this economic interest. Götz Aly and Susanne Heim have demonstrated that an economically oriented population policy did not contradict its racial foundation: "Full Germans therefore do not distinguish themselves primarily by a particular exterior, but by efficiency and adaptability." Population policy provided a concrete foundation for a heretofore vague racial policy.[73]

This policy had to be translated into a discourse for the interested public. In 1942 the geographer Wilhelm Sattler published a study of population policy and economy in Lower Styria for the Südostdeutsches Institut. It pointed out that the procedures of Germanizing and deportations were closely connected to Nazi economic interests. The demographic part of his study focused less on national categories and more on population density, age structure, the relationship of town and country, and occupational and social categories. The second part of the study detailed the economic resources of Lower Styria. His conclusion is revealing. The new German administration had abolished the previous "Serbian mismanagement," and "the failure of the government in Belgrade" in agriculture. A policy of modernization and the *Erzeugungsschlacht* (battle for production) replaced this policy: "Produce more and consume the products more economically!"[74]

Carstanjen, who in 1941 became responsible for the national policy of the civil administration in Lower Styria, wrote the introduction to Sattler's book. Even if there were linguistic differences in Lower Styria, a racial border could not be drawn in this "ancient German land," according to Carstanjen. The German and Slovene populations differed from

> [the] racial types, with whom they had to live together under Yugoslavia.... Also the Serbs clearly believe that a world separated them from the people of Lower Styria. Their use of the disparaging term "Schwaba" was encouraged by the feeling that the people of Lower Styria, attached to their home country, do not belong to the cultural sphere of the Balkans but to the German people.

Now, language, the last blockade, had to be run in order to make the population really "German." In addition, colonization by Germans resettled from Southeastern Europe in Lower Styria would provide improved economic efficiency.[75]

Yugoslavia and the Serbs

The Nazi discourse on the Serbs was embedded in two other discourses: one on Southeastern Europe in general and the other on Yugoslavia in particular. Demographers and economists considered Southeastern Europe an important part of the Nazi *Ergänzungswirtschaft* (supplementary economy). It was a semi-colonial supplier of agricultural products.[76] This relationship was established during the first years of Nazi rule, and enforced in the early phase of the Second World War. By early 1940, the Nazis had established the *Südosteuropagesellschaft* to coordinate economic policy vis-à-vis Southeastern Europe from Vienna.[77] The dimensions of Nazi policy in the Balkans became apparent after April 1941, when, having defeated Yugoslavia, the *Wehrmacht* and other officials of the Third Reich came to the region. Nazis from the former Republic of Austria participated in this colonialist approach to the Balkans, since they could refer to Austria's historical role in the Balkans before 1918. Because Nazi discourse on Yugoslavia and the Serbs was dependent on political circumstances, it is useful to consider publications before April 1941 separately from later ones.

The Serbs as Supporters of the State:
The Short and Treacherous Flirtation with Yugoslavism (1938-1941)

"Each people honors itself, if it honors the history of another people, because the praise of honor, liberty, and fatherland constitutes the history of each people...."

Furthermore, for each people, studying the history of a strange people, it is useful to keep to the saying: "Do unto others as you would have them do unto you."[78] This maxim was the starting point for the Austrian Nazi Gilbert in der Maur's three-volume *Die Jugoslawen einst und jetzt* (1936-1938). In the introduction to these volumes he tried to fight stereotypes of Balkan "rascal peoples and the mutton-thieves" and considered Yugoslav unification a mirror of the situation in Germany. In his account, the Serbs played a prominent part in the foundation of Yugoslavia, and he was more sympathetic to them than to other Yugoslav peoples. According to in der Maur, the political history of the Serbs had two zeniths—the empire of Tsar Dušan in the fourteenth century and the regaining of their own state in the first decades of the nineteenth century. The Croats had only a short historical period of glory, since their kingdom had become part of Hungary in the early twelfth century, while the Slovenes were a nonhistorical people.[79] This account was critical of the political system of the Habsburg Monarchy and its policy against Serbia until the First World War, since in der Maur generally considered the Habsburg Monarchy an "obstacle" to itself. He also interpreted the fusion of the South Slav peoples into one Yugoslav nation as irreversible. He concluded that this fusion of the Yugoslav peoples adumbrated the Austrian *Anschluß* in March 1938 with the Third Reich. In June 1938 he wrote: "Like the Yugoslavs had to struggle for their freedom from the Habsburg Monarchy, we Germans from the *Ostmark* will gain our freedom from the 'straitjacket' of the dictated state of 'Austria'—our belief was not disappointed."[80]

Camillo Morocutti, a physician from Lower Styria, was responsible for the section of *Des Reiches neue Nachbarn*, edited by Walter Schneefuß (1939), on Yugoslavia. He argued that of all the states founded by the Western powers after the First World War, Yugoslavia had the best preconditions for survival. He asserted that the Serbs, the mainstay of the state, had their origin in Germanic remnants of the Goths, the "prime Slavs," and the Dinaric race. Due to centuries-long Ottoman domination, a pronounced class distinction could not develop, even after the successful uprisings in the early nineteenth century. At that time, "country and people were poor, exploited under the Turkish rule; only folk songs remained of their cultural assets. Everyone was familiar with them and they recalled the memories of a great past. What counted as an important value was their fame as fighters." This value had marked the political culture of the Serbs, which was determined by self-help, blood feuding, murder, and conspiracy. Morocutti also argued that modernization had reached Yugoslavia. Yugoslav foreign policy was pro-German, more than two-thirds of Yugoslav foreign trade was with Germany, and the fusion of Serbs, Croats, and Slovenes into a Yugoslav nation was underway.[81]

Why this relatively positive image of the Serbs and of Yugoslavism? The answer lies in the Nazi conception of history. After the defeat of France in 1940, "the last hour of the democracies had come" and peoples were "supporters of a new order."[82] The Nazis considered the Serbs a great historical nation and the main supporters of the Yugoslav state, who had started the fusion of three South

Slavic peoples into one Yugoslav nation, as the Nazis had done with the incorporation of German lands into the Reich since 1938. Consequently, Nazi discourse favored Serb-led centralism and was against any federalism or even separatism of Croats or Slovenes.

But this positive image was not only a result of political sympathy. It also corresponded to the idea that a homogeneous Yugoslav space could be more easily penetrated by German political and economic interests. If that failed, the Nazis were flexible enough to work out another option, which focused on the division of Yugoslavia in order to secure economic and political control on regional levels: with respect to the Slovenes, the systematic realization of the second option—the annexation of parts of Slovenia to the Third Reich—could be based on the precautionary labor the Südostdeutsches Institut had undertaken since 1938. With respect to Serbia, however, the Nazis had to work out plans virtually overnight. This rashness corresponded with the sudden change in the ranking of the Serbs.

On the "Nature of the Serbs" (1941-1944)

Since German troops were stationed in Romania in the winter of 1940-1941 and marched into Bulgaria in February 1941, the Yugoslav government, which had come under pressure from Hitler, finally decided to join the Axis. This decision provoked a coup d'état, providing the Germans a pretext to attack Yugoslavia on April 6. The Germans conquered the country in eleven days. On the territory of Croatia and Bosnia-Herzegovina the Axis Powers established the "Independent State of Croatia" under the fascist *Ustasha* Party. Serbia was reduced to its pre-1913 borders under German military control. Mass murder and other excesses against the Serbs in Croatia, the extermination of Jews and Roma throughout the former Yugoslavia, and cruel measures against the civilian population in Serbia formed the background of the radically changed Nazi discourse on the Serbs. This turn consisted of a general revision of the discourse of 1938-1941, a positive, new discourse on the Croats, a revival of the discourse on cultural borders, and recourse to the pre-First World War Austro-Hungarian stereotypes of the Serbs. Joseph Goebbels, Nazi Minister for Propaganda, created the ideological guidelines for this change, which was put to force in a few days before the attack on Yugoslavia and was almost immediately accepted by the academic henchmen of the Nazi regime.[83]

Since 1939, the popular science monthly *Volkstum im Südosten* had reported on ethnic issues in Southeastern Europe. In March 1941 chief editor Felix Kraus wrote that the decision of the Yugoslav government to join the Axis "expressed the will of the Yugoslav people to finally eliminate the criminal policy of England and to participate in the reorganization of Europe, side by side with the 'young nations.'" Only "the affirmation of *Volkstum* as the supporter of national life" would lead to reconciliation among the South Slav "tribes."[84]

One month later, following the 6 April attack, the same Felix Kraus wrote, "elements of chaos from the Balkans had attempted to disturb reorganization."

Now the former Yugoslavia was considered a state previously dominated by a Serb minority. The centralism of Belgrade had tended to distort the new State of the Serbs, Croats, and Slovenes into a Greater Serbia. Kraus now spoke of a "Croatian space," which since the Middle Ages had been part of the cultural and political framework of Central Europe. The Yugoslav idea could not be realized, since "the historical and intellectual development in regions that had been isolated from one another through centuries, and the religious split had prevented cultural development, gaps that could not be bridged in a few years."[85] "The superficial ideology of a Slav community based on linguistic relationship was renounced, after it had been realized that the differences between the individual Slavic-speaking nations are greater than was formerly thought."[86] "'Yugoslav' had become simply another word for the Serb who had advanced as far as the river Drava" in Lower Styria.[87] In 1939 the Viennese writer Heinz Scheibenpflug had published a book on the Danube and the Danubian region. It treated the Serbs better than the Croats, with the author paying particular attention to the founding of the medieval Serbian state and admiring the purity of the Dinaric race to which the Serbs belonged. Since the Croats were related to the Serbs, the antagonisms between the two peoples were explained by cultural differences. They both spoke the same language, Serbo-Croatian. The only difference was the characters, which the Serbs wrote with Cyrillic and the Croats with Latin letters.[88] Four years later, after the engagement of the *Wehrmacht* in Southeastern Europe and Operation Barbarossa, a revised edition of Scheibenpflug's book appeared. In it, the order and also the evaluation of the two peoples was reversed. Scheibenpflug dealt with the foundation of the medieval Croatian state, which he had not mentioned earlier, while describing the emergence of the Serbian state as "more difficult and tedious" than the Croatian one. Moreover, the author stressed that in Serbia each succession to the throne was accompanied by dynastic conflicts, murder of relatives, and civil war.[89] He concluded,

> In almost all European conflicts with intrigue and intervention, Serbia remained a disruptive element on the continent until recently, because England and France had harnessed Serbia to their political apparatus. Serbia also used its power to subjugate the Croats and Slovenes. These peoples all too soon regretted their decision to form a joint state. But the clique of political adventurers from Belgrade exceeded all bounds and consciously set itself against a European order![90]

What remained of the former positive image of the Serbs? The "heroic struggle of the peasant" against the Ottoman Empire, the admiration of patriarchal values, and "the historical memory" reflected in heroic and epic songs. In other words, the Nazis reduced their imagination of the Serbs to those archaisms that belong to the mainstream of general Western imagination of the Balkans since the nineteenth century.[91]

With a fascist puppet regime in Croatia, a new Nazi discourse on the Croats was developed. This discourse focused on the racial relationship between Germans and Croats. The relationship was based on the assumed Aryan, either

Gothic or Iranian, roots of the Croats, including the hypothesis of a different origin of Croats and Serbs. Croatian scholars had developed this hypothesis before 1941, and it gained popularity among German scholars after the establishment of the new political framework in Southeastern Europe.[92]

In the early 1940s, the geographer Wilhelm Sattler published two books on the German minority in Croatia. The first appeared in 1941, perhaps before the German attack on Yugoslavia. It criticized the Croat majority's treatment of the German minority.[93] The second book, published in 1943 in the series of the Südostdeutsches Institut, was positively disposed to the "Independent State of Croatia." Derogatory references to the period of the Yugoslav kingdom, addressed as the "Serbian period" and the "Serbian yoke," became part of an oft-used rhetorical formula in the discourse on Croatia: "In the Yugoslav state Croatdom found itself betrayed because of the Serbian demand for sole rule."[94] Since the Serbs were not the focus of the study, the author did not explain anti-Serb stereotypes, which were nonetheless indispensable for the intrinsic cohesion of the text. In discussing the Croatian absorption of the Germans, Sattler noted that no similar process occurred in Serbian majority areas, since "their different religious confession and their considerably inferior culture impede racial approximation." The Croats, on the other hand, had learned from history:

> Like the Hungarians, the Croats were able to absorb foreign ethnic groups in their area, and they seemed to achieve splendid success in that, particularly at the turn of the century. Under Serbian rule in the Yugoslav kingdom, however, they had to suffer such a treatment for twenty-three years, and it is apparent that they, having had such experiences, now judge the existence of the German ethnic group in a different way than in earlier times.[95]

Schneefuß dealt with the political geography of Croatia. His image of the Serbs is outlined in a manuscript dating from 1942. It was not, however, hectographed by the Südostdeutsches Institut until 1944. He noted that "Yugoslavism determined by Serbia" was an historical option that could not be realized, since it was contravened by the Croat struggle for the recreation of an independent Croat state that had existed in the Middle Ages. Schneefuß treated the medieval period as if modern national struggles had already occurred at that time. He argued that by the tenth century the Serbs, from their base in Bosnia, had tried to reach the Croatian heartland. But the Croats managed to defeat the Serbian "wedge." The Serbs had then been incorporated into the Ottoman Empire and consequently suffered "for centuries an interruption of their historical continuity," while the Croats experienced "the full continuity of their culture, and this culture was essentially richer and superior to the Serb one." A common language was founded, but *Volkstum* rested not only on a joint language, as the Serbian propagators of Yugoslavism asserted, but "the community of blood and fate that is expressed by a specific history and culture also belongs to *Volkstum*. Since that was lacking, there was little reason to believe in unification." The alternate notation of the Serbo-Croat language, either in Cyrillic or in Latin letters, indicated the affiliation to different civilizations. He spoke clearly of the

"Croatizing, respectively re-Croatizing of all disputed citizens." Schneefuß did not mention the mass murder, expulsion, and compulsory conversion of the Serb population within the criminal framework of the Independent State of Croatia. Being a "dispassionate" observer of the technology of power, he rather dealt with the issue if this fusion really would only shape a common Croat nation formally, or would result wholesale in a rooted Croat *Volk*.[96]

A special discourse on cultural borders was already present in the separation of German *Volksboden* from *Kulturboden*. In 1941 the geographer Hugo Hassinger posited an additional cultural border between "Southeastern Central Europe," which included Croatia, and the Balkans with Serbia south of the Danube. Thus, in the case of Yugoslavia "the cultural borders cut through the body of the nation."[97] That same year another geographer, Norbert Krebs, concretized this cultural border, which was "more than a thousand years old," by designating the river Sava and the lower reaches of the Danube on the territory of former Yugoslavia as boundaries between Central Europe and the Orient. He considered the foundation of Yugoslavia the short-term triumph of Serbian "Dinarism," which had imposed an inferior culture on the peoples living north of the cultural border.[98] Belgrade, the capital of both Serbia and Yugoslavia, "was at the Southern bank of the Danube, not at the northern bank, in the Balkans, not in Central Europe," Schneefuß concluded in *Donauräume und Donaureiche*.[99] He included also Bosnia, which was south of the River Sava into the German *Kulturboden*, since it had been under Austrian, that is, German administration from 1878 until 1908 [sic]. So Bosnia-Herzegovina and the former Habsburg Military Border, both now part of the Independent State of Croatia, shaped the natural border against Serbia.[100] The new context also implied a revision of the image of the Habsburg Monarchy. This can be seen in the case of Bosnia's Muslims, who had been a bone of contention between Croats and Serbs: "Croats and Muslims were the pillars of the Austrian regime, in spite of all complaints and of all the awkwardness of the administration; both of them jointly led the resistance against Serbian intentions of conquest, against South Slav egalitarianism."[101]

In a 1942 essay on the historic role of the Germans in Southeastern Europe, historian Mathilde Uhlirz of the University of Graz emphasized the importance of the Habsburg Monarchy as frontier guard: the "rush of Pan-Slavism against the Danube monarchy" in the nineteenth century meant "the clash of Slavdom against the German world and the thrust into the Central European space." Emperor Francis Joseph should have grasped "the historical importance of the problems in the Southeast in its meaning for the whole of Germandom."[102]

In 1944, Fritz von Reinöhl of the State Archive in Vienna, by order of the German Ministry of Foreign Affairs, edited a collection of sources for the years 1900 to 1917 on the Greater Serbian "machinations" against Austria-Hungary. He sought to demonstrate that Serb propagators tried to detach those parts of the Monarchy that were populated by Serbs in order to incorporate them into the Kingdom of Serbia.[103] The Nazi discourse on the Serbs explicitly referred to arguments that had been raised in the final years of the Monarchy. These arguments pointed out that the authorities of the Monarchy lacked the energy to fight the Greater Serbian "machinations."[104]

Did the Evil Come from Germany?

During the interwar period Austrian academic discourse on the South Slavs, with some exceptions, was limited to the "unjust" border and to Slavic minorities within the borders of the Republic of Austria. This discourse of mourning and accusation focused mainly on the Slovenes. At the same time, racial science—thinking and talking about race in a scientific way—was increasingly applied to this discourse. In Germany a new discourse on German *Volksboden* and *Kulturboden* fostered the foundation of institutions to pursue the so-called *Südostforschung*. This new interdisciplinary approach replaced the earlier *Balkanforschung*, which, until 1918, had had one of its centers in the Habsburg Monarchy.[105] Now the research focus shifted to the German minorities in Southeastern Europe. The new approach was consistent with the ideology of the Nazis, who seized power in Germany in 1933. In Austria, a similar *Südostforschung* had been pursued only by German nationalist Societies like the Deutscher Schulverein Südmark. Major studies were published in Germany. After the *Anschluß*, *Südostforschung* was also established in Austria. Its major exponents were the Südostdeutsches Institut in Graz and the Südostdeutsche Forschungsgemeinschaft Wien. Both were in contact with the Institut zur Erforschung des deutschen Volkstums im Süden und Südosten in Munich.[106] The discourses of Luschin and Wutte, which had developed in another context, were transformed into an instrument of National Socialist population and space policy that was crudely realized following the German attack on Yugoslavia in April 1941.

The attack was also a caesura within the German discourse on the Serbs and Yugoslavia. This discourse had been relatively positive from 1938 to 1941 since the Yugoslav unification was represented as a mirror of the German unification of 1938. But after the defeat of Yugoslavia, there was a need for a new concept. This time it was overwhelmingly anti-Serb. The upgrading of the Croats as an ally, the enforced application of the concept of cultural borders, which had already been employed by Erwin Hanslik in 1910, and the partial rehabilitation of the Habsburg Monarchy as bulwark against Slavdom served to stabilize the intrinsic economy of the new discourse on the Serbs.

Although institutionalized *Südostforschung* came from Germany, the Viennese geographer Hugo Hassinger had already applied the concepts of German *Volksboden* and *Kulturboden* in the early 1930s.[107] Moreover, Fritz Valjavec, the leading figure in the institute in Munich, came from the former Habsburg Monarchy. And the highest degree of cooperation between science and policy was achieved in the Südostdeutsches Institut. It is too simple to say that the evil came from Germany. Austrian scholars, primarily the young ones, also participated.

Some Conclusions

Whether Slovenia constitutes part of Central Europe or Southeastern Europe was long disputed and has been again since the wars of Yugoslav succession in the 1990s. The Slovenes shared common territory with Germans in Styria and still share it in Carinthia. Like the Czechs, they became a major target of German nationalism in the late nineteenth century. Today there is still strong evidence of a vivid anti-Slovene discourse in Carinthia, where local Slovenes continue to be treated as a threat to Germandom, rather than as bilingual Austrian citizens. Serbia, however, is considered part of the Balkans. Here the conflict between "West" and "East," between "civilization" and "barbarism," is connected with the issue of Balkanism. In the Austrian imagination, Serbia was the reason for the First World War, and in the Nazi view Serbs were the reason for the German attack on Yugoslavia in 1941. A recent reflection of this discourse is the negative image of the Serbs in the Austrian media after the fall of the second Yugoslavia in 1991. This anti-Serbism did not help unmask the responsibility of local nationalist élite, in particular Serbian, for massacres and mass flights during the 1990s, but rather reinforced old patterns of xenophobia and confirmed an image of the Balkans as a powder keg of barbarian peoples.

Was Grillparzer's anti-Slavism part of a tradition that led to the Nazi discourse on the Slovenes and on the Serbs? Grillparzer used derogatory terms to criticize "backwardness" and "Slavic nationalism." His criticism of underdevelopment was part of the dark side of the Enlightenment's legacy, in which Central and Western European civilization was the yardstick for the assessment of the culture of the people. Since nation-building among the peoples of the Habsburg Monarchy was proceeding in the nineteenth century, Grillparzer's anti-Slavism was above all part of a general aversion to any nationalism, including German nationalism. Such an attitude did not, however, question the traditional distribution of power in the Monarchy, which favored German preponderance in the cultural and political fields.

At the turn of the century a younger generation of scholars established a new form of general anti-Slavism that met the needs of German nationalism in the Monarchy. After the First World War, the new discourse led to the founding of *Südostforschung* and later toward the Nazi discourse on Slavs in general. The older anti-Slavism remained a stock from which some stereotypes were borrowed to strengthen the new discursive formation that unfolded under new circumstances. So, despite some elements of continuity, a clear line can be drawn between Grillparzer's attitude and the anti-Slavism of the twentieth century.

While the discourse on the Slovenes fits into this general scheme, the discourses on the Serbs were more ambiguous and underwent several modifications, the result of changing political constellations. Imagining the Serbs was a matter of daily politics. Since the political constellations changed more than once, there were positive and negative stocks of stereotypes of the Serbs, which could be applied according to the respective policy toward the Serbs. The discourses on the Serbs, however, were embedded into a metadiscourse on the Balkans that had its roots in the age of Enlightenment and consisted of several unchangeable stereotypes that appeared in every discourse on the Serbs: "underdevelopment," "backwardness," "heroic culture," or "patriarchalism." Maria Todorova and Vesna Goldsworthy have already analyzed British, French, Russian, and American accounts of the Balkans.[188] Delving deeper into Austrian discourse on this part of Europe remains a task for the future.

Notes

1. Quoted in Gerhart Reckzeh, *Grillparzer und die Slaven*, Forschungen zur neueren Literaturgeschichte LIX (Weimar: Alexander Duncker, 1929), 24.

2. See Kiril Petkov, *Infidels, Turks, and Women: The South Slavs in the German Mind, ca. 1400-1600* (Frankfurt am Main: Peter Lang, 1997). For other approaches toward the Slavs see Franc Rozman, ed., *Der Nachbar im Spiegelbild des Nachbarn von 1848 bis heute* (Ljubljana: Nacionalni komite za zgodovinske vede, 1993); Felix J. Bister and Peter Vodopivec, eds., *Kulturelle Wechselseitigkeit in Mitteleuropa. Deutsche und slowenische Kultur im slowenischen Raum vom Anfang des 19. Jahrhunderts bis zum Ersten Weltkrieg* (Ljubljana: Oddelek za zgodovino Filozofske fakultete, 1995); "Österreich-Slowenien: Geschichte und Gegenwart," *Europäische Rundschau* 29, no. 1 (2001): 3-98; Ferdinand Mayer-Grünbühel and Miroslav Polzer, eds., *Avstrija-Slovenija; Preteklost in sedanjost* (Ljubljana: Cankarjeva zalozba and Klagenfurt: Wieser, 2002).

3. Maria Todorova, *Imagining the Balkans* (New York: Oxford University Press, 1997), 7.

4. Elisabeth List, "The Fantasy of Unity: Body Imaginary and the Construction of Collective Identity," in *Otherhood and Nation. Selected Papers from the International Conference*, ed. Rada Iveković and Neda Pagon (Ljubljana: Institutum Studiorum Humanitatis, 1998), 13.

5. Todorova, *Imagining the Balkans*, 19.

6. Larry Wolff, *Inventing Eastern Europe: The Map of Civilization on the Mind of the Enlightenment* (Stanford, Calif.: Stanford University Press, 1994), 107.

7. See Ernest Gellner, *Nationalismus und Moderne* (Berlin: Rotbuch, 1991), 14, 21.

8. Moritz Csáky, *Ideologie der Operette und Wiener Moderne. Ein kulturhistorischer Essay zur österreichischen Identität* (Vienna: Böhlau, 1996), 179-80.

9. Anton Thomas Linhart, *Versuch einer Geschichte von Krain und der übrigen südlichen Slaven Österreichs* (Nürnberg, 1796); quoted in Alfred Fischel, *Der Panslawismus bis zum Weltkrieg. Ein geschichtlicher Überblick* (Stuttgart: J.G. Cotta, 1919), 232.

10. "Annalen der Literatur und Kunst in den österreichischen Staaten," no. 7 (October 1803), 687, quoted in Gertraud Marinelli-König, *Die Südslaven in den Wiener Zeitschriften und Almanachen des Vormärz, 1805-1848*, Philosophisch-historische Klasse, Sitzungsberichte 603/Veröffentlichungen der Kommission für Literaturwissenschaft 14 (Vienna: Österreichische Akademie der Wissenschaften, 1994), 417.

11. Joseph Rohrer, *Versuch über die slawischen Bewohner der österreichischen Monarchie* (Vienna: Kunst- und Industrie-Comptoir, 1804).

12. Adolf Ficker, "Die Völkerstämme der österreichischen Monarchie 1868," *Mittheilungen aus dem Gebiete der Statistik* 15 (1869): 34.

13. See Peter Stachel, *Ethnischer Pluralismus und wissenschaftliche Theoriebildung im zentraleuropäischen Raum. Fallbeispiele wissenschaftlicher und philosophischer Reflexion über die ethnischkulturelle Vielfalt der Donaumonarchie* (Ph.D. Dissertation, University of Graz, 1999), 12-16.

14. Quoted in Reckzeh, *Grillparzer und die Slaven*, 4.

15. Anton Šantel, "Moji spomini," *Srce in oko. Obzornik Prešernove družbe* 13 (1990): 126-27.

16. "Österreichische Blätter für Literatur und Kunst," no. 40 (17 August 1844), 320, quoted in Marinelli-König, *Die Südslaven in den Wiener Zeitschriften*, 114.

17. Solomon Wank, "The Habsburg Empire," in *After Empire: Multiethnic Societies and Nation-Building: The Soviet Union and the Russian, Ottoman, and Habsburg Empires*, ed. Karen Barkey and Mark von Hagen (Oxford: Westview Press, 1997), 50.

18. Janez Cvirn, "The Slovenes from the German Perspective," *Slovene Studies* 15, nos. 1-2 (1993): 51-62.

19. See, in detail, Janez Cvirn, *Trdnjavski trikotnik. Politična orientacija Nemcev na Spodnjem Štajerskem (1861-1914)* (Maribor: Obzorja, 1997).

20. Quoted in Hugo Suette, *Der nationale Kampf in der Südsteiermark. 1867 bis 1897*, Veröffentlichungen des Instituts zur Erforschung des deutschen Volkstums im Süden und Südosten in München und des Instituts für ostbairische Heimatforschung in Passau 12 (Munich: M. Schick, 1936), 52.

21. R[ichard] Foregger, *Zur Zillier Gymnasialfrage* (Vienna: R. Foregger, 1894).

22. Richard Pfaundler, "Die Grundlagen der nationalen Bevölkerungsentwicklung Steiermarks," *Statistische Monatsschrift* 12, new serial (1907): 560, 561, 571, 574, and 591.

23. Miroslav Hroch, *Social Preconditions of National Revival in Europe: A Comparative Analysis of the Social Composition of Patriotic Groups among the Smaller European Nations* (Cambridge: Cambridge University Press, 1985), 10.

24. Martin Wutte, "Die sprachlichen Verhältnisse in Kärnten auf der Grundlage der Volkszählung von 1900 und ihre Veränderungen im 19. Jahrhundert," *Carinthia I* 96 (1906): 153-78.

25. Wilhelm Hecke, *Volksvermehrung, Binnenwanderung und Umgangssprache in den österreichischen Alpen- und Südländern* (Brünn: Irrgang, 1913) (Offprint from the Statistische Monatsschrift); Wilhelm Hecke, *Die Verschiedenheit der deutschen und slawischen Volksvermehrung in Österreich* (Stuttgart: Enke, 1916).

26. Erwin Hanslik, "Kulturgeographie der deutsch-slawischen Sprachgrenze," *Vierteljahrsschrift für Sozial und Wirtschaftsgeschichte* 8 (1910): 103-27, 445-75.

27. Vincenz Goehlert, "Untersuchungen über die Augen- und Haarfarben der Schulkinder in der Steiermark," *Statistische Monatsschrift* 6 (1880): 407-16.

28. See for example, Emil Zuckerkandl, "Physische Beschaffenheit der Bevölkerung," in *Die österreichische-ungarische Monarchie in Wort und Bild. Steiermark* (Vienna: Kaiserlich-königl. Hof- u. Staatsdruckerei, 1890), 238-44.

29. See Brigitte Hamann, *Hitlers Wien. Lehrjahre eines Diktators* (Munich: Piper, 1998), 285-333.

30. "Vaterländische Blätter für den österreichischen Kaiserstaat," no. 4 (15 May 1810), 41, quoted in Marinelli-König, *Die Südslaven in den Wiener Zeitschriften*, 252; see, in general, Emmanuel Turczynski, "Austro-Serbian Relations," in *The First Serbian Uprising*, ed. Wayne S. Vucinich (Boulder, Colo.: Brooklyn College Press, 1982), 175-206.

31. Marinelli-König, *Die Südslaven in den Wiener Zeitschriften*, 244-47, 289, 334, 340, and 354.

32. "Archiv für Geographie," nos. 52 and 53 (1 May and 3 May 1811), 230, quoted in Marinelli-König, *Die Südslaven in den Wiener Zeitschriften*, 370-71.

33. Kanitz became a member of *Matica srpska*, one of the most important Serbian national cultural societies, and was treated as a "Serbian author." The king of Serbia awarded Kanitz his country's highest order. On Kanitz see Zoran Konstantinović, *Deutsche Reisebeschreibungen über Serbien und Montenegro*, Südosteuropäische Arbeiten 56 (Munich: R. Oldenbourg, 1960), 94-107.

34. Ibid., 122-24.

35. Hugo Bach, "Die Bevölkerung des Königreiches Serbien und ihr Bildungsgrad," *Statistische Monatsschrift* 14 (1888): 1, 7, 19, 22.

36. Stojan Novaković, *Die Wiedergeburt des serbischen Staates, 1804-1813*, Zur Kunde der Balkanhalbinses 2.3 (Sarajevo: B.-H. Institut für Balkanforschung, 1912).

37. By the 1880s Novaković had served in several ministerial posts; he briefly became Prime Minister of Serbia in 1909.

38. Heinrich Friedjung, *Aktenstücke zur großserbischen Bewegung in Österreich-Ungarn* (Vienna: Waizner, 1909).

39. Leopold Mandl, *Österreich-Ungarn und Serbien nach dem Balkankriege. Materialien zum Verständnis der Beziehungen Serbiens zu Österreich-Ungarn* (Vienna: Perles, 1912), 8, 12, 26, 34, 35.

40. Ibid., 35.

41. Ibid., 39, 40, 54.

42. Friedrich Salomon Krauss, "Vom serbischen Volkstum," *Süddeutsche Monatshefte* 12 (1915): 986-91.

43. See Mechthild Golczewski, *Der Balkan in deutschen und österreichischen Erlebnisberichten 1912-1918*, Quellen und Studien zur Geschichte des östlichen Europa XVI (Wiesbaden: Franz Steiner, 1981); Konstantinović, *Deutsche Reisebeschreibungen*, 164.

44. See Arthur Haberlandt, *Kultur- und wissenschaftliche Beiträge zur Volkskultur von Montenegro, Albanien und Serbien*, Zeitschrift für Volkskunde, suppl. vol. 12 (Vienna: Gerold, 1917), 162-63.

45. See Fischel, *Der Panslawismus bis zum Weltkrieg*, 31, 41, 55, 125-26, 211-17, 504, 549, 576-81.

46. See Arnold Luschin-Ebengreuth, *Die Zerreißung der Steiermark. Zwei Denkschriften* (Graz: Moser, 1921).

47. Wilhelm Fischer, "Die steirische Mark," *Mitteilungen des Vereines Südmark* 14, no. 4 (1919): 71.

48. Martin Wutte, *Deutsch-Windisch-Slowenisch. Zum 7. Jahrestag der Kärntner Volksabstimmung* (Klagenfurt: Kärntner Heimatbund, 1927).

49. See, in detail, Tom Priestly, "Zur Rechtfertigung des Unentschuldbaren: Politische Manipulationen ethnischer Bezeichnungen in Gebieten mit slowenischen Minderheiten in Österreich und Ungarn," in *Slowenische Steiermark. Verdrängte Minderheit in Österreichs Südosten*, ed. Christian Stenner, Zur Kunde Südosteuropas 2, no. 23 (Vienna: Böhlau, 1997), 322-28.

50. See, for example, the monthly periodical *Grenzland. Zeitschrift des Deutschen Schulvereines Südmark*, vol. 1-14 (1925-1938).

51. Gustav Kraitschek, *Rassenkunde mit besonderer Berücksichtigung des deutschen Volkes, vor allem der Ostalpenländer*, Urgeschichtliche Volksbücher 1 (Vienna: Burgverlag, 1923), 38-41, 55, 59-60, 112, 114.

52. Rudolf Polland, "Die rassische Zusammensetzung der Bevölkerung der Steiermark," *Volk und Rasse* 1 (1929): 16-17.

53. Robert Routil, *Völker und Rassen auf dem Boden Kärntens*, Schriften zur Geistesgeschichte Kärntens (Klagenfurt: Artur Kollitsch, 1935), 52, 57, 75, 76. The process of cranial measurement, however, has no value and no role in current physical anthropology. Blood types, disease patterns, and DNA are the current markers; see Luigi Luca Cavalli-Sforza and Francesco Cavalli-Sforza, *The Great Human Diasporas: The History of Diversity and Evolution* (Reading, Mass.: Addison-Wesley, 1995).

54. Karl Nehring, "Geschichte des Südost-Instituts," in *Südost-Institut München 1930-1990. Mathias Bernath zum siebzigsten Geburtstag* (Munich: R. Oldenbourg, 1990), 21. On the upsurge of Ostforschung see Michael Burleigh, *Germany Turns Eastwards. A Study of Ostforschung in the Third Reich* (Cambridge: Cambridge University Press, 1988), 22-39.

55. Burleigh, *Germany Turns Eastwards*, 26-27. How the academic approach of *Südostforschung* was integrated into the general Nazi approach toward social science and humanities can be seen best in Michael Fahlbusch, *Wissenschaft im Dienst der nationalsozialistischen Politik?*

Die "Volksdeutschen Forschungsgemeinschaften" von 1931-1945 (Baden-Baden: Nomos, 1999), 260-63.

56. Doris Kraft, *Das untersteirische Drauland. Deutsches Grenzland zwischen Unterdrauburg und Marburg,* Veröffentlichungen des Instituts zur Erforschung des deutschen Volkstums im Süden und Südosten in München und des Instituts für ostbairische Heimatforschung in Passau 10 (Munich: Schick, 1935), 95, 125-26, 138.

57. Suette, *Der nationale Kampf,* VI, 13-14, 125.

58. Fritz Valjavec, "Wege und Wandlungen deutscher Südostforschung," *Südostdeutsche Forschungen* 1 (1936): 12.

59. See Robert Mayer, "Das Südostdeutsche Institut in Graz, seine Aufgaben und Arbeiten," *Mitteilungen der Geographischen Gesellschaft in Wien* 86 (1943): 277-79.

60. See Tone Ferenc, *Nacistična raznarodovalna politika v Sloveniji v letih 1941-1945,* Knjižnica NOV in POS 35 (Maribor: Obzorja, 1968), 85-91.

61. See Götz Aly, Karl-Heinz Roth, *Die restlose Erfassung. Volkszählen, Identifizieren, Aussondern im Nationalsozialismus,* Rotbuch 282 (Berlin: Rotbuch, 1984), 10.

62. Gerhard Werner [i.e., Helmut Carstanjen], *Sprache und Volkstum in der Untersteiermark,* Forschungen zur Deutschen Landes- und Volkskunde XXXI, 3 (Stuttgart: Engelhorn, 1935), 161; see also Fahlbusch, *Wissenschaft im Dienst der nationalsozialistischen Politik?,* 320-21.

63. Mayer, "Das Südostdeutsche Institut in Graz," 278.

64. See Ferenc, *Nacistična raznarodovalna politika,* 100.

65. "Lebensfragen der Grenzbevölkerung untersucht an der steirischen Südgrenze. Reichsberufswettkampf der deutschen Studenten, Kennummer 967, Gau Steiermark," vol. 1, nos. 3-4 (Graz: unpublished manuscript, 1938/39) (University Library of Graz: #II 199.142), vol. 2 (Graz: Styrian Provincial Archive: manu. #1858), 151-59, 165, 324.

66. Ibid., 150-51.

67. Ibid., vol. 4, 336-43.

68. See Herman Ibler, "Des Reiches Südgrenze in der Steiermark. Vergewaltigtes Selbstbestimmungsrecht" (Graz: unpublished manuscript, 1940).

69. See Ferenc, *Nacistična raznarodovalna politika,* 732; Fahlbusch, *Wissenschaft im Dienst der nationalsozialistischen Politik?,* 311-12, 665.

70. Helmut Carstanjen, *Die Untersteiermark. Eine politische Aufgabe an der Südostgrenze des Großdeutschen Reiches. Nur für den Dienstgebrauch* (Marburg: Steirischer Heimatbund, 1943/44), 10-11.

71. See, in detail, Ferenc, *Nacistična raznarodovalna politika,* 731-813; Horst Seidler and Andreas Rett, *Rassenhygiene. Ein Weg in den Nationalsozialismus* (Vienna: Jugend und Volk, 1988), 201-12.

72. American Historical Association: American Committee for the Study of War Documents, Records of the National Socialist Labor Party (NSDAP) [National Archives Microcopy No. T-81] (Washington, D.C., 1956), National Archives Microcopy No. T-81 Roll No. 284, VOMI/267-293 (Deutsches Ausland-Institut), VOMI 279, 4-5.

73. Götz Aly and Susanne Heim, *Vordenker der Vernichtung. Ausschwitz und die neuen Pläne für eine neue europäische Ordnung* (Frankfurt am Main: Fischer, 1993), 140-41, 289.

74. Wilhelm Sattler, *Die Untersteiermark. Eine Darstellung der bevölkerungspolitischen und wirtschaftlichen Grundlagen,* Schriften des Südostdeutschen Institutes Graz 8 (Graz: Steirische Verlagsanstalt, 1942), 70-71.

75. Helmut Carstanjen, "Untersteiermark, ein deutsches Grenzland," in Sattler, *Die Untersteiermark,* 10-12.

76. See, for example, Hugo Hassinger, "Lebensraumfragen der Völker des europäischen Südostens," in *Lebensraumfragen europäischer Völker,* ed. K.H. Diezel, O. Schmieder, and H. Schmitthenner, vol. 1 (Leipzig: Quelle & Meyer, 1941), 611-12.

77. See Aly and Heim, *Vordenker der Vernichtung,* 232-42.

78. Gilbert in der Maur, *Die Jugoslawen einst und jetzt, Vol. 1: Aus der Geschichte der Südslawen* (Leipzig, Vienna: Johannes Günther, 1936), XIII.

79. Ibid., XIII, 23.

80. Gilbert in der Maur, *Der Weg zur Nation. Jugoslawiens Innenpolitik 1918-1938. Stojadinovic als Vollstrecker* (Berlin: Payer & Co., 1938), 607.

81. Camillo Morocutti, "Südslawien," in *Des Reiches neue Nachbarn*, ed. Walter Schneefuß (Salzburg: Pustet, 1939), 265, 176-77, 191-93, 204-6, 209.

82. [Felix] K[raus], "Südosteuropa an der Schwelle der neuen Zeit," in *Volkstum im Südosten*. Volkspolitische Monatsschrift, vol. 2 (1940), 117.

83. See Werner Augustinovic and Martin Moll, "Deutsche Propaganda im Balkanfeldzug 1941," *Österreichische Militärische Zeitschrift* 38, no. 4 (2000): 459-60.

84. Felix Kraus, "Der Neuordnung entgegen!" *Volkstum im Südosten* 3 (1941): 44-45.

85. Felix Kraus, "Das Ende der südslawischen Idee," *Volkstum im Südosten* 3 (1941): 73-75.

86. E[gon] Lendl, "Wandlungen des Geschichtsbildes südosteuropäischer Völker," *Volkstum im Südosten* 3 (1941): 156.

87. F[elix] K[raus], "Rückblick," *Volkstum im Südosten* 4 (1942): 58.

88. Heinz Scheibenpflug, *Donau und Donauraum. Der Schicksalsweg eines Stromes* (Vienna: Adolf Luser, 1939), 35, 38-39.

89. See Heinz Scheibenpflug, *Donau und Donauraum. Landschaft, Völker und Staaten Südosteuropas* (Vienna: Wiener Verlagsgesellschaft, 1943), 41-42.

90. Ibid., 42.

91. See Albert Klein, "Vom inneren Reichtum der 'Balkanier,'" *Volkstum im Südosten* 4 (1942): 184-88; N.N., "Vom alten Rascien," *Volkstum im Südosten* 5 (1943): 204-9; [Felix] K[raus], "Kosovo," *Volkstum im Südosten* 6 (1944): 38-39. Walter Wünsch, "Volkslied und Volkstum der slawischen Bauern und Hirten auf dem Balkan," and "Die slawische Volksepik in Südosteuropa," in *Deutschland und Südosteuropa. Die natürlichen, völkischen, kulturellen und wirtschaftlichen Beziehungen des Deutschtums mit den Völkern im Südosten*, Schriften des Südostdeutschen Institutes Graz 7 (Graz: Steirische Verlagsanstalt, 1942), 96-102. In general see Todorova, *Imagining the Balkans*.

92. Walter Schneefuß, "Politische Geographie Kroatiens" (Graz: unpublished manuscript, 1942), 99-106.

93. Wilhelm Sattler, *Die slawonische Drauniederung als deutsche Volksinsellandschaft*, Deutsche Schriften zur Landes- und Volksforschung 11 (Leipzig: Hirzel, 1941).

94. Wilhelm Sattler, *Die deutsche Volksgruppe im Unabhängigen Staat Kroatien*, Schriften des Südostdeutschen Institutes Graz 9 (Graz: Steirische Verlagsanstalt, 1943), 7, 38, 57.

95. Ibid., 45, 48.

96. Schneefuß, *Politische Geographie*, 12-14, 23, 111, 116, 124-35.

97. Hassinger, "Lebensraumfragen der Völker," 594, 600. See also Hugo Hassinger, "Mitteleuropa, Donaueuropa, Südosteuropa," *Volkstum im Südosten* 3 (1941): 173-76; on Hassinger see Fahlbusch, *Wissenschaft im Dienst der nationalsozialistischen Politik?*, 253-54.

98. See Norbert Krebs, "Die geographische Struktur der südslawischen Länder," *Geographische Zeitschrift* 47 (1941): 242, 255-56.

99. Walter Schneefuß, *Donauräume und Donaureiche* (Vienna: Braumüller, 1942), 44.

100. Schneefuß, *Politische Geographie*, 168.

101. Ibid., 120.

102. Mathilde Uhlirz, "Das Gesamtdeutschtum und derSüdosten von dem Einbruck der Türken bis zum Beginn des Weltkrieges," *Deutschland und Südosteuropa* (1942): 39, 43.

103. Fritz von Reinöhl, ed., *Großserbische Umtriebe vor und nach Ausbruch des Ersten Weltkrieges. I. Der Fall Jeftanović-Sola-Gavrila* (Vienna: Holzhausen, 1944).

104. See Ludwig Bittner, "Geleitwort," in ibid., IV.

105. See Fritz Valjavec, "Der Werdegang der deutschen Südostforschung und ihr gegenwärtiger Stand," *Südost-Forschungen* 6 (1941): 18-19.

106. See Karl Nehring, "Der Briefwechsel von Fritz Valjavec 1934-1950. Personen und Institutionen," *Südost-Forschungen* 53 (1994): 323-54.

107. See Siegfried Mattl et al., eds., *Willfährige Wissenschaft. Die Universität Wien 1938-1945* (Vienna: Verlag für Gesellschaftskritik, 1989), 233.

108. Vesna Goldsworthy, *Inventing Ruritania; The Imperialism of the Imagination* (New Haven, Conn.: Yale University Press, 1998).

Chapter 10

PEOPLES OF THE MOUNTAINS,
PEOPLES OF THE PLAINS

Space and Ethnographic Representation

Karl Kaser

This essay examines and decodes the ethnographical representation of the Balkans by two outstanding historical figures, the Serbian geographer Jovan Cvijić and the Croatian sociologist Dinko Tomašić, each a scientific authority in his country.[1] Their scholarly publications represent either differently imagined or realistic pictures of the Balkans. In 1991, the Serbian Academy of Sciences and Arts published a reprint of Cvijić's famous *Balkansko poluostrvo* (The Balkan Peninsula), which originally appeared in French (1918) and was translated into Serbo-Croatian in 1922. Following decades of official condemnation, Tomašić has recently enjoyed a revival in Croatia. This revival is reflected in the scholarly writings of Croatian-born Stjepan G. Meštrović, a professor of sociology at Texas A&M University, who promotes Tomašić's ideas in American academia. (In addition, Meštrović has recently published books on Anthony Giddens[2] and Emile Durkheim.[3])

Geography and ethnic perspectives are closely related in the Balkans. Although Cvijić and Tomašić have similar research objectives, the conclusions of the South Slavic-Serbian-oriented Cvijić differ greatly from those of the Croatian-oriented Tomašić. The difference cannot easily be explained merely by their differing approaches. The nationalist struggles of the former Yugoslavia, founded in 1918 as the Kingdom of the Serbs, Croats, and Slovenes, are reflected in scholarly work. Cvijić writes during the period of Yugoslavia's inception, Tomašić after its dissolution. How did these two authors construct the Other and create Otherness? What are the results of their efforts in Balkanizing the Balkans? How at the end of the twentieth century could sociological theory be used misleadingly to explain the wars in the former Yugoslavia? To answer these questions, we must decode the mechanisms of how the Dinaric people could become synonymous with both "good" and "bad" or "evil."

Jovan Cvijić and Dinko Tomašić

Jovan Cvijić (1865-1927) studied physical geography and geology at Vienna University from 1889 to 1892, where he earned his Ph.D., with a dissertation entitled *Das Karstphänomen*. Upon returning to Belgrade he became a professor at the *Geografski institut* (Geographic Institute), which he founded. After 1902, he became editor of *Naselja i poreklo stanovništvo* (Settlement and origin of the population), an important series on the settlement and origins of the Serbs, which is still published. Cvijić spent most of the First World War in Paris, where he taught at the Sorbonne. In 1921, he was elected president of the Serbian Academy of Sciences and Arts, a position he held until his death.[4] The 1991 edition of his main scholarly work, *Balkansko poluostrvo*,[5] is the source used in this article.

Dinko Tomašić (1902-1975) was educated in Split and Zagreb, earning his Ph.D. in law and social sciences from Zagreb University. After several positions in Zagreb, Belgrade, and the United States, Tomašić taught sociology at Zagreb University from 1935 to 1941. In 1941, following the destruction of Yugoslavia at the hands of the Germans and Italians, he migrated to the United States where he taught at a variety of universities.[6] During his first years in exile he wrote the articles that serve as sources for this paper: "Personality Development in the Zadruga Society,"[7] "Personality Development of the Dinaric Warriors,"[8] and "The Structure of Balkan Society,"[9] which would later be published as a monograph.[10]

The publications of the two scholars share some common features. Both deal with the personality or psychological development of the Dinaric Mountain population and the population of the Pannonian Plains, especially the Croatian parts. Moreover, to a certain degree, the authors were convinced that geography had a determining influence on the human psyche. Both believed in a strong connection among soil, climate, biotic factors, and the human being, Tomašić more so than Cvijić. Tomašić's approach is that of a psycho-ethnologist, while Cvijić's approach is that of an anthropo-geographer, which he described as the study of the psychic constitution of populations in different natural environments and the impact of geographic factors upon those populations. But he also incorporated historical, ethnic, and social elements, which he believed contributed to the constitution of the psyche of a people.[11] Cvijić divided the geographic influences into three types: direct influences, such as climate and landscape; indirect influences, such as natural resources that had an impact on types of dwellings, forms of economy, food, and clothing; and geographic factors that influenced the movement of human groups and shaped the zones of their civilizations.[12]

Contemporary anthropologists might be more cautious in their explanations of the interaction between geography and psyche than either Cvijić or Tomašić was. About the time Tomašić was writing, the French historian Fernand Braudel had just completed *The Mediterranean and the Mediterranean World in the Age of Philip II*.[13] The first section of this book, "The Role of the Environment," developed an approach very similar to that of Cvijić and Tomašić, discussing the impact of mountains and plains on the mentalities of peoples and the impact of climate on history. However, Braudel differed from these two authors because he compared the different cultures of the Mediterranean world in history. The Balkans was only one part of his broad perspective. The advantages of the Braudelian approach are twofold: his comparative approach relativizes one-sided conclusions, and he considers the historical actor not only structured by environmental constraints, but also as an actively structuring human being. This is why man can never be considered merely a result of environmental pressure. Perhaps this is why Braudel drew different conclusions than Cvijić and Tomašić.

The Context

Until the twentieth century, pastoralism had long been the primary economic activity in the Dinaric Mountains. The notion of pastoralism usually involves herding in natural pastures and implies that animal husbandry is economically dominant. Pastoralists in the Dinaric Mountains derived most of their income or sustenance from keeping livestock (sheep, goats) in conditions in which their livestock consumed primarily natural forage rather than cultivated fodder. Other factors were the two pastoral strategies for overseeing the livestock; one was the permanent stability of the main residential group, with certain specified individuals taking the livestock and living away from the main residence. This pattern was common in the Mediterranean as well as in the Dinaric Mountains. The other strategy was coordinated movement of both the residential group and the flock, the nomadic strategy. Both strategies had an impact but not necessarily a determining function on household and kinship structure and labor division. For this, additional factors have to be considered. They include the kind of animals that comprised the flocks, security, the kind of society the pastoralists came in contact with, the persons who made up the pastoral labor unit, the relation of pastoral and nonpastoral labor activities of household members, the interrelationship of pastoralism with other forms of production, and the capacity to expand the capital resources of livestock, pasture, and water.

At first glance there seems to be a pronounced interaction between pastoralism and the existence of both the joint family household (*zadruga*) in the context of a patrilineal kinship structure and explicit patriarchal patterns.[14] Although this relation between pastoralism, family complexity, patriarchy, and patrilineality is obvious, there is no explanation why complexity, patriarchy, and patrilineality should have been necessarily confined to herding areas in the Balkans. In fact, this was also the case among the land cultivators of the Eastern European and Croatian plains. The structure of the complex family seems similar to those in the Dinaric Mountains, but the economic background was completely different. The cultivation of land rather than herding was the primary economic activity. Large households usually ran big farmsteads. The household members specialized in certain branches of economic activity (the cultivation of crops, cattle breeding, etc.). In contrast to the Dinaric mountain areas, which had been historically attached to the Ottoman Empire, the Habsburg Monarchy, which administrated Croatia until 1918, was able to establish security for the people and their economic activities. This made living conditions much more favorable. Because of the presence of the administration and guarantied security, the patrilineal group no longer played a significant role. The great impact of Roman Catholicism, which opposed the concept of patrilineality, on daily life was also important.[15]

In short, there were both similarities (patrilocality, early age at marriage, family structure) and differences (patrilineality, tribal organization, deep-rooted patriarchy, an economy of goat and sheep breeding, and forms of ancestor worship in the Dinaric Mountains) between people of the plains and those of the mountains. These differences probably meant that people thought and approached certain problems in different ways, but far-reaching conclusions regarding, for example, the organization of political life cannot be drawn.

Ethnographic Representation of the Dinaric and the Plain Peoples

The images of the character and mentality of the Dinaric Mountain population and the Croatian plains population differ significantly. Cvijić drew his conclusions through systematic fieldwork and participant observation, undertaken annually from 1887 to 1915. His conceptual guideline was the ethnic entity of the South Slavs, including the Slovenes, Serbs, and Croats as well as the Bulgarians. Cvijić observed common psychic characteristics and a common mentality among these peoples. Different historical developments and cultural influences led to regional differences, however. The most significant was between the Southeastern Slavs (the Bulgarians) and the Southwestern Slavs (the Serbs, Croats, and Slovenes). He differentiated four basic types: the "Dinaric," which included people who lived in or migrated from the mountainous regions of the Dinaric Mountain chain; the "Central," which consisted of people from the Southern Morava Valley, Vardar Valley, and the Šopi, in western Bulgaria; the "East Balkan," that is, the remaining Bulgarians; and the "Pannonian," inhabitants of the Great Pannonian Plains and the surrounding mountains. These four types were subdivided into "varieties" and "groups."[16] The first and fourth types fit into Tomašić's typology. Whether coincidentally or not, it seems as if these four types represented a hierarchy. Type one held the highest ranking; obviously he invested significantly more time in studying the Dinaric people, whereas type four had the lowest evaluation, and the ethnographic representation of the Pannonian people was rather limited. In Tomašić's terminology, "Dinaric" did not contain negative associations, but was positively connoted. He did not articulate this differentiation, but a close reading of his book indicates that the Dinaric people—two-thirds of whom were Serbs—represented the most "valuable" part of the South Slav population for him.

The Dinaric people's general psychological characteristics were the same everywhere despite state boundaries. They practiced a patriarchal way of life, were lively, intelligent, and sensitive, and had a rich imagination. They easily became very enthusiastic or angry. Materialistic considerations were of little significance; greed and selfishness were therefore absent. The majority of their activities were related to their sentiments and feelings and to fostering individual and group pride, honor, justice, and freedom. Violation of these virtues was the main reason for quarrels, because success in life depended on maintaining such values. The Dinaric people instinctively sensed their roles in the world and had unlimited trust in their abilities to solve any problem they might encounter.[17]

Aside from these general psychological characteristics, Cvijić observed a series of much more detailed features such as very strong ties to the land, to place of birth, and to their ancestors who had worked and lived on the land. The Dinaric people were more closely tied to their homeland than other South Slav peoples because their lives were so largely shaped by the difficult ecological conditions of the Dinaric Mountains. Their thoughts centered on images of mountains, sources, karst rivers, huge forests, old oak trees, and the scenery of mountain peaks. Spirits inhabited oil, water, and trees.[18] They imagined nature as being alive and treated it as a living being.

According to Cvijić, the most important element in shaping the Dinaric mentality was probably living in *zadruga,* including common ancestors and an elected elder *(starac).* While the tribe was predominantly a fighting organization, the *zadruga* was a place of peaceful living, functioning as an economic unit that produced everything necessary for survival. Age and ability determined the division of labor. The strongest men did heavy fieldwork while the elderly and younger household members carried out lighter duties. Women did housework and girls worked on their dowries. Life in an extended family was based on a patriarchal civilization that was not as archaic as is generally assumed. On the contrary, patriarchy was a well-organized moral system based on customary law. The *zadruga* was the site where national epic poetry and folklore were created and fostered. In the *zadruga* the highest level of solidarity, sympathy, and emotional warmth could be reached. These features were stronger among the Dinaric people than among the other South Slavs.[19]

Additional elements of the Dinaric psychology observed by Cvijić were a high level of interpersonal solidarity, particularly in difficult situations, combined with a warm cordiality, resulting from the tradition of the *zadruga,* and fighting skills that developed through centuries of opposing Ottoman domination. As a result the Dinaric people could not work as servants as most people of the plains could.[20]

While Cvijić developed the psychology of the Dinaric type in great detail, he was unspecific concerning the Pannonic type. To compare his views to Tomašić's, who focused on northwestern Croatia, I will analyze Cvijić's comments on the so-called Slavonic variety and the Zagreb-Zagorje group. Cvijić's assessment of the plains people was unenthusiastic, if not entirely negative. In sharp contrast to the Dinaric region, he described the soil as fertile, the villages were well-organized, and the animals, especially the pigs, were numerous. He obviously liked people of the Slavonic variety; he appreciated their sense of delicacy toward other people and their extreme goodness, which he believed could often turn into weakness. Their "national soul" was close to that of Russians, but was also full of joy of life. Women especially knew how to enjoy themselves. This mentality can be explained by the easy life in this region due to fertile soils and rich harvests. The *zadruga* lifestyle was not essentially different from that in Serbia, although gender relations were more liberal and morals of women looser than elsewhere.[21]

Cvijić's view of the rural population of the Zagreb-Zagorje region was different. Centuries of Austrian administration, Austro-Hungarian nobility, and German customs shaped its psychology. On the one hand the population was closely tied to the soil; although the increasing population made life difficult, it was industrious, persistent, and acted with circumspection. On the other hand, the peasants were cold and brusque in their behavior. Everyone considered himself a "genuine" Croat. Those who did not speak the Croatian dialect were called foreigners. These were suspicious people who lacked solidarity. They did not know their historical traditions, and the vivid metaphors of the Dinaric people were absent from their dialect. As a result of long feudal oppression, from which they never freed themselves, they lacked the democratic spirit of the Dinaric people. They thought that nobility, and not ordinary people, should form the government. Without a lord there was no order. They served in a disciplined manner and submitted themselves to the will of the older generation.[22]

Some two decades later Tomašić drew a very different picture, one that clearly differentiated the good from the bad. The good was the plowman of the plains while the bad was the sheep breeder of the Dinaric Mountains. His focus on northwestern Croatia allowed Tomašić to paint an idyllic picture of *zadruga* life in the early nineteenth century, comparing it to the Russian village community *(mir)* described by great Russian novelists. The favorable environment of this region—the soil, the supply of wood, and the climate—made the production of most required goods possible. Communal work increased production, "combined with singing and a general spirit of gaiety. Common work was often followed by a feast which was again an occasion for singing, drinking, and merry-making. A few *zadrugas* might unite to help each other in order to make the work more efficient and the time merrier."[23] Singing and merry-making were the predominant activities of happy Croatian peasants. There was no particular discrimination between *zadruga* members at meal times and nothing of importance could be decided by the *zadruga* elders *(gospodars)* without consulting the whole community. The oldest man was not automatically elected *gospodar* but rather the best manager, and there was no rivalry for this position. This democratic spirit was reflected annually. A couple of weeks before the New Year the *gospodar* would tender his resignation and on New Year's Eve the community would choose the new elder: someone who was strong, healthy, industrious, prudent, and intelligent. Despite his authority the *gospodar* could not concentrate all power into his own hands.[24]

Kinship relationships and rules of exogamy did not play a decisive role in communal life. There was often intermarriage within the same *zadruga*, mainly because girls preferred to marry boys from their own households. The division of labor was gendered: men did the hard labor while cooking, cleaning, and lace work were reserved for women. Men also helped women in the agricultural work, such as hoeing, reaping, and sometimes weaving. In Tomašić's eyes, the organization of labor indicated a tendency to distribute wealth so that everybody shared equally in the benefits of *zadruga* life.[25]

No wonder children were born under happy circumstances; they were considered assets rather than burdens. Everyone showed them much affection, and each married couple wanted to have at least a few. No matter how many children were born to the *zadruga*, they were welcomed with tenderness. Parents wanted a family with both boys and girls. There was no difference in the upbringing of boys and girls, nor were sexuality and magic kept secret from them. Community members were expected to treat pregnant women well. While a mother was nursing she was spared from work. During the course of a child's first year the mother spent most of her time looking after the child.[26]

Interpersonal relations were ideal. People tried to avoid clashes, and everyone was aware that their existence depended on cooperation and collaboration. The elderly were respected. The parents were more concerned with protecting than with disciplining their children. Women enjoyed a high social position, and the division of labor favored them. Sometimes a woman even chose her husband. *Zadruga* members felt neither superior nor inferior to others. There was a remarkable lack of sexual offenses, abortions, extramarital sexual relations, and divorces. Suicide was unknown.[27]

According to Tomašić this idyllic society in the plains and valleys stood in sharp contrast to the Dinaric sheep-raising society that had for ages "bred outlaws, guerrilla fighters, mercenaries, military leaders, dynasts and political terrorists."[28] Families were not organized in *zadrugas*, but by household *(kuća)*. Life in this kind of family organization had warlike characteristics. First, family relations were based on paternal status and age. The concentration of power in the hands of the elder, who ruled autocratically, was considered a moral and natural order.[29] The elder was expected to ask for advice, but the final decision rested with him. He was not only autocratic, but also restricting and crafty.

The chief occupation of the men was herding, usually in a seminomadic way. Women did most of the work in the house, in the fields, and with the cattle. Conflicts were frequent in Dinaric households. Tensions often resulted in violent clashes. Blood feuds, poverty, and aversion to agricultural labor had for centuries sent large numbers of Dinaric emigrants into neighboring regions. This, and their lust for power, led to the group exerting a significant influence in the politics of Balkan countries.[30]

The birth of a son was greeted with particular joy, since men held exclusive power in this society. The main purpose of marriage was to produce warriors. A father had the power of life and death over his sons, resulting in frequent father-son clashes. But there were also fathers who did not punish their children at all. Some of them even encouraged children to misbehave.

Women were held in low esteem throughout the Dinaric regions. Pregnant women were not spared work even on the day they gave birth or immediately thereafter. In Montenegro women never ate at the same table with their men. They ate only what was left when the men had completed their meals. Male children, no matter how young, always held higher rank than female members of the family. Women were quite capable of aggressive behavior. Illicit premarital and extramarital affairs might have been a form of aggressive compensation for women who were maltreated by brothers or husbands. The ill will of Dinaric women often took the form of exposing breasts.

In order to show his strictness and to test his power and dominance, the husband apparently beat his wife periodically. Wife beating and wife hating, combined with child beating, were socially approved, and institutionalized, and developed into a social duty.[31]

Another element of the Tomašić construct was the remarkable lack of emotional balance—a feature noted by all observers of Dinaric society, including Cvijić. They were ready to shed tears and to go to extremes in their grief. In moments of anger the Dinaric people might lose self-control and kill an offender. This lack of emotional balance might explain why the Dinaric warriors were more successful and efficient as guerilla fighters than as regular army soldiers. As soldiers of a regular army they were exceedingly brave in a successful venture, but reacted with cowardice when faced with superior forces.[32]

As a result of the lack of a well-established and accepted central authority, violence was another specific characteristic of Dinaric society, according to Tomašić. There was no protection against their aggressive tendencies. Physical force was identified with order and law. Dinaric ballads were known for glorification of violence. They often used blood as a symbol of society, and blood vengeance was deep-seated. As soon as a young man could carry arms, he was expected to retaliate by killing the person who insulted him or any of his kin. This conformed to their general deceitfulness and distrust. The prevalence of perfidy in social relations might explain the Dinaric male's lack of confidence. He was suspicious of not only the enemy, but also of members of his own community. Banditry and professional robbery were institutions.[33]

In the historical explanation Tomašić provided, the origin of this system can be traced back to the early Middle Ages when small bands of warriors, clans, and pastoral nomads conquered the Dinaric regions and forced their rule upon the Slavic democratic society. The Altaic origin of the conquerors was echoed in the Dinaric social organization, and the personality of the Dinaric warrior still resembled their Mongol prototypes.[34]

As for the political future of the Balkans after the Second World War, Tomašić concluded that the "former outlaws and mercenaries became military leaders and statesmen."[35] Many political leaders came from families of mountaineers who had migrated into urban centers as professional soldiers and traders. These people were trained at Western universities, but their own cultural heritage was too strong: "Extremely ambitious, power-seeking, and aggressive in their political behavior, they were not ready to compromise on issues."[36] They split into numerous parties and clan-like party factions. They fought among themselves; a type of sham parliamentarianism and only a resemblance of representative democracy developed.

The primary result of the Second World War was that former outlaws and mercenaries became statesmen and political leaders, taking power and leadership with the help of the Red Army. Therefore, political tensions in this part of the world would last until a radical reconstruction of the Balkan political structure occurred.

In contrast to the political systems shaped by Dinaric sheep breeders, the systems of the peaceful plains people led to the institution of universal suffrage and to political parties that guaranteed stability and democracy. Plains people in power would lead to demilitarized, democratic, and economically and politically independent states. This would be the only way the age of Dinaric warriors would end rapidly.[37]

I have summarized both Cvijić's and Tomašić's views of the Dinaric people and the plains people. They employed similar approaches, but their ethnographic representations were different. For a historian of the Balkans this is unsurprising, since representations of the cultural Other often produce quite different portraits of one and the same group. This is not the place to decide who was right and who was wrong. All we can do is to decode the intended messages.

Different Ethnic Perspectives and Constructions of the Other

It is, of course, not the intention of this article to discredit either scholar. Cvijić's and Tomašić's work on the Dinaric and plains peoples are, however, characteristic examples of the construction of cultural Otherness. They portray the Other not from different scholarly positions, but rather from different national perspectives and historical contexts. Cvijić worked and wrote at the end of the nineteenth and the beginning of the twentieth centuries when the Yugoslav movement was strongest. His work reflects this. He proclaimed the ethnic unity of the South Slavs, including the Bulgarians, while he differentiated culturally defined types, varieties, and groups in one nation. This was his first guideline. The other was his Serbian perspective. He knew his own people best and he believed his people were ready to fight for a Yugoslav state. He did not, however, want to exclude the people of the Pannonian Plains from Yugoslavia. His construct was not black and white, but nevertheless, the Dinaric people would fight and create a state based on its positive values, whereas Croatian plowmen were not prepared to fight their oppressors.

Tomašić's's message was more definitive. When he wrote some two decades later, the failure of the Yugoslav experiment was evident. He asserted that a state led by Dinaric warriors was bound to end in chaos and authoritarian rule, because the fighting warrior rather than the peaceful plowman had come to power. His construction was an obvious oversimplification in which the plains *zadruga* produced happy, democratic people ready for parliamentarianism, and the Dinaric *zadruga* was the breeding ground for an authoritarian, warlike, and demonic people unfit for democracy. His ideological mystification of the *zadruga* is of interest insofar as, according to him, its distribution was limited to the plains and the peaceful Croatian plowman, although the Serb historian, philologist, and writer Vuk Karadžić invented the term at the beginning of the nineteenth century. The Dinaric population that also lived in joint families was not worthy of the word *zadruga*. Cvijić's mystification of the *zadruga* was similar, but it referred to the Dinaric one.

Cvijić's popularity in Serbia after 1989 is understandable, as is Tomašić's in Croatia. Their messages are political ones, which are welcome in times of war and struggle; scholarship often takes a back seat.

War and Actualization of the Construction of the Other

War and conflict between Serbs and Croats in Croatia (1991-1995) actualized the traditional images of the Other on both sides. Meštrović's book *Habits of the Balkan Heart*, one of several he has written on the Balkans, examines this phenomenon.[38] He contributed to Tomašić's popularity with the *Habits of the Balkan Heart*, since he rediscovered him and his theories about the peoples of the mountains and the plains.

The central importance of Tomašić's arguments is that they help explain the details surrounding the Yugoslav War of 1991—Bosnia-Herzegovina, Croatia, and Slovenia seeking independence on the one hand versus Serbia and Montenegro seeking to preserve the old power structure on the other—as well as the events that led up to it. In particular, Tomašić's theory helps to explain the Serbian desire for territory at Croatia's expense, its human rights abuses in Kosovo, and its clinging to communism, although most of Eastern Europe voted for democratic forms of government, and Serbian domination of the government bureaucracy of what used to be communist Yugoslavia.[39]

The author employs the concept of social character as popularized by Alexis de Tocqueville in the first half of the nineteenth century, which is a substitute for biological instinct among humans and which explains the diversity among the world's many cultures. In every culture, social character has good as well as bad aspects; there are also good as well as bad forms of nationalism. [39] Yugoslav communism was shaped by the barbaric aspects of the Dinaric social character. The consequences were similar to those of German fascism. He suggests that it is possible to argue that pockets of social character unsuited for democracy as practiced in the West exist in the Balkans, and that there is a real danger of regression to earlier, undemocratic forms of government. [40]

Differing social characters divided the peoples in the former Yugoslavia. The demarcation runs along today's border between Croatia and Serbia. The Serbs and Montenegrins adhere to a sort of cult of the warrior: "They habitually own guns and engage in hunting as part of a machismo set of values. Within Yugoslavia, they are known for being stubborn, irascible, and emotionally unstable."[41] Meštrović arrives at the hypothesis that a precondition for the establishment of democracy in the former Yugoslavia is overcoming the Dinaric social character and its barbaric influence. Slovenia and Croatia lean toward Western cultural values, European political values, and free-market economy, whereas Serbia and Montenegro have espoused a neocommunist orientation, a tendency toward a unitary state, and tendencies to dominate existing power structures; the Western model is not appreciated. The scenarios for postcommunist Serbia and Montenegro include Balkanization, conflict, isolation, seperation, chaos, and the rise of new forms of totalitarianism. [42]

Meštrović argues that recent studies, like Thomas Sowell's,[43] emphasize the role that geography plays in the ways that cultures can borrow from each other. People who live in mountainous regions tend to be more insulated and isolated. This may explain their general backwardness and inability to borrow innovations. It was no accident that fighting broke out in the Balkans, Georgia, Azerbaijan, and other remote regions of the Urals following the collapse of communism. Although Meštrović does not hypothesize that remote mountainous regions tend to produce power-seeking personalities, he asserts that the Dinaric Alps have been and continue to be a hot spot in the world. In Meštrović's view, the problem is that the savage violence of the Dinaric social character has never been adequately constrained. In the modern West, this phenomenon has been muted, controlled, and perhaps sublimated. In contrast, the Yugoslav civil war exhibited barbaric acts of cruelty, massacres, and the mutilation of the living as well as the dead. His explanation is that such savagery appears to be fairly typical in the history of the Balkans. [44]

Meštrović asserts that his arguments are cultural, but they are politically motivated. The concept of the social character he applies leads to a polarization of good and bad, mountaineers and plains people—and this after three decades of discussion in which cultural anthropologists have questioned such ethnographic representation. In addition to the political construction, however, there is also a cultural one that can be decoded as "Balkanism" or the Balkanization of the Balkans.

The Balkanization of the Balkans

The term Balkanism derived from Edward W. Said's term, Orientalism.[45] His book deals with the construction of a specific image of the Orient by the West, an image that has little to do with reality. In analyzing the reasons for this development, Said argues that the Orient was one of the West's deepest and most recurrent images of the Other. The Orient helped Europe to define itself as its contrasting image and idea. Orientalism is a mode of ideological discourse to express and represent cultural Otherness. It is a means of establishing European hegemony over the Orient.[46]

Orientalism has become a critical term denoting a specific discourse about the Other. It inspired the Bulgarian-American historian Maria Todorova to investigate how the Western image of the Balkans came into being and what its functions were. In *Imagining the Balkans*,[47] Todorova argues that at the beginning of the twentieth century "Balkanization" came to denote the parceling of large political units into small ones, synonymous with reversal to the tribal, the backward, and the barbarian. In the same manner as the Orient, the Balkans became the Other of Europe. Todorova asserts that Balkanization and Balkanism are not mere subspecies of Orientalism. She accepts the idea of the crises of representation, which to her is also a crisis of representing the Balkans. This has considerable relevance for the work of Cvijić, Tomašić, and Meštrović.

Both Orientalism and Balkanism are inventions, but the two terms differ insofar as Balkanism refers to a concrete geographic entity and to Byzantine and Ottoman histories. What Todorova defines as Balkanism is a concept formed over two centuries mainly by Western travelers. It crystallized in a specific discourse about the Balkans around the time of the Balkan Wars and the First World War. In the ensuing decades this discourse attained additional features, and the rest was discursive hardening.[48]

Todorova provides an interesting theoretical framework that enables us to clarify Cvijić's, Tomašić's, and Meštrović's contributions to the discourse on the Balkans. Cvijić was one of the first Balkan scholars to contradict the image of the Balkans constructed by the West. At the same time he related his image of the Balkans to the Dinaric society and preached cultural relativism by pointing out the different value systems in the Dinaric culture. His message appeared to be, "Yes, we are the Balkans, we are different from the West, but Balkanism is not *a priori* negative, the Balkans have a right to be understood." This does not mean that he was right or wrong in his positive representation of the Balkans, but that is the function of his book.

Tomašić's contribution, more than twenty years later, and Meštrović's book some seven decades later, can be seen in light of what Todorova called discursive hardening. In this period the peoples of the plains were ascribed to the West, while the peoples of the mountains, bearing the negative image, became representative of the Balkans. In the twentieth century, the negative image has become fixed and further details have been added to the general picture by the two authors. They wanted to present the reader with a cultural explanation of communism and war. They were not cultural relativists, but dogmatists. They preached the superiority of one culture over the other and left no space for differentiation. Again, the issue is not if they were correct or not, but the kind of discourse they produced.

Secondly, the concreteness of Balkanism engenders the problem of representing the Balkans. One cannot say that our two authors invented the Dinaric warrior and the plains plowman. Both were real, so there is little use in saying, "Throw their publications away and let us look at the Balkans as they really were." What the two authors describe was reality, but a selective one. What we must do, then, is to correct the one-sided, politically biased Balkanizing image of the Balkans that resulted from their selective perceptions.

Let us return to Fernand Braudel. Without detailing his thoughts about the impact of mountains and plains on the mentalities of the peoples, one can conclude that his book on the Mediterranean world contains no Balkanizing statements. This was due to his comparative approach, which avoids singling out the uniqueness of each Mediterranean region, and seeks to portray the common aspects of different cultures. It is necessary to explore both local and regional cultures as well as overriding phenomena. Braudel's approach, which is profoundly cultural, historical, and anthropological, is comparative. To compare Balkan cultures with other cultures and to seek relativistic explanations are concerns for both the historian and the anthropologist working in the Balkans.

Notes

1. A colleague at the University of Chicago, Marko Živković, has been working on a similar topic. We share many of the same ideas and a common point of departure, but our conclusions are different. See Marko Živković, "Violent Highlanders and Peaceful Lowlanders: Uses and Abuses of Ethno-Geography in the Balkans from Versailles to Dayton," in *Republika* 2(1997), 107-19.
2. Stjepan Meštrović, *Anthony Giddens: The Last Modernist* (London: Routledge, 1998).
3. Stjepan Meštrović, *Emile Durkheim and the Reformation of Sociology* (Lanham: Rowman & Littlefield, 1994).
4. *Enciklopedija Jugoslavije*, vol. 2 (Zagreb: Leksikografski institut, 1956), 510.
5. Jovan Cvijić, *Balkansko poluostrvo* (Beograd: Državna Stamparija, 1991).
6. Dinko Tomašić, "Personality Development in the Zadruga Society," *Psychiatry* 5 (1942): 229.
7. Ibid., 229-61.

8. Dinko Tomašić, "Personality Development of the Dinaric Warriors," *Psychiatry* 8 (1945): 449-93.
9. Dinko Tomašić, "The Structure of Balkan Society," *The American Journal of Sociology* 52 (1946): 132-40.
10. Dinko Tomašić, *Personality and Culture in East European Policy* (New York: Stewart, 1948).
11. Cvijić, *Balkansko poluostrvo*, 325.
12. Živković, "Violent Highlanders and Peaceful Lowlanders," 109.
13. Fernand Braudel, *The Mediterranean and the Mediterranean World in the Age of Philip II* (New York: Fontana, 1972).
14. Karl Kaser, *Familie und Verwandtschaft auf dem Balkan. Analyse einer untergehenden Kultur* (Vienna: Böhlau, 1995), 167-416.
15. Ibid.
16. Cvijić, *Balkansko poluostrvo*, 325-35.
17. Ibid., 337.
18. Ibid., 338.
19. Ibid., 339.
20. Ibid., 341-48.
21. Ibid., 510.
22. Ibid., 513.
23. Tomašić, "Personality Development in the Zadruga Society," (1942), 230.
24. Ibid., 231-34.
25. Ibid., 235.
26. Ibid., 237-41.
27. Ibid., 241-49.
28. Tomašić, "Personality Development of the Dinaric Warriors," (1945): 449.
29. Ibid., 449.
30. Ibid., 450.
31. Ibid., 452, 471-79.
32. Ibid., 455.
33. Ibid., 457-67.
34. Ibid., 489, 493.
35. Tomašić, "The Structure of Balkan Society," 133.
36. Ibid.
37. Ibid., 133-40.
38. Stjepan Meštrović et al., *Habits of the Balkan Heart: Social Character and the Fall of Communism* (College Station, TX: Texas A&M University Press, 1993). See also Stjepan Meštrović, *The Balkanization of the West: The Confluence of Postmodernism and Postcommunism* (London: Routledge, 1994); Stjepan Meštrović, ed., *Genocide after Emotion. The Postemotional Balkan War* (London: Routledge, 1996); Stjepan Meštrović and Ahmed S. Akbar, eds., *The Conceit of Innocence: Losing the Conscience of the West in the War Against Bosnia* (London: Routledge, 1997).
39. Meštrović, *Habits of the Balkan Heart*, 51.
40. Ibid., x f., 13, 25, 148.
41. Ibid., 30.
42. Ibid., 30, 36, 47.
43. Thomas Sowell, "Cultural Diversity: A World View," *The American Enterprise* 2 (1991): 44-55.
44. Meštrović, *Habits of the Balkan Heart*, 56, 61, 72.
45. Edward W. Said, *Orientalism* (New York: Vintage Books, 1978).
46. James Clifford and George E. Marcus, eds., *Writing Culture: The Poetics and Politics of Ethnography* (Berkeley: University of California Press, 1986); Eberhard Berg and Martin Fuchs, eds., *Kultur, soziale Praxis, Text. Die Krise der ethnographischen Repräsentation* (Frankfurt am Main: Suhrkamp, 1993).

47. Maria Todorova, *Imagining the Balkans* (New York, Oxford: Oxford University Press, 1997).
48. Ibid., 11.

Chapter 11

MARKING THE DIFFERENCE OR LOOKING FOR COMMON GROUND?

Southeast Central Europe

Oto Luthar and Breda Luthar

Employing research from northeastern Slovenia, this essay discusses the historical circumstances and dynamics of formation of an idea about the Other in southeast Central Europe. The first part addresses the notion of Central Europe as an objective geographic, social, historic, and economic reality on the one hand, and the historical formation of Central Europe as an imaginary concept and ideological construction on the other. The formation of an Other in Slovenia, where four European cultures—Germanic, Hungarian, Roman, and Slavic—meet, is examined. The second part of the essay focuses on the "We" group construction based on biology and the essentialist version of the past in Slovenia. It discusses three "technologies" of exclusion and their carriers: "nationalizing nationalism," the reinterpretation of the past in the attempt to recover the authentic history, and the role of media narratives in the construction and maintenance of an essentialist version of identity that includes the reproduction of traditional mythologies in the marking of difference. Conceptualizing identities and histories as arbitrary, as a product of political and cultural discourses, permits us to challenge the hegemony of the notion of ethnic citizenship in Central Europe and the politics and practices of exclusion and marginalization.

Notes for this section begin on page 241.

The Poetics of Space

Central Europe has long been defined more by its internal differences than by its common traits. Its collective identity has been constructed and sustained by the existence of the Oriental Other, whose personification has been historically unstable and represented by the Turks, the closest southern neighbor, or the Balkan peoples in general. Since the wars of Yugoslav succession and the Serb occupation of Kosovo in the 1990s, the notion of Central Europe has regained importance. The longing for the reconstruction of the concept of Central Europe as a space of a common historical memory is no longer merely an issue of nostalgic admirers of the Austrian fin-de-siècle. In the middle of Europe is a space that, because of its transitional and exposed geographic location and distinct history, is different from the European East and West. The difference lies in its linguistic, ethnic, and cultural diversity as well as in the historical and contemporary institutionalization of these differences. Discussion of the practices and discourses of exclusion in Central Europe should contribute to the recognition of difference within nation-states and make possible the search for new forms of collectivity and consensus beyond ethnicity that would replace exclusionist regressive reassertion of "traditional" identities and allegiances.

Central Europe is not solely a geographic notion but rather an idea linked with the myths of western civilization and shaped by the encounters with the Balkans as its Oriental Others. The geographic shape of Central Europe has been regularly redefined, and the region has long been a dynamic historical, ideological, and cultural concept. Along with its objective quality, Central Europe has a subjective dimension, a constructed notion of what Central Europe is.

A brief summary of the historical genealogy of the idea of Central Europe can help to connect this imaginative reality to concepts of Otherness and contemporary practices of exclusion. Before the First World War, *Mitteleuropa* (Central Europe) referred to the German Empire, the Habsburg Monarchy, and neighboring areas, which were considered regions of Germanic political interest and cultural hegemony. After 1918 the notion of the center of Europe was widened to include Baltic nations and all of the nascent countries formed from the now-defunct Monarchy. In the 1960s and 1970s, the meaning of Central Europe again narrowed. Its geographic axis was formed around the Eastern European cities of Bratislava, Budapest, Ljubljana, Prague, Warsaw, and Zagreb. Eastern European dissidents transformed the concept of Central Europe from a geostrategic, historical, or geographic site into an ideological concept and a constituent part of their movement. Being historically part of Central Europe meant sharing a common Western cultural background of democratic civilization, in contrast to "Oriental totalitarianism."

The concept of Central Europe is closely linked to changing ideas of Europe and its eastern territories in European history over the last two centuries. Before the eighteenth century, Western European notions of Europe were significantly narrower than today's understanding of Europe. Its eastern borders remain today a site of struggle over inclusion and exclusion. Up to the end of the seventeenth century the northwestern borders of the Ottoman Empire reached as far as what would later become the center of Europe. Following the Ottoman conquest of Constantinople in 1453, Aeneas Silvius Piccolomini (from 1458, Pope Pius II) developed a new geopolitical conception of the Western Christian world. The central part of newly established Europe became distinct from the southeastern regions governed by "cultureless Turks—eating horse meat, hating science, and persecuting humanist studies."[1] In the seventeenth century, Europe as a cultural concept expanded eastward only when Austria's victories over the Turks and Central Europeans began to make Austrians into representatives of Western European culture.

The second geographic and conceptual expansion of the idea of Europe was to include Russia following its "Europeanization" under the reformers Peter the Great and Catherine the Great. Thus, Europe acquired its eastern border in the eighteenth century. Russia became an internal Other, providing Western Europe with its first model of underdevelopment. This model became a stereotype for the West, which since then has been applied to various countries across the globe.

After marking its western and eastern boundaries, Europe began to explore its "central" part. The center was not geographically and politically determined until Napoleon dissolved the Holy Roman Empire of the German states in 1806. At that point, the center became important for sustaining the balance of power in Europe. At the Congress of Vienna in 1815, following the defeat of Napoleon, the European powers had to define new European borders. A major problem was, of course, the German alliance. The establishment of a stable political equilibrium was dependent on the balance between the rising military and political importance of multinational Prussia and Austria on one hand, and the Slavic neighbors on the other. This was a recurring problem until the end of the Second World War.

In the 1960s and 1970s historians in Austria, Czechoslovakia, northern Italy, Slovenia, and Hungary found the forerunners of a Central European idea among the German economic and political scholars of the nineteenth century, including Friedrich List, Karl Ludwig von Bruck, Lorenz Stein, and Constantin Franz. At the same time, they discovered elements of later Central European political concepts in the Austrian-Slavic federalist plans of František Palacký and Karel Havlíček, as well as in the ideas of those authors who advocated German expansion eastward. Friederich Neumann's pathbreaking book *Mitteleuropa*, published in 1915, which proposed an economic and military transnational union between Austria-Hungary and the German Empire on the territory between Great Britain and Russia, introduced today's notion of Central Europe. Neumann's *Mitteleuropa* would have been not only a product of German territorial expansion but also a place of tolerance and equal rights for nations. In 1917, Tomáš G. Masaryk, the future president of Czechoslovakia, dreamed of a new European federation of states extending from the Baltic to the Aegean Sea that would separate Russia from Germany.[2]

Echoes of these ideas were heard in the Germany of the 1930s, but they were driven by different ambitions. There is no trace of Neumann's notion of equality within the united states of Central Europe in the writings of such German authors as Albert Haushofer and Heinrich von Srbik. Their ideas were used mainly to legitimize German expansionist policy in the East and the Balkans. It is thus unsurprising that with the collapse of the German Reich in 1945, discussions of Central Europe ceased. The concept of the space in the center of Europe mediating between the East and the West disappeared both on maps and as an idea. Europe consisted of the East and the West, divided by the Iron Curtain. From that point, Europe was understood as the territory west of the line that divided two political and economic orders.

The revival of the concept of Central Europe in the 1960s and 1970s was the result of regional economic and cultural initiatives in northeastern Italy, bordering Austria and Yugoslavia (today's Slovenia). It was motivated primarily by the need of the neighboring three regions (Friuli in Italy, Slovenia and Croatia in Yugoslavia, and Carinthia in Austria) to establish cultural communication and economic relations in the region, regardless of the political order.

In the mid-1970s, and particularly at the beginning of the 1980s, Central Europe became a major topic of the intellectual-dominated Eastern European dissident movements in Czechoslovakia, Hungary, and Poland. Central European intellectuals traditionally had not been confined to academic enclaves and had played a crucial political role there. This role gained new dimension in the work of Václav Havel, Milan Kundera, Gyorgy Konrad, Adam Michnik, and Czesław Miłosz. They shared the argument that Central Europe had its own "historical destiny," which was necessarily influenced by the small size of its ethnic constituent parts that had been colonized by large empires and forgotten as cultural and historical entities. Some ten years ago, Konrad wrote that to feel like a Central European was not a question of citizenship, it was a philosophy of life.[3]

The English historian Eric Hobsbawm has a similar opinion of Central Europe, which he considers an ideological construction, one having more to do with politics than with geography, and more with politically and ideologically inspired national programs than with geographic and social reality. Metaphorically, the objective space of the house (its corridors, rooms, and so on) is far less important than what it is poetically endowed with.[4] This does not mean, of course, that the space between East and West does not have its own historical reality, even if this reality is only in the history of ideas.

Although Central Europe is an imaginary concept, the region objectively possesses its own expressly multinational character. Every empire in this region was necessarily multinational. Prior to 1989, it is impossible to speak of one Central European history. There are instead

> a number of conflicting national accounts colored by moral indignation, historical
> speculation, and nostalgic transfiguration.... Central Europeans ... have in their heads
> a number of different historical maps and milestones that are not particularly well

known outside the region or necessarily respected by their neighbors, and they still regularly use them as points of orientation.[5]

Thus, the same process that occurs with space also occurs over time. Space (central territories of the European continent) acquires political and emotional meaning as Central Europe. Similarly, historical milestones are imaginative knowledge that help constitute a sense of collectivity and difference. Time and space are therefore "something *more* than what appears to be merely positive knowledge."[6]

Lucky to Live North of the Land of Barbarian Orientals

Beyond its positive existence—geography, history, that is, its social reality—Central Europe also has a fictional reality. The practices of inclusion and exclusion are dependent on the way Central Europe imagines itself and others. Though Central Europe has long been perceived as a melting pot, the people of the region regularly draw attention to national and cultural peculiarities and designate those different from themselves as Other. Their sense of collective identity is derived predominantly negatively (for example, as different from the Orientals living south of them); the "We" group identity is almost entirely based on ethnicity.

How far does the symbolic practice of drawing the line between "our civilized world" and a foreign world—the land of barbarian Orientals—take on in Central Europe a specific form, different from practices of identity formation in the Western world? The perception of being trapped between Western cultural imperialism and local attempts to revive or reinvent indigenous regional cultures and identities that can be maintained only by the existence of the "Oriental threat" from the south or the southeast increases the difficulty of living with difference in contemporary Central Europe. This is a typical example of what Emmanuel Levinas would call "self-centered 'egology,'"[7] where all of the national history is seen from the viewpoint of the nation itself. It originates from the existential fear that sees enemies everywhere and takes advantage of the narcissism of nascent or reborn nations. It is a matter of selfish national and social emancipation, which, in the eastern regions of Central Europe, sets up boundaries to separate the nation in question from regions farther south and east in an attempt to reject association with the Balkans and the Orient.

One of the indicators of the setting of cultural boundaries is the establishment of the imaginary borders of civilization in southeastern Europe in which the borders are always located south of one's own geographic territory. From the Austrian perspective this border lies in the Karavanke Mountains, on the top of the southernmost Alpine peak on the border with Slovenia, separating the Oriental Slavic world from the civilized European Germanic world. In the Slovene imagination, the border separating civilization from barbarians lies south of Slovenia on the Kolpa, the river separating Slovenia (Central Europe) from Croatia (the Balkans). Croats place the edge of civilization on the border between Croatia (Central Europe) and Serbia (the Balkans). And the Serbs understand themselves as the last defense of European civilization against underdeveloped Islam personified most recently by either the Bosnian Muslims or the Kosovar Albanians. The uncivilized, of course, rarely acknowledge this designation. In this network of discourses of Otherness, everyone has an Other who serves as a basis for a typical innocent view of the West, and considers the southern neighboring territory as a space of primitive ethnic conflicts and exotic underdevelopment.

The Threat from the South Has Not Disappeared: Contemporary Mythologies of the Turks

In recent history, Central Europe has been a space of antisemitism, marginalization, and exclusion. But it has also been a space of myriad interactions of different cultures and structures of feeling. Time of "transition" is a time of fragmentation, transformation, and large-scale reorganization of economic, political, and cultural life. It is a time of risk, of breaking down the existing identities, and of the reemergence of marking differences and erosion of intercultural sociality. Along with new elective "postmodern" sociality in Central Europe, earlier forms of exclusion are being reconstructed. Old ethnic certainties, and a more culturally homogenous notion of collective identity based on biology and an essentialist version of the past, are being reinvented.

It appears that each newly reconfigured state in this region goes through a stage we can call "nationalizing nationalism."[8] The concept implies that a core nation or nationality, defined in ethno-cultural terms, distinguishes itself as the legitimate "owner" of the state. Despite its "ownership" of the state, this dominant or core nation conceives itself as being weak in a cultural, economic, or demographic position within the state. The weak position—understood by the interpreters of the national interest as a legacy of discrimination against that nation before it attained independence—is considered to justify "remedial" or "compensatory" projects using state power to promote the specific interests of the core nation. "We" group solidarity is almost exclusively based on ethnicity, obscuring or omitting other identities, for example, class and gender. This form of nationalism is the consequence of large-scale reorganization of political space along national lines and the dominant role of ethnicity at the expense of the notion of citizenship.

The construction and maintenance of nationalizing nationalism through public discourse, primarily the mainstream media, are important issues. People are largely dependent on the media for the images of the "normal" Slovene or the "ordinary" Austrian. Mass media do not simply report or transmit nationalism outside into the "real" world; they also reproduce it by stereotyping and naturalizing the socially and historically constructed images of "Us" and "Others" and legitimate identities. The Slovene media, for the most part, has legitimized nationalistic politics and practices by creating the community in which the "We" is defined almost exclusively in terms of ethnicity.[9] Media representations of

Others include Bosnian refugees; illegal immigrants from Iran, India, Turkey, and Albania;[10] or "Southerners," that is, ethnic minorities from the former Yugoslavia, who stand for everything Slovenes are not—uncivilized, dirty, lazy, criminal, uncontrolled, and violent. Dominant narratives that shape the perceptions of "Us" and "Others" both legitimize marginalizing discourse and practices and lead to a sense of "secondariness" and inferiority on the side of the minorities such as "Southerners" or Roma.

As in Slovenia, in post-communist Central Europe in general, racist discourse is not marginalized and confined to the nationalistic discourse of tabloid journalism. Ethnocentrism and nationalism are normalized and considered legitimate public discourse in most central national media organizations and diverse genres of mediated public culture. Oppositional voices that might subvert the ethnocentric notion of the community are rare, and the media routinely rely on the supposed general consensus on the "Others" and "Us," reproducing it and repeatedly telling Slovenes that only ethnic Slovenes have legitimate claim to the Slovene state. The stereotype of the threatening Oriental barbarian from the south (the Turk), which was constructed in the fifteenth century, has been recycled and appears in right-wing political discourse and media narratives. Popular media narratives place actors and events in already-existing models; new situations are adapted to old definitions. This placement in existing categories offers a formulaic understanding of the social world within the oppositional relationships: "We" versus "Other," civilized versus uncivilized, individual versus system, and good versus bad. The characteristics that personalize the civilized and uncivilized, or good and bad, are regularly replaced, but their functions remain stable.

Such exclusionary nationalist policy has profound influence, even in a stable democracy such as Austria, where a standard propaganda phrase of the far right-wing Austrian Freedom Party (*Freiheits Partei Österreichs*) leader Jörg Haider has been, "Why did our ancestors defend our country against the Turks if they now let them in again?"[11] The same historical Turk has become the retrospective referent for a whole range of "Oriental" immigrants, including "refugees or migrant laborers, students or tourists from anywhere to the east, southeast, or south."[12] The rhetorical question—"Why did our ancestors defend our country?"—is based on a cultural discourse that is much older than the political discourses of either the former Austrian president and Secretary-General of United Nations Kurt Waldheim or Jörg Haider. Haider's language is politically mobilizing and effective as long as it is embedded in popular mythology as "strong … associations outside the realm of political discourse that can be effectively tapped into to animate public rhetoric."[13] His language has its origin in the discursive culture or the conceptual framework that his supporters inhabit.

Recently, however, Haider's concept of ethnic citizenship has become less exclusive. In the campaign for the European Parliament elections in 1996, he broadened the meaning of "Us" and gave new meaning to the concept of the Austrian. He incorporated "assimilated" and long-term immigrants into the "We" group; those excluded were recent immigrants.

In addition to the construction of cultural and national difference and reliance on the negative definition of identity (that is, "different than"), the politics of exclusion involve the radical reinterpretation of the past and the rewriting of history.[14] The rewriting is to be understood as the mobilization of interpretative resources in the struggle over the present and the future where the story of the past is presented as an unchanging truth waiting to be discovered. The process of rewriting recent milestones of Slovene national history began in 1991 as a political project to rehabilitate Second World War collaborators and later became a part of a historical discourse. The revisionist idea was that the new understanding of national identity (independent from and in contrast to Yugoslav identity) has to correspond to both the reconstruction of national history and the challenge to the communist version of the meaning of the resistance movement, which therefore must have been authenticated and supported by the "real version" of the Slovene past.

Attempts to reclaim national history are characteristic of almost all transitional postsocialist countries in Central Europe. They represent a present- and future-oriented history in which the past is employed to construct the "true" future. As a result, historical representations have become a battlefield over meaning as well as over how the national interest will be defined and space where the present and the future political power may be gained. The struggle over the authentic version of the past has taken place during the last ten years in public discourse outside academia. The battle over the supposedly authentic version of the past is an articulation of the essentialist notion of history and national identity, based on the notion of the possibility of homogenization of the "We" group, on a fixed notion of identity, and on a unified national subject. Because no unproblematic national subject exists, there are inevitably many possible ways of being Slovene. The belief in an ethnic group's uniqueness and unity is contradictory in a world that "can no longer be contained within the limits of 'nations' and nation-states.'"[15]

A tendency of conservative politics toward religious differentiation and the efforts of the Roman Catholic Church to gain a hegemonic position, thus marginalizing other religious communities, represent attempts to define group uniqueness and colonize the concept of the national subject. Religious differentiation is part of an attempt to re-Catholicize public culture and the life-world of the individual. The essence of the political project of re-Catholicization is to reestablish and naturalize the unity between Sloveneness and Catholicism. The project's notion of identity basically suggests that there is one authentic set of characteristics shared by all Slovenes. These characteristics remain consistent over time. Being Slovene in a postcommunist era should therefore include the reinvention of one's own pastoral life organized around the Catholic Church. The Slovene branch of the Catholic Church and its local loyal élite propagate the discursive project of re-Catholicization, which is part of the struggle over the definition of the "We"-community. Based on the larger discourse of the essentialist and fixed definition of Slovene identity, it produces conflicts on a local level and invents crises.

An example of the "invention of crises" at the local level is the reinvention of conflicting religious identities in otherwise traditionally multinational/multiethnic Prekmurje, in northeastern Slovenia. This region—north of Croatia, south of Austria, and west of Hungary—is the only Slovene province where Slovene and Hungarian Protestant communities, a Catholic community, and the Roma have lived together with little notable religious conflict since the Thirty Years' War.[16] Before the Nazi deportation of the Lendava Jews in 1944, Prekmurje was also home to two thriving Jewish communities. This region is known as the Bible Belt of Slovenia (almost half of all Slovene Roman Catholic priests come from Prekmurje) and religiously mixed marriages are common. The region also has a double heritage: traditional tolerance based on the Habsburg tradition of cohabitation of different Central European cultural and religious entities, and the modernizing contribution of socialism with its emancipatory legal framework concerning the rights of ethnic minorities. Despite a multiethnic history, in the mid-1990s, five Slovene Roman Catholic villages caused a local furor by demanding the establishment of new municipalities, arguing that they were "trapped" between the Slovene Protestant community and the Hungarian ethnic minority, as an isolated island within "their own homeland." They argued that a new Catholic Slovene municipality should be established.[17]

Beyond Exclusion: Core and Marginal Culture

Intercultural practices still thrive in Prekmurje. One of the most marginalized ethnic groups in Central Europe, the Roma,[18] and "civilians" (the term the Roma of Prekmurje employ for those different from them, that is, the "white" population) still enjoy much interaction in everyday life. Historically, in the Prekmurje region the contacts among the German, Hungarian, and Slavic cultures on the one hand, and the "Oriental" cultures or structures of feeling (Roma, Jews, migrants from southern parts of Yugoslavia) on the other, contributed to the tolerance and acceptance of different identities.

Although the majority of Roma in Prekmurje remain segregated in the suburbs of Murska Sobota, the provincial capital, and in hamlets outside villages, there is a great sense of local solidarity. In a referendum during the late 1970s Prekmurje's population voted to finance construction of a local community center (which houses a medical care center and a kindergarten) for the Roma settlement just outside the capital. The situation of Roma in Prekmurje illustrates how a history of intercultural tolerance, where it is not easy to sustain a hegemony of core culture, supported during Yugoslav socialism unites, in the long term, a core culture and a group traditionally marked as taboo. Identity is maintained through symbolic inclusion or exclusion as well as through social and material conditions. Symbolic marking is "lived out" in social and economical differentiation as one aspect of marking difference.

The Roma of Prekmurje attempt the imaginary by establishing a connection to themselves and the core culture through changing both their surnames and first names. Although this process involves the complicated procedure of changing personal documents, some Roma change their names several times during their lifetimes. It is not unusual for a man with the common Roma name Sarkezi or Baranje to alter his name to a typical Slovene name. More common is to take a name of a minor local celebrity, someone who enjoys the respect of the "borrower" or who helped him or her in some way. Most new names are those of popular local officials, obstetricians, surgeons, and other physicians from a local hospital. Another source of inspiration is the mediated popular culture, either names of fictional characters or famous performers. Among the names the Roma of Prekmurje have adopted are those of the Italian singer Romina Power and the late Diana Spencer. Gender differences are unimportant and the "bricoleurs" imaginatively change the names of female and male celebrities for their own use. A male fan of Sophia Loren slightly transformed Sophia to Slavko Loren. The names appropriated by the Roma population have varied over time, reflecting the changing celebrities produced by the global culture industry and locally distributed by the indigenous popular culture through which the stars' images gain their symbolic meaning for the Roma "users."

The practice of renaming is connected with the relationship of the Roma to mainstream culture. While this practice may be influenced by traditional cosmology, it more likely arises from the historical genealogy of names in Roma culture. In the seventeenth century, when Roma began using surnames, they borrowed most of them from surrounding objects or domesticated animals, and later from the region of their origin (Baranja, now part of Croatia) or the ethnic groups among whom they lived (for example, the family name Horvat, that is, Hrvat, or Croat). In addition to names such as Baranja and Horvat, which are of "Croat origin," there are also surnames like Cener (in German, Zehner), which attest to their Austrian or German origin. The assimilation practices of "urban" and "suburban" Roma, or "real" and "authentic" Roma, differ considerably. While the latter, by using popular culture as the imaginative source, establish an imaginary relationship with the mainstream culture, the first use the renaming as a means of individualization. Contemporary urbanized Roma change their names to stress their individuality. Taking over a new name enables them to reidentify, to emphasize a distinctive individual identity different from collective Roma identity. Naming is a first step in the active construction of identity or difference and an example of both the resistance to marginalization within the generally welcoming "core" culture, and a manifestation of an entirely nonessentialist view of identity. Roma perspectives on identity are fluid. There is no "true" identity that would be fixed and persistent across time with an authentic source in "true" history.

To imagine new forms of collectivity, conceptualize citizenship as political instead of ethnic, and transgress the regressive reassertion of traditional essentialist identities and allegiances in Central Europe and beyond, it is important to explore the constructed nature of national identities and the fictional dimension of Central Europe as a concept together with its real nature (its economic, historical, social, geographic, and political dimension). Identity is the product of political, cultural, and other discourses and history. In contemporary Central Europe, we cannot think of identity as having one authentic set of biological characteristics that would prevent someone from being a Slovene, Croat, or Austrian. Nor should such characteristics endow one group with their own state and exclude those who are marked as Other. Ethnicity should not be the determining force that shapes all relationships. What is conceptualized as historical can be changed and what is constructed can be reconstructed, but what is understood as essential and based in biology and "true" history (that is, a shared past) denies the possibility of human action to change conditions and to include the outsiders into the notion of "We"-community. When thinking about Central Europe as a space of exclusion but, at the same time, as a space of intercultural sociality, we should avoid falling into one or the other of two opposite errors: the illusion of the "never-been-seen-before" and its counterpart, "the-way-it-always-has-been."[19]

Notes

1. Tomaž Mastnak, *Evropa: med evolucijo in evtanazijo* (Ljubljana: Studia Humanitatis, 1998), 59.
2. Peter Vodopivec, "Srednja Evropa je, Srednje Evrope ni," in *Srednja Evropa,* ed. Peter Vodopivec (Ljubljana: Mladinska knjiga, 1991), 7.
3. Ibid., 10.
4. See Eric J. Hobsbawm, *The Age of Extremes: A History of the World, 1914-1919* (New York: Vintage, 1996). The house metaphor is used by Edward W. Said, *Orientalism* (London: Penguin Books, 1978), 55.
5. Lonnie Johnson, *Central Europe: Neighbors, Enemies, Friends* (Oxford: Oxford University Press, 1996), 5.
6. Said, *Orientalism,* 55.
7. István Bibo, et al. *Regije evropske povijesti* (Zagreb: Niprijed, 1995), 47.
8. See Rogers Brubaker, *Nationalism Reframed: Nationhood and the National Question in the New Europe* (Cambridge: Cambridge University Press, 1996), 4.
9. Examples include slow administrative work on citizenship and asylum requests and repeated denial of a building permit for a mosque in Ljubljana for a large Bosnian Muslim minority, a discriminatory legal framework concerning immigration, discriminatory social policy, and many others, including everyday interaction and symbolic practices of exclusion.
10. Slovenia has become a transit country for asylum seekers and immigrants from the Third World to the West. Traditionally, the Other was represented by Bosnians, Serbs, and so on, that is, by the ethnic minorities in Slovenia (or "Southerners"), consisting of immigrants from the southern republics of the former Yugoslavia.
11. Andre Gingrich, "Frontier Myths of Orientalism: The Muslim World in Public and Popular Cultures of Central Europe," in *MESS, Mediterranean Ethnological Summer School Vol. II,* ed. Bojan Baskar and Borut Brumen (Ljubljana: Institute of Multicultural Research, 1996), 104.
12. Ibid.
13. Ibid., 105.

14. On the rewriting of history see Oto Luthar, "Possessing the Past: The Problem of Historical Representation in the Process of Reinventing Democracy in Eastern Europe—the Case of Slovenia," *Filozofski vestnik—Acta Philosophica*, vol. 18, no. 2 (1997): 233-56.

15. Eric Hobsbawm, *The Age of Extremes*; idem., *Nations and Nationalism since 1870* (Cambridge: Cambridge University Press, 1992), 182.

16. The Prekmurje region is—in an otherwise ethnically and religiously quite uniform Slovenia—a mixture of languages, ethnicities, and cultural practices. The approximately 89,000 people who live in this region include some 2,000 Roma, 8,500 Hungarians, and an unknown number of Croats who commute to work daily from neighboring Croatia.

17 See the minutes of the Council of Commune of Morarske Toplice, which includes Bogojina; 26, 27 May 1996, as well as articles in *Delo*, Slovenia's most influential daily, May 1996.

18. Roma from Prekmurje call themselves "Gypsies" and, at least, in unofficial communication reject the politically more accepted "Roma."

19. Pierre Bourdieu, *On Television* (New York: The New Press, 1998), 68.

Chapter 12

THE PSYCHOLOGY OF CREATING THE OTHER IN NATIONAL IDENTITY, ETHNIC ENMITY, AND RACISM

Peter Loewenberg

> Poets are the unacknowledged legislators of the world.
> — Percy Bysshe Shelley

> Nationhood is the extension of real or symbolic love felt for the corner of land which belongs to the commune, to an entire valley, an immense plain, the steppe, and the great city such as Paris or Vienna.
> — Arnold van Gennep

> History … is a nightmare from which I am trying to awake.
> — James Joyce, *Ulysses*

The Construction of National Identity

In the late afternoon of 16 June 1904 a dialogue takes place in Barney Kiernan's saloon on Little Britain Street in which Leopold Bloom is baited by a one-eyed Fenian fanatic known simply as "the citizen." Bloom's is the voice of humane cosmopolitan reason:

- Persecution, says he, all the history of the world is full of it. Perpetuating national hatred among nations.
- But do you know what a nation means? says John Wyse.

– Yes, says Bloom.

– What is it? says John Wyse.

– A nation? says Bloom. A nation is the same people living in the same place.

– By God, then, says Ned, laughing, if that's so I'm a nation for I'm living in the same place for the past five years.

So of course everyone had a laugh at Bloom and says he, trying to muck out of it:

– Or also living in different places.

– That covers my case, says Joe.

– What is your nation if I may ask, says the citizen.

– Ireland, says Bloom. I was born here. Ireland….

– And I belong to a race too, says Bloom, that is hated and persecuted. Also now. This very moment. This very instant….

– Robbed, says he. Plundered. Insulted. Persecuted. Taking what belongs to us by right. At this very moment, says he, putting up his fist, sold by auction off in Morocco like slaves or cattle.

– Are you talking about the New Jerusalem? says the citizen.

– I'm talking about injustice, says Bloom.

– Right, says John Wyse. Stand up to it then with force like men….

– But it's no use, says he. Force, hatred, history, all that. That's not life for men and women, insult and hatred. And everybody knows that it's the very opposite of that that is really life.

– What? says Alf.

– Love, says Bloom. I mean the opposite of hatred….

– Ireland my nation says he (hoik! phthook!) never be up to those bloody (there's the last of it) Jerusalem (ah!) cuckoos….

John Wyse saying it was Bloom gave the idea for Sinn Fein to Griffith to put in his paper….

– Isn't that a fact, says John Wyse, what I was telling the citizen about Bloom and the Sinn Fein? …

– He's a perverted jew, says Martin, from a place in Hungary and it was he drew up all the plans according to the Hungarian system. We know that in the castle….

– A wolf in sheep's clothing, says the citizen. That's what he is. Virag from Hungary! Ahasuerus I call him. Cursed by God.[1]

Amid the sweet stench of beer in Barney Kiernan's pub, James Joyce dramatizes the emotional valences of exclusion and inclusion, of violence and single vision, that make up the discourses on national identity. He plays with the problematic politico-legal definition of "nation," which may mean whatever one wishes it to mean, and with the complexity of distinguishing "national identity" from "ethnicity," "peoplehood," and "race." Joyce's caricature-in-voice monocular Irish "citizen" is evocative of Homer's "violent and lawless tribe … these Cyclopians have no parliament for debates and no laws."[2] The Cyclopian episode of *Ulysses* displays chauvinism without irony, vision without perspective. Bloom offers us a series of attempts at defining national identity. First is the legal positivist definition: a nation is constituted by those living in the same place. It is expressed in the third person: "He or she belongs ..." The second definition is cultural: a national identity is composed of those who believe they belong to a nation, and is affirmed in the first person: "I belong ..." The xenophobic, one-eyed "citizen" offers a third definition, which is prescriptive: national identity consists of particular characteristics—racial, religious, ideological, spiritual, physical—that circumscribe belonging and is pronounced in the second person: "You do ..."; or, as is asserted to Bloom: "You do not belong ..."

The dialogue alludes to a complex and neglected Hungarian-Jewish-Bloom-Griffith-Fenian-Irish nationalist relationship with which Joyce played.[3] Bloom was born of a Hungarian-Jewish father in the year of Hungary's rebirth, 1866, the year of Habsburg Austria's defeat by Bismarck's Prussia in the Seven Weeks' War, a war that began on "Bloomsday," 15-16 June 1866. Bloom is rumored in Dublin to be the secret Jewish advisor to Arthur Griffith (1872-1922), founder of the Sinn Fein.[4] The Hungarians had exploited Austria's defeat to negotiate a new constitutional arrangement, the *Ausgleich* of 1867, which gave Hungarians home rule and influence on national policy in a dual monarchy, while accepting the Austrian emperor as the constitutional head of state. In 1904 Griffith advocated the "Hungarian Plan" as a viable blueprint for Ireland's future relationship with Great Britain. He concluded: "None who reflect can doubt that, carried out with the same determination, the policy which resurrected Hungary ... can end the usurped authority of England to rule our country."[5] The citizen's curse "Virag from Hungary!" speaks of virago, a malelike woman. Bloom's character had androgynous qualities, and *virag* in Hungarian means bloom or flower.[6] When Bloom is attacked by the citizen, he bids farewell to Dublin as Lipóti Virag, and the orchestra follows "Come Back to Erin" with "Rakoczy's March."[7]

Joyce left Dublin for the Continent in 1904; his final line in *Ulysses*, "Trieste-Zürich-Paris, 1914-1921," speaks of cosmopolitan wandering, personal isolation, exclusion, and exile. He articulates in his modern odyssey the tensions of twentieth-century chauvinist identity politics. Odysseus tricked the Cyclops and made escape possible by telling him, "Noman is my name. Noman is what mother and father call me...."[8] Leopold Bloom is for Joyce "Everyman or Noman."[9] He is the universal hero: Irish, Jewish, Hungarian, Hellenic, the quintessential modern man—a rootless, dispossessed wanderer, "Ahasuerus," without a national home, and not the master in his own house. He is four times exiled, as a Jew, a Hungarian, and an Irishman, and displaced at home by Blazes Boylan. Bloom is an ethnic and religious cosmopolite: uncircumcised, multiply baptized, half Irish, half Jew, born of a gentile Irish mother and a Hungarian father who gave him a Jewish name and visage, married to a half Spanish, half Irish woman, affirming a proud historic Jewish identity. He suffers the torments and the ambiguities of the rise of militant twentieth-century nationalism, which continue to tear asunder both his country and his people. The Fenian "citizen" and the Protestant Orangeman Crofter, political and religious enemies, can unite in their antisemitic hatred of Bloom. "Nothing," said Joyce's friend Frank

Budgen, "brings people nearer to one another than community in fearing, loving and hating."[10]

Joyce's central European contemporary, Robert Musil, challenged the concept of "national character" by describing the multiple identities possessed by each person:

> The inhabitant of a country has at least nine characters: a professional one, a national one, a civic one, a class one, a geographical one, a sex one, a conscious, an unconscious and perhaps even a too private one; he combines them all in himself, but they dissolve him, and he is really nothing but a little channel washed out by all these trickling streams, which flow into it and drain out of it again in order to join other little streams filling another channel. Hence every dweller on earth also has a tenth character, which is nothing more or less than the passive illusion of spaces unfilled.... This interior space—which is, it must be admitted, difficult to describe—is of a different shade and shape in Italy from what it is in England, because everything that stands out in relief against it is of a different shade and shape; and yet both here and there it is the same, merely an empty, invisible space with reality standing in the middle of it like a little toy brick town, abandoned by the imagination.[11]

Musil deconstructs and subverts the essentialist concept of identity. Yet he sees "the national" as not only one of the nine identity fragments, but ascriptively in the invisible interior space "without qualities" in which the essential spirit (*Geist*) resides. National identity is culturally, psychologically, and historically constructed, consisting of a different "shade and shape" in England or Italy, because relations to the nine identity fragments that people internalize are essentially different in each nation. Nationality is privileged in defining personal, subjective, political, and social identifications because it absorbs into itself all other identity fragments.

Social Science Theories of National Identity

The three main social science approaches to national identity are the reflexive sociological model of Pierre Bourdieu, Rogers Brubaker, and Benedict Anderson; the cognitive socialization model of Ernest Gellner and Eric Hobsbawm; and the family communication model of Erik H. Erikson and Karl Deutsch, which, I argue, offers the maximum utility and relevance for research in problems of national identity.

Most sociologists use "identity" ascriptively; as something that is assigned by others. Bourdieu, undoubtedly with the history of France in mind, views the state, through its administrative discourse of symbolic functions, official forms, certificates, records, and credentials, as the institution "which assigns everyone an identity."[12] Identity, suggests Bourdieu, can be self-assigned, as when a person intentionally alters language to adopt the style of a higher social class.[13] Identity is perception that "exists fundamentally through recognition by other people."[14] In seeking to explain the Chinese student protest movement of the night of 3-4 June 1989 in Tiananmen Square, Craig Calhoun tells us that:

Identity is a no more than relatively stable construction in an ongoing process of social activity.... Even at a personal level ... identity is not altogether internal to an individual but is part of a social process.... Identity is not a static, preexisting condition that can be seen as exerting a causal influence on collective action; at both personal and collective levels, it is a changeable product of collective action.[15]

Concordantly, on the national level Rogers Brubaker argues:

We should think about nation not as substance but as institutionalized form, not as collectivity but as practical category, not as entity but as contingent event ... as something that suddenly crystallizes rather than gradually develops, as a contingent, conjuncturally fluctuating, and precarious frame of vision and basis for individual and collective action, rather than as a relatively stable product of deep developmental trends in economy, polity, or culture.[16]

As Brubaker points out, nationality is not quantifiable precisely because it is a subjective category: "Nationality is not a fixed, given, indelible, objectively ascertainable property; and even subjective, self-identified nationality is variable across time and context of elicitation, and therefore not measurable as if it were an enduring fact that needed only to be registered."[17]

Benedict Anderson affirms that the rich multiplicity of historical, ethnic, and religious roots of national identity require acts of invention of a mythic common past, usually glorious but sometimes persecutory, and the suppression of the diversity of sectarian, clan, tribal, dynastic, and polyglot origins of the peoples who constitute the nation. Anderson cogently applies the metaphor of childhood memory amnesia in the creation of a national identity:

All profound changes of consciousness, by their very nature, bring with them characteristic amnesias. Out of such oblivions, in specific historical circumstances, spring narratives. After experiencing the physiological and emotional changes produced by puberty, it is impossible to "remember" the consciousness of childhood.... As with modern persons, so it is with nations. Awareness of being imbedded in secular, serial time, with all its implications of continuity, yet of "forgetting" the experience of this continuity ... engenders the need for a narrative of "identity."[18]

Both the power and the feigned quality of nationalism are apparent when we look at such synthetic nations as the United States, Brazil, Indonesia, and Israel. These are invented nations, each with an assertive, self-worshiping, and aggrandizing nationalism, and each worthy of special attention, study, and interest. But the power of "imaginary" nationalism should not to be underestimated or deprecated merely because it is "constructed." People are demonstrably willing to die for these national identities, which evoke deeply stirring identifications with family and home, tradition, and emotionally freighted symbolism.

Eric Hobsbawm detests nationalism, therefore discounts its power and wishes it would disappear to the trash heap of history with other bourgeois institutions. This wish also determines his analysis. In 1990 he doubted "the strength and dominance of nationalism," holding that it "will decline with the decline of the nation-state ... the phenomenon is past its peak."[19] Three decades ago Hobsbawm argued for nationalism as "a historic phenomenon, the product of the fairly recent past, and unlikely to persist indefinitely."[20] Bourdieu's critique of Marxist research into the national question reflects that "it is no coincidence that Stalin is the author of the most dogmatic and most *essentialist* 'definition' of the nation."[21]

Ernest Gellner stressed the role of school-transmitted culture, which he termed "exosocialization" or "education proper," as distinguished from family childhood socialization.[22] The historical development, which Gellner sees, is the nation as a culture/polity based on an educational machine running from grade school to university.[23] Gellner has a distinctively Darwinian view of human nature, and for that reason points to the superiority of the Freudian model over rational interest models of behavior: "All the assumptions, for instance, contained in the pervasive economist's model, of a *homo economicus* in pursuit of sharply specific aims, simply fail to do justice to the brutality, deviousness, tortuous obscurity of our inner life, to all the things which we know from experience to mask our real driving forces."[24] He therefore believes that "nationalism does not have any very deep roots in the human psyche. The human psyche can be assumed to have persisted unchanged through the many millennia of the existence of the human race, and not to have become either better or worse during the relatively brief and very recent age of nationalism."[25] Gellner subscribes to the classical Freudian idea of an unaltered, unconscious instinctual structure in humankind. He legitimately calls for a culture-specific explanation of nationalism, which should place him in the province of modern ego psychology. Our focus must, indeed, be on how political institutions and individual people adapt to the pressures and exigencies of historical forces.

Social scientists currently use the term "identity" widely and artlessly, without reference or acknowledgment to Erik H. Erikson, who first articulated and developed the concept. He drew on "internal" personal and "external" historical experience, calling the integration psychosocial identity. Social scientists critique Erikson's concept of identity because he redefined it often as he applied it in particular cases.[26] I find this flexibility to be a virtue that enhances the usefulness of psychosocial identity as a concept for comprehending nationalism in its multiplicity of forms. In all of his uses of identity, the sense of inner continuity between one's personal, ethnic, social, and politico-national past and one's present interactions with the world remains the important consistent factor. Erikson did field work on the Pine Ridge Indian Reservation of the Oglala Sioux in South Dakota in 1937. The Sioux children were forced to attend the U.S. government boarding schools, where the general affect was slow, apathetic, and depressed. A boy who was singled out by his teacher as a problem "radiates ... a sense of ideal identity" when he can, in the present moment, behave in a way that is in concord with his traditional tribal values of sharing and generosity: "The way you see me now is the way I really am, and it is the way of my forefathers."[27] The Eriksonian model assumes that identity is made up of identifications—the internalization of parents, family, kin, friends, peers, teachers, social and spiritual counselors, ethnic and religious heritage, transgenerational political and social traditions, geography, and all the elements that make up the growing person's psychosocial surround. But identity is more than the sum of childhood identifications. Ego identity, says Erikson,

> is the accrued experience of the ego's ability to integrate all identifications with the vicissitudes of the libido, with the aptitudes developed out of endowment, and with the opportunities offered in social roles. The sense of ego identity then, is the accrued confidence that the inner sameness and continuity prepared in the past are matched by the sameness and continuity of one's meaning for others.[28]

People will fight hard to maintain these identities when they are threatened because the alternative—identity diffusion—is a painful experience of inner fragmentation. We need operational definitions of national identity that allow space for the subjective experiences of people, including their sense of continuity and integration with their internalized personal, familial, and ethnic past.

Karl Deutsch, in a seminal work, which I think deserves renewed attention, emphasizes the intimate family socialization process as the essential building block of nationalism. Deutsch distinguishes between two kinds of communication, bureaucratic and social. Bureaucratic, or what Talcott Parsons termed "instrumental," communication connotes business, professional, and official transactions. Deutsch differentiates

> the narrow vocational complementarity which exists among members of the same profession, such as doctors or mathematicians, or members of the same vocational group, such as farmers or intellectuals. Efficient communication among engineers, artists, or stamp collectors is limited to a relatively narrow segment of their total range of activities.

The other field of communication, which Deutsch signifies as "social communication," denotes intimate spheres including "childhood memories, in courtship, marriage, and parenthood, in their standards of beauty, their habits of food and drink, in games and recreation, they are far closer to mutual communication and understanding with their countrymen than with their fellow specialists in other countries."[29] This is what Parsons termed the "affectual," as opposed to the "instrumental," functions, and it corresponds to the distinction Ferdinand Tonnies made between community (*Gemeinschaft*) and society (*Gesellschaft*). For Deutsch there is a fundamental relationship between a people and a community of mutual understanding. "Membership in a people essentially consists in wide complementarity of social communication. It consists in the ability to communicate more effectively, and over a wider range of subjects, with members of one large group than with outsiders."[30]

Deutsch draws on the concept developed by the Austro-Marxist Otto Bauer, that a nation is a community shaped by shared experiences. Bauer specified a common history: "a community of fate" that "tied together" the members of a nation into a "community of character." A "community of culture" remains entirely dependent on a preceding "community of fate" (*Schicksalsgemeinschaft*).[31]

Deutsch considers nationalism to be grounded in a common social culture, which is a personal, developmental, highly family- and home-oriented, learned pattern of life: "We found culture based on the community of communication, consisting of socially stereotyped patterns of behavior, including habits of language and thought, and carried on through various forms of social learning, particularly through methods of child rearing standardized in this culture."[32] He directly invokes the feeling of comfort and security in knowing that others understand one in the intimate realms of taste, play, family and sexual life, referring to

> the widespread preferences for things or persons of "one's own kind" (that is, associated with one's particular communication group) in such matters as buying and selling, work, food and recreation, courtship and marriage.... At every step we find social communication bound up indissolubly with the ends and means of life, with men's values and the patterns of their teamwork, with employment and promotion, with marriage and inheritance, with the preferences of buyers and sellers, and with economic security or distress—with all the psychological, political, social, and economic relationships that influence the security and happiness of individuals. Nationality, culture, and communication are not the only factors that affect all these, but they are always present to affect them.[33]

The obvious case to test the family socialization model of Deutsch and Erikson is the history of modern Poland, a naturally poor country with open forest and steppe frontiers, and the geopolitical misfortune of being surrounded by strong, voracious imperial neighbors—Romanov Russia, Hohenzollern Prussia, and Habsburg Austria. As Thucydides said, "Of the gods we believe, and of men we know, that by a necessary law of their natures they rule whenever they can." Poland was four times partitioned and occupied by hostile neighbors: in 1772, 1793, and 1795, and again from 1939 to 1945, between Hitler's Nazi Germany and Stalin's Soviet Russia. In the "long" nineteenth century, Poles were subjected to Russification and Prussification, their language was banned in schools and offices, their culture deprecated, their church persecuted. The Polish people revolted in 1830-31 and 1863-64, which the Russians suppressed with bloody severity. When Poland was re-created in 1919 after the First World War, there had been no Polish state for 124 years, or the equivalent of six demographic generations. But the flame of Polish national identity was kept alive and fueled in the Polish family, home, and church.

Erikson and Deutsch provide for the existence and instrumental effectiveness of Musil's reality of an interior space in the person. Their evocation and structuring of the most intimate interpersonal psychodynamic field and their relation of that field to ethnic and national conflict makes their models of nationalism richer, more complex, and superior to Anderson's, Bourdieu's, and Brubaker's reflexive understanding of nationalism, or Hobsbawm's and Gellner's structural models. Deutsch integrates the implications of developmental personality research with social science communication theory to build an integrated dynamic cultural—historical narrative explanation of how nationalism and nation-building function in individuals and groups. While Deutsch accurately locates the phenomenology of nationalism in the family and the home, he does not explain the dynamics of how these nationalist messages are communicated, transferred, inculcated, and internalized from caretakers to children in each case in the intimate family ambiance. This is the province of psychoanalytic research on the internalization of trust and fear.

Childhood Socialization and National Identity

Nationalism begins in the family and the home. There is a common folk saying in the Middle East: "I fight my brother, my brother and I are against our cousins, we and our cousins against the other clans, our people versus their people, our nation against the world." This maxim conveys the family socialization process, which begins early and which views outsiders and strangers as a cause for anxiety as well as curiosity and wonderment. The decisive questions appear early: "Mama, what are we? What am I? Who are they? Are they good or bad? Can I feel safe with them? Who dominates whom? Who has power, authority, and status?" And, immediately sensed but never articulated, "Why are you anxious?"[34]

By the second half of the first year of life the generalized smiling response is reserved for the mother and other special caretaking persons. This preferential smile to the mother is the crucial proof that a bond to another specific person has been established that distinguishes that loved person from all others in the world.[35] Projection, or casting away from the self, and introjection, or taking in, incorporating into the self, are among the most "primitive" defenses. Their roots are in the earliest "oral" phase of life. As Freud put it:

> Expressed in the language of the oldest—the oral-instinctual impulses, the judgement is: "I should like to eat this" or "I should like to spit it out"; and put more generally: "I should like to take this into myself and keep that out." That is to say: "It shall be inside me" or "it shall be outside me".... The original pleasure-ego wants to introject into itself everything that is good and to eject from itself everything that is bad. What is bad, what is alien to the ego and what is external are, to begin with, identical.[36]

Melanie Klein and her followers developed the concept of primitive "splitting" in early infancy, which explains the division of people and objects in the world into categories of "good" and "bad."[37] A child who has distinguished between internal and external, between self and nonself, may then use what Anna Freud categorized as the defense mechanisms of projection and introjection: It is then able to project its prohibited impulses outwards. Its tolerance of other people is prior to its severity toward itself. It learns what is regarded as blameworthy but protects itself by means of this defense mechanism from unpleasant self-criticism. Vehement indignation at someone else's wrong-doing is the precursor of and substitute for guilty feelings on its own account.[38]

The decisive variable is the level of basic trust and confidence based on a consistent, close, warm, and pleasurable interaction with the mother or other primary caretakers. Erikson refers to the conflict of "basic trust versus basic mistrust" as "the nuclear conflict" and "the first task of the ego."[39]

Stern argues that the leap from unpleasurable to "bad" and from pleasurable to "good" is an issue for later cognitive ego development, dependent on verbalization and symbol formation. He offers the concept of effectively toned clusters of interactive experiences between infant and mother, which constitute "working models" of mother for the child. At a later date these are reintegrated by the older child or adult into higher-order categorizations of "good" and "bad."[40] The important point for us is that "splitting" exists in adult attitudes toward conflict in personal, group, and international settings and that the analysis and understanding of this pervasive mechanism is relevant for coming to grips with nationalism, ethnocentrism, and racism.[41]

Year-old infants scan their mother's face for signals of anxiety, which in turn cue how the infant will respond to the new situation. As Stern describes it, they

> look towards the mother to read her face for its affective content, essentially to see what they should feel, to get a second appraisal to help resolve their uncertainty. If the mother has been instructed to show facial pleasure by smiling, the infant crosses the visual cliff [or other frightening object]. If the mother has been instructed to show facial fear, the infant turns back from the "cliff," retreats, and perhaps becomes upset. Similarly, if the mother smiles at the robot [or other stimulating object], the infant will too. If she shows fear, the infant will become more wary.[42]

The phase-specific distinctions between the secure "us" and the anxiety-inducing "other"   the "them" that children experience as they grow up can give us a grasp of the roots of national identity.

Models of Transcending Nationalism

There are a few places in Europe where serious political thought has been given to principles effecting a transcendence of the most virulent forms of nationalism consisting of murderous projections on the Other. The relevant case has its roots in wrestling with forces of nationalism in the final three decades of Austria-Hungary, a multinational, polyglot, multiethnic and religious dynastic monarchy. The most creative thinkers on nationalities questions were the Austro-Marxists, especially Karl Renner (1870-1950) and Otto Bauer (1881-1938). The essence of their proposals is to detach national identity from territory. Nationality would not be determined by birth or residence, but by personal choice, the personality principle (*Personalitätsprinzip*), which would be recorded in a national register. Cultural and educational life, including taxation to support these, would be determined by the various autonomous groups, who could thus occupy the same territory and share economic, governmental, and transport facilities.[43] This is the only viable alternative to territorial hegemony for national groups which necessarily has meant "ethnic cleansing" of one or another grade of severity.

Karl Renner was the president of Austria from 1945 to 1950, when Italy and Austria negotiated the Paris Agreement of 5 September 1946, which set the outline for a long-term settlement of the ethno-linguistic issues in the South Tirol.[44] In essence the agreement provides for Italian sovereignty and cultural autonomy for the German-speaking majority. A noteworthy feature of Austro-Italian diplomacy over the past forty-five years is a gradual structure, including a "Package" of 137 sections negotiated in 1969 and a "Calendar of Operations" for their implementation. These measures include the use of the German language in judicial, police, and other administrative procedures, regional finances, water courses, forestry, education, textbooks, and teacher credentialing, in agreements worked out in bilateral commissions.[45] Happily, in the year 1992 all 137 sections of the Austro-Italian Autonomy Package for the South Tirol were declared fulfilled.[46] The Italo-Austrian accommodation on the South Tirol (Alto Adige) should be of special relevance to tempering of nationalistic passions because Austria, the nonsovereign power, is guaranteed an international protective function (*internationalen Schutzfunktion*) for the German-speaking population under international law. The point for international conflict resolution is that not all issues can be settled in one adjudication. There are many disputes where the process itself over time constitutes a healing function.

Crosscutting of Identifications

Individuals are made up of many different introjects, identifications, partial identifications, and inner objects that may be in conflict. This knowledge becomes crucial for understanding the role of various group and regional identifications in national conflict or the equally complex problem of national cohesion.

What importantly distinguishes the Austro-Italian case from the tragedy of national conflict and "ethnic cleansing" in Israel-Palestine, the former Yugoslavia, or in the Caucasus is the willingness to forgo concepts of territoriality and sovereignty in deciding the daily lives and discourse of people who occupy the same piece of land. In the Italian Alto Adige-South Tirol both the Germanic and the Italian population are Roman Catholic. Because any individual is subject to cross-pressures of various identifications and allegiances, crosscutting encourages conciliation. Moderate attitudes and actions are encouraged and often prevail by mobilizing like introjects and common inner objects.

Hostility and aggression in the politico-social world are created through murderous rage, persecutions and foulness, in the conscious and unconscious inner fantasies of the perpetrators. A moment's reflection will convince us that we are only able to postulate a characteristic or trait in another because it has been to some degree known to us in fantasy. Peoples and nations find in their minorities and in their neighbors an available and vulnerable target on whom to project their bad internal objects—their hatred and urge to kill as well as their depreciated sense of inferiority, of being despised as slovenly parasites, cheats, and unscrupulous characters. In the passion of nationalism the enemy within becomes the enemy without.

To return in a Joycean mode to where we began, with *Ulysses*, Joyce knew and portrayed the nightmarish side of Irish, Hungarian, and Jewish identity. An important personal and political meaning of his novel is that national identity may haunt us, but it is also essentially who we are—internalized identifications with loved and hated persons and places, dreams and disasters, wounds and triumphs, grievances and entitlements, rituals and symbols, that constitute meanings for life. Nations as polities can exist, at least in theory, with only an "imaginary past." The imaginary, however, carries great demonstrable power to move individuals to action. However, persons and nations that believe they are reborn anew each day are living a fantasy of denial that will exact a cost in pain and destruction. I have undertaken to demonstrate that humanistic and psychoanalytic understandings of national identity incorporate inner subjective dimensions of experience that are needed for understanding politics and history in as much as they make us conscious that we are not born anew daily—we carry internalized pasts within us. Persons and groups have histories that interact with current crises and opportunities. Perspectives that include a place in the personality and the polity for the continuity of history and cultural discourse are a prerequisite for a satisfying contemporary social science understanding of national identity.

Notes

1. James Joyce, *Ulysses* (1922; reprint, New York: Random House, 1961), 331-38, passim. I am indebted to the thoughtful analysis of Joyce by James J. Sheehan in "National History and National Identity in the New Germany," *German Studies Review*, Special Issue: "German Identity" (Winter 1992): 163-74. I benefited from the discerning discussion of this topic at the fifth annual meeting of the University of California Interdisciplinary Psychoanalytic Consortium at Lake Arrowhead on 10 May 1997.
2. Homer, *The Odyssey: The Story of Odysseus*, trans. W.H.D. Rouse (New York: Penguin, 1937), 102.
3. Little scholarly attention has been paid to the Hungarian identity theme in *Ulysses*. A rare exception is Roger Tracy, "Leopold Bloom Fourfold: A Hungarian-Hebraic-Hellenic-Hibernian Hero," *Massachusetts Review* 6 (Spring-Summer 1965): 523-38.
4. Hugh Kenner, *Ulysses* (London: Allen & Unwin, 1980), 133; Vincent Sherry, *Ulysses* (Cambridge: Cambridge University Press, 1994), 12.
5. Arthur Griffith, *The Resurrection of Hungary: A Parallel for Ireland*, with appendices on Pitt's Policy and Sinn Fein, 3rd ed. (1904; Dublin: Whelan and Son, 1918), 95.
6. I thank Professor Gyula Gazdag for translation from the Hungarian.
7. Joyce, *Ulysses*, 342-43.
8. Homer, *The Odyssey*, 107.

9. Joyce, *Ulysses*, 727.

10. Frank Budgen, *James Joyce and the Making of Ulysses* (Bloomington: Indiana University Press, 1960), 274.

11. Robert Musil, *The Man Without Qualities*, vol. 1, A Sort of Introduction: The Like of It Now Happens (I), trans. Eithne Wilkins and Ernst Kaiser (New York: Perigee, 1953), 34. Musil disliked Joyce's work and the comparison with *Ulysses* annoyed him.

12. Pierre Bourdieu, *In Other Words: Essays Towards a Reflexive Sociology*, trans. Matthew Adamson (Stanford, Calif.: Stanford University Press, 1990), 136.

13. Pierre Bourdieu, *Language and Symbolic Power*, ed. John B. Thompson, trans. Gino Raymond and Mathew Adamson (Cambridge, Mass.: Harvard University Press, 1991), 88.

14. Ibid., 224.

15. Craig Calhoun, "The Problem of Identity in Collective Action," in *Macro-Micro Linkages in Sociology*, ed. Joan Huber (Newbury Park, Calif.: Sage Publications, 1991), 52, 59.

16. Brubaker, *Nationalism Reframed: Nationhood and the National Question in the New Europe* (Cambridge: Cambridge University Press, 1996), 18-19.

17. Ibid., 56, n. 1.

18. Anderson, *Imagined Communities: Reflections on the Origins and Spread of Nationalism*, revised ed. (London: Verso, 1991), 204-05.

19. E.J. Hobsbawm, *Nations and Nationalism since 1780: Programme, Myth, Reality* (Cambridge: Cambridge University Press, 1990), 182-83, and n. 22. This analysis prompted the *New York Times* to comment that Hobsbawm's "survey, conducted with the traditional Marxist loathing for anything so backward-looking, merely reveals nationalism's faults rather than proves that its emotions have lost their pulling power" (28 July 1990), and moved Stanley Hoffmann to write: "Mr. Hobsbawm on nationalism is a bit like a deaf man writing about music" (*New York Times*, 7 October 1990).

20. E.J. Hobsbawm, "Some Reflections on Nationalism," in *Imagination and Precision in the Social Sciences*, ed. T.J. Nossiter, A.H. Hanson, and Stein Rokkan (London: Faber and Faber, 1972), 406.

21. Bourdieu, *Language and Symbolic Power*, 288, n. 11.

22. Ernest Gellner, *Nations and Nationalism* (Oxford: Basil Blackwell, 1983), 36-38.

23. Ibid., 57.

24. Gellner, "Psychoanalysis as a Social Institution: An Anthropological Perspective," in *Freud in Exile: Psychoanalysis and Its Vicissitudes*, ed. Edward Timms and Naomi Segal (New Haven, Conn.: Yale University Press, 1988), 223-27. The quotation is from 226.

25. Gellner, *Nations and Nationalism*, 34-35.

26. John J. Fitzpatrick, "Erik H. Erikson and Psychohistory," *Bulletin of the Menninger Clinic* 40 (1976): 295-314; Howard I. Kushner, "Pathology and Adjustment in Psychohistory: A Critique of the Erikson Model," *Psychocultural Review* 1 (1977): 493-506; Paul Roazen and Erik H. Erikson, *The Power and Limits of a Vision* (New York: Free Press, 1976). For an appreciation, see Robert Coles, *Erik H. Erikson: The Growth of His Work* (Boston: Little, Brown, 1970).

27. Erik H. Erikson, *Childhood and Society*, 2nd ed. (New York: Norton, 1963), 129.

28. Ibid., 261.

29. Karl W. Deutsch, *Nationalism and Social Communication: An Inquiry into the Foundations of Nationality*, 2nd ed. (Cambridge, Mass.: MIT Press, 1966), 98.

30. Ibid., 97.

31. Ibid., 19-20. Otto Bauer, *Die Nationalitätenfrage und die Sozialdemokratie* (1907), *Werkausgabe* (Vienna: Europaverlag, 1975), 1, 172, 192. See also Peter Loewenberg, "Austro-Marxism and Revolution: Otto Bauer, Freud's 'Dora' Case, and the Crisis of the First Austrian Republic," in *Decoding the Past: The Psychohistorical Approach* (New Brunswick, N.J.: Transaction Publishers, 1996), 161-204.

32. Deutsch, *Nationalism*, 37.

33. Ibid., 101, 106.

34. Margaret S. Mahler, Fred Pine, and Anni Bergman, *The Psychological Birth of the Human Infant* (New York: Basic Books, 1975), 209. Mahler et al. stress the variety of reactions to strangers, of which anxiety is only one. They regard "stranger anxiety" as a "one-sided" and "incomplete" description (56), preferring the term "stranger reactions." "In addition to anxiety, the stranger evokes mild or even compellingly strong curiosity. That is why we have emphasized throughout this book that curiosity and interest in the new and the unfamiliar are as much a part of stranger reactions as are anxiety and wariness."

35. John Bowlby, "The Nature of the Child's Tie to His Mother," *International Journal of Psychoanalysis* 39 (1958): 350-73. See also Bowlby, *Attachment and Loss*, Vol. I, *Attachment* (London: Tavistock, 1969, 1982); Vol. II, *Separation: Anxiety and Anger* (London: Tavistock, 1973); Vol. III, *Loss: Sadness and Depression* (London: Tavistock, 1980).

36. Sigmund Freud, "Die Verneinung" (1925), *Studienausgabe*, ed. Alexander Mitscherlich et al., vol. 3 (Frankfurt am Main: S. Fischer Verlag, 1975), 374; "Negation," *Standard Edition of the Complete Psychological Works*, ed. James Strachey et al., vol. 19 (London: Hogarth Press, 1961), 237.

37. Melanie Klein, *The Psycho-analysis of Children* (London: Hogarth Press, 1932); *Contributions to Psycho-analysis, 1921-1945* (London: Hogarth Press, 1948); *Envy and Gratitude and Other Works, 1946-1963* (London: Hogarth Press, 1975). See also Otto Kernberg, *Borderline Conditions and Pathological Narcissism* (New York: Jason Aronson, 1975).

38. Anna Freud, *The Ego and the Mechanisms of Defence* (1936) trans. Cecil Baines (New York: International Universities Press, 1946), 128.

39. Erikson, *Childhood and Society*, 249.

40. Daniel N. Stern, *The Interpersonal World of the Infant: A View from Psychoanalysis and Developmental Psychology* (New York: Basic Books, 1985), 252-53.

41. Vamik D. Volkan, *The Need to Have Enemies and Allies: From Clinical Practice to International Relationships* (Northvale, N.J.: Jason Aronson, 1988), 28-29. See also Kurt R. Spillman and Kati Spillmann, *Feindbilder: Entstehung, Funktion und Möglichkeiten ihres Abbaus, Züürcher Beiträge zur Sicherheitspolitik und Konfliktforschung*, 12 (Zurich: ETH, 1989); and Group for the Advancement of Psychiatry, *Us and Them: The Psychology of Ethnocentrism* (New York: Brunner-Mazel, 1987).

42. Stern, *Interpersonal World of the Infant*, 132.

43. Renner, writing under a pseudonym because he was a Habsburg state employee, developed the personality principle at the turn of the century. Synopticus (pseudonym), *Staat und Nation: Zur österreichischen Nationalitätenfrage* (Vienna, 1899); *Der Kampf der österreichischen Nationen um den Staat* (Vienna, 1902). See Peter Loewenberg, "Karl Renner and the Politics of Accommodation: Moderation Versus Revenge," *Fantasy and Reality in History*, (New York: Oxford University Press, 1995), 119-141.

44. For an anthropological perspective on the cultural differences and conflicts between these two peoples, see John W. Cole and Eric R. Wolf, *The Hidden Frontier: Ecology and Ethnicity in an Alpine Valley* (New York: Academic Press, 1974); and Eric R. Wolf, "Cultural Dissonance in the Italian Alps," *Comparative Studies in Society and History: An International Quarterly*, vol. 5 (The Hague: Mouton & Co., 1962-63), 1-14.

45. Heinrich Siegler, *Die österreichisch-italienische Einigung über die Regelung des Sudtirolkonflikts* (Bonn: Verlag für Zeitarchiv, 1970); Siegler, *Österreichs Souveranität, Neutralität, Prosperität* (Vienna: Siegler & Co., 1967), Chap. 3; Siegler, "Das Problem Sudtirol," trans. as *The Problem of South Tyrol* (Bonn: Siegler & Co., 1959), 40-70; Siegler, *Austria: Problems and Achievements since 1945* (Bonn: Siegler & Co., 1969); Mario Toscano, *Alto Adige-South Tyrol: Italy's Frontier with the German World*, ed. George A. Carbone (Baltimore: Johns Hopkins University Press, 1975); Kurt Waldheim, *Der österreichische Weg: Aus der Isolation zur Neutralität* (Vienna: Verlag Fritz Molden, 1971), trans. as *The Austrian Example* (New York: Macmillan, 1973), see Chap. 9 "Sudtirol"; Antony Evelyn Alcock, *The History of the South Tyrol Question* (Geneva: Michael Joseph Ltd., 1970).

46. "Declaration of the Federal Foreign Minister to the Austrian Nationalrat," Vienna, 5 June 1992.

SELECT BIBLIOGRAPHY

Agnew, Hugh LeCaine. *Origins of the Czech National Renascence.* Pittsburgh: University of Pittsburgh Press, 1993.

Agnew, John A. *Place and Politics: The Geographical Meditation of State and Society.* Boston: Allen and Unwin, 1987.

Alliès, Paul. *L'invention du territoire.* Grenoble: Presses universitaires de Grenoble, 1980.

Anderson, Benedict. *Imagined Communities: Reflections on the Origin and Spread of Nationalism.* 2nd enlarged edition. London and New York: Verso, 1991.

Balić-Hayden, Milica. "Nesting Orientalisms: The Case of Former Yugoslavia." *Slavic Review* 54, no. 4 (Winter 1995): 917-931.

Berg, Eberhard and Martin Fuchs, eds. *Kultur, soziale Praxis, Text. Die Krise der ethnographischen Repräsentation.* Frankfurt am Main: Suhrkamp, 1993.

Black, Jeremy. *Maps and History: Constructing Images of the Past.* New Haven, Conn.: Yale University Press, 1997.

Bourdieu, Pierre. *Language and Symbolic Power.* Ed. John B. Thompson, trans. Gino Raymond and Mathew Adamson. Cambridge, Mass.: Harvard University Press, 1991.

Breuilly, John. *Nationalism and the State.* Chicago: University of Chicago Press, 1994.

Brubaker, Rogers. *Nationalism Reframed: Nationhood and the National Question in the New Europe.* Cambridge: Cambridge University Press, 1996.

Bucur, Maria, and Nancy M. Wingfield, eds. *Staging the Past: The Politics of Commemoration in Habsburg Central Europe, 1848 to the Present.* West Lafayette, Ind.: Purdue University Press, 2001.

Buisseret, David, ed. *Monarchs, Ministers, and Maps. The Emergence of Cartography as a Tool of Government in Early Modern Europe.* Chicago: University of Chicago Press, 1992.

Clifford, James, and George E. Marcus, eds. *Writing Culture. The Poetics and Politics of Ethnography.* Berkeley: University of California Press, 1986.

Felak, James Ramon. *"At the Price of the Republic": Hlinka's Slovak People's Party, 1921-1938.* Pittsburgh: University of Pittsburgh Press, 1995.

Gellner, Ernest. *Language and Solitude: Wittgenstein, Malinowski and the Habsburg Dilemma.* Cambridge: Cambridge University Press, 1998.

———. *Nations and Nationalism.* Oxford: Basil Blackwell, 1983.

Golczewski, Frank. *Polnisch-jüdische Beziehungen 1881-1922. Eine Studie zur Geschichte des Antisemitismus in Osteuropa.* Wiesbaden: Steiner, 1981.

Gordon, Avery F., and Christopher Newfield, eds. *Mapping Multiculturalism.* Minneapolis: University of Minnesota Press, 1996.

Guibernau, Montserrat, and John Rex. *The Ethnicity Reader. Nationalism, Multiculturalism and Migration.* Cambridge: Polity Press, 1997.

Habermas, Jürgen. *The Structural Transformation of the Public Sphere: An inquiry into a Category of Bourgeois Society.* Trans. Thomas Burger with the assistance of Frederick Lawrence. Cambridge, Mass.: MIT Press, 1992.

Hamann, Brigitte. *Hitler's Vienna: A Dictator's Apprenticeship.* Trans. Thomas Thornton. New York: Oxford University Press, 1999.

Harle, Vilho. "On the Concepts of the 'Other' and the 'Enemy'." *History of European Ideas* 19, nos. 1-3 (1994): 27-34.

Harley, Brian J. "Deconstructing the Map." In *Writing Worlds. Discourse, Text and Metaphor in the Representation of Landscape,* ed. Trevor J. Barnes and James S. Duncan. London: Routledge, 1992.

Himka, John-Paul. *Galician Villagers and the Ukrainian National Movement in the Nineteenth Century.* Houndmills: Macmillan, 1988.

————. "Ukrainian-Jewish Antagonism in the Galician Countryside during the Late Nineteenth Century." In *Ukrainian-Jewish Relations in Historical Perspective,* ed. Peter J. Potichnyj and Howard Aster, 111-58. Edmonton: Canadian Institute of Ukrainian Studies 1988.

Hobsbawm, Eric J. *Nations and Nationalism since 1780: Programme, Myth, Reality.* 2nd ed. Cambridge: Cambridge University Press, 1992.

Höbelt, Lothar. *Kornblume und Kaiseradler. Die deutschfreiheitlichen Parteien Altösterreichs 1882-1918.* Vienna: Verlag für Geschichte und Politik, 1993.

Hosking, Geoffrey, and George Schöpflin, eds. *Myths & Nationhood.* New York: Routledge, 1997.

Hroch, Miroslav. *Social Preconditions of National Revival in Europe.* New York: Columbia University Press, 2000.

John, Michael, and Oto Luthar, eds. *Un-verständnis der Kulturen. Multikulturalismus in Mitteleuropa in historischer Perspektive.* Klagenfurt: Hermagoras-Mohorjeva, 1997.

Johnson, Lonnie. *Central Europe: Neighbors, Enemies, Friends.* Oxford: Oxford University Press, 1996.

Kaser, Karl. *Familie und Verwandtschaft auf dem Balkan. Analyse einer untergehenden Kultur.* Vienna: Böhlau, 1995.

Kieval, Hillel. *The Making of Czech Jewry: National Conflict and Jewish Society in Bohemia, 1870-1918.* New York and Oxford: Oxford University Press, 1988.

King, Jeremy. *Budweisers into Czechs and Germans: A Local History of Bohemian Politics, 1848-1948.* Princeton: Princeton University Press, 2002.

Kirshenblatt-Gimblett, Barbara. *Destination Culture: Tourism, Museums and Heritage.* Berkeley: University of California Press, 1998.

Kiss, Csaba, etal., eds. *Nation und Nationalismus in wissenschaftlichen Standardwerken Oesterreich-Ungarns, ca. 1867-1918.* Vienna: Böhlau, 1998.

Kořalka, Jiří. *Tschechen im Habsburgerreich und in Europa 1815-1914.* Vienna: Verlag für Geschichte und Politik, 1991.

Kraft, Claudia. "Die jüdische Frage im Spiegel der Presseorgane und Parteiprogramme der galizischen Bauernbewegung im letzten Viertel des 19. Jahrhunderts." *Zeitschrift für Ostmitteleuropaforschung* 45 (1996): 381-409.

Křen, Jan. *Die Konfliktgemeinschaft. Tschechen und Deutsche 1780-1918.* Munich: Oldenbourg, 1996.

McCagg, Jr., William O. *A History of the Habsburg Jews, 1670-1918.* Bloomington: Indiana University Press, 1989.

Marjanovic, Vladislav. *Die Mitteleuropa-Idee und die Mitteleuropa-Politik Österreichs 1945-1995.* Frankfurt: Peter Lang, 1998.

Pynsent, Robert B. *Questions of Identity: Czech and Slovak Ideas of Nationality and Personality.* Budapest, London, New York: Central European University Press, 1994.

Rupp-Eisenrich, Britta, and Justin Stagl, eds. *Kulturwissenschaft im Vielvölkerstaat: Zur Geschichte der Ethnologie und verwandter Gebiete in Oesterreich, ca. 1780-1918.* Vienna: Böhlau, 1995.

Sack, Robert David. *Human Territoriality: Its Theory and History.* Cambridge: Cambridge University Press, 1986.

Said, Edward. *Orientalism.* New York: Random House, 1978.

Smith, Anthony D. *Nations and Nationalism in a Global Era.* Cambridge: Polity Press, 1995.

Sperber, Jonathan. *The European Revolutions 1848-1851.* Cambridge: Cambridge University Press, 1994.

Stauter-Halsted, Keely. *The Nation in the Village: The Genesis of Peasant National Identity in Austrian Poland, 1848-1914.* Ithaca, N.Y.: Cornell University Press, 2001.

Todorov, Tzvetan. *On Human Diversity: Nationalism, Racism, and Exoticism in French Thought.* Cambridge, Mass.: Harvard University Press, 1993.

Todorova, Maria. *Imagining the Balkans.* New York: Oxford University Press, 1997.

Urban, Otto. *Die tschechische Gesellschaft 1848 bis 1918.* Vienna: Böhlau, 1994.

Wank, Solomon. "Some Reflections on the Habsburg Empire and Its Legacy in the Nationalities Question." *Austrian History Yearbook* 28 (1997): 131-46.

Wolff, Larry. *Inventing Eastern Europe: The Map of Civilization on the Mind of the Enlightenment.* Stanford, Calif.: Stanford University Press, 1994.

Woodward, Kathryn. *Identity and Difference.* London: Sage Publications, 1997.

INDEX